Roger Protz's

WORLD BEER GUIDE

First published in 1995 under the title 'The Ultimate Encyclopedia of Beer'
This edition published in 2009

10 9 8 7 6 5 4 3 2 1

Text copyright © Roger Protz 1995, 2000, 2009
Design copyright © Carlton Books Limited 1995, 2000, 2009

A CIP catalogue record for this book is available from the British Library

Carlton Books Ltd
20 Mortimer Street
London W1T 3JW

ISBN 978-1-84732-135-0

Project editor: Martin Corteel
Project art direction: Brian Flynn
Jacket design: Elle Ward
Production: Sarah Corteel

Printed and bound in Great Britain

Roger Protz's

WORLD BEER GUIDE

CARLTON
BOOKS

Author's acknowledgements

Thanks to Conrad Seidl in Vienna and Graham Lees in Singapore for briefing me on changes in Austria and the Far East. Special thanks to David Lipman and Matthew Kirkegaard of *Beer and Brewer* magazine for hosting a visit to Australia, and to Glenn Cooper and Nick Sterenberg at Cooper's of Adelaide for their hospitality. Thanks to all my friends, family and acquaintances who kept me sane with the occasional libation. Special, heartfelt thanks to Martin Corteel at Carlton Books for his patience and forbearance.

Sources and further reading

Jackson, Michael, *Michael Jackson's Beer Companion*, London, 1993.
Lees, Graham, *The CAMRA Good Beer Guide to Munich and Bavaria*, St Albans, 1994.
Webb, Tim, *The CAMRA Good Beer Guide to Belgium and Holland*, St Albans, 1992.

Contents

Introduction

Fancy a beer? You've come to the right place. This is more than just a book about beer – it's a celebration of the world's oldest alcoholic drink, one which dates back to at least 3000 BC. It's also world's the most popular beverage. A survey in 2008 showed that beer is the most widely consumed drink on the planet, followed by soft drinks in second place and wine in third place.

That will surprise many people. The media in many countries is obsessed with wine. Wine columns and programmes proliferate. And yet, since the last edition of this guide appeared, a counter-culture has developed. Prompted by vigorous groups of both dedicated consumers and beer writers, brewers have put aside the mask of secrecy and now reveal detailed information about their recipes and ingredients. Beer lovers are becoming as knowledgeable about different varieties of malts and hops as wine drinkers are about the attributes of such grapes as Cabernet, Chardonnay and Pinot Noir. Pilsner, crystal, Munich, roasted and wheat malts give fascinatingly different flavours and colours to beer. Fuggles and Goldings is not the name of an English country law firm but are two types of hops, one used for bitterness, the other for aroma. If a beer has a rich, tingling, citrus/grapefruit character we know it's likely to have been brewed with hops from the Pacific North-west region of the United States, while the "noble" hops from the German Hallertau impose a delightful floral, piny and resinous note.

Greater appreciation of beer and its raw materials has also led to an increasing interest in style. Why, for example, do many beers made in Australasia, Britain and the US bear the curious rubric "IPA"? The answer is that it's short for India Pale Ale, a style first brewed early in the nineteenth century in England for the colonial trade. Genuine IPAs disappeared early in the twentieth century but they are now a vogue drink again. There are now many fine interpretations of a style that should be genuinely pale and bursting with tangy hop bitterness.

Pilsner – sometimes spelt Pilsener or Pils for short – is a bowdler-ized beer, often crude shorthand for a pale, bland and uninteresting lager. The collapse of the divisions in Europe means we can now distinguish a true Pilsner – complex, with toasted malt and floral hops – as well as other misunderstood European styles, ranging from Budweiser to Bock.

It's not only pale beers that create interest and diligent research. A century before both pale ale and lager appeared as a result of the new technologies of the Industrial Revolution, England created porters and stouts that not only transformed brewing in neighbouring Ireland but also reached as far as the United States in the west and central Europe and the Baltic States in the east. Today we can enjoy dark and roasty interpretations of porter and stout that stress there is far more to the style than just one version in Dublin.

There have been some fundamental changes to the structure of the brewing industry since the last edition. At the top, mergers have created such unlikely and awkward bed-fellows as A-B InBev, Coors Molson and SABMiller, combinations that do little to please either the English language or consumers seeking richness and memorable flavour in beer. At the other end of the industry, however, small craft breweries flourish. Britain, with around 550, now has more "micros" per head of the population than any other country. Craft breweries in the US have seen their market share grow from 2 per cent in 2000 to more than 10 per cent today. Australia and New Zealand are following a similar course.

Above all, this is a guide to pleasure. To this end, we list some of the best bars, pubs, cafés, gardens and kellers that serve good beer. We also add some of the growing number of festivals throughout the world that act as shop windows for beer and the craftsmen and women who fire their mash tuns and coppers to make it.

Cheers!

ROGER PROTZ
St Albans

The Art and Science of Beer-making

Beer is as old as civilization. The methods that produce some types of ale have scarcely changed for centuries. Modern lager brewing has introduced new technologies aided by yeast cultivation and refrigeration. But the essentials of making beer – turning barley into malt, extracting the sugars, boiling with hops and fermenting with yeast – remain today essentially the same as when early man first discovered the joys and mystery of brewing.

When water was turned into wine, it was described as a miracle. But making beer from barley is rather more difficult, since a harvest of golden grain produces beer only as a result of profound and natural chemical reactions, and enormous skill from maltsters and brewers. Along the way other cereals may be blended in, while the remarkable hop plant imparts quenching bitterness and tempting aromas.

In Germany, the biggest beer-drinking nation in the world, they do their best to keep it simple. The ingredients that can be used in brewing are controlled by a sixteenth-century law called the *Reinheitsgebot*, or "Purity Pledge", so German beer drinkers can be certain that only malted barley or wheat, along with hops, water and yeast, go into their favourite tipple. In the rest of the world, however, unravelling the contents of a glass of beer is more complicated. Many brewers use "adjuncts", either because they are cheaper, or because they help to produce the right balance of flavours. Germans turn their noses up at "impure" beers from abroad, but English pale ales and milds, as well as Belgian Trappist beers and Irish stouts, would change character noticeably if brewers were not able to use special sugars and unmalted cereals to give their creations their own unique colours and tastes.

In a few regions of the world, where it is difficult to grow barley, brewers are forced to use the raw ingredients available – such as rice in the Far East, or sorghum in Africa. Barley, though, is the preferred grain for brewing. In the Ancient World of Egypt, Mesopotamia and Sumeria, the first brewers found that, while wheat made excellent bread, it caused problems if it was the only grain used in the beer-making process. Barley, on the other hand, makes relatively poor bread, but was found to be the ideal grain for brewing. Even today, with the dramatic revival of interest in wheat beers, wheat makes up only one per cent of the total grain used in brewing worldwide. All modern "wheat beers" use between 30 and 50 per cent malted barley in their composition.

Cereals such as barley and wheat developed from tall grass. Barley, though, is unusual because it has a husk. The early brewers soon found that this husk acted as a natural filter in the first stage of brewing. This is known as "mashing", when the natural sugars are extracted from the malt. Other cereals, such as wheat, have no husk and so can clog up pipes and machinery in brewing vessels. The other important advantages of barley are that it has the highest "extract" of fermentable sugars, and also produces a cleaner-tasting beer. Wheat, on the other hand, has a distinctive, fruity tartness that does not blend well with the bitterness of hops, while oats and rye have to be used in small proportions or they will impart to the beer a flavour that is either too creamy or too grainy. Some specialist ale brewers in Britain, however, have rediscovered oats and are using small amounts in stouts that are radically different in flavour from the dry Irish style.

Making malt

Many people make the mistake of assuming that brewing is a simple process – unlike wine-making, which needs enormous skill. The opposite is the case. If you crush grapes, the natural yeasts on their skins will ferment the sugary liquid. But nothing happens if you crush an ear of barley. It needs the gentle craft of the maltster to take the raw grain and turn it into malt. During the malting process, natural chemical reactions begin to turn the starches in the barley into fermentable sugars.

The barley of choice

Brewers choose malt with great care, preferring to stick to a tried and trusted variety that they know yeast will work with in harmony. Change the barley, and the yeast will react badly or even refuse to ferment and produce alcohol. Brewers, if they can acquire it, prefer two-row barley. The name refers to the number of rows of grain within each ear. The finest two-row barley grows close to the sea on rich, dark soil and is known as "maritime barley" as a result. The East Anglia region of England, the Scottish Lowlands and Belgium produce some of the finest varieties of two-row maritime. In warmer climates – the Mediterranean countries and the United States – six-row barley is more common. As well as having six rows of grain in each ear, the barley has a thicker husk; this contains tannins known as polyphenols. Both the husk and the tannins can cause a haze in finished beer and brewers who use six-row barley tend to blend in substantial amounts of adjuncts, such as corn and rice, to counter this haze. Six-row barley is also particularly rich in enzymes that will convert the starches in corn and rice, as well as the malt, into sugar. American "lite" lagers are often made from six-row with large amounts of adjuncts. But master brewers in Germany and the Czech Republic, the birthplaces of modern lager brewing, will only use two-row barley. Pale ale brewers agree with them. They feel that six-row gives an astringent and harsh character to beer.

But whether it is two-row or six-row, only a small proportion of barley is suitable for brewing. It must be low in nitrogen to avoid hazy beer, and with the widespread use of pesticides and fertilizers, nitrogen is a growing problem. Ale brewers tend to prefer winter barleys – sown in the autumn and able to withstand frosts and snow – for their robust character, while lager brewers use spring varieties which possess softer, lighter qualities.

Under pressure from farmers and big brewers, seed merchants have developed new varieties of barley that have a high "yield". This means that they produce more grain per acre than some of the more famous barleys, such as Maris Otter in England and Golden Promise in Scotland, though traditional brewers are willing to pay a premium price for low-yield varieties of barley, since they produce the best flavours and ferment in harmony with yeast. Changing the barley variety can result in a "stuck" fermentation.

The maltings

When the brewer and the maltster are satisfied with the quality of the barley, it goes to a maltings to start the long journey that will end with beer. At the maltings, the grain is washed thoroughly to remove dirt, agro-chemicals and other impurities. This is done by "steeping", or soaking, the grain with water in a deep trough or, in modern maltings, in large metal tanks. During this process, a primitive type of fermentation occurs as bacteria attack wild yeasts on the grain and the water bubbles and froths alarmingly. The water is changed frequently to flush away both bacteria and any wild yeasts that could interfere with the natural development of the grain. At the same time, the grain is absorbing moisture – vital if germination is to start – and the moisture level of the grain will increase from 14 to 40 per cent.

At the end of steeping, the water is drained and the grain is left to stand for several hours. In a traditional floor maltings, the grain is spread on a floor to form a "couch". In a modern maltings, the grain goes into large revolving drums. In either system, the grain will begin to germinate, and it must be turned or raked frequently to allow it to breathe. Germination and the biochemical changes that take place within the grain lead to a build-up of heat that must be carefully controlled or the grain will suffocate.

Modification

What happens to the grain is known as "modification". The embryo of the grain, the acrospire, starts to grow while tiny roots break through the husk. The grain is composed of two parts, the starchy endosperm and a tough, outer, aleurone layer that protects the endosperm and also contains proteins. The growth of the acrospire causes natural chemical reactions to transform the proteins into enzymes and so make the starches soluble. While the acrospire becomes soft, the rootlets grow at great speed. The maltster tests the degree of modification by a simple test: he puts some grain in his mouth and chews it. If it is soft and "friable", then modification has gone far enough and the barley has become what is known as "green malt".

An ale brewer will want a fully modified malt with as much of its protein as possible turned to enzymes. This enables him to use a simple infusion mashing system that turns starches into brewing sugar. Lager brewers traditionally have used less modified malt with a lower rate of protein conversion, while a more complex decoction mashing system is needed to convert the sugar and avoid beer haze. The reason for the differences lies in the fact that lager brewers in central Europe didn't have access to maritime barley and so had to make do with inferior varieties. Today, all two-row barleys are of high quality, but many lager brewers – and German wheat beer brewers – prefer to stick with decoction mashing.

Drying the malt

The green malt has to be heated to dry it and preserve the vital enzymes. In a modern maltings, this is done inside a drum that is heated externally. A kiln in a traditional maltings is like a large chimney. A coke, gas or electric fire at the bottom heats the malt, which is spread out above on a mesh floor. The temperature is carefully controlled to produce the type and colour of malt needed by the brewer. The first temperature stage, around 60°C/150°F, stops the process of germination. To produce white malt for lager brewing, the heat is increased slightly and held for 24 hours, while a marginally higher temperature is used for pale malt, the classic type for ale brewing. Malt destined for darker beers, such as English mild, will be kilned at an even higher temperature. The important factor is that the heat must be maintained at a level that will not kill the enzymes which will turn starch into sugar in the brewery. Heavily kilned malts will have no fermentable sugars and so are used solely for producing colour and flavour.

Dark malts

Dark malts – amber, chocolate and black – are produced in machines similar to coffee roasters. Unmalted roasted barley, used principally in dry Irish stouts, is also made in this way. Green malt is loaded into the roasters where temperatures range from 200°C/ 430°F to 210°C/450°F, depending on the colour required. Roasted malts have an intense, bitter flavour.

Special types of dark malt are made in a different way. Carapils and caramalt used in lager brewing, and crystal malt used for ale, are produced by loading green malt into a sealed kiln. The moisture cannot escape and, as the temperature is raised to 45°C/ 113°F, the enzymes convert starches into sugar. The husks of grain contain soft balls of malt sugar. As the vents of the kiln are opened and the heat is increased, the sugar crystallizes and the colour deepens. Not all the starches are converted, however, and much of the sugar produced is dextrin rather than maltose. As dextrin cannot be fermented by brewer's yeast, it gives not only flavour and colour to the beer, but also "body", a roundness of fullness and flavour.

Brewers specify the colour of the malts they need by quoting a scale agreed by the European Brewing Convention. The scale applies either to the malt or to the colour of the finished beer. A classic pale-gold Pilsner will have around six to eight units EBC, an English pale ale using crystal malt will register between 20 and 40 units, while dark beers in the porter and stout category will be as high as 300 units on the scale. In the United States, brewers use a system known as Degrees Lovibond to measure colour. Under this system, pale lager will have 1.6 degrees, a pale ale three degrees, and a stout 500 degrees.

Pale or dark, the maltster has now taken raw grain and turned it into an ingredient rich in soluble starches. The first and staple ingredient in making beer is now ready to go to the brewery.

Hops

Wine-makers are fortunate. Everything they need to make wine is contained within the grape, including natural preservatives that single the grape out from other fruits. Brewers, however, have to balance malt, with its biscuity sweetness, with plants or herbs that not only add aroma and bitterness, but also prevent bacterial infections during the brewing process. For centuries brewers tackled the problem of how to offset both the poor keeping qualities of ale and its cloying sweetness by adding a variety of herbs and plants. These included yarrow, rosemary and bog myrtle. But from around the eighth century AD, hops started to be used in brewing in central Europe. In Britain, the hop, *humulus lupulus*, was eaten as a delicacy by the Romans, but was not used in brewing at the time. Knowledge of the hop and hop cultivation was taken into the Caucasus and Germany as part of the great migration of people that followed the collapse of the Roman empire. By the early ninth century, hops were being grown in the Hallertau region of Bavaria. Brewers who used other plants, or a mixture of herbs, plants and spices known as "gruit", fiercely resisted the hop, while in many countries the church controlled the gruit market and could rail against the demon hop from the pulpit.

The hop for brewing arrived late in England in the fifteenth century and was banned by such luminaries as Henry VIII and the aldermen of Norwich and Shrewsbury. But eventually the superiority of hopped beer put paid to ale and gruit. Though the term "ale" is still widely used in the British Isles and the United States to define a warm-fermenting style, today all ales are brewed with hops.

Pity the poor male

Left to itself, the hop will trail across the ground and grow wild in hedgerows. Hop farmers train it to climb up poles, its thick stalk or bine wrapping round the pole. This gives the plant maximum exposure to sun and light. The hop plant is dioecious: the male and female plants grow separately. Except in the British Isles, the male hop has a short and miserable existence. Lager brewers want unfertilized hops that will give aroma to their beers, but they avoid too much bitterness and shy away from any suggestion of astringency. In most countries the male hop is ruthlessly persecuted to stop it mating with female hops. Classic ale producers, on the other hand, want an earthy, peppery aroma and flavour in their beers and a deep and intense bitterness. As a result they use fertilized female plants and encourage the male to enjoy a healthy sex life.

The flower of the hop – the cone – contains resins known as alpha acids (or humulones) and beta acids (or lupulones), as well as oils. Alpha acids give bitterness to beer, while the oils impart flavour. The beta acids and tannins in the cone help to stabilize the beer and also have vital disinfectant qualities to ward off infections. The hops grown in such famous European regions as the Hallertau in Bavaria and Žatec (Saaz in German) in the Czech Republic are known as "noble hops" because of their superb aroma but comparatively gentle bitterness. Modern varieties, known as "high alphas", have been developed to give twice the level of bitterness to beer compared to noble varieties. Many brewers are wary of high alphas as they feel they give a harsh and astringent character to their brews. They prefer to blend in different varieties to achieve the right balance of aroma and bitterness. English ale brewers, for example, use the Fuggle for bitterness and the Golding for aroma. Both are named after their original growers.

Hops around the world
The major hop-growing areas of the world are the United States and British Columbia in North America, Kent and Worcestershire in England, Bavaria in Germany, Žatec in the Czech Republic, and Styria in former Yugoslavia. Hops are also grown in Poland and China, while the Pride of Ringwood variety from Tasmania is highly regarded and is much in demand from brewers of organic beer. Recently, leading growing areas, such as the German Hallertau and the English counties, have seen their hops attacked by pests and diseases, so new strains (including "dwarf hops" that grow to half the height of conventional varieties), resistant to attacks from the likes of downy mildew and red spider mite, have been developed. The United States is expected to dominate world hop-growing within a few decades as a result of the ideal climates in Idaho, Oregon and Washington State which produce such varieties as Cascade, Chinook, Cluster and Willamette. All hops give an appealing citric character to beer, and this is most apparent

in American varieties – the Chinook in particular imparts a powerful aroma and flavour of grapefruit.

Picking the hops

Hops are picked in the early autumn. (Before mechanization, hop picking provided a short paid holiday for working-class families who lived close to the hop fields. In England, special trains were used to take London Cockneys and "Brummies" from Birmingham to pick hops in Kent and Worcestershire respectively.) Hops have a high water content and they must be dried and packed quickly to stop them going mouldy. Drying is usually carried out close to the hop fields – in England it is done in attractive oast houses topped by cowls that keep a steady draught of warm air circulating over the hops. When they are dry, the hops are compressed into sacks and stored in dark, cool areas in breweries to avoid oxidation and photosynthesis.

Brewers with traditional equipment prefer whole hops, while breweries with modern hop whirlpools use pelletized hops that have been milled to a powder and reduced under pressure into pellets. Hop oils and hop extracts, produced by boiling hops with hydrocarbons or in an alkaline solution, are not popular with craft brewers, since they feel they give an unpleasant harshness and bite to the beer.

IBUs

The bitterness of beer is measured by an internationally agreed scale, International Bitterness Units, or IBUs. They are sometimes known as EBUs (from European Bitterness Units), but the scale is now used in North America as well. The measurement is based on the level of hop acids and the quantity of hops used in a beer. IBUs do not give an indication of hop aroma or flavour, since they have to be balanced against the alcoholic strength of a beer and the amount of malt used. A "lite" American lager may have around 10 IBUs, whereas a genuine Czech Pilsner will have 40. An English mild ale will have 20 units, an India Pale Ale 40 or higher, an Irish stout 55 to 60 and a barley wine 65.

Water

Even the strongest beer is made up of 90 per cent water. Yet, brewers apart, we tend to ignore the role of water in brewing, except when we accuse brewers of "watering" their beer. In fact, every brewer in the world has to water the beer, otherwise there would be nothing to drink. In a brewery, water is treated with a care bordering on religious fervour. For a start, it is never called water but "liquor": water is the stuff used for washing floors and equipment.

Hard versus soft

The quality of the brewing liquor is essential to the clarity and taste of the beer. It encourages malt and hops to give up their sugars, aromas and flavours, and it also stimulates yeast to turn sugars vigorously into alcohol. The purity of water destined for brewing helps to produce a beer that is free from infections, while its hardness or softness will help determine the "mouthfeel" of finished beer. Brewers who want to produce a genuine Pilsner beer will need a soft water, while a pale ale brewer will want a water that is hard and rich in mineral salts. The level of salts in the water of Pilsen in the Czech Republic, home of Pilsner beer, is 30.8 parts per million. Before the Industrial Revolution and the ability to make chemical changes to water, London's water, high in calcium carbonate, was ideal for brewing milds, porters and stouts. In Burton-on-Trent, where the classic flinty English pale ales were born, water is hard and salts add up to 1,226 parts per million. Centuries ago, when public water was unsafe to drink, breweries would be set up next to natural springs or wells, or water diviners would be paid to find a supply of fresh water that would not only provide clean brewing liquor, but could also be used to germinate barley.

All water, whether it comes from wells, rivers or ponds, is the result of rain falling on to the earth. As it falls, it picks up gases that acidify it. Carbonic acid is the main acid in rain water. When it hits the ground, rain water drains through the top soil and finds its way through porous rocks and mineral layers until it settles on a water table of impervious rock. During that long, slow passage, the water will absorb mineral salts. The type and quantity of salts will depend on the rock formation in a given area. Soft water collects on insoluble rock, such as slate or granite, and is virtually free of minerals as a result. Water returns to the surface by forcing its way as a spring or flowing into a river, or bores will be sunk to pump it to the surface.

Likes and dislikes
Calcium bicarbonate is the most common cause of temporary hardness in water. It comes from chalk and is a nuisance in a brewery because the salts impede fermentation and reduce the effectiveness of other minerals. As those who live in a hard-water district will know, calcium bicarbonate leads to a heavy build-up of deposits in kettles. Brewers remove as much of it as possible by boiling or filtration.

On the other hand, calcium sulphate − or gypsum − is as welcome as free beer in a brewery, since it encourages enzymes to turn starch into sugar during the mashing stage of brewing, maintains the correct level of acidity − the pH or "power of hydrogen" − in the unfermented beer, and ensures that the yeast works in a lively manner. The high levels of gypsum in the water of Burton-on-Trent enable brewers there to produce sparkling and clean-tasting pale ales of dazzling quality. The sulphury aroma on a true Burton beer is known locally as the "Burton snatch".

Yeast loves magnesium sulphate (Epsom Salts) and attacks the sweet sugars in the fermenters with enormous vigour thanks to the presence of magnesium. The salts also help to stabilize the sugar extract when it is boiled with hops. Edinburgh, which also became a leading pale ale centre, has water rich in mineral salts.

Burtonization

At the other end of the brewing scale, great brewing centres, such as České Budějovice and Pilsen in the Czech Republic, and Munich in Bavaria, have soft waters with a negligible mineral content. This enables them to produce lager beers with a satiny, rounded smoothness. When London was a great centre for dark beers, the chlorine in the water accentuated the sweetness of the malt. But London is now, on a much reduced scale, a pale ale centre and brewers there "Burtonize" their liquor to match the hardness of Burton-on-Trent. The expression "Burtonization" is now used worldwide to describe the addition of mineral salts. Even brewers in Bavaria, speaking in German, use the term, though the amounts of gypsum and Epsom Salts added to Munich brewing liquor must be small as the lager beers of the city are noticeably soft in texture. But it is a sign of the importance that brewers attach to the quality of water that they have universally adopted a method to replicate the liquor of a small town in the English Midlands.

With the aid of modern technology, almost any water can be used in brewing. While it is pure Irish folk lore that Guinness in Dublin uses water from the River Liffey, there is nothing to stop the company from doing so. Brewers are meticulous in filtering liquor several times to remove any impurities. Many use double osmosis systems. It is a sad reflection on modern life that brewers in the East Midlands of England, home of pale ale, can no longer use some of the natural wells due to their high levels of nitrates. They have turned instead to the public water supply and as a result have to add back calcium and magnesium to achieve the right levels of hardness.

Yeast

For centuries they called it "God-is-Good". Brewers didn't understand yeast, but they knew that if they saved the foam from one brew, it would magically turn sweet liquid into beer when used again. The earliest brewers probably did not even save the foam, but instead allowed deposits of yeast in their brewing vessels to ferment subsequent brews. Wild yeasts in the air would also attack the sugary liquid, while micro-organisms in storage containers added a lactic sourness. The production of lambic and gueuze beers by spontaneous fermentation in Belgium is a link with brewing's past.

It was not until the eighteenth century, with the pioneering work of the Dutch scientist Anton van Leeuwenhoek, followed by Louis Pasteur with his microscope in the following century, that the mystery of yeast was revealed. Today we know that yeast is a single-cell micro-organism – a fungus – that can turn a sugary liquid into equal amounts of alcohol and carbon dioxide by multiplying and reproducing itself. Pasteur's book *Etudes sur la Bière* changed brewing practice throughout the world. Prompted by the French scientist's work, brewers realized that yeast had to be cultivated and stored to remain pure and uncontaminated. They also had to keep their breweries scrupulously clean to avoid bacteria and wild yeasts infecting beer and turning it sour. With the aid of the microscope, brewers discovered that yeast was made up of several different, competing strains which fought each other and so impeded a successful fermentation. Gradually, yeasts were cultured, both to remove unnecessary strains and also to retain one or two that would attack brewing sugars with the most success. For example, Guinness in Dublin still uses Arthur Guinness's original yeast from the eighteenth century, though it has now been cultured down from five strains to one.

Banking on success

Today, nothing is left to chance. Brewers realize how vital yeast is, not just to a clean fermentation, but also to the flavour and character of their beers. After each brew, the yeast is collected, pressed to remove any liquid, then stored in refrigerators.

Yeast is not neutral. It picks up and retains flavour from one brew to the next. So if a brewer wishes to produce a classic Pilsner or Pale Ale, he will need not just the right malt, hops and water, but also the correct yeast strain. He can take a bucket to the brewery of his choice and ask for a supply, but he is more likely to go to a special yeast bank and buy a culture. All brewers keep samples of their yeasts in special banks.

A yeast infection is like a death in the family. If a brewery does get an infection, then it immediately orders a sample from a yeast bank. In Britain, the National Collection of Yeast Cultures, located in Norwich, has a vast range of cultures, as does Weihenstephan near Munich, VLB in Berlin and Jorgensen in Copenhagen. Craft brewers in the United States, anxious to produce ales and lagers in the true style, order their yeasts from these banks.

Ale and lager yeasts

There are two basic styles of brewer's yeast – ale and lager. Ale yeast, known by its Latin name of *Saccharomyces cerevisiae* – meaning literally "sugar fungus ale" – is a development of the type of brewing yeast that has been used since the dawn of time. It works at a warm temperature in the brewery, creating a vast blanket on top of the liquid. The temperature will start at around 15°C/59°F, but the heat created by fermentation will increase it to 25°C/77°F. Ale yeasts are used in the production of wheat beer and such German specialities as the Alt beers of Düsseldorf and the Kölsch beers of Cologne, as well as conventional British ales and Irish stouts. Although they are carefully cultured and scientifically analysed, these beers remain a throwback to the age before the Industrial Revolution. Unlike a pure, isolated, single-strain lager yeast, an ale yeast may be a two-strain variety with sugars turned into alcohol at different stages. Ale yeasts give a rich fruitiness to finished beer.

Ale yeast is often used in open fermenters. The heavy blanket it creates on top of the liquid keeps oxygen at bay, and it is this tendency to rise to the top of the fermenting beer that has given ale yeasts the name of "top fermenters", while lager yeasts fall to the bottom of the vessel and are known as "bottom fermenters". The terms, however, are seriously misleading, because any brewer's yeast must work at all levels of the liquid if it is to convert sugars into alcohol. Better terms are "warm fermentation" for ale yeast and "cold fermentation" for lager strains.

In some modern ale breweries, fermentation takes place in enclosed conical fermenters. The yeast gradually falls to the bottom of the vessel as though it were a lager strain. Brewers will replace such yeasts with a pure culture after just a few brews, otherwise it would not produce the correct ale characteristics.

Lager yeast is classified as *Saccharomyces carlsbergensis*, as the first pure culture was isolated at the Carlsberg brewery in Copenhagen. Today it is more commonly called *Saccharomyces uvarum*. Lager brewing began in central Europe in the fifteenth century, when brewers in Bavaria stored – *lagered* in German – their beers in deep, icy caves to keep them in drinkable condition during the long, hot summers. The cold stopped wild yeasts attacking and infecting the brews, and also forced the brewer's yeast to work more slowly and precipitate to the bottom of the vessels.

Golden Pilsner

In the nineteenth century, with the aid of ice-making machines and refrigerators, a brewer named Gabriel Sedlmayr II, working at the Spaten brewery in Munich, developed lager brewing on a commercial scale. These first commercial lagers, however, were dark. It was when a golden lager was produced in Pilsen, in neighbouring Bohemia, that the new method of brewing became an international craze and Pilsner a much-imitated – and ultimately, much-abused – style. Lagering became popular because the beer was more stable, with fewer flavour fluctuations from brew to brew. As a result of lower temperatures, brewers had better control over fermentation. The yeast turns more sugar into alcohol, producing a dryer beer with little or no fruitiness. Fermentation is in two stages: primary fermentation starts at around 5–9°C/41–48°F and lasts for as long as two weeks, twice the time ale fermentation takes. The beer is then stored – lagered – at 0°C/32°F. During lagering, a secondary fermentation takes place, with the yeast slowly turning the remaining sugars into alcohol and carbon dioxide.

Today, there is a trend towards shorter lagering periods. Some "international" brands enjoy a brief honeymoon of just a couple of weeks in the lagering tanks. But classic lagers, such as the Czech Budweiser Budvar, enjoy three months' lagering and emerge with clean, quenching palates, delicate aromas and a complex balance of malt and hops.

Wild fermentation

There is a further type of fermentation in the world of brewing. It is confined to the Senne Valley area of Belgium, based in Brussels, where a handful of specialist brewers produce beers by wild, or spontaneous, fermentation. These lambic and gueuze beers are left to cool under the roofs of the brewhouses; during the night, airborne yeasts enter through open windows and attack the sugars in the solution. The two main yeast strains have been identified as members of the *Brettanomyces* family and are labelled *lambicus* and *bruxellensis*, though more than 100 wild strains have been identified in lambic breweries. The resulting beers, some fermented with fruit, are vinous and cidery, and break down the boundaries between wine and beer.

The strength of beer

Alcoholic strength used to be expressed in many different and confusing ways. In Britain, beer was taxed on its "original gravity" before fermentation, while other European countries used degrees Balling or Plato. Fortunately, most countries have now adopted the system of Alcohol by Volume (ABV), which is, as the name suggests, a measure of the amount of alcohol in the finished beer. The only major exception is the United States, which prefers to use Alcohol by Weight (ABW). As alcohol is lighter than water, ABW figures are approximately 25 per cent lower than for ABV, so a 4 per cent ABV beer would be 3.2 per cent in the US. Not that you will find any indication of strength on most American labels, though a Supreme Court ruling in spring 1995 allowed breweries to state alcohol ratings if they wish. Some American craft breweries are now using ABV in preference to ABW.

In Canada strength is shown as Alcohol by Volume (ABV).

% Alcohol by weight	% Alcohol by volume
2	2.5
2.5	3
3	3.75
3.2	4
3.7	4.6
3.9	4.8
4	5
4.25	5.3
4.4	5.5
4.8	6
5.4	6.8
5.9	7.4
7	8.75
8.8	11
10	12.5
12	15

In the brewery

No two breweries are alike and many modern breweries blur the distinction between ale and lager. Some breweries use the same equipment for both types of beer, though ale and lager yeasts are kept strictly apart to avoid cross-fertilization. (The brewing processes for ale and lager described below are the classic methods for both styles.)

Both start in the same way, with the arrival of malt in the brewhouse. The malt is first screened to remove any small stones or other impurities that may have survived the malting process. It is then "cracked" in a malt mill to produce a rough powder called "grist", which gives us the expression "all grist to the mill". Most of the malt is ground to a fine flour, but it is also blended with coarser grits and the rough husks of the grain, which act as a natural filter during the mashing stage. The grist is then ready to start the brewing process.

Classic ale brewing

The first stage of ale brewing is an infusion mash. Grist and brewing liquor are mixed in a large circular vessel known as a mash tun, which may be made of copper, cast iron or stainless steel, and is covered by a lid that can be raised by pulleys. Balanced above the tun is a large tube, a nineteenth-century device called a Steel's Masher, after the Mr Steel who invented it. Exact proportions of grist and hot liquor are mixed by an Archimedes screw inside the masher and the mixture then flows into the mash tun.

Temperature is crucial at this stage. If it is too high, the enzymes will be destroyed; too low, and the enzymes will work sluggishly and fail to convert some starches into sugar. The liquor, which has been stored in special tanks in the roof of the brewery, is heated to 75°C/180°F. This is known as "strike heat". It is higher than mashing temperature – 65°C/150°F – but the coolness of the grist will quickly reduce the temperature of the liquor to the desired level. If the temperature falls too low, more hot liquor can be pumped into the mash tun through its slotted base. The brewer has to avoid "cold spots" in the mash where the grist would turn into a paste, refuse to release its sugars and block every pipe and outlet.

Adjuncts

At this stage, the brewer may blend in other cereals with the malt. These are known as adjuncts, and are used to help clarify the beer, reduce nitrogen haze and give the right flavour balance the brewer seeks. The usual adjuncts in ale brewing are torrefied wheat or barley, which are similar to popcorn. The grain is scorched – torrefied – and the heat pops the endosperm and gelatinizes the starch. Flaked maize, another popular adjunct, is made by steaming or milling the grain to gelatinize the starch. Wheat flour is also widely used and gives a fine flavour to beer, but it can only be used in tiny amounts or it will clog up the brewing equipment. Adjuncts do not contain enzymes. It is up to the enzymes in the malt to convert the adjuncts' starches into sugar. All adjuncts have to be used in small amounts: add too much popcorn to beer and it will taste like breakfast cereal.

Starches to sugar

The thick, porridge-like mixture is now left to stand in the mash tun for one or two hours as saccharification takes place. This means that starches turn to sugar as a result of enzymic activity. Enzymes are biological catalysts. The two most important ones in brewing are alpha-amylase, which converts starches into maltose and dextrins, and beta-amylase, which produces only maltose. Maltose is highly fermentable, while dextrin cannot be fermented by brewer's yeast and is important for giving "body" to beer. If all the sugars turned to alcohol, the beer would be high in alcohol, but thin in flavour.

The sugars dissolve into the liquor, producing a sweet liquid called wort, pronounced "wurt". The mash tun has taps fitted to the side and the brewer can run off a sample of the wort to check that saccharification is under way. He can usually tell just from the bready smell and taste of the liquid, but if necessary he can carry out a simple chemical test by mixing some wort with a few drops of iodine. If the iodine stays clear, sugar has been produced. If it turns blue-black, then starch is still present. It is important to stop the mashing process once saccharification has taken place, otherwise tannins in the wort will produce an unpleasant flavour, rather like stewed tea. Mashing is terminated by pumping more hot liquor into the tun to kill the enzymes.

The slotted base of the vessel is now opened and the sweet wort starts to filter through the thick cake of spent grain. Perforated tubes in the roof of the tun start to revolve and "sparge" the grains with more hot liquor to flush out any stubborn sugars that remain behind. Sparging was a Scottish invention and the word stresses the Old Alliance between Scotland and France, for sparge comes from the French word *esparger*, meaning "to sprinkle".

Waste not, want not

Next, the hot sweet wort flows from the mash tun into a receiving vessel known as the "underback". Several vessels in a brewery have "back" in their name, an old word that is derived from the same root as bucket. In medieval breweries, wort would have been ladled from the mash vessel into a series of metal or wooden buckets. The spent grains left behind are not wasted and are sold to farmers as protein-rich cattle feed. In the brewing industry, nothing is wasted. Used hops are in great demand as garden fertilizer, while excess yeast is sold to companies that make yeast extract.

Run-off from the mash tun takes two hours. The wort is then pumped from the underback to the coppers. Many modern "coppers" are made of stainless steel, but a genuine copper copper is a delight, a domed and burnished vessel, like a cross between a diving bell and a lunar module. In the days before hops were used in brewing, the wort had to be boiled in order to kill any bacteria. Today, boiling has a dual purpose: to ensure absolute purity of the wort, and to add the essential acids, oils and tannins of the hops. If an ale mash tun is like a giant tea pot, infusing malt and hot water, then the copper is akin to a coffee percolator. It has a central tube – the calandria – topped by a dome called a "Chinese hat". As the wort starts to boil, it gushes up the tube into the main body of the copper and begins what is known to brewers as a "good rolling boil".

Hops are then added through a porthole in the domed roof of the copper. They are not, however, added in one batch. Instead, the brewer will add them at stages, usually twice or three times. The almost magical qualities of the hop will kill any bacteria in the wort, destroy the enzymes to stop any further saccharification and force proteins in the wort to come out of suspension and coagulate at the bottom of the copper. If all the hops were added in one batch, many of the vital bittering and aroma qualities would be lost in the boil. So the brewer will add bittering hops in one or two stages and then will "late hop" just a few minutes before the end of the boil with aroma hops.

Invert sugar

Some brewers will add sugar during the copper boil. Sugar is often considered to be an adjunct, but it has no starches that need to be attacked by enzymes, which is why it is added in the copper, not the mash tun. It is totally fermentable and the problem with brewing sugar is that if too much is used, then the finished beer will be high in alcohol but thin in body. Brewing sugar is called "invert sugar", as it has been inverted into its component parts of glucose and fructose. It comes in different colours, depending on the brewer's requirements, and is simply labelled Number One Invert, Number Two Invert and so on up the colour scale. Some of the sugars from both the malt and the invert will be caramelized during the boil, adding colour to the finished beer.

At the end of the boil, a powdered seaweed called Irish moss is added to the copper to clarify the wort by encouraging any remaining proteins and other detritus to settle at the bottom of the vessel. The spent hops act as a filter as the wort flows out through the slotted base of the copper into a hop back, where it is left to cool. The residue left behind is known as "trub". Mixed with the spent hops, it makes a rich compost for gardeners.

Some brewers will add further hops in the hop back to give additional aroma to the wort. Three famous ales from England – Adnams Extra and Greene King Abbot Ale, both from Suffolk, and Timothy Taylor's Landlord, from Yorkshire – circulate over a deep bed of hops in the hop back and have a pungent "hop nose" as a result. If pelletized hops rather than whole flowers are used, the hopped wort is pumped from the copper to a whirlpool, where the spent hops are removed by centrifugal force.

Cooling the wort

Before fermentation can begin, the temperature of the boiling hopped wort has to be lowered to 18°C/64°F. In a few breweries, the wort is left to cool in an open shallow vessel called a "cool ship", but there is always the danger that it can be attacked by wild, airborne yeasts as it cools. The vast majority of breweries use heat-exchange units known as paraflows. The wort is pumped through a series of plates that look like old-fashioned school radiators. Each plate containing wort is next to one filled with cold water. As the wort flows along the plates, it will get progressively cooler, until it is finally ready to be turned into alcohol.

Pitching the yeast

The cooled wort is pumped into fermenting vessels and liquid yeast is then mixed or "pitched" into it. Before it is pitched, however, a sample of the yeast will have been checked under a microscope in the brewery laboratory. Yeast cells are invisible to the naked eye, but under the microscope they can be seen darting and diving around. What the brewery is looking for are white yeast cells. Blue cells are dead and would impede fermentation, while black rods among the cells indicate a yeast infection, which would require the entire batch to be poured down the nearest drain.

Fermenting vessels vary from one ale brewery to the next. (Specialist fermenters unique to certain areas, such as Burton union and Yorkshire squares, will be covered in Chapter Two.) Most conventional ale breweries use open vessels, though nowadays there is a trend towards covering them in order to stop CO_2 escaping into the atmosphere. Depending on their age, fermenters may be built from wood, stone or various metals. Stainless steel is used to build modern vessels. Older ones are normally lined with polypropylene to avoid a build-up of bacteria and old yeast in cracks and other rough surfaces.

The role of oxygen

Brewer's yeast respires in two ways: aerobically (with oxygen), and anaerobically (without oxygen). Pasteur described the ability of yeast to breathe without oxygen as *la vie sans air* – "life without air". Yeast works with oxygen at the start of fermentation. In fact, brewers agitate and aerate the wort to make sure there is plenty of dissolved oxygen present. The yeast works rapidly, with bubbles rising to the surface of the wort. Within a few hours, a brown slick covers the surface and within 24 hours this has grown to a dense, rocky head that rises to peaks known as "cauliflowers". The yeast head is streaked with brown and black from proteins in the wort. The yeast head will be removed, or "skimmed off", from time to time to stop dead cells and detritus from impeding the work of the yeast in solution.

Enzymes in the yeast – maltase and invertase – turn sugar into alcohol and carbon dioxide. The converted sugars are assimilated by the yeast cells which at the same time are growing by dividing and fusing into fresh cells. Maltase enzymes produce glucose,

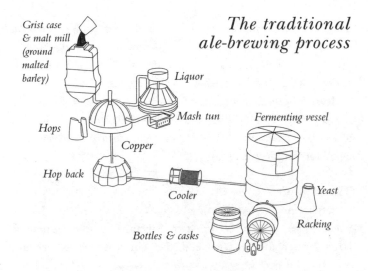

Grist case
& malt mill
(ground
malted
barley)

Liquor

*The traditional
ale-brewing process*

Hops

Mash tun

Fermenting vessel

Copper

Hop back

Cooler

Yeast

Racking

Bottles & casks

while invertase turns sucrose into glucose and fructose. Dextrins cannot be fermented, neither can lactose – "milk sugar" – which is sometimes added to sweeten stouts. They remain to give body and sweetness to beer.

Fermentation causes the temperature of the wort to rise. Yeast is pitched at around 15°C/60°F, but during fermentation this will rise to 25°C/80°F. Fermentation also creates chemical compounds, known as "esters", which are present in the atmosphere above the vessels in the form of fruity aromas. Depending on the strength of the beer and the balance of malts, adjuncts and sugars, the aromas may be reminiscent of apples, oranges, banana, pineapple, pear drops, liquorice or molasses. In some very strong beers, the esters can be reminiscent of fresh leather.

Eventually, the yeast will be overcome by the alcohol. After about seven days, the yeast cells will start to clump together and rise to the surface. This is known as flocculation. If it happens too early in the process, the brewer will have to aerate the wort again. When almost all the yeast has risen out of suspension, fermentation is at an end. Throughout the entire process, the brewer will check the transformation of sugar into alcohol by measuring the sweetness of the liquid with a hydrometer or saccharometer. Before the yeast is pitched, the wort may have a "gravity" of 1,040 degrees. Water has a gravity of 1,000 degrees, which means that 40 degrees of fermentable sugar is present in the wort. Since maltose, unlike brewing sugar, is not totally fermentable, the final gravity will be around 1,006 degrees, though stronger beers may have more sugar remaining.

Green beer

Brewers, being fundamentalists as well as traditionalists, like to give the beer seven days or "two Sabbaths" in the fermenters. When fermentation is at an end, the wort has been turned into beer, but it is not yet ready to drink. It is known as "green beer" and has to spend several days in conditioning tanks to mature. Some of the rougher alcohols and fruity esters will be purged, producing a cleaner and drinkable beer. When it is ready to leave the brewery, the beer may go in two different directions. Packaged beer, either for bottle, can or keg, will be filtered to remove any remaining yeast and then pasteurized. Carbon dioxide is pumped into the container as the beer is packaged to give it both sparkle and a lively head when poured.

Real ale

The beer style unique to Britain, "real ale", does not go through any of these processes. Instead, it is racked from the conditioning tanks straight into casks, though additional hops for aroma and sugar for a secondary fermentation may also be added. The beer leaves the brewery in an unfinished state because final conditioning takes place in the pub cellar, where the yeast in the cask continues to turn the remaining sugars into alcohol. As the beer matures, it gains not only a small amount of additional strength, but also rounded and fruity flavours. A glutinous substance known as "finings", made from isinglass, is added to attract yeast cells and other detritus to the bottom of the cask, leaving a clear beer above. Casks are vented by porous pegs hammered through a hole in the top of the cask to allow carbon dioxide to escape, though the cask has to be sealed when secondary fermentation is finished in order to keep sufficient gas in the beer to give it sparkle.

Classic lager brewing

The aim of a lager brewer is identical to that of an ale brewer: to extract the sugars from the malt, boil the wort with hops, ferment the hopped wort and produce beer. But the methods used are a variation on the theme, a variation that extends beyond the use of bottom-fermenting yeast, since it is based upon lower temperatures at almost every stage of production.

As lager malt is often less modified than ale malt, a decoction mashing system is used in which the grist is mixed with hot brewing liquor in a mash kettle at a starting temperature of around 38°C/100°F. Part of the mash will be pumped to a cooker, where it is heated to a higher temperature – between 43–56°C/120–130°F – and then returned to the kettle. Another portion of the mash will be pumped to the cooker and the temperature will rise to 65°C/150°F before being returned to the kettle. Returning the portions of heated mash to the kettle raises the temperature to around 50°C/120°F.

Rest period

The central feature of the decoction system is that the main body of the mash has a "protein rest" at around 45–55°C/113–130°F for periods of an hour of more. This rest period allows excessive protein, contained in malt that is high in nitrogen, to be degraded by a process known as "proteolysis". The heating of portions of the mash at higher temperatures gelatinizes the starch present in poorly modified malt, so allowing it to be attacked by enzymes.

Both protein and starch would cause haze in the finished beer if they were not tackled during mashing.

When double or triple decoction has taken place, the temperature of the kettle is raised to 75°C/167°F – the same as the mashing temperature in an ale brewery. At this heat, the mash is pumped to a third vessel, called a "lauter tun", which has a false bottom and clarifies the wort as it is run off. It also sparges the spent grain. Unlike an ale mash tun, though, this cannot be done in the mash kettle (which does not have a false bottom) because of the pumping required to the cooker and back.

Different coloured malts can be used during mashing but, if the beer is being produced in Germany, the Czech Republic or other countries that adhere to the German Pure Beer Pledge, no cereal adjuncts will be used. Similarly, no brewing sugars are added during the boil in a wort kettle. These days, most lager brewers use pelletized hops and they are added in two or three stages during the boil. The hopped wort is then pumped to a whirlpool and centrifuged to remove the mushy pellets and other detritus.

Fermentation

Next, the hopped wort is cooled and pumped to fermentation vessels. Lager fermentation is in two stages. The first stage – primary fermentation – may take place in either a tall, conical, stainless steel vessel, or in a more traditional, horizontal one. Temperature ranges between 5–9°C/41–48°F. At such temperatures, the yeast will work much more slowly than an ale strain as it converts sugars to alcohol and CO_2. As a result, there is much less build-up of yeast head and the purity of the single-strain variety creates few fruity esters.

Primary fermentation lasts for around two weeks. The green beer is then pumped to lagering tanks, where it is held at 0°C/32°F or just above. During this period of cold conditioning, which may last for several weeks or months, the yeast continues to turn sugars into alcohol as it precipitates at the bottom of the tank.

The finished beer will be clean and quenching, but it will deliberately lack the rounded, fruity quality of an ale, unless it is an exceptionally strong "bock" beer that has been lagered for as long as a year. The cool temperatures and slow conditioning enable the brewer to remove most of the flavour characteristics that an ale brewer seeks, leaving a lighter, malt-accented beer with a delicate hop character. Neither dry hopping nor the use of isinglass finings are permitted under the *Reinheitsgebot*.

Pasteurization

When lagering is complete, the finished beer will be filtered and often pasteurized. Louis Pasteur was a mixed blessing to the brewing industry. He solved the problems of infection in breweries and unravelled the mysteries of yeast. But he also introduced a heating

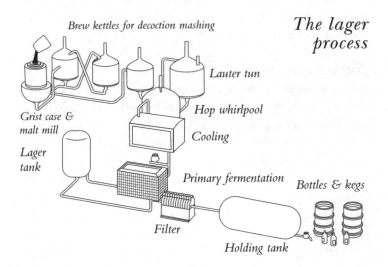

Brew kettles for decoction mashing

The lager process

Lauter tun

Grist case &
malt mill

Hop whirlpool

Cooling

Lager
tank

Primary fermentation

Bottles & kegs

Filter

Holding tank

method that can unbalance the subtle aromas and flavours of beer and give it hints of burnt toffee and cardboard. As the head brewer of the Brand brewery in the Netherlands once stated: "Pasteurization is for the cow shed, not the brew house". Grolsch, another leading Dutch lager brewery, does not pasteurize its beers. And what is good enough for them should be good enough for the rest of the world.

The families of beer

Ale is the world's oldest style of beer, and modern ales are descendants of the beers brewed 3,000 years BC in Ancient Egypt and other parts of North Africa and the Middle East. The British Isles remains the major centre of ale brewing. Though lager has made considerable incursions into Britain and Ireland, around half the beer produced in those islands is still in ale form. England is best known for bitter, a well-hopped beer that is best drunk in unpasteurized draught form in pubs. Bitter evolved from the India Pale Ales and other forms of pale ale introduced in the nineteenth century and brewed primarily in Burton-on-Trent, a town famous for its brewing since the twelfth century.

Porter and stout

Before the arrival of pale ale, the British Isles, like all other countries, produced brown and dark beers. Before the development of pale ale and lager, England's singular contribution to the history of beer was porter, a dark brown or black beer first brewed at the turn of the eighteenth century. In fact, the craze for porter created the modern commercial brewing industry. The strongest – stoutest – version of porter was called "stout". Although support for porter and stout declined in Britain as pale ale grew, it took deep root in Ireland and has never diminished. Irish ale and lager are both brewed in the Irish Republic, but dry stout remains the dominant beer. In Britain, mild ale, a dark brown and lightly hopped beer, which was once blended into porter, has kept some support, especially in areas of heavy industry where workers need to refresh themselves with light and slightly sweet beer. Britain also enjoys a growing range of seasonal beers. Rich and fruity old and winter ales have been joined in recent years by spring, summer and autumn beers.

Belgian varieties

In Belgium, ales are only a small proportion of a market dominated by such famous lager brands as Stella Artois and Jupiler. But the ale market is growing as both Belgians and the outside world have come to marvel at the enormous variety available in such a small country. Trappist monks, for example, brew ales of enormous complexity in their monasteries, while wheat beers, often flavoured with herbs and spices, have become cult drinks with the young. Pale ales and golden ales have enormous hop character, while in French-speaking Wallonia, seasonal or *saison* beers recall an earlier, bucolic time, when ale was brewed by farmers for their families and workers. In parts of Flanders, russet-coloured ales are stored in oak vats and have a sour and lactic taste. The most remarkable of all the Belgian ales are the wild beers of the Senne Valley, where lambic and gueuze beers are produced by spontaneous fermentation. When fruit – usually cherries or raspberries – is blended with these beers, they have a wonderful tart and quenching character. The success and interest in Belgian ales is creating a smaller revival in ale in the neighbouring Netherlands, dominated by the giant Heineken lager group.

German varieties

Germany is the world's leading lager-brewing nation, producing beers of awesome quality, a long way removed from the light, bland, international interpretations in other countries. There are also powerful variations in the style, with malty versions in

Bavaria, rounded but hoppier ones in Dortmund, and intensely bitter beers in the north. Not all lagers are pale. In the Munich region in particular, dark lagers – *dunkel* – are still popular. The Germans also brew seasonal beers and strong beers. "Bock" means strong and the name is a corruption of the name of the town of Einbeck, where the style was first brewed many centuries ago. Bock also means "goat" in German and many bock beer labels depict the animal. In the Munich area, exceptionally strong lagers have names ending in -ator, as in Celebrator or Triumphator. Seasonal beers are recalled in the Märzen (March) beers, brewed at the end of winter and stored until the autumn. Traditionally, it was Märzen beers that were served at the world-famous Oktoberfest in Munich. Other German specialities include the smoked beers of Bamberg, using wood-smoked malt, and beers in which the malt sugars are caramelized in the mash kettle by plunging in red-hot stones.

Germany also has some distinctive ales. Cologne has golden-coloured Kölsch beers, so treasured that they have the equivalent of an *appellation contrôlée* from the government, while nearby Düsseldorf has amber-coloured Alt – "old" – beers. Wheat beers have become vogue drinks, the spicy, fruity Bavarian style growing in recent years to 30 per cent of the beer market. In Berlin, the wheat beers are injected with a lactic culture to give them a mouth-puckering sourness.

The golden Pilsner

Bohemia, now the Czech Republic, was the home of the first golden Pilsner lagers. The name comes from the great industrial city of Pilsen, also famous for the S̆koda motor car. While Munich developed commercial lagering, the first pale beer of the style came from Pilsen at the height of the Industrial Revolution. Today, only two breweries brew genuine Pilsners, Pilsner Urquell – meaning "Original Source Pilsner" – and Gambrinus. Beers made in Prague or C˘eské Bude˘jovice (Budweis in German) are termed respectively "Prague" beers or "Budweiser" beers. Outside the Czech Republic, though, brewers are not so punctilious. Any light lager is termed Pilsner or Pils, even though it has little in common with the rich complexity of the genuine article.

In both Scandinavia and the Far East, lagers ranging from the bland to the complex are the norm, but there are small pockets of dark beer. The Japanese, for example, brew some flavourful dark beers, while Sweden and Finland brew porters produced by proper warm fermentation.

Brewed in the USA

The history of American brewing has been dominated by both immigration and politics. The first settlers from England took an ale culture with them across the Atlantic, but ale took second place to lager when the second wave of immigrants from central Europe arrived. During the long years of Prohibition in the 1920s, quality ales and lagers largely disappeared, and the breweries that survived dominated the market with increasingly bland light or "lite" lagers. Today, however, there are more than 1,200 small craft breweries producing ales and lagers of enormous quality, while the one true American beer style – steam beer, a hybrid lager–cum–ale – has been rescued and resuscitated by the Anchor Brewery in San Francisco.

In Australasia, ale was supplanted by lager early in the twentieth century. Today, famous brands such as Foster's and Castlemaine XXXX dominate the market, but the success of one traditional ale brewery in Adelaide, Cooper's, has prompted a small ale revival in other parts of the country. There are now several craft breweries in Australia and New Zealand that are concentrating on ale brewing. As the twenty-first century gets under way, ale, against all the odds, is the world's most sought-after revivalist beer style.

The Beer Family

ALE (WARM FERMENTING) TYPES AND STYLES

BELGIUM:	Ales. Golden ales. Lambic and gueuze spontaneous fermentation/kriek and frambozen. Brown ales/brown kriek. Flemish red ales. Trappist ales. Abbey ales. Saison. Wheat beers.
THE CARIBBEAN:	Stout.
ENGLAND:	Mild (pale and dark). Sweet/"Milk" stout. Stout and porter. Bitter. Northern brown ales. Special bitter/India Pale Ale. Strong bitter. Summer ale. Harvest ale. Old ale/Winter ale. Barley wine.
FRANCE:	Bière de garde. Bière de Mars. Bière de Printemps.
GERMANY:	Alt. Kölsch. Wheat beer (Berlin/Bavaria). Stone beer.
IRELAND:	Irish ale. Irish red ale. Dry stout.
THE NETHERLANDS:	Aajt. Amber. Bock. Oud Bruin. Trappist ale. Wheat beer.
SCANDINAVIA:	Porter. Sahti/Juniper beer.
SCOTLAND:	Light/60 shilling. Heavy/70 shilling. Export/80 shilling. Wee Heavy/90 shilling.
SRI LANKA:	Stout.
UNITED STATES:	Amber ale. Cream ale. Steam beer*. India Pale Ale. Porter/Stout. Wheat beer.

WOOD-AGED BEERS

This style is a new development and covers beers matured in wood, usually oak. The innovator was Innis & Gunn in Edinburgh, Scotland, and the process sees beer maturing in casks obtained from the American bourbon industry. The casks are stored in a Scottish whisky distillery. A number of Scottish and English brewers now mature ale in whisky casks: some casks are from the US, some from the Spanish sherry industry. Some 70 craft breweries in the US now produce wood-aged beers.

LAGER (COLD FERMENTING) TYPES AND STYLES

CZECH REPUBLIC:	Budweiser. Pilsner. Prague beer. Black lager.
GERMANY:	Munich Dunkel, Munich Helles. Dortmunder/ Export. Bock/Double Bock. Märzen/ Oktoberfest. Rauchbier. Black beer. German Pilsner.
JAPAN:	Dry beer. Black beer. American/German-style lager.
UNITED STATES:	Lite lagers. Malt liquor. Pilsner. Oktoberfest/ märzen. Steam beer★. Bock/Double bock. Ice beer.
CANADA:	Ice beer.
MEXICO:	Vienna-style dark lager. Light lager.

NOTE
★Steam beer is a hybrid, made with a lager yeast but fermented at an ale temperature. Most other countries brew international-style lagers, based loosely on the Pilsner style.

Serving beer

Temperature is crucial to the enjoyment of beer. Lager beers should be kept in a refrigerator and served at 9°C/48°F. Light American and Australian lagers are often served at a lower temperature of 6°C/42°F. Ales should not be over-chilled or they will develop a haze and their fruity flavours will be masked; 11–13°C/52–56°F are recommended. Very strong ales, such as barley wines, should be served at room temperature. Do not store bottle-conditioned beers in a fridge. Keep them cool and allow them to stand for several hours (a day is best) to allow the sediment to clear.

The World A–Z
of Beer

Fancy a beer? It is one of the oldest invitations in the world and one that sets the tastebuds tingling. Beer, more than any other drink, means conviviality, a pleasure shared. But simply to ask for "a beer" in a bar or a pub is to risk missing out on the diversity and the complexity of styles available on the world stage. If you ask for "a beer" in an English pub you may be handed the stock bitter or, if you're unlucky, the standard lager. An interested barperson, on the other hand, may ask you to specify. Perhaps a mild ale, or a pale ale, or a special bitter, a porter, a stout, an old ale, a barley wine or a winter warmer? You begin to see that beer is not such a simple thing; that not all brown liquids are the same.

In Germany it would be absurd and mildly irritating to call for "ein bier, bitte" or, even worse, "a lager", which to the Germans is a brewing term and certainly not a definition of a style. Again, you would be asked to be specific: a Helles (light), or a Dunkel (dark), a strong Bock, an export, a Pils, a Weizen (wheat) beer or the two proud and idiosyncratic warm fermenting styles of Cologne and Düsseldorf, a Kölsch or an Alt.

Belgium packs within its small territory such a manifold range of beers that a waiter confronted by the demand for just "a beer" would respond by handing you a drinks menu conveniently divided into pale ales, Trappist, Abbey beers, red beers, white beers and fruit beers – and that is just scratching the surface of the choice available.

Even in the United States, where for generations the call for "a beer" was synonymous with asking for a standardized bland, mass-marketed lager, the explosion of small craft breweries – there are now 1,200 with a 10 per cent market share – the beer world has been turned on its head. A bar specializing in craft beers may offer you an India Pale Ale, an amber ale, a red ale, a "London" porter or an "Irish" stout. If lager beers are the specialities, they will be far removed from a Bud or a Coors. You may get a genuine Märzen, a Bock, a Celebrator, an Oktoberfestbier, a Dunkel, a Pilsner, or a Dortmunder.

In Australia, where for decades beer drinking was epitomized by the "six o'clock swill" – as many schooners as possible knocked back before the shutters came down – more liberal opening hours have encouraged greater emphasis on quality and a willingness to experiment. Craft breweries and brewpubs may not challenge the hegemony of such mass market brands as Carlton Draught and Victoria Bitter, but choice is beginning to seep across the continent. The revival of ale, personified by the doughty Adelaide firm of Cooper's, founded by an emigrant from Yorkshire, has created interest in a beer style that pre-dates the lager revolution and proves that warm-fermented beer can be enjoyed in hot climates.

In countries considered to be quintessentially within the lager fold there are surprises. In Japan you will find black beers and stouts that offer welcome choice in a country where pale lagers dominate. And in pockets of Scandinavia warm-fermented porters and stouts stick their heads above the ice floes.

The world of beer is not noted for its conformity. As beer makes inroads even into great wine-making countries such as France and Italy, drinkers are discovering a multiplicity of flavours and aromas.

In Northern France – or "French Flanders", as the locals prefer to call it – the ancient style of *bière de garde* has been resurrected with considerable success. Similar to the saisons of Belgium, these French "keeping beers" were originally made by farmers for consumption during the summer and the harvest. They are members of the ale family and their critical acclaim has stimulated a number of small craft breweries to start production and introduce other interpretations of the style, such as March, autumn and winter beers. They have become a fashion beer in Lille, capital of French Flanders, where specialist cafés offer an abundance of choice and even brew on the premises. Jenlain, leading city of the revivalists, has its own café.

Not to be outdone, Italians who used to dismiss beer as a light summer refresher are taking a greater interest. The big commercial breweries have added some beers of distinction to their portfolios while several new craft breweries in the north of the country are producing ales, wheat beers and German-style lagers with great dedication to style.

The Beers of Europe

Europe is the cradle of modern brewing. The lagering or storing of beer – usually in icy caves – developed empirically in Central Europe from medieval times and then spread like a bush fire when ice making machines were invented during the Industrial Revolution. The first commercial lagers in Munich were dark in colour. It was Pilsen in Bohemia – today's Czech Republic – that produced the first golden lager and gave the world a style known as Pilsner or Pils. Britain and Ireland remained faithful to ale: pale ale or bitter in Britain and dark, roasty dry stouts in Ireland, while Belgium offers a remarkable choice of ales, including some brewed by Trappist monks.

Austria

Austria lost not only a great empire but a beer style as well. Today brewers will argue there was no such thing as a Vienna style based on "red" malt but history to proves them wrong. In far away Mexico, briefly and incongruously ruled by Austria, red-brown lagers such as Dos Equis and Negro Modela pay homage to a style that marked Vienna out from such all-conquering neighbours as Munich and Pilsner.

Anton Dreher was one of the great brewing innovators. He worked closely with Sedlmayr in Munich to develop commercial lager brewing in the nineteenth century. While the first Munich lagers were dark brown – Dunkel – Dreher's were amber-red. No information exists about Dreher's recipe, but he was known in Vienna as the "English maltster" and he may have brought from England a coke-fired kiln that enabled him to produce a paler malt than the wood-cured ones in Munich. The water in Vienna is harder than in

Pilsen, which would give the finished beer an amber colour not dissimilar to the pale ales of Burton-on-Trent. In the 1840s Dreher would not have had access to stewed malts such as caramalt and crystal, which did not appear until the turn of the century.

Vienna lager beers were first produced by Dreher around 1841 from his brewery in Schwechat in the Vienna suburbs. The brewery still exists, a remarkable group of buildings, both bucolic and baronial, parts dating back to a hunting lodge built in 1750 for Archduchess Maria Theresa, ruler of most of Europe, who is thought to have used the lodge for less than courtly purposes.

In Dreher's day, Schwechat was a vast enterprise challenging Pilsner Urquell in size. He built other breweries in Bohemia (at Michelob, a name still in use as Anheuser-Busch's premium beer in the US), in Budapest and in Trieste. The Italian brewery still bears Dreher's name though it is now owned by Heineken. In his heyday of the 1870s, with the Industrial Revolution going full bore and the world of beer turned upside down as a result of new technologies, Dreher was exporting beer far and wide. But his Vienna company went out of business in the 1930s and the style of beer he had created became just a fading memory for elderly Viennese. Today Austrian beers tend to ape the Bavarian style across the border, though they do not adhere to the *Reinheitsgebot*. Corn, wheat and rice are used as adjuncts and hop rates in general are not high. The result is pale, golden lagers that tend to be malty with a sweetish edge and only light bitterness.

Schwechat is now part of BrauUnion, a merger of Austria's two biggest breweries, Bräu AG and Steirische Bräuindustrie. The merged group was subsequently bought by Heineken but operates under the Austrian name, with head offices in Linz. **Schwechat Lager** (5.2 per cent ABV) is malty and rounded while the premium **Hopfenperle** (5.3 per cent ABV) has more hop character and a dry finish. It has no connection with the Swiss beer of the same name. Bräu AG also brews under the Kaiser and Zipfer labels. **Zipfer Urtyp** – Original

– (5.4 per cent ABV) has a fine perfumy hop aroma and finish with good balancing malt.

The Steirische section of the group is based in Graz. Steirische is the local name for Styria and is a major hop-growing region, though most hops today that carry the name come from a province also called Styria in neighbouring Slovenia. The most assertive and characterful beers from the group are brewed under the Gösser label. **Gösser Export** is 5.0 per cent ABV, brewed with pale malt, caramalt, maize and rice, with Hallertau, Spalt, Styrian and Goldings hops (20 IBUs). With just gentle hop bitterness, the beer has a rich malt and vanilla aroma and palate with some hop notes in the bittersweet finish.

Stiegl in Salzburg was founded in 1492, the year Columbus landed in the Americas. The connection is celebrated by **Columbus** (5.3 per cent ABV) a rich, malty but well-hopped lager.

Ottakringer in Vienna dates from 1837 and is still family-owned. Its beers are among the most characterful in the country due to the generous use of Saaz hops. Its **Helles** (5.1 per cent ABV) is tart, quenching and aromatic while its Gold **Fassl Spezial** (5.6 per cent ABV) has a more pronounced maltiness balanced by perfumy hops.

The Schloss Eggenberg Brewery in the town of the same name has a beer that panders to Scotch whisky drinkers while offering a colour akin to a genuine Vienna Red. **MacQueens Nessie Whisky Malt Red Beer** is a powerful 7.5 per cent ABV with 26.7 IBUs from Hallertau hops. The malt is imported from Scotland and imparts a delicious smoky, peaty character. The colour of the beer is amber and the finish is long and smoky with hop undercurrents. "It's like a whisky and soda," according to the brewer. He also makes an **Urbock 23°**, the number referring to its strength on the Plato scale which translates into 9.3 per cent ABV. It is lagered for an impressive nine months, has a rich fruity aroma, rounded malt and hops in the mouth and a big vinous and hoppy finish. It is made from Pilsner and Munich malts and Saaz and Hallertau hops (40 IBUs). Following the closure of the Hürlimann Brewery in Switzerland, Schloss Eggenberg now brews Samichlaus, the strongest lager beer in the world. See Swiss section for full details of the beer.

The Josef Sigl Brewery in Obertrum keeps the wheat beer tradition alive with a warm-fermenting **Weizen Gold** (5.2 per cent ABV). It is hopped with Hallertau and has a spicy cloves aroma, a tart and refreshing palate and a lingering bittersweet finish. Sigl's **Trumer Pils** (4.9 per cent) is a fine example of the style. It's aged for six weeks and has a toasted malt, noble hops and lemon fruit aroma, and a bitter, malty and gently fruity palate and finish. Since 2004, the beer has also been brewed under licence in Berkeley, California.

Three new craft breweries have been launched in recent years. The 1516 Brewing Company in Vienna brews a lager and – unusually – an ale, the latter brewed under licence from the Victory Brewery in Pennsylvania, United States. Handsbrauerei Forstner in Graz has a large portfolio for a small brewery: blonde, red, black and wheat. Brauhaus Gusswerk in Salzburg concentrates on organic beers, including a wheat beer.

Two brewpubs of note are the Fischer Gasthof at Billroth Strasse 17, Döbling in Vienna, which offers a Helles and a Bock. In Nüssdorf, Baron Hendrik Bachofen von Echte has a fine brewery and restaurant in the cellars of his castle. He makes warm-fermenting beers, including a Helles brewed with 30 per cent wheat malt, a malty Altbier and a chocolatey and dry Irish-style stout called Sir Henry's.

AUSTRIAN BREWERS

Braueueri Schloss Eggenberg,
Eggenberg 1, 4655 Vorchdorf.

Braueueri Kapsreiter,
A-4780 Schärding.

Josef Sigl Brauerei,
A-5162 Obertrum SLBG.

Bräu Union, A-4021 Linz.

1516 Brewing Co, A-1010 Wien.

Handbrauerei Forstner, A-401 Graz.

Brauhaus Gusswerk, 5020 Salzburg.

St Georgs-Bräu,
8861 St. Georgen ob Murau

The beer styles of Belgium

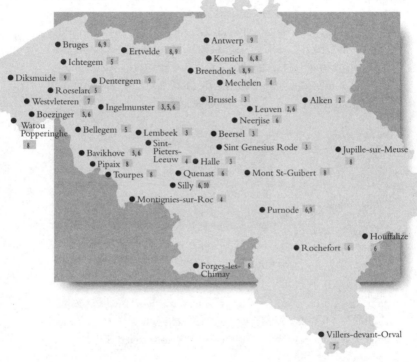

Key

1 Brewery

2 Pils brewers

3 Lambic producers and Gueuze blenders

4 Old Brown brewers

5 Red Beer brewers

6 White Beer brewers

7 Trappist breweries

8 Abbey breweries

9 Ale brewers

10 Saison brewers

Belgium

Belgians are passionate about beer. If you show an interest in the subject, waiters or bar owners tend to dive into cellars and return with dusty bottles they have been saving for "a special occasion". Often the bottles are wrapped in coloured tissue paper and have Champagne-style cradles and corks. Without hesitation or fear of being derided, they will call such offerings "Grand Cru" or the Bourgogne (Burgundy) of the beer world. Unlike the British, whose collective stiff upper lip refuses to acknowledge that they also make some amazing ales, the Belgians have no qualms about proclaiming their beers to be as good as fine wine.

BELGIUM	Diksmuide	Leuven	Schepdaal
	De Dolle Brouwers	Stella Artois (Pils)	De Neve Brouwerij
Alken	**Ertvelde**	Domus Brouwerij	**Silly**
Alken	Bios, Brouwerij van	(White beer)	Brasserie de Silly
Antwerp	Steenberghe	**Mater**	**Sint Genesius**
De Koninck	**Flobecq**	Roman Brouwerij	**Rode**
Brouwerij	Brasserie Voisin	**Mechelen**	Wets Gueuzestekerij
Recommended pub	**Forges-les-**	Het Anker	**Sint-Pieters-**
Kulminator	**Chimay**	Brouwerij	**Leeuw**
Bavikhove	Abbaye de Notre-	**Montignies-**	Moriau
Bavik-De	Dame de	**sur-Roc**	Gueuzestekerij
Brabandere	Scourmont	Brasserie de l'Abbaye	**Sint-Ulricks-**
Beersel	**Ghent**	des Rocs	**Kapelle**
Drie Fonteinen	*Recommended pub*	**Neerijse**	Girardin Brouwerij
Vandervelden	De Hopduvel	De Kroon Brouwerij	**Steenhuffel**
Brouwerij	**Halle**	**Ninove**	Palm Brouwerij
Bellegem	Vander Linden	Slaghmuylder	**Ternat**
Bocker Brouwerij	Brouwerij	Brouwerij	De Troch Brouwerij
Boezinge	**Hoegaarden**	**Oudenaarde**	**Tourpes**
Leroy Brouwerij	De Kluis Brouwerij	Clarysse Brouwerij	Brasserie Dupont
Breendonk	**Houffalize**	(Old brown/	**Villers-devant-**
Moortgat Brouwerij	Brasserie d'Achouffe	white beer)	**Orval**
Bruges	**Ichtegem**	Leifman's Brouwerij	Abbaye de Notre-
Recommended pub	Strubbe Brouwerij	(Old brown)	Dame d'Orval
't Brugs Beertje	**Ingelmunster**	**Pipaix**	**Vlezenbeek**
Brussegem	Van Honsebrouck	Brasserie à Vapeur	Lindemans
Belgor Brouwerij	Brouwerij	Brasserie Dubuisson	Brouwerij
Brussels	**Itterbeek**	**Purnode**	**Watou-Poperinge**
Belle-Vue	Timmermanns	Brasserie Du Bocq	Sint Bernardus
Cantillon Brouwerij	**Jupille-sur-Meuse**	**Quenast**	Brouwerij
Recommended pubs	Brasserie Jupiler	Brasserie Lefèbvre	**Westvleteren**
Falstaff	**Kobbegem**	**Rochefort**	Abdij Sint Sixtus
A La Morte Subite	De Keersmaeker	Abbaye de Notre-	
Moeder Lambic	Brouwerij	Dame de St	
Ixelles	**Kontich**	Rémy	
't Spinnekopke	Maes	**Roeselare**	
Dentergem	**Lembeek**	Rodenbach	
Riva Brouwerij	Frank Boon	Brouwerij	

Belgian Pils

The choice in this small country is astonishing. But the recent revival of interest in Belgian ales – pale, golden, red, Trappist, Abbey, wheat and lambic – cannot disguise the fact that for everyday drinking the people consume vast amounts of Pilsner-style lagers. Purists may argue that only lagers from Pilsen in the Czech Republic should carry the appellation, but it cannot be said that the Belgian interpretations of the style are anything less than good. The two leading (but not the best) Pils brands, **Stella Artois** and **Jupiler**, come from the giant Interbrew group, the result of a merger in the 1980s between Stella Artois of Leuven and Piedboeuf of Jupille-sur-Meuse near Liège. The merger not only brought two leading breweries under one roof but also, as their places of origin suggest, managed to bridge the linguistic divide. Interbrew is now the world's biggest brewer. It first merged with Ambev of Brazil to become InBev and then in 2008 bought America's biggest brewery, Anheuser-Busch, brewer of Budweiser, to become InBev A-B.

Stella Artois traces its origins to the Den Horen (the Horn) tavern that brewed beer from 1366 and began to supply the university from 1537. Sebastien Artois was an apprentice brewer at Den Horen, graduated as a master brewer and bought the brewery in 1717. His grandson Léonard busily expanded the business and bought two rival companies in Leuven. Den Horen Artois became one of the major commercial breweries in Europe and switched with enthusiasm to the new lagering methods in the late nineteenth century. Its first golden, cold-fermented beer was called **Bock** but unlike German Bocks, which are high in alcohol, this was weaker than a genuine Pilsner. The company achieved greater fame and fortune in 1926 when it brewed a stronger 5.0 per cent Pils-style beer, Stella Artois, that is now Belgium's best-known – though not best-selling – Pils. It is exported widely and brewed under licence in several countries. Stella Artois is made with great dedication to traditional methods. The brewery has a six-storey maltings in Leuven, using the floor method rather than modern tanks. Brewers believe that malt spread out on warm floors and regularly turned and aerated produces a cleaner, sweeter beer. In the brewhouses – Artois once had a dozen but is consolidating them – the wort is boiled with Czech Saaz hops along with some German Northern Brewer and Tettnanger, as well as Styrians. The Saaz dominate, giving the finished beer (30 IBUs) an aromatic, slightly spicy aroma. Stella is lagered for around two months and is clean and quenching in the mouth with a finish that becomes dry as the hops emphasize their character. The Artois side of Interbrew also produces a stronger (5.7 per cent ABV) lager beer called **Loburg**, designed to counteract Danish "super premium" imports.

Jupiler (5.0 per cent ABV, around 25 IBUs) is the biggest-selling Pils in Belgium. The Piedboeuf family founded its brewery in 1853 in Jupille, believed to be the birthplace of Charlemagne and with a history of brewing that dates back to 1256. Jupiler's rise to popularity is impressive as it was launched as recently as 1966. It is an easy-drinking, soft, malt-accented beer lacking the hop character of Stella. Interbrew also owns the **Lamot Pils** brand though the Lamot Brewery in Mechelen closed at the end of 1994.

Four-fifths of all Belgian Pils are accounted for by InBev and the second biggest brewing group, Alken-Maes. A–M was bought by Scottish & Newcastle, along with Kronenbourg in France, from Danone in 2000. S&N has closed the Maes plant at Waarloos and concentrated production at Alken. **Cristal Alken** is the Pils favoured by connoisseurs. It was formulated in 1928 to suit the tastes of miners in the Limburg region. As a result it is more aggressively hoppy than other leading Belgian Pils. Alken is close to the German border and it could be the German Pils brewing tradition that has prompted Alken to make its beer a shade dryer and more positively bitter, though the brewers who formulated the beer claimed they were attempting to recreate a genuine Czech Pilsner.

There are around 100 Pils brands in Belgium. Even some specialist ale brewers also produce a Pils in order to have a small slice of the substantial market. The most highly regarded Pils from a smaller brewer comes from Haacht near a village of the same name that is roughly equidistant from Brussels, Leuven and Mechelen. The Pils is called **Primus** and is a complex beer with a sweetish start leading to a refreshing palate and a dry finish with good hop influence. French and Dutch malts are joined by the ubiquitous Saaz and German varieties of hops. Other highly regarded interpretations of the style include an unfiltered, well-hopped **Redor Pils** from Dupont of Tourpes, an equally hoppy **Bel Pils** from Moortgat of Breendonk, two from Slaghmuylder of Ninove, Paasbier and Kerstbier, and Strubbe's **Super Pils**, a well-hopped version brewed in Ichtegem.

SELECTED PILS BREWERS

Alken, Alken-Maes,
Stationstraat 2, 3820 Alken.

Haacht Brouwerij,
Provinciesteenweg 28,
2890 Boortmeerbeek.

Dupont,
Rue Basse 5, 7904 Tourpes-Leuze.

Brasserie Jupiler,
Interbrew, rue de Vise 243,
4500 Jupille-sur-Meuse.

Duvel Moortgat,
Breendonkdorp 58, 2870 Puurss.

Slaghmuylder,
Denderhoutembaan 2, 9400 Ninove.

Stella Artois,
Interbrew,
Vaartstraat 94, 3000 Leuven.

Strubbe,
Markt 1, 8480 Ichtegem.

Lambic

Lambic, a beer produced by spontaneous fermentation as a result of action by air-borne yeasts, is a potent link with brewing's past. Before brewers understood the mysteries of yeast, they allowed wild strains either in the air or in brewing vessels to attack malt sugars and turn them into alcohol. With the aid of science and technology, ale brewers and later lager producers turned their back on such antiquated methods and produced their beers with the aid of carefully cultured yeast strains.

In the Payottenland area of Belgium centred on the Senne valley (Zenne in Flemish) a handful of dedicated brewers has remained faithful to a tradition that produces beers which, with their tart, vinous and even cidery characteristics, seem to break down all the barriers between cereal-based and fruit-based alcoholic drinks. They hark back to a period when all alcoholic drinks were bucolic, peasant ones, made from the raw ingredients to hand in the surrounding fields.

Lambic (sometimes spelt "lambik") is the world's oldest beer style still made on a regular commercial basis. It has existed for some 400 years and it is fitting that its area of production almost exactly matches that part of Belgium dubbed by the tourist board "the Breugel Route". For the paintings of the Breugels, Pieter the Elder in particular, personify a rural idyll in which the consumption of a rough ale called lambic was at the heart of family and communal life. The recent revival of interest in lambic and its off-shoots – gueuze, faro, mars, kriek and frambozen – has prompted both the Belgian government and the European Union to protect the style and to lay down strict rules for its production.

Lambic is a country beer style. It declined as industry sprang up and the great city of Brussels expanded into the Senne valley. City dwellers switched first to strong ales brewed in the conventional manner and then to the new Pilsner beers. Although one of the remaining lambic brewers, Cantillon, is based in Brussels, it remains a rustic beer in its methods of production. As with farm brewers of earlier times, brewing does not take place during the summer months because of the impossibility of controlling the temperature of a spontaneously fermenting ale.

In order to qualify as a genuine lambic, the beer must be brewed with at least 30 per cent wheat in the mash. Unlike a classic Bavarian wheat beer, the wheat in a lambic is unmalted. Busy farmers understood that barley malt provided sufficient enzymes to convert starch to sugar without the need to malt their wheat as well. The barley malt is as pale as Pilsner malt. With the addition of wheat, the resulting mash is cloudy and milky white. The starting gravity is around 1050 degrees with a finished ABV of 4.5 to 5.0 per cent.

The hop rate is high but the hops used are four years old. They have lost their aromatic quality and have a deliberate "cheesy" smell. The varieties are used primarily for their antiseptic qualities. Lambic brewers discovered, along with wheat beer producers in other regions, that the tart nature of fresh hops does not blend well with the spicy, fruity and slightly lactic character of wheat beer.

When the copper boil is over, brewing is left to nature. The hopped wort is pumped to a shallow, open fermenting vessel known as a "cool ship". The ship is always high in the roof of the brewery. Louvred windows are left open and a few tiles are even removed from the roof. During the night yeasts come in on the breeze and attack the inviting malt sugars in the ship.

After spontaneous fermentation, the green beer is transferred to oak casks where it is attacked by microflora. In the cellars, cobwebs and spiders abound, as nothing must be done to alter the eco-structure. Spiders are important as they attack fruit flies which would otherwise feast on the beers, especially those to which fruit is added. The casks, made mainly from wood with a few of chestnut, are bought from port producers in Portugal. Belle-Vue, the biggest producer of lambic, has 15,000 casks on five floors, ranging in size from 250 litres to 30 hectolitres.

Wild *Brettanomyces* yeasts give what brewers call a "horse-blanket" aroma to ale, a grainy, slightly musty character. But it takes some time for *Brettanomyces* to dominate other microflora active in lambic. The beer will stay and mature in cask for a few months, in some cases for as long as six years. A young lambic is yeasty and immature, and even after a year the beer will still have some "cheesiness" from the hops. At 18 months the beer takes on a sherry colour and *Brettanomyces* has started to dominate the aroma. An aged lambic of six years will have a pronounced vinous aroma, a deep sherry character in the mouth, and a sour and lactic finish.

Gueuze

Lambic is usually served on draught while its most widely available bottled form is known as gueuze. To counteract the green flavours of young lambic, gueuze is a blend of mature and young brews. The mature lambic gives gloss, depth and a tart vinous character to the beer while the young, which contains unfermented malt sugars, causes a second fermentation in the bottle. The blend is usually 60 per cent young to 40 per cent mature. The bottles are stoppered with Champagne corks and laid down horizontally in cellars for between six and 18 months. When a bottle is opened, the ale rushes, foaming, into the glass: it is truly the Champagne of the beer world. As more alcohol has been produced during the bottle-conditioning, a gueuze will have around 5.5 per cent ABV. It is tart, cidery and refreshing. Some gueuze makers have tended to sweeten their beers in order to reach a wider audience but the resurgence of interest in the style has concentrated brewers' minds. In 1993, Belle-Vue, owned by InBev, responded to its critics by launching **Séléction Lambic**, which met with critical acclaim. But InBev closed the Brussels Belle-Vue brewery, moved production to Sint-Pieters-Leeuw and Séléction Lambic has disappeared. The current Belle-Vue brewery, which also produces lambic and gueuze under the De Neve label, dominates the market but its beers tend to be sweet and its fruit lambics are made with concentrate rather than whole fruit.

Kriek and frambozen

In a world where there is a sharp but wholly absurd dividing line between beer and wine, a "fruit beer" sounds bizarre, but the origins of the style are functional and sensible. Before the hop was adopted both to make beer bitter and to act as a preservative, country brewers used all manner of herbs and spices to balance the malty sweetness of their brews. Brewers in the Low Countries found that cherries, which grow in abundance, added a further fermentation to their brews, increasing the level of alcohol and imparting a pleasing tartness. Fruit marries especially well with wheat beers, with their fruity flavours in which apple and banana predominate.

Kriek is the Flemish word for cherry. Raspberry beers are called both *framboise* in French and *frambozen* in Flemish. The preferred cherry is the small, hard Schaarbeek that grows around Brussels. Rather like "noble rot" grapes, the cherries are picked late so that the fermentable sugars are well developed. The cherries are not crushed but the skins are lightly broken and added at the rate of one kilo of cherries to five kilos of beer in the lambic cellars. Some young lambic is also added. The fruit sugars and the young beer encourage a new fermentation and the skins of the cherries add dryness to the beer. As fermentation proceeds, the yeasts even attack the pips which impart an almost almond-like quality. You can tell which casks in the cellar contain cherries as the brewers place some twigs in the open bung hole. These stop the cherries floating to the top of the beer, blocking the bung and preventing attack by fruit flies.

Fruit beers improve and deepen with age. A young kriek, with its luscious pink colour, will offer an aroma and palate of fruit whereas a year-old version will have developed a sour palate and a long, dry finish. At 18 months, a kriek will have taken on earthy, vinous characteristics. A frambozen of around one year will have a delicate perfumy aroma, bittersweet fruit in the mouth with a spritzy, refreshing finish.

The small craft lambic brewery of Cantillon in Brussels produces a magnificent range of beers. Its classic is considered to be **Rosé de Gambrinus**, a blend of kriek and frambozen. The brewery has further blurred the distinction between beer and wine by making a lambic that uses grapes as well as cereals. Cantillon has regular open days where visitors can taste the beers and see the brewing vessels. Cantillon and some of the other lambic brewers also occasionally make faro, a lambic produced by remashing the grains of the first brew and adding candy sugar to encourage fermentation. **Faro** is drunk on draught at around 4.0 per cent ABV as a good refreshing beer. The even lower-alcohol mars is no longer made.

LAMBIC PRODUCERS AND GUEUZE BLENDERS

Belgor Brouwerij,
Kerkstraat 17, 1881 Brussegem.
Belle-Vue,
1600 Sint-Pieters-Leeuw.
Owned by InBev: lambic, gueuze, kriek and frambozen.
Bokor,
8510 Bellegem-Kortrijk:
lambic, gueuze, kriek and frambozen.
Frank Boon BV,
Fonteinstraat 65, 1520 Lembeek:

lambic, gueuze, kriek, frambozen and faro.
Cantillon Brouwerij,
Gheudestraat 56, 1070 Brussels:
lambic, gueuze, kriek, frambozen and faro.
De Keersmaeker Brouwerij,
Brusselstraat 1, 1703 Kobbegem
(owned by Scottish & Newcastle, brews under the Morte Subite and Eylenbosch names): lambic, gueuze, kriek, frambozen and faro.
De Koninck Gueuzestekerij,
Kerstraat 57, 1512 Dworp (not

related to De Koninck of Antwerp):
gueuze and kriek.

De Troch Brouwerij,
Langestraat 20, 1741 Ternat-
Wambeck: lambic, gueuze and faro.

Drie Fonteinen,
H. Teirlinckplein 3, 1650 Beersel:
lambic, gueuze, kriek and frambozen.

Girardin Brouwerij,
Lindenberg 10, 1744 Sint-Ulriks-
Kapelle: lambic, gueuze and kriek.

Hanssens Gueuzetekerij,
Vroenenbosstraat 8, 1512 Dworp:
gueuze and kriek. Blender.

Lindemans Brouwerij,
Lenniniksebaan 257, 1712
Vlezenbeek: lambic, gueuze, kriek
and frambozen.

Moriau Gueuzestekerij,
Hoogstraat 1, 1600 Sint Pieters-
Leeuw: lambic, gueuze and kriek.
Brewed for the company by Boon.

Timmermanns NV,
Kerkstraat 11, 1711 Itterbeek: lambic,
gueuze, kriek and frambozen.

Vandervelden Brouwerij,
Laarheidestraat 230, 1650 Beersel:
Production stopped when the owner
retired. New, young owners are
restoring the tradition but it will take
a few years for aged lambic, gueuze
and kriek to come on stream. A
strong ale is currently brewed.

Van Honsebrouck Brouwerij,
Oostrozebekestraat 43, 8770
Ingelmunster (produces lambic and
fruit beers under the St Louis name:
uses mainly syrups, not whole fruit).

Brown ale

Tragedy has struck the historic waterside Flemish city of Oudenaarde, once the historic home of brown ales. The best known of the **Old Brown (Oud Bruin)** ales came from Liefman's, a brewery founded in 1679. The fame of the brewery spread in the 1970s when the owner died and the company was taken over by his former secretary, Rose Blancquaert-Merckx. With her son Olav, she expanded the business and won worldwide acclaim for the beers. But when she retired, the brewery was bought in the early 1990s by the Riva group, based in Dentergem, best known for its spicy wheat beer: Riva also acquired the Straffe Hendrik brewery in Bruges. Both Liefman's and the Bruges brewery closed though the group, without a blush, is now called Liefman's. As a result of consumer protest, brewing may restart at Oudenaarde at some unspecified time.

The basic Old Brown is brewed from a blend of Pilsner, Munich and Vienna malts and a little roasted barley. Hops are English Goldings, with some Czech and German varieties. The slow copper boil lasts for 12 hours. The 5.0 per cent ABV beer is fermented for seven days in open vessels and is then matured for four months. A stronger, 6.0 per cent ABV, version called **Goudenband** (Gold Riband) is a blend of the basic beer with one that has matured for six to eight months. The blend is primed with sugar, re-seeded with yeast and stored for three months. Goudenband can be laid down and will improve for several years, taking on a dark, sherry-like wineyness.

Once a year Liefman's makes both a kriek and a frambozen from fresh cherries and raspberries, with the basic Oud Bruin. The beers are stored and refermented for up to two months. The 7.1 per cent ABV Liefman's kriek has a delectable dry and tart fruitiness while the 5.1 per cent ABV frambozen has a lilting aroma of fresh fruit and is bittersweet on the palate. All the Liefman's beers come in tissue-wrapped bottles.

As a result of being incorporated into the Riva group, the Liefman's beers are mashed and boiled at Riva's main brewery at Dentergem. The wort is trunked to Oudenaarde for fermentation and maturation. Riva used to make brown ales at the Het Anker brewery in Mechelen but in 1998 the plant was sold to its management. As a result there has been considerable investment and expansion, including restoration of an old steam brewhouse dating from 1873 and the opening of a brewery hotel. Anker is best known for its bottle-conditioned **Gouden Carolus**, named after a coin from the reign of Emperor Charles V. There are now three versions of the beer, **Ambrio** (8 per cent ABV), **Classic** (8.5 per cent) and **Tripel** (9 per cent). There are also Easter and Christmas versions of the beer and an Anker-Bok (6.5 per cent) aimed at the Dutch market.

OLD BROWN BREWERS

Clarysse Brouwerij, Krekelput 16–18, 9700 Oudenaarde.

Cnudde Brouwerij, Fabriekstraat 8, 9700 Eine.

Het Anker Brouwerij, Guido Gezellaan 49, 2800 Mechelen.

Liefman's Brouwerij, Aalstraat 200, 9700 Oudenaarde.

Liefman's Riva Group, Wontergemstraat 42, 8720 Dentergem.

Roman Brouwerij, Hauwaert 61, 9700 Mater.

Among other brown ale brewers, the splendidly artisanal Roman, which dates from 1545, has a chocolatey 5.0 per cent ABV **Oudenaards** and an 8.0 per cent ABV **Dobbelen Bruinen (double brown)** packed with dark malt and hop flavours.

Red ale

If the brown ales of East Flanders are a rare style, the sour red beers of West Flanders are even more esoteric. They are beers that are matured for long periods in unlined oak vats where micro-organisms attack the malt sugars and add a lactic sourness. Such beers are yet another fascinating link with brewing's past, when beers were deliberately "staled" and were then blended with younger ales. The major producer of sour red ale is Rodenbach of Roeselare. The Rodenbachs came from Koblenz in Germany. Alexander Rodenbach bought a small brewery in Roeselare in 1820.

The St George's Brewery in Roeselare is supplied with brewing water from underground springs beneath a lake in the grounds of the brewer's stately home. The brewery site is dominated by an old malt kiln now used as a museum. Beer is made from a blend of pale malts, both spring and winter varieties, and darker Vienna malt. Vienna malt is similar to English crystal and adds both the red/copper hue and body to the beer. Malt accounts for 80 per cent of the grist, the rest made up of corn grits. The hops are Brewers' Gold and East Kent Goldings, used primarily for their aroma. Too much bitterness would not marry well with the tartness of the beer. Primary fermentation takes seven days and is followed by a second fermentation in metal tanks. The "regular" **Rodenbach**, 4.6 per cent ABV, is bottled after six weeks and is a blend of young and mature beers. Beer destined for ageing is stored in tall oak tuns for a minimum of 18 months and as long as two years.

As the beer matures in the wood, *lactobacilli* and *acetobacters* add a sour and lactic flavour to the beer. The blended beer has a sour, vinous aroma, is tart in the mouth with more sour fruit in the finish. **Grand Cru**, bottled straight from the tuns, is 5.2 per cent ABV and has 14 to 18 units of bitterness. It is bigger in body and flavour than the blended beer: woody, tannic, sour and fruity. Both beers have some sugar added to take the edge off the sourness and they are pasteurized. Rodenbach was bought in 1998 by the major ale brewer, Palm of Steenhuffel. There has been considerable investment in the plant, including new brewing vessels and an overhaul of the vital wooden tuns. Palm has opened some specialist Rodenbach cafes and introduced a new beer, **Oud Belegen Foederbier**, a cask-conditioned beer stored in wooden casks in the specialist cafes.

Among smaller West Flanders breweries, **Bavik Petrus Oud Bruin**, 5.5 per cent ABV, is fermented in oak casks for 20 months and then blended with young beer. The brewery also produces a 7.5 per cent ABV **Triple Petrus**.

RED BEER BREWERS
Bavik-De Brabandere,
Rijksweg 16a, 8752 Bavikhove.
Bockor Brouwerij,
Kwabrugestraat 5, 8540 Bellegem
(Ouden Tripel).
Leroy Brouwerij,
Diksmuidesweg 406, 8930 Boezinge
(Paulus).

Rodenbach Brouwerij,
Spanjestraat 133, 880 Roeselare.
Strubbe Brouwerij,
Markt 1, 8270 Ichtegem (Ichtegems
Oud Bruin).
Van Honsebrouck Brouwerij,
Oostrozebekestraat 43, 8770
Ingelmunster (Bacchus).

White beer

When Pierre Celis brewed a "white beer" in the 1960s he had no idea he would spark a small revolution in Belgium. Today white beers (*bière blanche/witbier*) are cult drinks. Celis revived a beer style that was once very important in the Low Countries, and to do so he chose the small town of Hoegaarden near Leuven, where 30 white beer producers operated in the nineteenth century. All had succumbed to the onslaught of lager brewing. The rich soil of Brabant, that produces barley, oats and wheat in abundance, encouraged farmers, peasants and monks to brew: monks were brewing in Brabant from the fifteenth century. Herbs and spices were added to the brews to balance the sweetness of the grains.

White beer is wheat beer, a member of the ale family, brewed by top or warm fermentation: centuries ago it was fermented spontaneously. The grist is a 50:50 blend of barley malt and unmalted wheat. Pierre Celis used oats as well in his early days but they are no longer used. The units of bitterness in Hoegaarden are around 20: the brewer is not looking for excessive bitterness. The varieties are East Kent Goldings for aroma and Czech Saaz for gentle bitterness. Coriander seeds and orange peel are milled to coarse powders and added with the hops to the copper boil. After fermentation the green beer is conditioned for a month, primed with sugar, re-seeded with yeast and then bottled or kegged. **Hoegaarden** is 4.2 per cent ABV and has a rich, appetizing spicy nose with a clear hint of orange. It is tart and refreshing in the mouth followed by a clean, bittersweet finish. It will improve with age for around six months and takes on a smooth, honey-like character. Hoegaarden is served in a heavy, chunky glass and is cloudy from the yeast and protein left in suspension. The beer is a pale lemon colour with a dense white head of foam. Hoegaarden is now owned by InBev. When InBev announced it would close the Hoegaarden plant and move production to its Jupille lager factory, there was an outcry in Hoegaarden: in Belgium, it was a remarkably insensitive decision to move a beer from a Dutch-speaking area to a French-speaking one. The beer brewed at Jupille was not well-received and InBev rapidly returned to the original site.

Among other wheat beer producers, the Riva group gives prominence to its **Dentergems Witbier** (5.0 per cent ABV), made without spices but with a pleasing apple-fruitiness. The Wallonian brewers have not been slow to spot a large niche in the market. Du Bocq's **Blanche de Namur** (4.5 per cent ABV) is named after a princess from the region (Snow White?) who became queen of Sweden. The beer has a herbal aroma and palate, while the small Silly Brewery's **Titje** (5.0 per cent ABV) is uncompromisingly spicy, tart and quenching.

WHITE BEER BREWERS

Bavik-De Brabandere,
Rijksweg 16a, 8752 Bavihove.

Brasserie Du Bocq,
Rue de la Brasserie 4, 5191 Purnode.

Brouwerij Riva,
Wontergemstraat 42, 8720 Dentergem.

Clarysse Brouwerij,
Krekelput 16-18, 9700 Oudenaarde.

Haacht Brouwerij,
Provinciesteenweg 28, 2980 Boortmeerbeek.

De Kluis Brouwerij,
Stoopkenstraat 46, 3320 Hoegaarden.

De Kroon Brouwerij,
Beekstraat 8, 3055 Neerijse.

Domus Brouwerij,
Tiensestraat 8, 3000 Leuven.

Brasserie Lefèbvre SA,
Rue de Croly 52, 1381 Quenast.

Leroy Brouwerij,
Diksmuidesweg 406, 8930 Boezinge.

Palm Brouwerij,
Steenhuffeldorp 3, 2901 Steenhuffel (Steendonk Witbier).

Roman Brouwerij,
Hauwaert 61, 9700 Mater.

Brasserie de Silly,
Ville Basse A141, 7830 Silly.

Van Honsebrouck Brouwerij,
Oostrozebekestraat 43, 8770 Ingelmunster.

Trappist ales

When Trappist monks were hounded from France during the French Revolution they stoically headed north into the Low Countries to establish new centres of religious devotion. Their simple life included eating the produce from the surrounding fields and making their own alcohol to sustain them during Lent and to help keep them healthy. In France they had made wine liqueurs. In the Low Countries the absence of grapes forced them to make beer from cereals. Thus was born one of the world's great beer styles.

The encroaching secular life has closed many of the abbeys in the Low Countries. Today just six abbeys in Belgium and one in the Netherlands still make beer and they need help from lay brewers to sustain production. Unless sufficient numbers of young people can be attracted to the austere way of life, there is a real fear that true Trappist beers could cease to exist.

Chimay is by far the most famous of the Belgian Trappist breweries. Its ales are sold worldwide. The success of Chimay is a fascinating example of God and Mammon pooling their resources: the monks are in charge of brewing but a few miles from their abbey in a complex of utilitarian buildings a large secular staff skilfully markets their beers.

Chimay once had a fine, traditional copper brewhouse but expansion and demand led to a new functional modern plant being installed. Most of the vessels are behind tiled walls. The monks, following a dispensation from the Vatican, are now allowed to talk but are disappointingly close-mouthed about the ingredients they use. The local water is soft and acidic and is not treated for brewing. It is thought that malts are a blend of Pils and cara-malt, with candy sugar used in the copper. German hops, possibly Hallertau, are blended, surprisingly, with some American Yakima. All the beers are primed with sugar for bottling. The three beers produced are known by the colour of their caps. **Chimay Red** is the original beer, 7.0 per cent ABV. It is copper-coloured with a fruity nose – blackcurrant is the dominant aroma – and great peppery and citric hop bitterness. Red is also known as **Première** when it is in large, Bordeaux-style bottles. **Chimay Blue** is 9.0 per cent ABV and is called **Grande Réserve** in large bottles. It has great depth of complex flavours, with spice and fruit from the hops and yeast. Dark malts give it a vinous character. **Chimay White** (8.0 per cent ABV) is sharply different from red and blue. It was first brewed in 1968 and, although the monks deny it, it is widely believed that white was introduced as a competitor to the beer from the nearby abbey of Orval. In common with all the true Trappist ales, Chimay's are bottle-conditioned. They will improve with age, red and blue taking on a port-wine character. They should be served at room temperature.

The Abbaye de Notre-Dame d'Orval is in the Belgian province of Luxembourg and is unusual in producing just one beer. The first abbey was built by Benedictines in 1070, but it was sacked and rebuilt several times: the present buildings date from the 1920s and 1930s. **Orval Trappist** ale is made from pale malt and caramalt, with candy sugar in the copper. German Hallertau and East Kent Goldings are the hop varieties: the brother brewers prize the earthy/peppery aromas of Goldings. The 5.2 per cent ABV beer in a club-shaped bottle has 40 units of bitterness. Following primary fermentation with an ale yeast, the beer has a second one lasting from six to seven weeks using several strains of yeast, including a wild one similar to lambic's *Brettanomyces*, circulating over a bed of Goldings. The beer is then bottled and seeded with the original ale yeast, which creates a third ferment. Not surprisingly, it is a highly complex ale, spicy with tart and quenching fruit, the finish becoming dry and dominated by hops.

Rochefort ales come from the Abbaye de Notre-Dame de Saint-Rémy in the Ardennes. There are three beers brewed from pale Pils and darker Munich malts, with dark candy sugar in the copper. Hop varieties are German Hallertau and Styrian Goldings. The beers are labelled Six, Eight and Ten from a now-defunct method of measuring alcohol. **Rochefort Six** is 7.5 per cent ABV, pale brown in colour and with a soft, fruity and slightly herbal palate. **Rochefort Eight** (9.2 per cent ABV) is a rich and round-ed ale, copper-coloured with a dark fruit character that recalls dates and raisins. **Rochefort Ten** is a mighty 11.3 per cent ABV. Hops meld with dark fruit, nuts and chocolate. The brothers point out that the strength of their beers and their malty/fruity character developed from their use as "liquid bread" during fasting.

There are two Trappist breweries in Flemish-speaking areas. Westmalle ale comes from the Abdij der Trappisten north of Antwerp. The 9.0 per cent ABV **Tripel** is extremely pale, with just 13 units of colour, with 35 to 38 IBUs. The monks use French and Bavarian pale malts with Czech, German and Styrian hops. Candy sugar is also added to the copper. The beer has a secondary fer-mentation in tanks lasting from one to three months and is then primed with sugar and yeast for bottle conditioning.

The Abdij Sint Sixtus in the hamlet of Westvleteren near Ypres (Ieper) is the smallest of the Trappist breweries and the least acces-sible. Visits are difficult but the full range of beers can be enjoyed in the Café De Vrede across the road. There is a malty/spicy **Green** corked **Dubbel** (4.0 per cent ABV), a **Red** (6.2 per cent ABV), fruity and hop-peppery, and the **Blue Extra** (8.4 per cent ABV) with great warming fruit and alcohol. The 10.6 **Abbot** is an explosion of raspberry and strawberry fruits (from the yeast, not from actual fruit) with a deceptively smooth drinkability.

A new Trappist brewery opened in 1999. Achel, in a village of the same name, brews only for consumption on the premises at present. The beers are **Achelse Blond** (4.0 per cent ABV), **Extra** (also 4.0 per cent), a 6.0 per cent **Blond** and a 5.0 per cent **Bruine**.

TRAPPIST BREWERS

Abbaye de Notre-Dame d'Orval,

6823 Villers-devant-Orval.

Abbaye de Notre-Dame de St-Rémy,

rue de l'Abbaye 8, 5430 Rochefort.

Abbaye de Notre-Dame de Scourmont,

rue de la Trappe 294, 6438 Forges-les-Chimay.

Achel,

St. Benedictusabdij De Achelse Kluis

De Kluis 1, 3930 Hamont-Achel.

Abdij Trappisten van Westmalle,

Antwerpsesteenweg 496, 2140 Malle.

Abdij Sint Sixtus,

Donkerstraat 12, 8983 Westvleteren.

Abbey beers

Abbey beers are modelled on Trappist ones. The original idea was a reasonable, even noble one: monks who no longer had the resources – money as well as manpower – licensed a commercial brewer to produce beer for them. But the success of genuine Trappist ales has encouraged scores of breweries to produce abbey beers, diluting the style as well as the intention.

The Norbertine abbey of Leffe has not brewed since the Napoleonic wars – the brothers struck a deal with the local brewer to make beers for them. In the way of the modern secular world, the brewery was taken over and Leffe beers finally ended up controlled by Interbrew (now InBev). The abbey of Grimbergen, once in the country and now in the northern suburbs of Brussels, has followed a similar fate: its beers are now brewed by Macs, a subsidiary of Kronenbourg of France. The beers from the Benedictine abbey of Maredsous south of Namur are produced by the Moortgat Brewery in Breendonk.

The best of the Leffe beers is the bottle-conditioned **Triple** (8.4 per cent ABV) which was brewed for a time by De Kluis of Hoegaarden. It is golden in colour with an appealing citric lemon from the hops on the nose and palate and an aromatic finish. **Vieille Cuvée** (7.8 per cent ABV) is a one-dimensional darker ale while the 8.5 per cent ABV **Radieuse** has a strong hop presence.

Grimbergen beers, perhaps unintentionally mimicking the style of Benedictine liqueurs, are sweet in the mouth. The 10.0 per cent ABV **Optimo Bruno** is a deep amber colour with a pear-drop character on the palate. The 6.1 per cent ABV **Tripel** is darker and its aroma and palate are dominated by sweet fruits. The 6.2 per cent ABV **Dubbel** is copper-coloured with toffee and vanilla on the palate.

The Corsendonk range of abbey ales is brewed for the priory at Turnhout by Bios and Du Bocq. The 8.1 per cent ABV **Agnus Dei** has good citric lemon notes from the hops and more hop perfume in the finish. The 7.0 per cent ABV **Pater Noster** has a pleasant chocolate-and-raisins character.

Heineken, a growing presence in Belgium, owns the Affligem brewery in Opwijk, which produces a large range of abbey beers in association with Affligem abbey. They include **Blond, Dubbel, Tripel** and **Paters Vat**, ranging from 6.8 per cent ABV to 8.5 per cent. The Bosteels independent brewery in Buggenhout produces **Karmeliet Triple** (8 per cent ABV), to celebrate a former Carmelite monastery. Three grains are used and this delicious, complex, malty and hoppy beer was judged the Best Beer in the World by *Beers of the World* magazine in 2008.

SELECTED ABBEY BREWERS

Brasserie de l'Abbaye des Rocs,
Chaussée Brunehaut 37, 7383 Montignies-sur-Roc. (Despite the name, this is a microbrewery; there is no abbey on the site.)
Affligem (Heineken),
Ringlaan 18, 1745 Opwijk.
Bios, Brouwerij van Steenberghe,
Lindenlaan 25, 9068 Ertvelde.

Bosteels,
Kerkstraat 96, 9255 Buggenhout.
Moortgat Brouwerij,
Breendonkdorp 58, 2659 Breendonk.
Sint Bernardus Brouwerij,
Trappistenweg 23, 8978 Watou-Poperinge. Licensed by St-Sixtus to brew under its name.
Slaghmuylder Brouwerij,
Denderhoutembaan 2, 9400 Ninove.

Ales

The most famous of Belgium's pale ales is **Duvel**. It looks like a lager and many think it is pronounced, in the French manner, "Duvelle". But it is warm-fermented and is pronounced Doovul in the Flemish manner. The golden beer dates only from the 1970s, but the Moortgat (Moorgate) Brewery was founded in 1871 as a specialist ale producer. When sales of Pilsner beers started to take off in Belgium, Moortgat remained true to ales but introduced Duvel alongside its darker brews to expand and protect its market. Two-row Belgian and French barleys are specially malted for Duvel, which has a colour rating of seven to eight, only a fraction more than for a Pilsner. The brewing process is complex and intriguing. The ale is infusion-mashed in the traditional manner. Saaz and Golding hops are added to the copper boil in three stages to produce between 29 and 31 units of bitterness. Dextrose is added before primary fermentation to give body to the beer. Two strains of yeast are used in the first stage of fermentation: the hopped wort is split into two batches, which are fermented by two different yeast strains. A second fermentation takes place during cold conditioning, which lasts for a month. It is then primed with dextrose and re-seeded with yeast to encourage a third fermentation in the bottle. The end result is a beer of 8.5 per cent ABV. It throws such a dense, fluffy head that it has to be poured into a large tulip-shaped glass to contain both foam and liquid. Duvel is such an enormous success that several rivals have been launched with similar names, including **Judas** from Alken-Maes, **Joker** from Roman and **Rascal** from du Bocq.

Belgium's biggest-selling pale ale is **Palm** (5.2 per cent ABV), brewed by a family-run brewery in Steenhuffel. **Spéciale Palm** has a citric aroma from the hops, is bitter and quenching in the mouth and has a fruity/hoppy finish.

Antwerp is home to a superb ale rightly called **De Koninck** – "the king" (5.0 per cent ABV). The brewery began life in 1833 as a brewpub and its owners have resisted any suggestion that they should move from ale to lager. The copper colour of De Koninck comes from pale and Vienna malts. No sugars are used in the brewing process. Saaz hops are added three times during the copper boil. Following fermentation the beer has two weeks' cold conditioning.

SELECTED ALE BREWERS

Bios, Brouwerij van Steenberghe,
Lindenplaan 25, 9068 Ertvelde
(Piraat, 9.7 per cent ABV).

De Block Brouwerij,
Nieuwbaan 92, 1880 Peizegem
(Satan Gold, 8.0 per cent ABV).

Brasserie du Bocq,
rue de la Brasserie 4, 5191 Purnode
(St Benoit Blonde, 8.0 per cent ABV;
Gauloise, 9.0 per cent ABV).

De Koninck Brouwerij,
Mechelsesteenweg 291, 2018
Antwerp.

Moortgat Brouwerij,
Breendonkdorp 58, 2659 Breendonk.

Palm Brouwerij,
Steenhuffeldorp 3, 2901 Steenhuffel.

Riva Brouwerij,
Wontergenstraat 42, 8898 Dentergem
(Lucifer, 8.0 per cent ABV).

Straffe Hendrik,
Walplein 26, 800 Bruges (Bruges
Straffe Hendrik, 5.4 per cent ABV).

Wallonia

Brewers in the French-speaking region of Belgium complain that, with the exception of the Trappist ales, their contributions are overshadowed by those from the Flemish areas. But the saison or seasonal ales of Wallonia are worthy of respect, a beer style in their own right. They date from the time when farmer-brewers produced strong beers in the winter and spring that would survive the long, hot summer months. Saisons are warm fermenting, dark malts are often used and they are generously hopped. The classic of the style comes from Dupont at Tourpes. The brewery was founded on a farm with its own natural spring in the 1850s. The small brewhouse uses pale and caramalts with East Kent Goldings and Styrian hops. **Vieille Provision** (Old Provision) is 6.5 per cent ABV and has a peppery hop aroma and palate. Dupont also brews beers under the **Moinette** (Little Monk) label, a blonde and a brune, both at 8.5 per cent ABV. The blonde is hoppy and perfumy, the brune sweet and fruity.

There is nothing *Monty Python*-ish about the Silly Brewery. It is based in the village of Silly, on the river Sil. Like Dupont it is a farm-brewery that once ground its own grain. The 5.4 per cent ABV **Saison Silly** is brewed from French and Belgian malts with English Goldings hops. In common with several smaller saison brewers, the mash tun doubles as a hop back: after the copper boil, the hopped wort is pumped back to the mash tun for filtration. The beer is warm fermented for a fortnight, then matured in tanks for a further two weeks. The finished beer is copper-coloured with a pronounced earthy hop aroma and dark vinous fruit in the mouth. Silly also brews an "artisanal" **Double Enghien** – the name comes from the neighbouring village which had its own brewery – and a hoppy, perfumy and fruity **Divine** (9.5 per cent ABV).

SELECTED SAISON BREWERS

Brasserie Dupont,
rue Basse 5, 7911 Tourpes-Leuze.

Brasserie de Silly,
Ville Basse A141, 7830 Silly.

Brasserie à Vapeur,
rue de Marechal 1, 7904 Pipaix.

Brasserie Voisin,
rue Aulnois 15, 7880 Flobecq.

Speciality beers

The strongest beer in Belgium is brewed by a small company in Wallonia called Dubuisson. In the style of the region, Dubuisson is a former farm in Pipaix. Dubuisson means "bush" in French and the name of the 12 per cent ABV beer, **Bush**, was Anglicised in the 1930s to cash in on the popularity of strong British ales in Belgium. The amber-coloured Bush is made from pale and cara malts, with Styrian and East Kent Goldings. It is sold in the US as **Scaldis**, the Latin name for the major Belgian river, the Scheldt, to avoid confusion with Busch beer brewed by Budweiser giant Anheuser-Busch.

"Mad beer" can surely not be a style, yet it vies to become one as a result of the success of the Mad Brewers – De Dolle Brouwers – in Esen. The small brewery was on the point of closing in 1980 when some keen home-brewing brothers bought the site. Architect Kris Herteleer runs the enterprise with a rag-bag of equipment: a pre-First World War mash tun, a copper fired by direct flame, and an open wort cooler or cool ship. The main beer, **Oerbier** (Original Beer) is 7.5 per cent ABV and is brewed from six malts, including caramalt and black malt, with Belgian hops from Poperinge and English Goldings. It has a sour plums aroma – the yeast came originally from Rodenbach – and is bittersweet in the mouth with a fruity finish. An 8.0 per cent ABV **Arabier** is bronze-coloured, with a fruity and spicy aroma and more ripe fruit on the palate and finish. **Boskeun** (Easter Bunny) is an 8.0 per cent ABV season ale sweetened with honey, while the 9.0 per cent ABV Christmas ale, **Stille Nacht**, is packed with fruit and a hint of sourness.

La Chouffe, in the Belgian province of Luxembourg, takes its name from the village of Chouffe which in turn is named after a legendary local gnome. The brewery was opened in the 1980s. As well as using Pils and pale malts, Kent Goldings and Styrian hops, the beers are spiced in the medieval fashion with coriander, honey and bog myrtle. **La Chouffe**, 8.5 per cent ABV, has a sweetish start but a dry and spicy finish. **McChouffe**, inspired by Scottish ales, is 8.8 per cent ABV, bottle-conditioned with a big spicy aroma and palate.

The Vapeur (Steam) Brewery in Pipaix specializes in beers brewed with "botanicals" – herbs and spices. The range includes **Vanille** (5 per cent ABV), **Saison de Pipaix** (6.5 per cent ABV), and the massively spicy **Cochonne** (9 per cent ABV). Fantôme in Soy, province of Luxembourg, was founded in 1988 and brews a vast range of ever-changing beers, some with fruit and spices added, sometimes, it's said, with fruit added by mistake! **Fantôme** (8 per cent) is an intoxicatingly fruity regular beer and you may find **Blonde**, **Brune** and **Christmas Ale**, ranging from 4.5 per cent ABV to 10 per cent. Malheur is an even newer small brewery, founded in 1997, in Buggenhout. It produces strong pale ales in Champagne-style bottles, wonderfully rich and complex bottle-conditioned beers. The beers include **Malheur 6, 10, Brut** and **12**, ranging from a mere 10 per cent ABV to 12 per cent, which tests the tolerance of brewer's yeast. Malheur means "bad luck", a curious name for a brewery and possibly an obscure Belgian joke.

SELECTED SPECIALITY BREWERS

Brasserie d'Achouffe,
Route de Village 32,
6666 Achouffe-Houffalize.

Brasserie Dubuisson,
Chaussée de Mons 28, 7904 Pipaix.

De Dolle Brouwers,
Roeselarestraat 12b,
8160 Esen-Diksmuide.

Fantôme,
Rue Préal 8, 6997 Soy.

Malheur,
Mandekensstraat 179,
9255 Buggenhout.

Vapeur,
1, rue du Maréchal,
7904 Pipaix-Leuze.

The beer styles of the Czech Republic

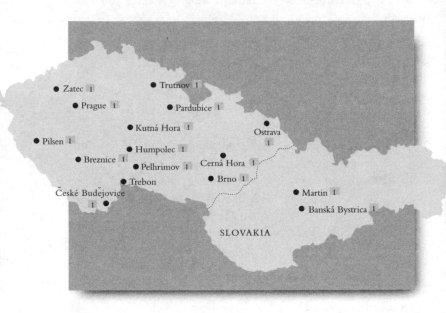

Key

1 Brewery

CZECH AND SLOVAK REPUBLICS	České Budějovice	Ostrava	Staropramen
	Budejovicky Budvar	Ostravar	*Recommended pubs*
	Samson	**Pardubice**	U Fleku
Banská Bystrica	*Recommended pub*	Pardubice	U Kalicha
Urpin	The Budvarka	**Pelhrimov**	U Cerného Vola
Breznice	**Humpolec**	Platan	U Zlatého Tygra
Breznice	Bernard	**Pilsen**	**Trebon**
Brno	**Kutná Hora**	Gambrinus	Regent
Starobrno	Kutná Hora	Plzenské Prazdroj	**Trutnov**
Černá Hora	**Martin**	(Pilsner Urquell)	Trutnov
Cerná Hora	Martin	**Prague**	**Žatec**
		Branik	Žatec

Czech Republic

It is one of the great unsolved mysteries of the world of brewing: why did Pilsen in Bohemia brew the first golden beer by the method of cold or bottom fermentation? It seems remarkable that this small country, locked at the time into the Austro-Hungarian Empire and, before that, part of the German Empire, was the first to break out of the dark beer straitjacket before such mighty cities as Vienna and Munich.

The true answer is complex and rooted in history. Bohemia – which now with Moravia makes up the Czech Republic – has a long brewing tradition. A brewery was recorded in Cerhenice in 1118 and both Pilsen and Budweis had breweries from the thirteenth century. As in other European countries, monasteries dominated beer production for centuries until the power of the church waned. From the thirteenth century many towns and cities had "citizens' breweries" – essentially co-operatives – while the aristocracy supplied beer from their castles. The Moravian capital, Brno, had been granted rights to brew beer from the twelfth century and King Wenceslas I (Václav I in Czech) decreed in 1243 that no one could brew within a mile of the Blue Lion inn in the city. Similar brewing rights were given to Pilsen in 1295.

Hops had been grown in the region from as early as 859 AD. While the first Bohemian beers were spiced and flavoured with berries and leaves, the superiority of the local hops encouraged their early use in brewing. From the twelfth century there are records of hops from the region being shipped to the hop market in Hamburg. Meanwhile Moravia had established a reputation for the quality of its malting barley, though for centuries wheat beer appears to have been the dominant style in what is now the Czech Republic.

For all its "Bohemian" associations with an unconventional lifestyle dominated by writers and artists living in Ruritanian surroundings, the real Bohemia was never a bucolic backwater. Tadeas Hájek wrote one of the first books on brewing technology in 1585, Professor C.J.N. Balling studied the role of enzymes in the mashing and fermentation processes while the Jecmen brothers developed the Czech method of cold fermentation.

The history of Bohemian brewing fused with the present in 1842 when the new "Burghers' brewery" of Pilsen employed a German brewer to make beer for them. Josef Groll or Grolle was employed because he was an expert in the new method of cold fermentation and came from the old brewing town of Vilshofen in Bavaria. The reputation of Pilsen beer was poor at the time and the brewery, a co-operative of tavern keepers, needed good beer because they faced stiff competition from the new brown lagers from neighbouring Bavaria. While no records survive, it is possible that Groll was supplied with an English coke-fired malt kiln that enabled him to produce a pale malt. The exceptionally soft waters of Pilsen would have helped produce a pale-coloured beer.

The golden Pilsner beer was a sensation. Its clarity in the glass was immediately appealing while its complexity of aromas and flavours, at once rich and malty yet enticingly hoppy and bitter, entranced all who drank it. Its reputation spread at great speed, aided by canals and a new railway system that carried supplies to all the great cities of the Austrian Empire, across into Bavaria and up the Elbe to Hamburg and beyond. A Pilsen Beer Train left every morning for Vienna. It became a cult drink in Paris and by 1874 it had reached the United States.

The success of the first Pilsen lager brewery prompted a second to be built in 1869. The Gambrinus Brewery, funded among others by Škoda the car manufacturer, was named after Jan Primus, the thirteenth-century toping Duke of Brabant, and built on land adjacent to the other brewery. In the German fashion, the beers from the town of Pilsen were known as "Pilsners", just as the rival brews from Budweis were called "Budweisers". In 1898, the first Pilsen lager brewer registered "Pilsner Urquell" as its official name. It is the German for "Original Source Pilsner" (Plzensky Prazdroj in Czech). The document referred to the "absurdity and illogicality of using the word 'Pilsner' for beers brewed in towns outside of Pilsen".

It was too late. With the exception of the British Isles, brewers throughout Europe rushed to emulate, replicate and too often denigrate the original with their versions of pale lagers. Germans and Czechs emigrated in large numbers to the United States, taking with them the technology to brew cold-fermenting beers.

The preponderance of German Pilsners tended to hide the originals. Drinkers could be forgiven for thinking the beer was a German style. The misunderstanding was heightened by the Cold War when Czechoslovakia disappeared from Western eyes. When it surfaced briefly during the "Prague Spring" of 1968 visitors from the West returned with the news that Czech beer was one of the wonders of the world. Beer had such deep roots in the Czech way of life that the Communist regime did not tamper with it. The breweries were state-owned but a surprisingly large number were allowed to operate, providing a wide choice, albeit within one general style. Even the fact that most of the breweries were starved of funds for modernization had its positive side as managements were forced to remain true to methods of production considered old-fashioned, conservative and quaint in other countries. While other Eastern bloc regimes forced breweries to use inferior ingredients so that the best barley and hops could be exported for hard currency, the Czech government stayed true to the German *Reinheitsgebot* for its premium beers. The Purity Law had been imposed on Bohemia and the other Czech regions when they were under German domination.

Now the walls are down and the West can marvel at Czech brewing. But the move to a market economy and the double-edged sword of modernization pose threats to the finest Czech traditions. There are around 70 breweries there but the number is falling as market forces take effect. Under the old regime the price of beer was kept low, but prices are rising and consumption is falling.

Ingredients

The quality of Czech beer is based on the ingredients used and the balance between them. The barley from the plains of Moravia and the Elbe produces a luscious sweet malt. Brewing liquor is soft and low in salts, allowing the sweetness of the malt and the aroma of the hops to best express themselves. The hop-growing area around the town of Žatec is in the north-west of Bohemia between Karlovy Vary (Carlsbad) and the capital, Prague. There is a smaller region north of Prague in Mustek. Žatec is known as Saaz in German and most Western brewers who buy the hops use the German name. Žatec hops grow in areas protected by mountains from high winds and rains. The soil is limestone and red clay. The hops are renowned for their fragrance, their softness, their ripe yet delicate aroma. They are not high in bittering acids but are rich in the tannins that give a distinctive piney, resiny aroma to beer. As a result of their aroma, Pilsner and other Czech beers have a late addition of hops towards the end of the copper boil.

Strength

The strength of Czech beers is expressed in degrees Balling, devised by Professor Balling. Most exported beer is 12 degrees, which is equivalent to 4.5 to 5.0 per cent ABV. But for everyday drinking, Czechs choose 10-degree beers, around 4.0 to 4.2 per cent ABV. Eight-degree beers are consumed in large quantities in industrial areas, and they are low in alcohol, around 3.2 per cent ABV. Some speciality beers are stronger, with 13-, 14-, 16- and even 19-degree ratings. Twelve-degree beers are all-malt but adjuncts are permitted in 8- and 10-degree beers, usually unmalted barley, wheat and sugar. The proportion of adjuncts does not usually exceed 10 per cent of the total grist. Premium beers are lagered for long periods – three months for Budweiser Budvar – but 21 days is normal for the lower strength beers.

Pilsner

The **Pilsner Urquell** Brewery is a temple of brewing. At night its neon-lit name blazes out over the city. By day visitors enter through a great triumphal arch to be confronted by tall chimneys, an almost Moorish water tower, and a warehouse complex that looks remarkably like London's King's Cross railway station. A meeting room in the grounds, with polished oak and stained glass windows, is like a chapel. In the 1980s the brewery yard was filled by giant oak casks, brought up from deep sandstone cellars to be re-pitched, the air rich with the smoky, autumnal aroma of fresh pitch. Both primary and secondary fermentation took place in pitch-lined oak vessels. Was it just the water, or did the oak vessels help impart a comforting softness to the beer?

In the two brightly lit, tiled brewhouses the mash is a thorough triple decoction system. Žatec hop flowers are added three times in direct-flame coppers. Until changes were introduced, the hopped wort went first to a vast, cool dimly lit room packed with small oak tubs each set at a slight angle as though the vessels were about to raise imaginary hats. The angle was designed to allow brewers to clamber up and check the progress of fermentation. When primary fermentation was complete, the green beer was pumped to six miles of sandstone cellars where the beer was lagered for 70 days at a natural temperature of 0–3.5°C/32–38°F. The oak lagering vessels were barrel-shaped and arranged horizontally.

The beer has 40 units of bitterness. Under the old lagering system, the original gravity was 1048 degrees with a finished alcohol of 4.4 per cent. This meant the beer was not fully attenuated – not all the malt sugars turned to alcohol.

The use of the past tense in describing fermentation and flavour profile is deliberate. For fundamental changes have taken place at the brewery since the fall of the old regime and the arrival of the market economy. Mashing and boiling remain the same but fermentation now takes place in modern stainless steel conical fermenters. The brewery claims that change had been under way since the 1970s but there had been no sight of conical vessels during the 1980s when Western journalists visited the brewery. It is more likely that the 10-degree version of the beer was brewed in modern vessels not open to inspection and the 12-degree beer was switched to them in the early 1990s following privatization.

In spite of claims to the contrary, the character of the beer has changed. The reason lies in the nature of conical fermenters. Unlike a horizontal lagering tank, where the yeast works slowly, almost lazily, turning remaining sugars into alcohol, a conical causes yeast to work more voraciously, hungrily attacking the sugars. The result is a more fully attenuated beer. Pilsner Urquell now has more in common with a German version of Pilsner: it is drier and more assertively bitter. It will be a tragedy if the inexorable demands of the market economy lead to any further blurring of its distinctiveness.

The **Gambrinus** Brewery next door is now part of the same privatized company as Pilsner Urquell. The brewery has also switched to fermentation in stainless steel conicals. Oak vessels were not used at Gambrinus: stainless steel replaced cast-iron. It is 4.5 per cent ABV and has 33 IBUs with a fresh-mown grass aroma, a more delicate bitterness than Urquell and a malty/hoppy finish that becomes dry. The 10-degree version, made with a proportion of sucrose, is the most popular beer of that strength in the Czech Republic. In late 1999, the Pilsner Urquell-Gambrinus group was bought by South African Breweries, now SABMiller.

Budweisers

Deep in the south of Bohemia and close to the Austrian border, the town of České Budějovice, with its magnificent central square and a fountain topped by a statue of Samson, vies with Pilsen as the great brewing centre of the Czech Republic. Its two breweries are smaller but Budweis, to use the old German name, had 44 breweries in the fifteenth century and was home to the Royal Court brewery of Bohemia. The royal connection allowed beers from the court brewery to be known as the "Beer of Kings" while all the town's brews became famous under the generic title of "Budweisers".

The standing of Budweiser beers can be seen in the decision of the American Anheuser-Busch company to give the name to its main product when it was launched in 1875 in St Louis, Missouri. Further confusion was added by the American sub-title "the King of Beers".

Twenty years later, in 1895, the Budejovicky Pivovar company started to brew. The name means the Budejovice Brewery, and its beer is always known simply by the contraction "Budvar" at home. But it is exported as **Budweiser Budvar** and the clash of names has led to endless law suits and wrangles over copyright. Anheuser-Busch can claim that it has precedent over Budvar for the use of the name but this ignores the fact that the older surviving brewery in České Budějovice, now called Samson, exported beer under the Budweiser name long before the American company took up the title. The Czech Budvar brewery cannot export to the United States using Budweiser on its labels while the American giant has to call its beer simply "Bud" in such countries as Germany and Spain where the Czechs registered the title first.

Since the arrival of the market economy, Anheuser-Busch has lobbied hard to win a stake in its smaller Czech rival. It has offered to buy 34 per cent of the shares, to inject capital to allow Budvar to expand, and to help Budvar market its beer worldwide. A-B has opened a St Louis Center in Cˇeské Budeˇjovice, donated to Prague University and taken full-page advertisements in newspapers to tell the Czech people that its intentions are honourable towards Budvar. So far the Czechs are unimpressed and the brewery remains in state hands, thought it may be privatized at some stage.

The Budvar Brewery is one of the most modern in the country. The old regime invested money in new plant to enable Budvar to export. Ironically, the beer had for years been hard to find in the Czech Republic as so much of it went for export. The brewhouse is magnificent, with large copper mash and brew kettles on tiled floors. A double decoction mash is used. Primary fermentation is in open vessels, lagering in horizontal ones. Lagering lasts for three months for the 12-degree beer, one of the longest periods in the world. It is an all-malt beer, using Moravian malt and Žatec hops. The original gravity is 1049 with a finished alcohol of 5.0 per cent ABV. The beer is well attenuated and has 20 units of bitterness. The balance of a Budweiser beer is therefore demonstrably different from that of a Pilsner. Budvar has a rich malt and vanilla aroma, it is quenching and gently hoppy in the mouth, while the finish has a balance of malt, hops and a delicate hint of apple fruit from the yeast. There is also a 4.0 per cent ABV version of **Budvar**, widely drunk in Czech bars, and in 2007 the brewery added a new, easy-drinking beer called **Pardál**, aimed at blue-collar consumers and sportsmen.

The Samson Brewery was the result of a merger in 1795 of two breweries, Velky (Great) and Maly (Small). It became the Citizens' Brewery and moved to a new site in the town in 1847. It changed its name to Samson but exported for some time under the Budweiser name until the arrival of the Budvar Brewery. Samson's management felt it received a bad deal under the old regime as all the investment available went to Budvar. Today Samson is independent and plans to stop sharing yeast with Budvar. It is a classic Czech lager brewery, with cast-iron mashing and boiling vessels, open squares for primary fermentation and horizontal ones for lagering. The management plans to install conicals but will continue to ferment its 12-degree beer in the old vessels to avoid any changes to the flavour profile. The premium product (4.3 per cent ABV) has a creamy note from the malt, some citric fruit from the hops and a well-balanced finish.

Both Budvar and Samson have been awarded "a guarantee of geographical status" from the European Union. To confuse visitors even further, Samson now also uses the name of the town in its branding. Further legal disputes could follow. In the meantime, Anheuser-Busch was bought by InBev and the new global giant may have less interest in pursuing the legal battle with Budvar.

Prague beers

Three of the Czech capital's four breweries merged in 1992 to form Prague Breweries. The biggest of the three in the group is the Staropramen (Old Spring) Brewery in the Smichov district, which started to brew in 1871. Its beer was praised by Emperor Franz Josef I and production soared. It is one of the biggest breweries in the Czech Republic, producing more than a million hectolitres a year. It is a classic lager brewery with secondary fermentation in horizontal tanks. In 1994 the British Bass group took a 34 per cent stake in Prague Breweries and said it would not change the brewing method as horizontal tanks were crucial to the flavour of the beer. The 12-degree **Staropramen** is 5.0 per cent ABV. It has a superb hop aroma, is well-balanced in the mouth between malt and hops and the finish is dry and bitter.

The second partner in the group is the Holesovice Brewery which brews under the **Méstan** name. Méstan comes from the original title of the brewery when it was founded in 1895 as První Prazsky Méstanský Pivovar – First Prague Burghers' Brewery. Its 12-degree beer is aromatic, soft, malty and bitter in the finish. The third member of Prague Breweries, Braník, started production in

1900 but was closed by InBev, which bought Prague Breweries from Bass. In 2009 InBev anounced it planned to sell the whole group. Fermentation now takes place in conical vessels and beer is canned for export.

The most celebrated beer in Prague comes from the world-famous beer hall, brewpub and beer garden known as U Fleků at 11 Kremencova in the New Town, the entrance marked by a large hanging clock. Beer has been brewed on the site since at least 1499: isotopic measurements of the remains of paintings on the wooden ceiling of the brewhouse have dated them back to 1360. The present name of the establishment stems from 1762 when Jakub Flekovský and his wife bought it. In the Czech fashion, the tavern was known as U Flekovskych, which over time was shortened to U Fleků. In Czech "U" serves the same purpose as the French "chez" – "at the house of". The tiny brewhouse, with a capacity of 6,000 hectolitres, is the smallest in the republic. With its open "cool ship" fermenter, it is reminiscent of a Belgian lambic brewery but no wild fermentation is allowed here. New brewing vessels are made of copper and date from 1980. The one beer is a dark lager, **Flekovaky**, 13 degrees (4.5 per cent ABV). It is made from four malts: Pilsner pale (50 per cent), Munich (30 per cent), caramalt (15 per cent) and roasted malt (5 per cent). A double decoction mash is used and Žatec hops are added in three stages.

Brno

The capital of Moravia has a long history of brewing, dating back to monastic times. The Starobrno (Old Brno) Brewery dates from 1872 when the family firm of Mandel and Hayek built the plant. Expansion was rapid, with exports moving from horse-drawn wagons to the railway in 1894. In the economically turbulent decades of the 1920s and 1930s, Starobrno bought several smaller breweries in the area. The plant was severely damaged by an air raid in 1944. It was nationalized in 1945 and during the course of rebuilding was considerably modernized. It now produces some 700,000 hectolitres of beer a year. Its 12-degree **Lezak Export** (Export Lager) is rounded and soft in the mouth, with a delicate hop aroma, and a gentle, bittersweet finish.

Country breweries

"Baker, priest, farmer, butcher, all drink beer from Breznice" an old slogan says. Brewing in the town dates back to 1506 and the town brewery was in the hands of the aristocratic Kolowrat Krakowsky family for 150 years. The coats of arms of the family with the emblem of an eagle adorns the labels of today's Herold beer. The Breznice brewery produces 10- and 12-degree Herold pale lagers but its main claim to fame is the first wheat beer seen in the Czech lands for at least a century. **Pivo Herold Hefe-Weizen** is a cloudy wheat beer in the Bavarian style, 12 degrees, unpasteurized and bottle-conditioned with a spicy, fruity aroma, a rich palate with apple fruit, and a long quenching finish. The brewery also makes kits for home-brewing: the Czech Republic has learnt an early lesson in basic capitalism – when commercial beer becomes expensive, drinkers turn to home-brewing.

The entrance to the **Krušovice** Brewery is guarded by an old wooden lagering tank bearing the company symbol of a cavalier. Krusovice malts its own barley using a traditional floor maltings where the grains are turned by hand. The 12-degree beer is one of the most highly prized beers in the Czech Republic, a fine blend of sweet malt and aromatic Žatec hops, a quenching palate and a long, delicate finish with good hop notes.

The **Platan** Brewery in Protivin is one of the finest in the country. Platan means plane tree and an avenue of the trees leads down to a complex of brewing buildings surrounded by woodland. There has been brewing on the site since the late sixteenth century. The feudal Schwarzenberg family built a new brewery between 1873 and 1876 and adopted all the new methods for producing lager beer. The first cultivation plant for Bohemian yeast was set up in the brewery and the beer was so highly prized that it was sold not only in Prague and Pilsen but also in Vienna, Trieste, Zagreb, Berlin, Leipzig, Geneva and as far afield as New York and Chicago. The brewery was nationalized in 1947 but has now been restored to its original owners. The 12-degree beer is closer to a Budweiser than a Pilsner in style, due to Protivín's proximity to Cˇeske Budeˇjovice. It is soft and and malty in the mouth, with a rounded, well-balanced malt and hops finish.

Closer to Prague, the beer from **Velké Popovice** would be declared a world classic if it were better known. The original brewery was built by monks in 1727, using the master of Czech baroque architecture, Kilian Dienzenhoffer. The plant was extensively expanded in 1871 and brewing capacity has been extended further in recent years. It is planned to build capacity to more than one million hectolitres, making it one of the biggest Czech breweries. The brewery has always been able to draw on natural water supplies from surrounding woodland and today takes its supply from 12 wells. The 12-degree beer has an enticing citric aroma of oranges and lemons, which dominate the palate and the finish, balanced by a sweet maltiness. The beer can be sampled in U Cernéha Vola, the Black Ox, in Prague, opposite the Loretto church at 1 Loretanské námesti, Hradcany, Prague 1.

The **Žatec** Brewery is in the heart of the great hop-growing region north of Prague and enjoys the pick of the crop. The brewery was built in 1801 as a citizens' brewery on the site of a former castle. The ancient castle cellars are used to lager the beers. It is a small brewery producing 120,000 hectolitres a year, concentrating on quality and supplying surrounding towns.

Dark lager

Bohemia did not turn its back on dark beers as a result of the success of golden Pilsners. Many breweries still produce dark beer (tmavé), all cold fermented today though there have been occasional spottings of beers called "porter", an indication that in its day London porter had an impact as great as those of Pilsner.

The Regent Brewery in Trebon has one of the finest brewhouses in the country. The brewery was founded in 1379 and came to be owned by the Schwarzenbergs, who moved the plant into their castle armoury and had it rebuilt, complete with its own maltings, by the Italian master builders, the brothers De Maggi, the Viennese Martinelli and the Prague architect Bayer. It has been privatized since the "Velvet Revolution" and recent investment has restored the brewhouse to its former glory. The brewing process is meticulous: mashing and boiling takes 12 hours, followed by primary fermentation for up to 12 days and lagering, for the 12-degree beers, for 90 days. Although Regent makes splendid pale lagers – closer to Budweiser than Pilsen in style – its classic beer is **Dark Regent** (12 degrees: 4.8 per cent ABV). Brewed from pale, caramalt and dark malts, it is ruby red in colour, with an appealing aroma of hops and bitter chocolate, dark malt in the mouth, and a hoppy/malty finish reminiscent of cappuccino coffee.

The Breclav Brewery has a 12-degree dark **Breclav Speciál**, sweet with a burnt sugar, caramel character. As the Czechs are a little late in learning about Political Correctness, this sweet style of dark lager is often referred to as "women's beer". C̆ernà Horà's 12-degree **Granát** is highly complex, with a sweet aroma but a dry finish and a smooth palate. The name means "garnet", a reference to the beer's appealing red-black colour. The Bernard Brewery in Humpolec also has a **Granát** (11 degrees) made from pale and caramalt. **Nová Paka Granát** is 12 degrees and has a bitter coffee finish after a malty start and palate. Velké Popovice has a dark version of its **Kozel** billy-goat lager, malty and chocolatey.

The Ostravar Brewery is in the mining town of the same name. It was founded by Czechs in 1897 to rival another brewery controlled by Germans. The present brewery's 10-degree **Vranik** has a delicate bitterness and dark maltiness and avoids the sweetness of other brands. Gambrinus markets **Purkmistr** (4.7 per cent ABV) brewed for it by the Domazlice Brewery.

The most memorable dark beer comes from the Pardubice Brewery in eastern Bohemia close to the Slovakian border. The 19-degree **Pardubice Porter** (7.0 per cent ABV) has a fine roasted malt aroma with powerful hop notes, a big palate of dark fruit and bitter hops, and a long finish bursting with coffee, chocolate and hop notes. Budvar has also introduced a new beer, **Budvar Dark**, following an intense debate at the brewery. Some members of the management felt a dark lager would have an old-fashioned "cloth cap" image but the brewing staff prevailed and Budvar Dark (5 per cent ABV) has a good peppery hop character as well as rich chocolate, coffee and roasted grain notes. The beer is sold in Britain where many drinkers like to mix the original golden beer with Dark to create "Half and Half".

Slovakia

Slovakia is a wine-making country with only a handful of breweries. The **Urpin Brewery** in Banská Bystrica produces a fine interpretation of the Pilsner style using Pilsner malt and Žatec hops. The 12-degree beer has a marked hop aroma, a firm malty body, and a long finish, hoppy and becoming dry.

The Martin Brewery in the town of that name was formed in 1893 with Jan Mattus, former head brewer at the Pilsen Brewery, in charge. As well as 12- and 14-degree pale beers, both delicately hopped, the brewery also produces the strongest known beer in both republics, **Martin Porter**. The 20-degree beer, around 8.0 per cent ABV, has a complex bittersweet palate after a hefty start of dark malt and bitter hops. The finish is long and deep with a charred malt character. It is only brewed occasionally.

SELECTED CZECH BREWERS

Bernard,
5 Kvetna 1, 396 01 Humpolec.

Branik,
Udolni 212/1, 101 00 Prague 4.

Breznice,
Zámecký obvod 31, 262 72 Breznice.

Budějovicky Budvar,
Kar. Svetlé 4, 370 21 České Budějovice.

Černá Hora,
Pivovarská 5, 679 21 Černá Hora.

Gambrinus,
U Prazdroje 7, 304 97 Pilsen.

Krušovice,
Krušovice 1, 270 53 Krušovice.

Kutná Hora,
U Lorce 11, 284 1t Kutná Hora.

Nová Paka,
Marantova 400, 509 01 Nová Paka.

Ostravar,
Hornoplni 57, 728 25 Ostrava.

Pardubice,
Palackého 250, 530 33 Pardubice.

Platan,
Pivovarská 856, 393 01 Pelhrimov.

Plzeňské Prazdroj (Pilsner Urquell),
U Prazdroje 7, 304 97 Pilsen.

Regent,
Trocnovské nám. 379 14 Trebon.

Samson,
Lidická 51, 370 54 České Budějovice.

Starobrno,
Hlinky 12, 661 47 Brno.

Staropramen,
Nádrazni 84, 150 54 Prague 5-Smichov.

Trutnov,
Krizikova 486, 541 01 Trutnov.

Velké Popovice,
Ringhofferova 1, 251 69 Velké Popovice.

Žatec,
Zizkovo nám. 78, 438 33 Žatec.

Note: In Czech, Prague is Praha, Pilsen is Plzen.

SLOVAKIAN BREWERS

Martin,
Hrdinov SNP 12, 036 42 Martin.

Urpin,
Sládkovicova 37, 975 90 Banská Bystrica.

Eastern Europe

With the exception of the former Czechoslovakia, the beers of the old Eastern bloc were hidden from Western eyes. All the breweries were state-owned and the switch to market economies has led to fundamental changes. Western brewers are hurrying to establish bridgeheads and to brew their strongly branded products locally.

Hungary

The great Austrian brewmaster Anton Dreher stamped his mark on Budapest. When Buda's twin city, Pest, was being constructed, large caves were dug in the rocky foundations and Dreher seized on them to lager his beer after he set up a company there in the middle of the nineteenth century, when Hungary was linked to Austria politically and economically. His Köbànya Brewery has survived and among its beers **Dreher Lager** and **Dreher Pils** pay homage to the founder while **Rocky Cellar** underscores the brewery's origins. The 12-degree beer – approximately 5.5 per cent ABV – uses a substantial amount of adjuncts and is lightly hopped with 20 IBUs. More interesting brews are all-malt – a hangover perhaps from the days when the Bavarian *Reinheitsgebot* held sway – and include a 5.0 per cent **Köbànyai** with delicate hop bitterness and a dark and sweet beer with some sultana fruitiness called **Bak** (7.5 per cent ABV), a local interpretation of the German Bock, and a pale lager of 5.5 per cent called simply **Budapest**.

BrauUnion of Austria has bought the Sopron brewery in the town of that name and has built a 30 per cent market share. Its main brand is **Soproni Aszok**. The Pécs brewery, founded in 1848 in Pécs, also has a major Austrian influence, with Ottakringer and BrauUnion holding a substantial investment. The beers include **Gold Fassl Pils** (4.8 per cent ABV) and **Gold Fassl Spezial** (5.3 per cent ABV). InBev has a majority stake in the Borodi group while Heineken has bought Komáromi and brews Amstel as well as local beers Talléros and Matroz.

The Kanizsa brewery in Nagy-kanizsa was founded in 1892 in an important barley-growing and malting region. In 1984 the brewery went into partnership with Holsten of Hamburg: both are now owned by InBev. The brewery produces Holsten Pils while its own brand is a malty lager called **Sirály (Seagull),** a full-bodied Export style called **Korona** and a dark lager known as **Göcesji Barna**.

Poland

Poland is a major brewing country with a sizeable hop-growing industry in the Lublin region and a well-developed barley and malting industry. As a result its lager beers have both good malt character and a strikingly perfumy and resiny hoppiness.

The Zywiec brewery in the town of that name dates from the time of the Austro-Hungarian empire and was built by a member of the Habsburg dynasty. Its brewing liquor comes from the Tatra Mountains and the plant is close to the hop fields of Krasnystaw. The group has been bought by Heineken and its Dutch lager is brewed along with **Zywiec Full Light**, a soft, malty beer with a good peppery hop note and light citrus fruit. The group's original brewery in Cieszyn, close to the Czech border, brews an excellent Pils called **Brackie** and the remarkable **Zywiec Porter**, once a warm-fermented beer but now a black lager with a redoubtable strength of 9.5 per cent ABV and a rich coffee, chocolate, roasted grain and bitter hops character.

Okocim Brewery, owned by Carlsberg, has a goat on its label, though this comes from the heraldic sign for the city of Okocim and is not a reference to a Bock beer. **Okocim Pils** is 5.1 per cent ABV, has a rounded malty aroma, with rich vanilla and hops in the mouth, and a big bittersweet finish. The biggest-selling Pils in Poland is **EB Specjal** (5.4 per cent ABV), a rich, malty/hoppy beer from the Elb Brewery, now owned by Heineken. The brewery makes much of the fact that EB is triple filtered for purity.

The Warsaw Brewery (Browar Warszawksi) in the Polish capital produces two full-bodied lagers in the Pilsner and Export styles, **Stoteczne** and **Krolewskie**. Of most interest is a beer called Porter, a cold-fermenting dark beer with plenty of dark malt and coffee character, a further reminder that porter and stout were once exported in vast amounts from Britain to the Baltic states. When the Napoleonic Wars closed the trade to Britain, local brewers responded to demand with their own versions but preferred to use lagering techniques.

Kompania Piwowarska is owned by SABMiller in Poznan, and produces some of Poland's most popular beers. They include **Lech**, **Lech Pils** and **Tyskie**. The Grodzisk brewery near Poznan recalls an older style of Polish beer with its warm-fermented **Grodzisk**, a blend of malted barley cured over oak fires, with some wheat and help from wild yeast during fermentation. It has a slightly sour, tart and refreshing character with a smoky, oaky tang.

Serbia

With the regions and new states of the former Yugoslavia in turmoil, the brewing picture is complicated. Except in Muslim areas, the region has powerful brewing traditions dating back to the thirteenth century. Slovenia has been a major hop-growing area for centuries and the quality of the hops from the Žatec region has stamped its mark on beers that are broadly in the German and Austrian moulds, though cold-fermented dark beers and porters have been spotted occasionally. Austrian practices, from the time when the Austro-Hungarian empire included the Slav regions, are evident in the use of the Plato scale to indicate strength. The Apatin Brewery was built in 1756 with financial support from the Imperial Chamber of Commerce in Vienna.

In Belgrade, Bip was founded in 1850. Its **Belgrade Gold** is a full-bodied malty lager of around 5.0 per cent ABV with a tart and citric hop character. Serbia's oldest brewery was built in Pancevo in 1722 and brews a **Standard** lager of around 4.5 per cent ABV and a stronger, malty/vanilla **Weifert** of 5.5 per cent.

The Trebjesa Brewery at Niksic was founded in 1896 and takes its brewing liquor from the natural spring waters of the surround-ing mountains. Its main product is **Big Nik Gold Beer** – the name suggests it's a steal at the price.

Estonia
The Tartu Olletehas brewery launched a German-style Bock beer in 1995. Called **Rüütli Olu**, the 7.5 per cent alcohol beer is dark brown in colour and is lagered for 70 days. It is the strongest beer brewed in Estonia. It has a dark fruit and spicy hops character, is rich and warming and is promoted as the ideal beer for festivals.

Russia
Russia is best known for vodka. During the Soviet period, beer was a minor drink and was sold only in bottled form in state shops and from street kiosks. Brewing has developed rapidly since the end of Communism. Draught beer is now widely available, while Western companies have rushed to participate in the potential offered by the vast market.

The biggest group by far is BBH – Baltika Beverages Holding. It owns two breweries in St Petersburg, Vena (Vienna) and Baltika and a third plant in Rostov-on-Don. In total, it now owns or has a stake in 12 breweries in Russia and two in Ukraine. BBH started life as a group run by Synebrychoff in Finland but that company was bought by Carlsberg of Denmark, which went into partner-ship with Scottish & Newcastle to run the group. S&N has since been bought by Heineken, leaving Carlsberg as the sole owner of BBH. Around 40 per cent of Carlsberg's profits now come from BBH, which accounts for a quarter of the Russian beer market.

Forty-five million dollars has been invested in the giant St Petersburg Baltika plant alone: with Vena, the two breweries produce around 14 million hectolitres a year. All the beers carry the Baltika brand name and range from **Lite** (3.2 per cent ABV), through **Nevskoye** (4.6 per cent), **Classic** (5 per cent) and **Original** (5.7 per cent).

The Stepan Raizin brewery was founded in the eighteenth century and changed its name following the Russian Revolution, when many industries were named after Russian heroes: Raizin was a seventeenth-century Cossack who attempted to assassinate the Tsar. The brewery has a full range of beers, including **Gold**, **Special**, **Admiralty** and a Bavarian-style Bock called **Old Recipe**. It has an 8 per cent ABV **Porter,** originally warm fermented but now a black lager, with a roasted grain, coffee and chocolate aroma and palate, underscored by generous hopping. It's cold-matured for an impressive 90 days. Stepan Raizin is now owned by Heineken and the ubiquitous Dutch lager has been added to the range. The brewery has an excellent museum devoted to the history of brewing in Russia, with fascinating artefacts from the Soviet period: the brewery was awarded the Order of Lenin.

SABMiller has bought the Kaluga brewery and brews two Czech lagers, **Kozel** from the Velké Popovice brewery near Prague and the world-famous **Pilsner Urquell** from Pilsen.

A group jointly owner by InBev and SUN of India is a major player in Russia and operates eight breweries in St Petersburg, Perm, Ivanovo, Kursk, Ekaterinburg, Suransk and Volsky. The beer range includes **Klinskoye**, **Sbirskaya Korona** and **Tolstink** as well as Stella Artois.

Many towns and cities in Russia have a branch of Tinkov, restaurants that brew on the premises. The beers include Bock, Pils, porter and a Bavarian-style wheat beer, but it has since been bought by InBev. Tinkov now produces 250,000 hectolitres a year.

The Moscow Brewery, established in 1863, makes a 4.6 per cent **Moskovkoye Lager** broadly in the Pilsner style, and a fuller-bodied, almost amber **Radonej**. It has added **August** (4.5 per cent

ABV), an all-malt beer named after the failed August coup that brought Boris Yeltsin to power. It is bronze-coloured with a rich toffee/vanilla aroma, hops on the palate and a light but fruity and hoppy finish.

"Russian stout"

In the nineteenth and early twentieth centuries the Baltic states had a love affair with the dark porters and stouts brewed in Britain. The strongest versions became known as Imperial Stout as a result of their popularity with the Russian court. The Empress Catherine was a devotee and encouraged the beer to be given to the sick. Imperial stouts were brewed in London by several companies based along the Thames. They were black and viscous, and heavily hopped in order to withstand long sea journeys to the Baltic. The sole surviving example, **Imperial Russian Stout**, came from the Courage group, which began life as Henry Thrale's brewery in London, founded in the seventeenth century. It was bought by a Scottish-American called Barclay, and became Barclay-Perkins before joining the Courage group founded by John Courage, a Scot of French Huguenot origins. There is a further convoluted ethnic twist to the story, for Imperial Russian Stout was exported to the Baltic for Barclay Perkins by a Belgian named Albert Le Coq. Monsieur Le Coq produced a booklet in Russian extolling the healthy attributes of the beer. He boosted the popularity of Russian Stout by giving away cases of the beer to Russian soldiers injured in the Crimean War. At the turn of the century Le Coq bought a brewery in Tartu in what is now Estonia to brew both porter and stout for the Baltic market. His success was short-lived for the brewery was nationalized by the Bolsheviks in 1917. Records show that the brewery last brewed a cold-fermenting porter in 1969.

Back in Britain, Courage continued to produce Imperial Russian Stout in small batches every other year. When it closed its

London brewery, it moved production to its John Smith's subsidiary in Tadcaster in Yorkshire. In London the beer used to be conditioned in the brewery for 18 months before being released. The bottle-conditioned beer had a starting gravity of 1104 degrees and was declared 10 per cent ABV, though 11 has been reached. Its complex grist included some Pilsner malt as well as pale, amber and black malts with some brewing sugar: perhaps the habit of using Pilsner malt stems from boats that had been full of stout returning to England with cargoes of European barley. It was hopped with the Target variety in the region of 24 pounds per barrel – four times the normal rate. Bitterness units were in the region of 50. Tragically, when Courage merged with Scottish and Newcastle Breweries in the 1990s, Imperial Russian Stout was discontinued. But Harvey's of Lewes in Sussex reached agreement with the family of Albert Le Coq and now brews a bottle-conditioned Imperial Russian Stout.

Lithuania

Lithuania has a long brewing tradition that dates back to the Middle Ages. Commercial brewing developed in the seventeenth and eighteenth centuries. Svyturys was founded in 1784 and is now the oldest brewery in the country and the last remaining producer in Klaipedia, once a major brewing town. **Ekstra** is its flagship brand, widely distributed in the United States. It's in the Dortmunder Export style, 5.2 per cent ABV, with a rich malty and biscuit aroma and palate backed by spicy hops imported from Germany.

Ukraine

Ukraine has two breweries owned by BBH/Baltika. The independent Obolon brewery near Kiev was built in the 1980s with Czech technology. The modern plant produces a wide range of beers including **Magnat** (5.3 per cent ABV), **Lager** (5.2 per cent), **Porter** (7 per cent) and two wheat beers in the Bavarian and

Belgian styles, **Weizen** (5 per cent) and **White** (also 5 per cent), which has an addition of coriander. Radomyshl in Kiev also brews wheat beer while the Slavutich brewery in Zoporozhyia Oblast, owned by Carlsberg, and the Yantar brewery in Mykolayiv, owned by Sun and InBev, both produce light lagers.

SELECTED BREWERIES IN EASTERN EUROPE

Baltika (BBH),
Rostov-on-Don &
6 Verkhny per., d. 3,
194292 St Petersburg, Russia.

Stepan Razin (Heineken),
Stepan Razin Str., 9,
198035 St Petersburg, Russia.

Vena (BBH),
Farforovskaya ul., d. 1,
192171 St Petersburg, Russia.

Svyturys,
Kūlių Vartų g. 7, Klaipėdia, Lithuania.

Obolon,
Bogatyrska, 3, 04655 Kiev, Ukraine.

Radomyshl
Ul. Mykgorod 71, 12200 Radomyshl, Ukraine.

France

The French make beer. The French drink beer. If that sounds trite, it is because the international image of France is inextricably linked to wine; beer needs to be dragged from the giant shadow cast by the vine. Beer is drunk throughout the country, often in bars and cafés called brasseries – breweries. Beer was once brewed all over France, too. The Gauls were famous for their cervoise, from the Latin cerevisia – ale. At the end of the nineteenth century there were still 3,000 French breweries, many of them tiny and run from farms, operating in Nice, Limoges and Toulouse as well as in beer's northern heartlands.

Today there are just 33 breweries left, plus a handful of micro-breweries. That marks a fall from 76 breweries in 1976. The decline of beer is remarkable in a country that is still largely rural and with a powerful agricultural lobby. But, outside the far North, beer was never treated as seriously as wine, was never so much part of the tapestry of life. It was a refresher, not a drink to savour or ponder. As a result, it became prey to industrialization. Today brewing is dominated to an astonishing degree by just two companies: Kronenbourg, acquired by Carlsberg in 2008 when it bought Scottish & Newcastle's French interests, and Heineken. Kronenbourg controls 50 per cent of the market, Heineken 25 per cent. InBev also busily sells beer in France, though it no longer brews there. Most production takes place in the North, mainly in Alsace-Lorraine, an area under German rule from 1871 to 1919 and also during the Second World War, experiences that stamped their mark on the language, the cuisine and the beer. And even within the region, brewing is concentrated in Alsace and its capital, Strasbourg. The last independent brewery in Lorraine (Amos of Metz) closed in 1992. The last regional brewery of any size or note outside the North, Schneider of Puyoô, closed in 1990 and even here there was an obvious German influence. Heineken has a plant in Marseille but it scarcely ranks as a French brewery.

Change is taking place, though. Consumption is increasing and there is a flowering of brewing of a quite different kind to the German-influenced lagers of Alsace. In the Nord-Pas de Calais region, strung out along the border with Belgium, ales are flourishing, albeit on a small scale. The brewers of the region, many of them new, small micros, concentrate in the main on the style known as *bière de garde*, a warm-fermenting beer that has powerful links with the farmhouse saison and vieille provision ales of Wallonia. The sudden interest in French ales has not gone unnoticed and even the giants of French brewing are reviving such long-lost styles as Christmas and March beers.

Alsace-Lorraine

This is lager-brewing territory. The German influence is obvious in the names of breweries, cities, towns and villages as well as in the cuisine, in which pork dishes abound. But the beer is a long way removed from the influence of the German *Reinheitsgebot*. Twenty to 30 per cent of cereal adjuncts are not uncommon in the lagers of the region. Hopping rates are not high, with bitterness units in the low to middle 20s. The results are beers of between 5.0 and 6.0 per cent ABV that are pleasant, refreshing but in general unremarkable.

Kronenbourg is based in Strasbourg, though the original brewery there is now a museum. It brews at Obernai in the biggest production plant in Europe, while its subsidiary Kanterbräu brews at Champigneulles in Lorraine, and Rennes in Britanny. The history of Kronenbourg is stamped on the label of one of its best-known brands, 1664, for that was the year when Jérôme Hatt started to make beer in a tavern called Au Canon (Zur Karthaune in German) on the Place de Corbeau (the Raven) in Strasbourg, close by the Customs House on the banks of the Rhine (Le Rhin).

Hatt had qualified as a master brewer and cooper and he quickly won acclaim for the quality of his beer, which would have been warm-fermenting in those days. His tavern became the top meeting place for the Strasbourgeois (the tavern has survived but now sells beer from the Schützenberger Brewery).

In 1850 Frédéric-Guillaume Hatt moved the brewery to a new site in the suburb of Cronenbourg, meaning the crown or brow of the hill. In the Germanic fashion, the brewery took on the name of its place of domicile and the spelling was subsequently changed to Kronenbourg. It achieved national status in the 1920s with a bilingual beer called Tigre Bock which frustratingly no longer exists. In the 1950s Kronenbourg began to expand aggressively. It pioneered beer in 25-centilitre bottles and made a big play for supermarket sales with disposable containers. Kronenbourg 1664 was launched in 1962, two years short of the brewery's double centenary, and a second brewery known as "K2" was opened at Obernai in 1969.

The main brand is simply called **Kronenbourg**, with medieval lettering on a quartered red and white label that is supposed to emulate a shield but looks more like a rugby shirt. The beer is 5.2 per cent ABV, with 23 IBUs. The aroma is light, delicate, unobtrusive, with a clean palate and finish, and some hop and malt notes. The 5.9 per cent ABV **1664** has a more pronounced aroma but is disappointingly light for a beer of the strength. The version brewed under licence in Britain is 5.0 per cent ABV. A brown version, **1664 Brune**, is a percentage point stronger and has a pleasant chewy, dark caramel character. A 4.7 per cent ABV **Bière de l'Eté** is a light summer refresher while a Christmas beer, **Bière de Noël**, has a fuller golden colour with a hint of red – perhaps a dash of Munich or caramalt – and more body.

The Kanterbräu subsidiary came about as a result of series of mergers and takeovers. Its origins are as Les Grandes Brasseries de Champigneulles, founded in 1897 by Victor Hinzelin and Victor

Trampitsch. Victor Trampitsch was a Slovenian who had learned his brewing skills in Pilsen, an impressive pedigree. Following the Second World War the company swallowed many other breweries in the region, becoming Société Européene de Brasseries (SEB) before being bought up by BSN in 1970 and renamed Kanterbräu. At one stage SEB had 11 breweries but now only two operate. The main brand, Kanterbräu, takes its name from a German brewmaster, Maître Kanter, who came to France from Germany. A romantic interpretation of him, in broad-brimmed hat and holding a foaming jug of beer, adorns the beer labels. **Kanterbräu** (4.5 per cent ABV) is light in aroma and body. A stronger **Kanterbräu Gold** is in similar vein to 1664 while a recent revival of **Bière de Mars** (March Beer) is disappointingly thin. The group has had considerable success with **Tourtel**. It is a low-alcohol beer named after another closed brewery: surely the ultimate indignity.

The small town of Schiltigheim – "Schillick" to the locals – is called "ville des brasseurs" (brewers' town). It is home to four brewing companies that provide jobs for around 2,000 people. The Grande Brasserie Alsacienne d'Adelshoffen was founded in 1864 by the Ehrhardt brothers. It was renamed Strassburger Münsterbräu during the years of German control and was bought by the Fischer/Pêcheur group in 1922, though it has always been given a considerable degree of independence to run its own affairs. It has an everyday light lager in the Alsatian style but a more characterful **Adelshoffen Export** (4.5 per cent ABV). It is brewed from pale malt and maize (corn) with Hallertau and Styrian hops (20 IBUs). It has a clean malt aroma with some citric notes from the hops, a malty palate and a bitter-weet finish that becomes dry. The company created enormous interest in 1982 with **Adelscott**, a beer made with some peated whisky malt. It cashed in on the French fascination with Scotch malt whisky. The beer is 6.6 per cent ABV, made from pale malt, whisky malt and maize. It is hopped with Alsace Brewers' Gold, Hallertau and Styrian varieties and has 16 to

20 IBUs. It is lagered for two months and has an appealing aroma of smoked malt, rich malt in the mouth and a light smoky finish.

Fischer was the largest independent brewery in France. It hedges its bets with its name, having used both at various times when under French and German control but today is known simply as Fischer. It was founded in 1821 in Strasbourg by Jean Fischer, who moved to Schiltigheim in 1854. Its ebullient chairman, Michel Debus, caused a storm of controversy in 1988 when he instigated the court case against the German *Reinheitsgebot* (see German section). He is a great innovator, constantly creating new brands that have considerable public relations impact but are a dubious contribution to the greater appreciation of beer. He has produced an aphrodisiac beer **36.15 – La Bière Amoureuse**, flavoured with ginseng, a rum-flavoured beer, and non-alcoholic beers for dogs and cats called **Mon Titi** and **Mon Toutou**. A 6.5 per cent ABV kriek is an attempt to replicate a Belgian cherry beer, using a fruit concentrate rather than whole cherries.

Among the standard brews, **Fischer Gold** (6.4 per cent ABV) in a Grolsch-style swing-top bottle, has a perfumy aroma and good hop character. A soft, malty, smooth *bière de mars* is brewed for the spring. In 2008, Fischer was bought by Heineken. The brewery closed a year later and production was transferred to the Espérance brewery: see below. The beer range is likely to change.

The brewery that became Schützenberger was founded in Strasbourg in 1740 but may be older. It was bought by Jean-Daniel Schützenberger in 1768. It was called the Brasserie Royale until the revolution of 1789 when it was hastily renamed Brasserie de la Patrie, which translated into Brauerei zum Vaterland – the Fatherland Brewery – under German rule. It moved to Schiltigheim in 1866. It is run today by Rina Müller-Walter, who succeeded her father. She is believed to be the only woman running a major brewing company in Europe. The company brews some rich and beautifully crafted beers, a long way removed from the general

Alsatian style. Its **Jubilator** and **Patriator** brews (7.0 per cent ABV) are pale and dark German-style double Bocks, with great hop character. The pale is smooth and perfumy, the brown rich and fruity. **Schutz 2000** was brewed to mark the two-thousandth anniversary of the founding of Strasbourg. It is an unfiltered, bottle-conditioned beer (6.5 per cent ABV) bursting with rich, tart fruit and resiny hops. Another celebration beer, **Cuivrée** (house brew) marked the brewery's own 250 years. This is a luscious, 8.0 per cent Vienna-style strong lager, gold-red, malty and fruity, underscored by perfumy hops. There are seasonal March (5.2 per cent ABV) and Christmas (6.0 per cent ABV) brews.

The cuckoo in the Schillick nest is Heineken, which went on the rampage in Alsace in the 1970s and 1980s. It is based on the site of the old Brasserie de l'Espérance (ironically, the Great Expectations Brewery) which was founded in Strasbourg in 1746 and moved to Schiltigheim in 1860. It merged with four other breweries, including Mützig, to form Alsatian Breweries, Alba for short. In 1972 Alba was bought by Heineken, which then staged a mammoth three-way merger in 1984 with Union de Brasseries, famous in Africa and South-east Asia for its 33 brand, and Pelforth of Mons-en-Baroeul, whose pelican trade mark is recognized throughout France. The new group, with a quarter of French beer sales, went through several changes of name until the dominant partner exerted its influence. It is now Brasseries Heineken. As well as the Schillick plant, it has the Pelforth Brewery near Lille and one in Marseille. The major emphasis goes into promoting the ubiquitous Dutch Heineken. The fate of other brands is less clear. It is likely that the Pelforth beers will continue because of their popularity in the Lille area. **Pelforth Blonde** and **Pélican** (4.8 per cent ABV) are standard French lagers but **Pelforth Brune** (6.5 per cent ABV) has plenty of rich dark chocolatey malt character. It is to be hoped that the characterful Mützig brands, **Mützig** (4.8 per cent ABV) and **Old Lager** (7.3 per cent ABV), both with rich malt and dry, hoppy finishes, will survive. The Pelforth plant produces **George Killian's Bière Rousse**, based on Killian's Irish Ale. It is sold in the Netherlands under the name of Kilyan.

Météor is in the Alsatian village of Hochfelden. Brewing dates back to 1640 and beyond: beer was supplied to a local abbey and to farms in the area. The present brewery was bought by the Metzger family of Strasbourg in 1844 and is now owned by their relations through marriage, the Haags. The name **Météor** was adopted in 1925 and the company launched a Pilsner-style beer under the name two years later. It signed an agreement with Pilsner Urquell to use the term "Pils", the only such agreement in the French brewing industry. The beer is 4.9 per cent ABV and is brewed with pale malt and corn grits. Hops used are Czech Saaz (Žatec) and Alsatian varieties. The beer, by local standards, is well-hopped, achieving 35 IBUs. A single decoction mash is used and the beer is lagered for one month. It has a toasty malt and hops aroma, with sweet malt and bitter hops in the mouth, and a long dry finish with more hops and some honey/vanilla notes. It lacks the depth and finesse of a true Pilsner but is a well-made and attractive beer. **Ackerland Blonde** (5.9 per cent ABV) is a rich and malty pale lager. A brown version, **Ackerland Brune** (6.3 per cent ABV), is packed with dark malt and hops character. The brewery has cashed in on the Scotch malt whisky craze with **Mortimer** (8.0 per cent ABV), an amber-coloured beer, fruity and lightly hopped.

Nord-Pas de Calais

If Alsace is a triumph of modernization, of state-of-the-art brewing, then Nord-Pas de Calais is a time-warp where beer is made by ancient, hand-crafted methods. This is the region of "artisanal beer". Some lagers are produced, but in general the beers of border country recall a more ruminative and rural period when beer was made on farms and in homes as naturally as bread would be baked and the land tilled and harvested. It is a region of flat land, lowering skies and distant horizons where political borders do not impinge on the reality of everyday life, a region rich in Flemish as well as French traditions. The locals speak of "French Flanders" and cock a snook at history.

On the coat-tails of the Belgian revival, beer lovers have discovered the ales of French Flanders, Artois and Picardy, once just a footnote in the brewing books, now a recognizable style in their own right. Between Calais and Lille there is a tradition known as "bière de garde". These were beers brewed on farms, usually in the winter, to provide important sustenance for farmers and all those who worked the land.

Many of the breweries are still small and are based on farms, though farming is no longer the major preoccupation as the interest in beer from Flanders grows. The beers are often pale as well as brown, but the original versions would have been dark. Wherever possible brewers use barley and hops from the region, which allows them to carry the appellation "Pas de Calais/Région du Nord" on their labels. From Ypres across the border in Belgium down into French Flanders stretches a small and very ancient hop-growing area, while Flanders, the Champagne region and Burgundy produce malting barley of the highest quality.

The classic style is a strong beer of between 6.0 and 8.0 per cent ABV, malty and spicy from the use of well-cured malts. Mashing is often long to achieve some caramelization of the brewing sugars. Hop rates are not high, with IBUs in the 20s: the brewer is seeking roundness, fullness, a certain alcoholic warmth rather than a hard bitterness. Finished beers are stored for a month: centuries ago this would have been a far longer period.

Commercial success has brought problems in its wake. Some brewers have switched from the use of traditional top-working yeasts to lager cultures. They say this gives them greater control over fermentation and the beers are more stable once out in the trade. But at the same time they are still fermenting at ale temperatures in order to achieve a fruity ale character. Nevertheless, it would be a tragedy if the true concept of a warm-fermenting bière de garde is lost in the rush to embrace all the demands of the modern market with its insatiable belief in "shelf life".

The beer that breathed life back into the style is Jenlain. It became a cult drink with students in Lille in the 1980s and features prominently in festivals and celebrations in the city. Jenlain comes from the Brasserie Duyck in the village of Jenlain south-east of Valenciennes. Brewing started on a farm and in 1922 Félix Duyck, of Flemish stock, started brewing there. The business is now run by his son Robert and grandson Raymond. Production has grown to 90,000 hectolitres a year but brewing has remained traditional in copper vessels. Malts from Flanders, Champagne and Burgundy are used along with four hop varieties from Belgium, France, Germany and Slovenia. **Jenlain**, 6.5 per cent ABV, is russet-coloured, spicy and malty. It is a highly complex beer with great depth (25 IBUs). The Duycks did experiment with a bottom-fermenting yeast but latest information is that they have returned to proper ale brewing. They also brew a Christmas beer and a pale spring (Printemps) beer.

Beer was brewed in the region for coal miners as well as farm workers – Lille was once at the heart of the mining industry of northern France. The Castelain Brewery at Bénifontaine near Lens once made a special 2.0 per cent alcohol beer for miners, but all the pits have gone and the only reminder of the industry is the ghostly figure of a coal miner with his lamp on the label of the brewery's main brand Ch'ti. The name comes from Picardy dialect and means "c'est toi" – "it suits you". The brewery, part of a farm, was built in 1926 and was bought by the Castelain family in 1966. The handsome brewhouse with gleaming copper kettles produces 28,000 hectolitres a year. Yves Castelain uses Flemish and French barley and hops for pale and brown versions of Ch'ti as well as for an organic beer called Jade, Christmas and March beers, and an abbey-style beer called Sint Arnoldus. Yves Castelain has switched to lager yeast but ferments at 15°C/59°F. The beers are fermented for 10 to 12 days and then conditioned for up to two months. **Ch'ti Blonde** is made from four malts, the **Ch'ti Brune** from eight, including Munich, cara-Munich and torrefied varieties. The 6.5 per cent ABV beers are rich and fruity, with the Brune in particular having a strong hint of raisins in the mouth. The 4.6 per cent ABV **Ch'ti Jade** has more hop character, pungent and perfumy, with sweet malt in the mouth and a fruity finish that becomes dry.

In the hills of French Hainaut, close to the Belgian border, the Bailleux family runs the Café Restaurant au Baron in Gussignies and also brews on the premises. All the products are true warm-fermenting, bottle-conditioned bières de garde, though one is called a saison in the Belgian fashion. The **Cuvée des Jonquilles** does not, in spite of the name, use daffodils in the brewing process but it has an entrancing golden colour and flowery-fruity aroma and palate. The 7.0 per cent ABV beer is brewed in the spring, which explains the daffodil associations. Four malts and four hop varieties are used. The **Saison Saint Médard**, also 7.0 per cent ABV, has a fine cherry colour and a fruity aroma similar to a Belgian kriek but without the lambic sourness. There is also a chocolatey and spicy Christmas beer.

The Brasserie d'Annoeullin is in the small town of the same name between Lens and Lille. The brewery was once a farm and Bertrand Lepers' wife, Yvonne, comes from farmer-brewers at Flers. When they married they merged the two breweries. The mash tun doubles as a copper after the wort has been clarified. The beer ferments in horizontal tanks in cellars that were once cattle byres. Primary fermentation lasts for a week, followed by two weeks' conditioning. The bière de garde is called, tongue-in-cheek,

Pastor Ale with the sub-title "C'est une symphonie". It is 6.5 per cent ABV and is made from pale malt only. It has a rich gold colour, pronounced orange fruit and earthy hops on the aroma, more tart fruit in the mouth and a dry and fruity finish. A 7.3 per cent ABV **Angelus** is a wheat beer, using 30 per cent buck wheat in flour form. It is bronze-coloured and has a powerful citric tangerine aroma backed by spicy hops, with more tart fruit in the mouth and a long, bittersweet finish: a magnificent beer.

The St Sylvestre Brewery at Steenvoorde, in the heart of the hop country, produces a gold bière de garde called **3 Monts** (8.5 per cent ABV). It is named after three local hills, worthy of celebration in such flat country. The beer is dry and winey with good hop character from local Brewers' Gold and German Tettnang.

The depth of support for beer in the region can be seen in the annual summer festival in Douai where ale is the main lubricant. The two legendary giants that lead the parade are known as Monsieur and Madame Gayant and the local brewery calls itself Les Enfants de Gayant. The enterprising brewery has a large portfolio of beers, including an Abbey beer and a 12 per cent ABV perfumy lager, **Bière de Démon**. Its interpretation of the bière de garde style is called **Lutèce Bière de Paris** – Lutèce comes from the Roman name for Paris, Lutetia. Brewers in Roman Paris were based in an area known as La Glacière, fed by the waters of the river Bièvre, named after beavers that bred there. Beer was stored in icy caves – an early form of lager brewing. The beer style was called Brune de Paris. The Lutèce Brewery was founded in Paris in 1920 on the site of an old Brasserie de Glacière and, although brewing has been switched to Douai, the style of the original beer is meticulously maintained. It is 6.4 per cent ABV and is made from pale, Munich, crystal and caramel-amber malts. Spalt and Saaz hops achieve 23 IBUs. The beer is conditioned for 60 days. It has a rich malt and fruit aroma, with malt and raisins in the mouth and a deep finish with hints of chocolate and liquorice.

Visitors to Lille can find instant refreshment when they leave the railway station in Les 3 Brasseurs at 22 Place de la Gare. It is a large, beautifully appointed brewpub, the first in a small chain owned by Patrick Bonduel in Northern France (other pubs are in Angers, Mulhouse, Paris and Strasbourg). The beers are all-malt and unpasteurized, brewed in a tiny brewhouse. Customers can order La Palette du Barman, four taster glasses of each beer. The Blonde has a malty, perfumy aroma with a bittersweet palate; the Ambré has a dark toasty character; the Brune has hints of sweet nuts and bitter chocolate; while the cloudy wheat beer – Blanche – has a tangy apples-and-cloves aroma, citric fruit in the mouth and a dry finish with a powerful hint of apples. There are also March and Christmas seasonal beers.

SELECTED FRENCH BREWERS

Grande Brasserie Alsacienne d'Adelshoffen, 87 route de Bischwiller, 67300 Schiltigheim.

Brasserie d'Annoeullin, 4 Place du Général de Gaulle, 59112 Annoeullin.

Brasserie Bailleux, Café-Restaurant Au Baron, Place du Fond des Rocs, Gussignies, 59570 Bavay.

Brasserie Castelain, 13 rue Pasteur, Bénifontaine, 62410 Wingles.

Brasserie Duyck, 113 rue Nationale, 59144 Jenlain.

Brasserie des Enfants de Gayant, 63 Fauborg de Paris, 59502 Douai.

Brasseries Heineken SA, 19 rue des Deux-Gares, 92565 Rueil-Malmaison.

Kanterbräu SA, Tour Chenonceaux, 92100 Boulogne.

Brasserie Kronenbourg SA, 86 route d'Oberhausbergen, 67067 Strasbourg.

Brasserie Météor Haag-Metzger & Cie, 6 rue du Général-Lebocq, 67270 Hochfelden.

Brasserie Saint Sylvestre, 1 rue de la Chappelle, 59114 Saint-Sylvestre-Cappel.

The beer styles of Germany

Key

1	Pils	5	Ice	9	Alt bier
2	Wheat	6	Helles	10	Weiss
3	Black beer	7	Kölsch	11	Bock
4	Smoked beer	8	Dortmunder Export	12	Dunkel

Germany

Germany is the world's greatest beer nation. Beer is rooted in the lifestyle and culture of the people. It underscores every celebration. And in the Catholic south, the Bavarians seem to find good reason to celebrate all year round. Their Munich Oktoberfest is the world's most famous beer festival but it is not sufficient to satiate the Bavarians. They have winter beers, March beers, May beers and strong Lent beers they call "liquid bread".

GERMANY
Aying
Brauerei Insel-
   kammer Aying
Bad Köstritz
Köstritzer Schwarz-
   bierbrauerei
Bamberg
Heller-Trum
   Schlenkerla
Kaisderdom Privat-
   brauerei
Bayreuth
Maisel
Berlin
Berliner Kindl
   Brauerei
Schultheiss-Brauerei
Bitburg
Bitburger Brauerei
   Theo Simon
Bremen
Brauerei Beck/
   Haake Beck/St
   Pauli Girl
Cologne
Gaffel, Privat
   Brauerei Gaffel-
   Becker
Helaler, Brauhaus
   Heller
Küppers Kölsch
   Brauerei
Malzmühle, Brauerei
   Schwarz
P. J. Früh Cölner

Hofbräu
Päffgen, Gebrüder
   Päffgen
Heller brewpub
Malzmühle
Donaueschingen
Fürstlich Fürsten-
   bergische
   Brauerei
Dortmund
Dortmunder Actien
   Brauerei
Dortmunder Kronen
Dortmunder Union
   Brauerei
Düsseldorf
Diebels, Privat-
   brauerei Diebels
Zum Eurige Ober-
   garige
   Haus-brauerei
Steinecker brew-
   house
Im Füchschen
Zum Uerige
Zum Schlüssel
Einbeck
Einbecker Bräuhaus
Erding
Erdinger Weissbräu
Frankfurt
Brauerei Binding
Henninger-Bräu
Fürstenfeldbruch
Schlossbrauerei
   Kaltenberg

Hamburg
Bavaria-St Pauli
   Brauerei Holsten
   (InBev)
Hanover
Gilde Brauerei
Herford
Brauerei Felsenkeller
   Herford
Jever
Jever, Friesisches
   Bräuhaus zu
   Jever
Kelheim
G. Schneider &
   Sohn
Kreuztal-
Krombach
Krombacher
   Brauerei
Kulmbach
EKU Este Kulm-
   bacher Actien
   Brauerei
Kulmbacher
   Mönschshof-Bräu
Reichelbräu
Mannheim
Eichbaum-
   Brauereien
Munich
Augustiner Brauerei
Bayerische Staats-
   brauerei
   Weihenstephan
Hacker-Pschorr

Bräu
Löwenbräu
Paulaner-Salvator-
   Thomasbräu
Gabriel Sedlmayr
   Spaten-
   Franziskaner-
   Bräu
Staatliches
   Hof-bräuhaus in
   München
Augustiner Gast-stätte
Donisl
Hofbräuhaus
Mathäser Bierstadt
Schneider Weisses
   Bräuhaus
Paulaner Bräuhaus
Forschungsbräu-stuberl
Unionsbräu Keller
Beer Gardens
Am Nockherberg
Chinesischer Turm
Hofbräu Keller
Münster
Pinkus-Müller
Nuremberg
Alstadthof
Stuttgart
Dinkelacker Brauerei
Schwaben Bräu
Warstein
Warsteiner Brauerei

115

It is not just "lager" that Germans drink. Ask for a lager in a German bar and you will get a puzzled look. You may be shown the storage area or the refrigerator instead of being served a cool, pale beer. Lager, from *lagerung* meaning "to store", is a stage in the brewing process. The term lager is mainly confined to exports to the British Isles where it is used to distinguish beers brewed by cold fermentation from warm-fermented ales. In Germany drinkers need to be more specific. Bavarians will call for a Hell or a Dunkel or, depending on the season of the year, they might demand a Märzen or a Bock. In the North, the call may be for an Export. And everywhere the shout for "a Pils" will bring forth a dry and bitter interpretation of the Bohemian Pilsner.

And Germans do not only drink beers made by cold fermentation. Members of the ale family of beer are growing in favour. Bavarian wheat beers are enormously popular and have grown to around 30 per cent of the total beer market. Berlin has its own idiosyncratic version of wheat beer while Cologne and Düsseldorf proudly brew golden Kölsch and copper-coloured Alt beers.

Reinheitsgebot

The history of the *Reinheitsgebot*, the sixteenth-century Bavarian "Pure Beer Pledge", is covered in the history section. It is still in force throughout Germany. It stipulates that beer can only be brewed with malted barley and wheat, hops, yeast and water: sugars and "adjuncts" – cheap unmalted cereals – are outlawed. The pledge is adhered to with fierce pride by brewers who were angered by a decision of the European Court in 1987 to declare the pledge "a restraint of trade". The case was taken to court by French brewers based ironically in the former German region around Strasbourg. French and other European brewers were irritated that they could not export beer to Germany as they did not brew according to the *Reinheitsgebot*. But, despite a court ruling in favour of non-German brewers, imported beer has made little headway in Germany. The German brewers launched a campaign against what they call "chemi-beer", an attempt to suggest that beers from other countries are grossly inferior to their own and brewed using chemicals. While some poor quality packaged beers are sometimes brewed with the help of small amounts of chemicals to speed up fermentation and to create a thick head on beer, the use of chemicals or natural compounds is in the main confined to water treatment to enable brewers to harden or soften their brewing liquor. And nothing in the *Reinheitsgebot* stops German brewers treating their water.

Every brewery in Germany, and many bars, too, display plaques announcing that the beers produced or on sale adhere to the *Reinheitsgebot*. Consumers are intensely loyal to their local breweries and the German brewing industry has been largely untouched by imports, though Czech beers, which are brewed to the Purity Pledge, are popular. It should be noted, however, that with the exception of Bavaria, German beers brewed for export do not have to meet the requirements of the *Reinheitsgebot*.

Bavaria

Germany has around 1,400 breweries. While there has been some contraction in recent years, the country has not been overtaken by the merger mania of the rest of the world, though Carlsberg, Heineken and InBev have made some inroads. Some 750 of the total are located in Bavaria. Every town and just about every village has a brewery, sometimes more than one, brewing to traditional recipes, producing seasonal specialities, ignoring the outside world and pressures to produce beers by faster and less perfect methods. Monasteries and even convents brew beer, often for just their own and visitors' consumption. Bavaria remains a largely rural region and brewing is a time-honoured, bucolic ritual, as natural as baking bread, using the barley and the hops from the surrounding fields and pure, icy water from the Alps. The choice is

literally staggering, around 5,000 different beers, in a wide variety
of styles and strengths. By avoiding mergers, only a handful of
brewers, mainly in Munich, are large, producing more than half a
million hectolitres a year. Five hundred Bavarian breweries make
no more than 10,000 hectolitres a year and some of those produce
as little as 2,000 hectolitres.

The only major change in brewing practice in Bavaria has
been the switch from warm to cold fermentation. The earliest
empirical attempts to store or lager beer came in the great Bavarian
capital of Munich. The city was founded in 1158 when a Bavarian
duke built a bridge across the River Isar and Munich became a
major trading town on the salt route from Austria to the north
German ports. Munich – München in German, from Mönchen,
"the monks' place" – is close to the foothills of the Alps and brewers stored their beers in deep caves to withstand the rigours of hot
summers. The low temperatures encouraged yeast to settle at the
bottom of the fermenting vessels and to turn malt sugars into
alcohol much more slowly than conventional warm fermentation.
The result was a cleaner-tasting, less fruity and more stable beer.

As massive industrial innovation swept across Europe in the late
eighteenth and nineteenth centuries, brewers rushed to embrace
all the new technologies available to them. Steam power, temperature control, yeast propagation, better hop utilization, kilning of
malt over coke fires and, above all, refrigeration led to fundamental
changes in the way beer was brewed. Gabriel Sedlmayr the
Younger, a member of the great Munich brewing dynasty that
owns the Spaten group, travelled widely in Europe to learn his
brewing skills. He returned to Munich in 1834 to put his knowledge into operation and to use new technology to develop lager
brewing. From the late 1830s Sedlmayr became famous throughout the world of brewing as the man behind the new
cold-fermenting beer. He collaborated with Anton Dreher, another innovative brewer in Vienna, and the two worked with Carl von

Linde, builder of ice machines, to develop a commercial refrigerator that would enable beer to be stored not in caves but in brewery cellars at near-freezing temperatures.

Dark lagers

The first Munich lagers were dark. Malting techniques must have been behind those in England, where pale ales appeared early in the nineteenth century. Coal was notoriously expensive in Bavaria and coke, made from coal, was vital to produce pale malt on a large scale. And continental varieties of barley, high in protein, were more difficult to work with, needing a triple-decoction mashing regime. So the revolutionary new beer that emerged from Sedlmayr's Spaten brewery was a dark copper-to-mahogany colour. The style survives and is called Dunkel, sometimes rendered as Dunkles, which means dark. Today the malt grist for the beer will be a careful blend of pale and darker malt. The latter is known worldwide as Munich malt, which has been kilned in the maltings to a high temperature but avoids the bitter, roasty character of a much darker English black or chocolate malt. A Munich brewer looks for sweetness from his malt which he can balance with aromatic Bavarian hops.

Spaten's **Ludwig Thoma Dunkel** is the classic Munich dark beer. It is 5.5 per cent ABV, with 47 colour units and a gentle 20 IBUs. It has a malty, slighty spicy aroma, a malt-and-coffee palate and a finish that begins bittersweet and becomes dry. Among the other Munich brewers, Augustiner's **Dunkel** is 5.0 per cent ABV, exceptionally dark with russet tints, a malty nose, a nutty palate and a dry finish. Hacker-Pschorr's **Dunkel** (5.2 per cent ABV) is rich, malty and chocolatey with a dry finish. The Hofbräuhaus, the world-famous "royal court brewhouse", with oompah bands and a large beer garden, has a distinctive 5.2 per cent ABV **Dunkel** with a complex malt and vanilla aroma, tart dark fruit in the mouth and a long finish with hints of hops, dark fruit and chocolate. Paulaner's

5.2 per cent ABV **Dunkel** is both extremely dark and well-hopped for the style, with an aromatic malt and hops aroma, dark fruit in the mouth and a dry and bitter finish.

Outside Munich, the Kaltenberg Brewery has turned its dark lager into a speciality. The brewery is based in a splendid neo-Gothic castle and is owned by an aristocratic brewer, Prince Luitpold of Bavaria. He is a member of the German royal family that lost power at the end of the First World War. When he took over the family castle and brewery in 1976, he decided to beef up the Dunkel and make it his leading brand.

The 5.6 per cent ABV **König Ludwig Dunkel** – named after a royal ancestor, King Ludwig – is well-attenuated, with most of the brewing sugars turned to alcohol. The mashing is an exhaustive triple decoction one and hops – Hersbruck and Tettnang – are added three times during the copper boil. The British practice of dry-hopping – adding a handful of hops to the beer in cask – is used for additional aroma: this is frowned on by most German brewers. The finished beer has 24 to 26 IBUs. The beer is kräusened during lagering, which means that some partially fermented wort is added to the beer to encourage a powerful second fermentation. Lagering takes place in the castle cellars in small stainless steel conical vessels. The beer has a pronounced bitter-hoppy character from aroma to finish, balanced by dark malt, coffee and bitter fruit. It is a splendidly refreshing beer.

Franconia, the northern region of Bavaria (Franken in German), is packed with breweries. The main towns of Amberg, Bamberg and Nuremberg have 18 breweries between them, nine of them in the half-timbered, medieval splendour of Bamberg. The relative isolation of Franconia, heightened by its proximity to East Germany and Czechoslovakia during the years of the Cold War, has made it a conservative region with a great belief in traditional values, including a devotion to dark lagers. Many of the breweries are tiny, no more than brewpubs. A classic is the Hausbrauerei

Altstadthof in Nuremberg, which means "the house brewery in the old town courtyard". Based in sixteenth-century buildings, the brewhouse has copper mashing and boiling vessels and wooden fermenters and lagering tanks. Using organically-grown barley and hops, the 4.8 per cent ABV dark beer is red-brown in colour, has a yeasty and malty aroma, a creamy palate and a malty finish with some hints of dark fruit.

In Kulmbach, the Kulmbacher Mönchshof was once a monastic brewery, secularized at the end of the eighteenth century. Its speciality is **Kloster Schwarz Bier** – cloister black beer – a 4.7 per cent ABV brew known locally as "the black Pils" because of its unusual hoppiness for the style. It begins malty and yeasty on the nose but picks up hop character on the palate and finishes dry and bitter.

Also in Kulmbach, EKU, the brewery famous for its 13.5 per cent ABV Doppelbock, one of the strongest beers in the world, also makes a 4.8 per cent ABV **Rubin Dunkel**, rich and malty with a hint of tart fruit and a dry finish.

The monastery in Bamberg had its own brewery for several centuries but it has closed and has been converted into a fine museum that traces the history of brewing in the region and explains on video the brewing process. Part of the museum is in the deep vaulted cellars where the monks once stored their beers. Beers on sale in the bar and restaurant in the grounds of the monastery include a dark lager specially brewed by a commercial company for the church. It's a dark brown, almost black beer, hoppy on the nose, with coffee and dark fruit on the palate and a bittersweet finish.

In Bayreuth, with its Wagner associations, Maisel brews a 5.1 per cent ABV **Dunkel** with a pleasant nutty palate, dry finish and delicate hop bitterness.

Pale lagers

To call the pale lagers of Munich and Bavaria "everyday beers" is
to diminish the quality and the respectable strengths of brews of
between 4.5 and 5.0 per cent ABV. They are known as Helles or
Hell for short, meaning pale. (The only exception is Franconia
where the style is often referred to as *Vollbier*.) Helles beers sit just
below Pilsners, which are slightly stronger and a shade dryer and
more hoppy. Helles is the drink of the beer garden and the keller,
refreshing, spritzy, malty and delicately hopped.

The first pale lager appeared from the Spaten Brewery in 1894.
Paulaner, which now includes Hacker-Pschorr, busily promoted
the style in the 1920s and 1930s. But Helles did not overtake
Dunkel in popularity until the 1950s, rather as pale ale replaced
mild in British beer drinkers' affections. Helles beers tend to be
extremely pale while a Pilsner is golden. Spaten's **Hell** is 4.8 per
cent ABV, its **Pilsener** – note the variation in spelling – is 5.0 per
cent ABV. But the Pilsner has 38 IBUs, the Hell just 22. The Hell
is a Bavarian classic, with an entrancing bittersweet, malt-and-hops
aroma, malty in the mouth and finish that becomes dry but not
bitter.

Augustiner's **Hell** (5.2 per cent ABV) is the most popular
among Munich's beer lovers, perhaps as a result of its more robust
strength, with a malty-creamy aroma, malt in the mouth and on
the finish. Hacker-Pschorr's 4.9 per cent ABV **Hell** is darker with
a fruity aroma and palate, and a dry finish (20 IBUs). Löwenbräu's
Hell (5.3 per cent ABV) is soft and malty from aroma to finish. In
sharp distinction, Paulaner's **Original Münchner Hell** (4.9 per
cent ABV) has a dry edge to the finish and is much more
generously hopped.

The oddest beer comes from Forschung at Perlach, an outer
suburb of Munich. As well as brewing, the Jakob family also carries
out research work for other breweries. The name of the 5.4 per
cent ABV **Pilsissimus** suggests it is a junior version of a Pilsner

but the strength belies this. It is copper-coloured with a big floral hop aroma, soft malt in the mouth and a finish packed with great hop character.

Another brewery close to Munich, Bachmayer of Dorfen near Erding, brews a 4.7 per cent ABV **Hell** that is exceptionally pale with a fruity aroma and palate and a dry finish. The 4.8 per cent ABV **Hell** from Dimpfl in Fürth im Wald is golden in colour, sharp and tangy on the aroma, with a rounded maltiness offset by good hop character: the character of the beer is clearly influenced by its proximity to the Czech border.

Examples of Franconian **Vollbier** include Bärenbräu's 4.8 per cent ABV in **Staffelstein**, hoppy and dry, Brauhaus's crisp and quenching 4.6 per cent ABV offering in **Amberg**, the bittersweet 5.1 per cent ABV from Eichorn of Forcheim, and the apple-fruity 4.8 per cent ABV from Falkenloch of Neuhaus.

Pilsener

In spite of the geographical closeness of Bavaria and Bohemia, the brewing of golden lagers was slow to spread from their town of origin, Pilsen, to Munich. But now "Pils" is such a widespread style that most beer drinkers think of it as German rather than Czech beer. Unlike the more austere Pils of Northern Germany, with their flinty dryness, Bavarian versions have much in common with the genuine article from Pilsen: a rich maltiness offset by generous bitterness, using hops from the Hallertau that have a similar aromatic quality to Bohemian Žatec or Saaz varieties. Most Bavarian breweries include a Pilsener – the German interpretation of the spelling – in their portfolios. Drinkers invariably shorten the word to demand "ein Pils".

In Munich, Löwenbräu's **Pilsener** (5.4 per cent ABV) is the hoppiest of the city's contributions to the style. With bitterness units in the high 30s from Hallertau and Saaz hop varieties, it has a superb citric aroma, a fine balance of malt and hops in the mouth and a shatteringly long finish packed with hop bitterness. Löwenbräu buys malt from Bavaria and also from the Champagne region of France. Paulaner's 4.8 per cent ABV **Pilsener** has a floral, aromatic hop nose, a big malty body underpinned by hops and a long, dry finish. In the manner of German winemakers, Paulaner describes the beer as "Extra Trocken" – Extra Dry. The world-famous brewing university of Weihenstephan ("Holy Stephen") at Freising on the Munich outskirts and close to the new airport is connected to a brewery of the same name. Its **Edelpils** (4.9 per cent ABV) is extremely dry with a fine perfumy hop aroma, a malty body and a dry and bitter finish. Löwenbrau and Spaten are now owned by InBev but the two breweries continue to brew separately.

Elsewhere in Bavaria, Aukofer of Kelheim brews a 4.8 per cent ABV **Pilsener** with a complex hoppy aroma, bittersweet malt and hops in the mouth and long, lingeringly hoppy finish. In Franconia, Becher of Beyreuth produces a 4.7 per cent ABV **Pilsener** that, in the Franken fashion, is unfiltered, with a yeasty aroma balanced by good bitter hops. In Amberg, the Brauhaus 4.7 per cent ABV **Pilsener** has a big hop attack on the aroma and palate, with some malt in the mouth and big bitter finish. At Zapfendorf near Bamberg, the Drei Kronen – Three Crowns – brewery has a superb 4.8 per cent ABV **Pilsener** with a dense head, firm body, malty palate and long dry finish. EKU's **Pilsener** (4.9 per cent ABV) from Kulmbach has a rich, floral hop bouquet, bitter hops in the mouth backed by sweet malt and a bittersweet, malt and hops finish. In Bamberg, Mahrs's **Pilsener** (4.7 per cent ABV) is rich and malty balanced by aromatic hops, with a dry and bitter finish. In the heart of the great Hallertau hop-growing area, the Schlossbräu (Castle Brew) **Pilsener** is 4.9 per cent ABV and, fittingly, has a nostril-expanding hop aroma, more hops with balancing malt on the palate and a bitter finish.

March beer

In spite of the enormous interest in Bavarian beers both within and without the region, one style is under threat. Märzenbier means March beer, an ancient style from the days before refrigeration. March was the last month when it was safe to brew before the hot summer weather arrived. So in that month beers strong in alcohol and high in hops were made and stored for drinking during the summer, with any left over consumed in September and October. The Märzenbiers of Bavaria took on a special significance in the nineteenth century with the arrival of the Munich Oktoberfest in 1810, followed by the moves towards commercial lagering of beer in the 1830s. March beers became an Oktoberfest treat, a special beer to mark a special occasion. The beers at first were dark brown but when Gabriel Sedlmayr at Spaten began his work on cold fermentation he worked closely with Anton Dreher in Vienna where beers had a reddish tinge as a result of using a well-kilned amber malt. Spaten's Märzenbier became the benchmark for other brewers to copy, a reddish-brown brew developed by Gabriel Sedlmayr's brother Josef at his own Franziskaner Brewery in Munich (the two breweries were to merge in 1920). The 5.6 per cent ABV beer today, called **Ur-Märzen** (Ur being short for Urtyp, or Original) is lagered for three months, has 32.5 colour units and 21.5 IBUs. It is a malty beer but the maltiness is clean, quenching and slightly spicy, not cloying, underpinned by a delicate but firm hoppiness, with a bittersweet finish.

Sales of Märzenbier are declining – down to less than 10 per cent of the total Bavarian beer market – as a result of the changing nature of the Oktoberfest. The festival is now so renowned that it attracts a vast number of visitors from abroad, mainly from the English-speaking world: it is packed with Americans, Australians and New Zealanders. Most of them are unaware of the history of Märzenbier and come to Munich expecting to drink pale lagers. The brewers oblige and some Oktoberfestbiers, though of good quality, are in every way a pale shadow of the brews originally proudly stored for the occasion. Even Spaten, with its classic Märzen, also produces a separate Oktoberfestbier today.

Fortunately the Hofbräuhaus sticks to tradition. Its 5.7 per cent ABV **Märzen** is another classic brew, red-brown in colour, with a rich malty aroma, a light and quenching palate and a gently dry finish. Outside Munich, the Bräuhaus at Fussen close to the Austrian border has a suitably dark red **Märzen**, with a honey aroma, a rich and fruity palate and malty finish that becomes dry. The Eichorn Brewery at Forcheim has a much paler **Märzen** (5.7 per cent ABV) with an apple-fruit nose, malt and hops in the mouth and big bittersweet, well-balanced and complex finish. Fässla of Bamberg has a 5.3 per cent ABV **Märzen**, also known as **Zwergla**, that has a dark amber colour, a nutty palate, and firm hops in the mouth and the finish. Goss's interpretation of the style in Deuerling is a 5.5 per cent ABV pale amber brew, more hoppy than most, with malt and light fruit on the palate and a clean, quenching finish. The St Georghen Brewery in Buttenheim in Franconia produces a magnificent **Gold Märzen** (5.6 per cent ABV) which, despite the name, is a true amber colour with great hop attack on the aroma and palate, a rich and rounded maltiness with a dry finish and a hint of apple fruit. Wagner in Eschenbach plays all the right tunes with its 5.3 per cent ABV **Märzen**: rich malt arpeggio, spicy and fruity notes with a good hop glissando.

Bock

Outside Bavaria the most popular theory for the origin of the term Bock is that it comes from the town of Einbeck in Lower Saxony. For centuries Einbeck has been associated with brewing strong beers, known as Einbecker beers and corrupted to just Beck (which has nothing to do with Beck's Brewery in Bremen). In the Bavarian dialect Beck became further corrupted to Bock. The style of beer had spread to the south as a result of a marriage in the seventeenth century between a duke of Brunswick in Lower Saxony and the daughter of an aristocrat from Bavaria. They were married in Munich and a century later there were records of an "Oanbock" beer being brewed in the Hofbräuhaus, the royal court brewery, in the Bavarian capital.

The Bavarians will have none of these airy Northern theories. For them Bock is a local style, a strong seasonal beer associated with Lent and brewed by monks as "liquid bread" to help them sustain themselves during the fasting period.

The early Bocks would have been dark and warm-fermented. Today there are pale Bocks, amber Bocks and copper Bocks as well, and they are cold-fermented. They are strong in alcohol, ranging from 6.0 to 8.0 per cent by volume. There are several seasonal versions: winter Bocks, Maibocks for the early summer and even stronger Double Bocks for Lent. The Double Bocks are also known as Starkbier (Strong Beer) and are drunk on draught for Starkbierzeit, "Strong Beer Time", in Munich.

The classic Maibock comes from the Hofbräuhaus in Munich, where the first casks are tapped on May Day by the Mayor and Prime Minister of Bavaria who, like a bibulous double act, perform the same ceremony at the Oktoberfest. Although the beer is described as "Helles Bock" (pale Bock) it is a burnished amber colour with 7.2 per cent alcohol. It has a dense head of foam through which springs the punch of alcohol balanced by a rich nutty maltiness and floral hop background leading to a deep malty palate and a finish that becomes dry with malt, fruit and hops.

Hacker-Pschorr's 6.8 per cent ABV **Hubertusbock** is a copper-coloured Maibock with hops and rich, dark fruit on the aroma, a massive malt and hops palate and a long bittersweet finish that becomes dry. The Union brewpub in Munich, owned by Löwenbräu, produces a 6.3 per cent unfiltered **Maibock** with a pronounced hoppy aroma, nutty in the mouth from the malt, and a bittersweet finish. South of Munich, the Ayinger Brewery in

Aying brews a delicious 7.2 per cent **Maibock**, straw-coloured, with a rich, perfumy hop aroma, apple and apricot fruit in the mouth and a dry, superbly balanced finish.

Franconian interpretations of Bock include the Malteser Brewery's **Rittertrunk** Bock (6.5 per cent ABV) in Amberg, reddish-brown, malt and hops aroma and a fruity palate and finish, and Mönchshof of Kulmbach's **Klosterbock** (6.3 per cent ABV), amber-coloured, with a malty start and a long, bitter and dry finish.

Double Bock (Doppelbock in German) is not double the strength of a Bock but is an indication that the beer is stronger than an "ordinary" Bock. They are Lent beers and are meant to be sustaining, a meal in a glass and a blanket round the shoulders. They are usually dark, warming, rich, glowing, more heavily malty and less hoppy than a Bock. The benchmark Double Bock comes from the Paulaner Brewery in Munich. So famous is the beer that the company is officially named Paulaner Salvator in order to incorporate the name of the beer in the title. The brewery was founded by monks of the order of St Francis of Paula in 1634, who naturally made a Lent beer. (This Saint Francis came from Calabria in Italy and must not be confused with the founder of the Franciscan order, St Francis of Assisi.) Beer from the monks' brewery was sold commercially from the late eighteenth century, and early in the nineteenth a brewer named Franz-Xavier Zacherl began to develop the Salvator brand. Salvator means "Holy Father Beer". The impact of the Double Bock that honours him led to all other God-fearing brewers adding the letters "-ator" to their versions of the style.

Paulaner Salvator Doppelbock is 7.5 per cent ABV and is brewed from three malts and Hallertau hop varieties. It is a deep, dark brown in colour, has a big malty-fruity aroma with a good underpinning of hops, a malty, yeasty, fruit-bread palate and an intense finish packed with dark fruit, malt and hops. The beer is lagered for around three months. Löwenbräu's **Triumphator** is

7.0 per cent ABV and has an intriguing and complex aroma and palate of roasted malt, nutmeg and spices, hints of chocolate, and a big, fruity, bready finish. Hofbräu offers a rich, warming, malty-hoppy Delicator (7.4 per cent ABV).

Ayinger brews a **Fortunator** (7.5 per cent ABV) with a Dundee-cake aroma and palate, warming and rich, with a dry finish. Eck in Böbrach brews a 7.0 per cent **Magistrator**, a slightly sinister name that suggests those who over-indulge will appear before the bench next morning. It is dark brown verging on black, with a deep malt and hops aroma, bitter chocolate in the mouth and a long bittersweet finish. With his determination to boost dark lagers, Prince Luitpold of Kaltenberg's **Dunkel Ritterbock** (6.8 per cent ABV) has a pronounced coffee aroma, a good balance of malt and hops in the mouth, and a dry, smooth finish. The monastic Klosterbräu Brewery in Ettal produces a 7.3 per cent **Curator**, reddish-brown, with a big malt aroma, a winey palate and a late burst of hops in the finish. The Klosterbräu at Irsee, South-west of Munich, uses the alternative **Starkbier** name for its strong Bock (6.8 per cent ABV). It is unfiltered with a yeasty, malty aroma, hops and fruit in the mouth and a dry, quenching finish.

The most famous Double Bock beers to drinkers outside Germany come from the EKU Brewery in Kulmbach. The letters stand for Erste Kulmbacher Unionbrauerei: Erste means first and Union indicates a merger of two former breweries in 1872. Using local barley, Hallertau hops (Perle, Hersbruck and Tettnang) and mountain water, EKU brews a 7.5 per cent **Kulminator** with an appealing claret colour, big malt on the aroma and palate, and hops and dark fruit in the finish. Not satisfied with this rich brew, the brewery then packs even more malt into its mash kettles to produce **Kulminator 28**, known abroad as **EKU 28**. For many years the beer vied with Samichlaus of Austria as the strongest lager in the world, though the Austrian beer is now the acknowledged leader. But 13.5 per cent alcohol by volume at EKU tests to the limits the ability of conventional brewer's yeast to ferment malt sugars before being overcome by the sheer weight of alcohol it has produced.

The beer is brewed from only pale malt but the amount of malt and some caramelization of the malt sugars gives the beer an amber glow. The alcohol gives a glow as well, backed by rich malt on the aroma, some citric fruitiness on the palate and a long, deep, intense, rich and warming finish with more fruit, malt and hops (30 IBUs). The beer is lagered for nine months and towards the end of the storage period ice forms in the lager tanks. But the brewery does not claim this makes it an "Eisbock" in which the creation of ice crystals concentrates the beer: there is quite enough alcohol in EKU 28 without any additional help. Some aficionados claim the beer is a cure for the common cold. It would certainly take your mind off it.

Close by, the Kulmbacher Reichelbräu brews a definably ice beer in the Bock style, known both as **Eisbock** and **Bayrisch G'frorns** ("Bavarian frozen"). The beer is 10.0 per cent alcohol and is made from five malts, including a dark variety and one that is deliberately slightly sour and lactic to avoid any cloying sweetness in the finished beer. It has 27 units of bitterness from Brewers' Gold, Perle, Hersbruck and Tettnang varieties. After primary fermentation, the beer is frozen for two weeks. Water freezes at a higher temperature than alcohol, forming ice crystals in the brew. The ice is removed, concentrating the alcohol. The beer is then kräusened with partially fermented wort to start a strong second fermentation. The finished beer is warming, aromatic from both malt and hops, rich and fruity in the mouth, and with a long, rich finish with coffee from the dark malt and an alcoholic kick. Eisbock may have been the inspiration for the heavily hyped Ice Beers developed in Canada. The Franconian version has the advantage of strength and a long lagering to give it great depth of character. The beer is brewed every year in August and September and stored until the last Saturday in March when a frozen cask is ceremonially broached at the Eisbock Festival in Kulbach's Rathaus – town hall.

Franconian specialities

The smoked beers of Bamberg are a powerful link with brewing's past and a more tenuous link with Scotch malt whisky where the grain is cured over peat fires. In the Bamberg area, the beers get their smoky character from barley malt kilned over beechwood fires. Until the Industrial Revolution and the switch from wood to coke, it is likely that all beers had a slightly smoky note from the kilning of the malt.

Bamberg, with its impressive blend of Romanesque, Gothic and Baroque buildings, is a malting centre as well as being rich in breweries. Beechwood is gathered from the surrounding forests to supply fuel for the malting kilns. The classic smoked or Rauchbier comes from the Heller-Trum Brewery which started in the Schlenkerla tavern in the town in 1678, when the beer was lagered in caves in the nearby hill of Stephansberg. The need for more space in the tavern and a growing demand for the beer forced the brewers to move to new premises. The brewery yard is packed with beechwood logs. Inside, there is a smokehouse where the barley lies on a mesh above a beechwood fire that throws up marvellous aromas reminiscent of autumnal garden fires. The copper brewhouse uses a double decoction mashing regime with primary fermentation in open vessels followed by two months' lagering. The main beer produced is **Aecht Schlenkerla Rauchbier** (5.0 per cent ABV; 29–32 IBUs), dark brown in colour and with an intense smoked malt aroma and palate, with dry malt in the mouth and a deep smoked malt finish. The brewery also makes an autumn smoky Bock and a Helles, which also has a hint of smoked malt.

The Christian Merz family's Spezial Brewery in Bamberg is a brewpub dating from 1536 that produces only smoked beers. Malt is made in a courtyard at the back of the pub. The Rauchbier is called, simply, **Lagerbier**. It is 4.9 per cent ABV with a light brown colour, with a malty-smoky aroma and palate, and a dry and fruity finish with a hint of burnt toffee. The Bürgerbräu-Kaiserdom Brewery has a full range of beers; its speciality is a 4.8 per cent **Rauchbier**, amber-coloured, with a malty/smoky aroma and palate leading to a dry finish.

Steinbier is a Franconian speciality even though the brewery using the method has moved from Neustadt, near Coburg, to Altenmünster in Southern Bavaria. Before metal kettles were widely used in brewing, it was dangerous to build fires under wooden vessels and it was a widespread custom in Northern Europe to lower hot stones into the mash. In 1982 Gerd Borges bought the brewery in Neustadt and decided to revive the fashion. Stones are brought from a nearby quarry and heated to white-hot temperature in an oven fired by beechwood logs. The stones are then lowered by the jaws of a small crane into a copper kettle. The mash boils, foams and steams while some of the malt sugars are caramelized and stick to the stones. When the stones have cooled they are placed in the maturation tanks where the caramelized sugar acts as a priming agent for a second fermentation. A top-fermenting yeast strain is used. **Steinbier** is 4.9 per cent alcohol, brown in colour, with a smoky aroma, toffee-like palate and a long, well-balanced malt, hops and dark fruit finish. The mash is a 50:50 blend of barley and wheat malts. Hersbruck and Tettnang hops are used and create 27 IBUs.

A version of the beer, using 60 per cent wheat malt, is called **Steinweizen** and is bottle-conditioned.

Bavarian wheat beers

The beer world has turned upside down in Bavaria. A warm-fermenting type of ale that was doomed to extinction with the development of lager brewing in the nineteenth century is undergoing a revival of Biblical proportions. Wheat beer, derided for decades as a beer for pensioners, enjoyed spectacular growth in the 1980s and achieved cult status among the young. As a result of bottle-conditioning, which leaves a sediment rich in yeast and proteins, it is perceived by the "green generation" as being a healthier drink than lager beers.

In the fifteenth century the barons of Degenberg appropriated the right to brew wheat beer and passed the right on to the Wittelsbachs, the Bavarian royal family. Their Royal Court Brewery – the Hofbräuhaus – in Munich was opened in 1589 and by the early part of the next century was producing large quantities of wheat beer. At one stage there were around 30 royal brewhouses in Bavaria producing the style. The ordinary people had no choice in beer, for the royal family controlled the grain market and refused to release wheat for brewing. Wheat beer only became available commercially in 1850 when the royal family licensed a Munich brewer named Georg Schneider to brew it in their Munich Hofbräuhaus. Perhaps the royals were losing interest in wheat beer and were casting envious eyes on Sedlmayr's new lager beers. Georg Schneider later moved a short distance to a brewery in Im Tal (the Dale), just off the Marienplatz with its stunning Gothic town hall, the Rathaus. Even though lager beer was being developed in the same city, Schneider's wheat beer was a sensation and he had to buy a second brewery in Kelheim in the heart of the Hallertau hop-growing area to keep up with demand. The Munich brewery was destroyed by the British Royal Air Force in the Second World War. It has been rebuilt as a beer hall but no beer is brewed there now.

Many Bavarian brewers followed in Schneider's footsteps and brewed wheat beer as a sideline, something to have in their port-folio alongside mainstream dark and pale lagers. But now wheat beer accounts for 30 per cent of the vast Bavarian beer market and, along with low alochol (Alcoholfrei) beers, is the only growth sector. Although some brewers have introduced draught versions of wheat beer, they are usually bottled. A secondary fermentation in bottle gives the beers a high level of natural carbonation, creating a dense and foaming head and adding to the refreshing character. Wheat beers are made from a blend of wheat and barley malts: wheat malt by law must make up at least half of the grist. Barley malt is essential as it has a greater number of enzymes that turn starch into sugar and it also has a husk that acts as a filter during mashing. Wheat is a huskless grain and used on its own would clog up brewing vessels. The main contribution wheat malt makes to the beer is an appealing pale and hazy yellow colour and a characteristic aroma and flavour of spices and fruit: cloves are the dominant spice while apple and banana are typical fruit aromas.

The surge in popularity of wheat beer has encouraged some brewers to cut corners in its production. Ale yeasts for the second fermentation in bottle are being replaced by lager yeasts because of their greater stability and ability to give beer longer "shelf life". The use of lager yeasts removes some of the fruity and spicy flavours that only an ale yeast can impart. Some brewers even pasteurize the beer after primary fermentation before re-seeding with lager yeast and adding sediment to give a false impression of natural cloudiness. Most wheat beer producers make two versions: Hefe Weisse or Hefe Weizen, which means wheat beer with yeast, and a filtered version called Kristall or Ohne Hefe, without yeast. The unfiltered versions are by far the most popular and flavourful. Connoisseurs like to pour the beer slowly until the glass is almost full then twirl the bottle and deposit the sediment of yeast into the glass. The habit of placing a slice of lemon in the glass is declining. The reasons for doing this are lost in time but it may have played a similar role to the addition of fruit or herb syrup to Berlin wheat beers to reduce some of the acidity.

Schneider – the name means Taylor in English – is the wheat beer brewer by whom all others are judged. The Kelheim Brewery produces nothing but wheat beer, though the family owns a smaller plant near Regensberg where it brews lagers. The Kelheim Brewery, an odd but fetching blend of Spanish and Gothic architecture, was built in 1607 and is thought to be the oldest continuous wheat beer brewery in the world. It is run today by Georg Schneider V and his son, Georg VI, who will take over when his father retires. The brewery has open fermenters, a rare sight in Germany where brewers prefer to keep their beers locked away from possible air-borne infections. But the Schneiders will do nothing to interfere with the workings of the single-strain yeast culture, which has been used for as long as anyone can remember. Nothing is altered in the fermentation hall. Rather like whisky distillers who will replace one vessel with a slight kink with a new one with an identical kink built in to it, the Schneiders will replace one fermenter with another of exactly the same dimensions. They will not change the specification of their malts in case it upsets the temperamental yeast.

Schneider makes 300,000 hectolitres a year, 90 per cent of which is a 5.4 per cent **Weisse**. The rest is made up of an 8.0 per cent wheat Bock named **Aventinus** and a lighter beer called **Weizen Hell**. The brewery uses half a million tonnes of Bavarian barley and wheat. In the Weisse they are blended in the proportion of 60 per cent wheat to 40 per cent barley. Some Vienna and darker malts are added to give the beer its attractive bronze colour. Hersbrucker hops from the surrounding Hallertau are used in pellet form with a small amount of hop extract. The Weisse has 14 to 15 units of bitterness: hops in wheat beer are used primarily for their antiseptic and preservative qualities as too much bitterness will not blend with the spicy, fruity character of the beer. The local well water is softened by osmosis to remove some of the natural salts.

The modern brewhouse was built in 1988 with stainless steel mashing and boiling kettles standing on marble floors. A double decoction mash is used: portions of the mash are pumped from one vessel to another, heated to a higher temperature and then returned to the first vessel, raising the temperature of the entire mash. As modern continental European malts are "well modified", with the cell walls of the grain easily broken to enable the starches to be attacked by enzymes, double decoction mashing is probably not necessary but the Schneiders will not tamper with tradition. Mashing starts at 38°C/100°F, a lower temperature than a typical English infusion mash.

As the wort is pumped from one vessel to another the temperature rises by stages to 43°, 48° and 56°, reaching a final 65°. The spent grains are sparged at 75°. Hops are added in two stages during the copper boil, then the hopped wort is cooled and pumped to the fermentation hall. Sixteen stainless steel vessels hold 350 hectolitres each. The hall is heady with tempting aromas of fruit, with banana dominating, underscored by delicious hints of apple. Fermentation lasts between three and five days at 20°C/68°F. Twice a day the yeast is skimmed from the top of the wort, cleaned and then pitched back into the vessels. At the end of primary fermentation the green beer is not filtered and is bottled with a blend of the same top-fermenting yeast and some sugar-rich wort to encourage a second fermentation. The bottles are warm conditioned at 20° for a week, which causes a lively carbonation as fermentation gets under way. The beer is then cold conditioned at 8°C/47°F for a fortnight to stabilize it.

Schneider Weisse has a complex bouquet of banana, cloves and nutmeg, tart fruit in the mouth and a creamy, fruity finish with hints of bubblegum. **Aventinus** is bronze-red in colour due to the addition of caramalt. It has a rich spices and chocolate aroma and palate, with more spices, vinous fruit and cloves in the finish. It makes a splendid nightcap or winter warmer.

Schneider may be the flagship wheat beer producer but the biggest brewer of the style is Erdinger. The company in the town of Erding, on the far outskirts of Munich, is based in a modern brewery built in the early 1980s. The original site in the town centre brewed from the mid-1850s and is now a tavern. Erdinger has specialized in wheat beer since the 1930s and now produces two million hectolitres a year.

All the wheat and most of the barley is grown locally by farmers who work to specifications drawn up by the brewery. The wheat is low in protein, producing a soft-tasting beer. Water comes from an underground lake believed to be two million years old.

A double decoction mash is used and Perle and Tettnang hops are added three times, achieving 18 IBUs. Primary fermentation is unusual, taking place in horizontal tanks just 2.8 metres high – the brewers think this produces a cleaner-tasting beer. Breaking with tradition, Erdinger uses a lager yeast for bottle conditioning and the bottles are warm conditioned for a month.

Hefe-Weissbier is 5.3 per cent ABV. It has a relatively restrained aroma for the style, with hints of apples and cloves, more fruit in the mouth, and a gently fruity finish. A filtered version is sold as **Kristallklar**. A dark **Dunkel Weissbier** (5.6 per cent ABV) has pleasant chocolate and liquorice notes while **Pikantus Bock** (7.3 per cent ABV) has spices and chocolate on the aroma and palate.

The most remarkable revival of wheat beer is seen at the Spaten Brewery in Munich. Even though the brewery is the cradle of lager brewing, it now devotes 50 per cent of its capacity to wheat beer production. The wheat beers are sold under the Franziskaner name, the bottle labels showing a cheerful monk holding a mug of beer. The original wheat beer brewery, bought by Josef Sedlmayr and merged with his brother Gabriel's plant, was the oldest in Munich and was next to a Franciscan monastery. The main Spaten wheat beer, **Franziskaner Weissbier** (5.0 per cent ABV) has an ususually high wheat malt content of 75 per cent. The brewer admits this occasionally causes problems during mashing but feels it gives a better flavour to the finished beer. The other brands, Hell, Dunkel, Kristall and Bock, are made more conventionally from a 50:50 blend of German and French barley and wheat malts. A complex hops recipe is made up of Hallertau, Tettnang, Spalt, Perle and Orion varieties. Fermentation takes place in conical fermenters where a "top" yeast sediments to the bottom of the vessels. The beer is then centrifuged to remove the ale yeast and is re-seeded with a lager culture for bottle conditioning. The main wheat beer has a gentle fruity aroma, tart fruit and spices in the mouth and a light but quenching finish. The **Dunkel** (also 5.0 per cent ABV) is bitter for the style with dark fruit on the palate and finish.

Elsewhere in Munich, Löwenbräu's 5.0 per cent **Löwenweisse** has a strong apples and cloves aroma, hints of banana in the mouth, and a dry and spicy finish. Augustiner's **Weissbier** at 5.2 per cent has a malty aroma and palate and tart, lingering finish. Hacker-Pschorr's **Weisse** (5.5 per cent ABV) is light and undemanding. Höfbräuhaus honours its royal tradition with a crisp, lemon–fruity, tart and marvellously refreshing 5.1 per cent beer.

Outside Munich, Prince Luitpold brews a **Hell** and a **Dunkel** wheat beer, both 5.5 per cent ABV, in Fürstenfeldbruck. The Dark is a delight, packed with malt-loaf fruitiness with a slightly sour and quenching finish. In an idyllic setting in the Obberbayern mountains, the Hopf Brewery of Miesbach brews only wheat beer. As the German for hop is Hopfen, the owner, Hans Hopf, has a head start over his competitors in the brand image stakes. The small brewery has had to be substantially extended to cope with demand. Old copper vessels nestle against modern stainless steel ones in the brewhouse, which produces 50,000 hectolitres a year. The brewing liquor is Alpine water. German and French malts are used, with wheat malt making up 65 per cent of the mash. Hops are Hallertau and Spalt varieties. After primary fermentation the beer is kräusened with brewhouse wort and mixed with a blend of top and bottom yeasts for a second fermentation. The main beer, **Hopf**

Export (5.3 per cent ABV; 12 IBUs) has a nostril-widening spicy and peppery aroma underpinned by banana and bubblegum.

In Passau, the Andorfer Brewery's 5.3 per cent **Weissbier** is amber-coloured and balances a malty palate with a tart, fruity finish. South-west of Munich, Karg in Murnau has a coppery, yeasty, fruity and tartly uncompromising 5.0 per cent **Weissbier**. In Bayreuth, the Maisel Brewery's 5.2 per cent **Hefe-Weissbier** is a deep reddy-brown, with a delightful apple aroma and palate and a tart, dry finish.

Throughout Bavaria most breweries now have wheat beers in their portfolios. The success and revival of the style, like the cask-conditioned ales of Britain, mark another victory for consumer preference over marketing zeal.

Baden-Württemberg

The adjacent state to Bavaria is known by a variety of names: Schwaben, Schwabian-Bavaria or, to the outside world, the Black Forest. Swaben was an independent duchy from the tenth to the fourteenth centuries: Schwabia today in Germany means an area famous for its distinctive cuisine and spectacular countryside. It tends to be overshadowed by its better-known Bavarian neighbour but hits back with its own beer festival held at the same time as the Munich Oktoberfest. The Cannstatter Volkfest (the "People's Fest" in the suburb of Cannstatt in Stuttgart) begins at the end of September and runs for two weeks.

Stuttgart's three breweries, Dinkelacker, Stuttgarter Hofbräu and Schwaben Bräu, produce Volkfestbiers broadly in the Munich Märzen style. Local custom determines that these beers are lower in strength – around 4.5 per cent ABV – than the Munich versions but, like their Bavarian cousins, they are amber in colour, rich, malty and satisfying with a good hop character. Almost identical beers are produced for Christmas and the New Year under the name of Weihnachtsbier.

The Stuttgart breweries concentrate on Pilsners – soft, malt-accented, with gentle hop character – all in the classic 4.8 to 5.0 per cent alcohol range. Dinkelacker is the major brewery in the region and its biggest brand is the oddly named **CD-Pils**. The CD tag has nothing to do with either Compact Discs or the Corps Diplomatique but comes from the initials of the founder of the brewery, Carl Dinkelacker. The Dinkelacker family has been brewing since the late eighteenth century, built the present city-centre plant in 1888 and still controls the company at a time when most larger breweries are owned by banks or other financial institutions. CD-Pils is mashed and hopped in fine, traditional copper kettles and kräusened during the secondary fermentation. It is hopped four times, the final addition being with Brewers' Gold for aroma as the hopped wort is pumped from the kettle. The finished beer has a malty nose and palate with delicate hop notes in the mouth and a soft finish. Dinkelacker owns the Cluss Brewery in Heilbronn which produces a 5.0 per cent **Cluss Pilsner** and a dark, creamy **Bock Dunkel**.

Schwaben Bräu, in the district of Vaihingen, has an impressive copper brewhouse and vast cellars where the comparatively dry **Meister Pils** is lagered. The Hofbräu, once a royal court brewery but now a public company, is on the edge of Stuttgart and produces malty-sweet beers, the main brand being **Herren Pils**, which translates as Pils for Men, surely Politically Incorrect today.

Fürstenberg from the Black Forest is the best-known of the region's beers as it is widely exported. The beer has noble connections: the Fürstenberg family are aristocrats who have been involved in brewing for more than 500 years. They are renowned patrons of the arts and have a fine collection of paintings in their museum at Donaueschingen, which is also the site of the brewery. **Fürstenberg Pilsener** (5.0 per cent ABV) is decidedly hoppy for the regional style, with an aromatic and malty aroma, a full palate and a dry and bitter finish. **Export** (5.2 per cent ABV) is a deep gold colour with hints of fruit in a big malty body and crisp, dry finish.

In the north of the region, Eichbaum of Mannheim dates from 1697 when Jean de Chaîne founded a brewery called Zum Aichbaum in the Stammhaus tavern: the brewery moved to its present site in 1850 but the tavern has survived as a main outlet for the brewery. At one stage Mannheim had 40 or more breweries but only Eichbaum has survived. It brews both a cloudy and filtered wheat beer (5.3 per cent ABV) with a spicy and fruity palate and an **Apostulator Doppelbock** (7.5 per cent ABV), using caramalt and dark malt. The main product is a 4.6 per cent **Ureich Pils**: Ur means Original and Eich means Oak, the oak tree, Eichbaum, being the brewery's symbol. It is hopped with Hallertau and Tettnang varieties. The beer has malt and citric fruit from the hops on the aroma, a malty-hoppy palate and a dry finish with delicate hop notes. A 5.3 per cent **Export**, in the Dortmund style, has a more rounded and malty character.

Dortmunder Export

One city in Germany that has been badly affected by mergers and closures is Dortmund on the Ruhr. The decline of what was once called the capital of German brewing – the equivalent of England's Burton-on-Trent – has been blamed on the loss of Dortmund's once mighty steel and mining industries. But the truth is that brewing has been hit as much by self-inflicted wounds as industrial wind-down.

Dortmund once produced more beer than any city in Germany or Europe yet it's absurdly shy about its main style of beer, Export. Today, the one remaining large brewery, DAB, prefers to emphasise its Pilsners. But from the nineteenth century, a rounded and malty beer that restored lost energy to industrial workers was once sold so widely within and without Germany that it acquired the name of Export. You will come across

"Dorts" brewed today in Belgium and the Netherlands but it's hard to find the style in its city of origin.

Dortmund has had a brewing tradition since the thirteenth century. It specialized in dark wheat beers until the Kronen (Crown) brewery switched to cold fermentation. In the 1870s, the large Dortmunder Union Brewery (DUB) began to make lager beer and Export rapidly became the city's signature style. The two giants of Dortmund brewing from the nineteenth century were DUB and Dortmunder Actien Brewery or DAB. DAB and DUB sound like two cartoon characters but they were massive companies that produced more than four million hectolitres of beer each every year. The DUB tower became a famous symbol of brewing. The giant letter "U", 17 metres or 55 feet high, blazed out from the 1920s functional building. Union in Germany has nothing to do with labour unions let alone the fermentation system in far-off Burton-on-Trent but refers to a merger, in this case the spectacular joining together of a dozen breweries under one roof in 1873. Actien, on the other hand, indicates a public company that makes its shares available on the stock market. Dortmunder Actien, founded by the Fischer family in 1868, went public in 1872, a step that was the springboard for the creation of DUB a year later.

Kronen claimed to be the oldest brewery in the region of Westphalia. It traced its roots to a brewery and tavern called the Krone in 1430. It, too, switched to Export production in the nineteenth century. All three breweries survived until sweeping changes arrived in the 1990s. Kronen was the first to close in 1995 after 565 years of brewing, its brands merged with DAB's. It was replaced a year later by a brand-new brewing complex called Dortmunder Ritter – Ritter means knight in German – built by the major company Brau und Brunnen. The modern facilities offered by Ritter led to the closure of DUB in 1997, with production moved to the new plant. In 2002, Ritter was renamed Brinkhoff in honour of a former brewer in Dortmund, who must have scratched his head in wonder from the Great Saloon Bar in the Sky at the weird activities below. Brinkhoff No 1 **Premium Pilsener** (5 per cent ABV) became the main brand. In 2006 Brau and Brunnen was bought by the Oetker group, best known for its pizza and pasta brands. Reaching great intellectual depths, a director of Oetker said: "Brewing goes well with pudding and pizza". In spite of its modern facilities, Brinkhoff closed in 2005 and Oetker concentrated production at DAB, which can now produce around six million hectolitres a year. **DAB Export** (5 per cent ABV) survives as the last remaining version of the style. It has a sweet malt aroma, a fully malty body and a bittersweet finish with a late flourish of hops. Other beers in the range include **DAB Pilsener** (4.8 per cent), **DAB Diät Pils** (4.8 per cent), and **Hansa Pils** (4.8 per cent). A wide range of beers is produced for companies throughout Germany.

Oetker has made a clean sweep in Dortmund. It also owns Hövels, a large brewpub on the city's ring road. The range includes **Clarrisen Alt** (4.8 per cent ABV), a warm-fermented beer in the Düsseldorf style, and **Original Bitterbier** (5.5 per cent), the closest any German brewery comes to making an English bitter.

Münster

In Münster, the delightful old university city of Westphalia, Pinkus Müller produces a fascinating variety of highly individualistic beers using organic malt and hops. Pinkus Müller is well-known throughout Germany even though it is no more than a beer tavern, making around 10,000 hectolitres a year. The tavern has four dining rooms, specializing in local cuisine. Founder Pinkus Müller started in business producing beer, bread and chocolate and the company has been on the same site since 1816.

The best-known brand today is **Pinkus Münster Alt**. Alt means "old" and is a major beer style in Düsseldorf. The Pinkus brand is not a true Alt in the Düsseldorf style as 40 per cent of the grist is composed of wheat malt, the remainder being Bioland organic Pilsner. Organic hops come from the Hallertau, the mash is single-decoction and the brew is kräusened during secondary fermentation, which lasts for four months. A top-fermenting yeast is used and a lactic culture is allowed to breed in the lagering tanks, imparting a deliberate hint of sourness to the finished beer. It is 5.1 per cent ABV, with a rich, slightly vinous aroma, malt and tart fruit in the mouth, and a long and fruity finish with slight acidity.

The brewery does not claim the beer is a wheat one and could not legally do so, as less than 50 per cent of the mash comes from wheat. It underscores the point by producing a **Hefe Weizen** (5.2 per cent ABV) with 60 per cent wheat malt. It is conditioned for one month and has a light fruit aroma, delicate malt and fruit in the mouth, and a dry and fruity finish. Pinkus Müller makes two cold-fermenting beers, a hoppy and dry **Pils** and a stunning **Special** (5.2 per cent ABV), lagered for three months and producing a full malty aroma and palate with hops developing in the dry, quenching finish.

One of the specialities of the tavern is a syrup made from fresh fruit – strawberries or peaches in summer, oranges in winter – which is added to the Alt to cut the beer's acidity.

Frankfurt and Hesse

A cynic might say that it is because Germany's biggest brewing group, Binding Oetker, is based in Frankfurt that this area of the country produces the least interesting beers. Certainly Frankfurt and its environs has no distinctive beer style and Binding Oetker, which also owns DAB in Dortmund and the Berlin Kindl Brewery and makes in total 2.5 million hectolitres a year, is best known abroad for its Clausthaler low-alcohol lager. Its main brand for the Frankfurt market is broadly in the style of a Dortmunder Export. **Export Privat** has some hops on the nose, a firm, malty body and some delicate fruit in the dry finish.

The second Frankfurt brewery, Henninger, is no slouch in the production stakes, making around 1.75 million hectolitres a year. Its main products are a smooth and undemanding **Kaiser Pilsner**, brewed principally for the international export market, and a slightly stronger and marginally hoppier **Christian Henninger Pilsener**.

Cologne and Kölsch

The golden, top-fermenting ales of Cologne (Köln in German) are so highly regarded that the style is protected by federal law. Brewing has been rooted in the culture and way of life of Cologne, capital of the Rhineland, since Roman times. The name Cologne stems from "colonial" and it was an important city of the Roman Empire. Monasteries dominated the production of beer for centuries and gave way to commercial brewers and tavern owners. The modern Kölsch beers are pale but would have been darker in previous centuries when all malt was brown. But they remain warm-fermenting, a member of the ale family. The determination of brewers in Cologne, along with their kin in nearby Düsseldorf, to stick to the old tradition may be the result of temperature as well as temperament – cool summers do not demand a chilled beer – and the city's proximity to the Low Countries. The region has long had close links with what is now Belgium and was influenced by the beers enjoyed by such bibulous luminaries as Duke Jan Primus (Gambrinus). Cologne's Guild of Brewers dates from 1396 and has been in the van of protecting the city's beer culture. Today the city and its surroundings have some 20 or so breweries dedicated to brewing Kölsch. Cologne has more breweries than any other major city in Germany or the world. Kölsch came under great pressure at the turn of the century to switch to lager brewing but the offer was refused: one brewer has even removed Pilsner from his portfolio.

The language of the style can be confusing. Kölsch beers look like lagers. They are often called "Wiess", a local spelling of white, but they are not wheat beers even though some brewers use a proportion of wheat malt in the mash. A typical Kölsch is around 5.0 per cent ABV with a malty aroma and some gentle fruitiness. It will be soft due to the local water and there will a delicate, perfumy hop character. Bittering units will be in the high 20s but extreme bitterness is avoided. Hallertau and Tettnang hop varieties are preferred. The Kölsch yeast is a greedy strain, busily turning most of the malt sugars into alcohol, with a dry beer as the result.

The biggest producer of Kölsch today is the Küppers Brewery, founded just 20 years ago. It has built market share through clever promotions that have not pleased some traditionalists. **Küppers Kölsch** is soft, easy-drinking and undemanding. An unfiltered version call **Wiess** is more fruity, yeasty and distinctive. Küppers has merged with other smaller brewers to form Kölner Verbund Brauereien and is based in the former Bergische Löwen-Brauerei. There are three taverns serving the beers, often under the names of former breweries: Gilden Brauhaus, Peters Brauhaus and Sion Brauhaus. Brewery and taverns are part of the ever-expanding Oetker group.

The best-known and most highly-regarded of the Cologne brewers is P. J. Fruh's **Cölner Hofbräu**. The beer used to be brewed in a tavern on the Am Hof in the city centre but the house brewery became too small to meet demand and a new plant has been built a short distance away. **Früh Echt Kölsch**, all malt without wheat, is wonderfully drinkable, with delicate fruit on the aroma, and hops from Hallertau and Tettnang in the finish. Gaffel in the Old Town district has been brewing since 1302 and produces a beer of considerable pedigree: intriguingly nutty for a pale beer and a dry finish. The Heller brewpub in Roon Strasse offers a malty-sweet **Kölsch** and an unfiltered, fruitier and slightly tart version called **Ur-Wiess**. The Malzmühle (malt mill) brewpub on Heumarkt – Haymarket – uses some wheat malt in the mash and produces a rounded, malt-accented beer with a hint of spice and some delicate hop character from Hallertau. Päffgen in Frisen Strasse has a distinctive floral hop bouquet and a hoppy finish: by far the hoppiest of the style.

It is part of the delight of drinking Kölsch beers that most of the producers are small and many operate from taverns. Discovering the beer makes for a splendid pub crawl.

Düsseldorf Alt

Alt means old but the young have taken it to their hearts. Düsseldorf is another great industrial city that was once at the heart of the mining industry. The copper-coloured, warm-fermenting beers of the region again have a link with the malty, refreshing milds of industrial England, brewed to refresh people after a shift at the coal-face or the furnace. But unlike English mild or Dortmunder Export, the Alts of Düsseldorf have not declined in step with heavy industry but have found a new audience among white-collar employees, the young in particular. As with Cologne, there is a Low Countries connection: Düsseldorf is close to the Low Countries, in particular the tongue of the Netherlands that includes Maastricht, and the influence of Dutch brewers has seeped across the border.

Alt beers superficially are the closest to English ale, but the similarities should not be over-stressed. Decoction mashing is used by some brewers and all the beers are cold-conditioned for several weeks, though at higher temperatures than for lager beers, around 8°C/47°F. Hop bitterness will range from the mid-30s IBU to 50. Open fermenters for primary fermentation are used by some of the smaller producers, many of them based in charac-terful city brewpubs where the beer accompanies vast platefuls of local cuisine. Typically, an Alt will be around 4.5 per cent alcohol by volume.

The fortunes of Alt brewing have waxed and waned. Two of the biggest producers, Hannen and Schlösser, lost market share as a result of mergers: Hannen is owned by Carlsberg of Denmark, Schlösser by the Oetker group. The major brewer is the once family-owned Diebels in the hamlet of Issum a few miles from the city. The brewery was founded in 1878 by Josef Diebels and was in the family for four generations before it was bought by InBev. It produces more than one and half million hectolitres a year and doubled production between 1990 and 1991.

Diebels **Alt** has a gravity of 1045 degrees and is 4.8 per cent ABV, which means it is well attenuated. The beer has an appealing burnished copper colour with a peppery hop aroma balanced by rich malt. It is bitter in the mouth with a dry and nutty finish and a hint of orange fruit. Ninety eight per cent of the grist is pale Pils malt. The remaining two per cent is provided by roasted malt, more a Scottish practice than a German one. (Other Alt brewers prefer to use Vienna or black malt for colour and flavour.) Hops are Northern Brewer for bitterness and Perle for aroma, producing 32 to 33 IBUs.

Diebels' modern Steinecker brewhouse has tiled walls deco-rated by a mosaic showing the old brewery at the turn of the century. Four mash kettles feed four wort kettles, where the hops are put in in one addition. A decoction mashing regime is used. The 50-year-old yeast culture is a top-fermenting strain but is cropped from the foot of conical vessels. As with Guinness in Dublin, primary fermentation is rapid and lasts for just two days. The green beer then has a short "diactyl rest", which purges toffee-like flavours, and is stored in tanks for between 10 days in summer and three weeks in winter.

The best way to taste Altbier is to visit the taverns of the Alt Stadt, the cobbled and gas-lit Old Town of Düsseldorf. Im Füchschen, the Little Fox, at 28 Ratinger Strasse, is a cavernous building with tiled walls, red-tiled floors and wooden bench seats. The house beer is tapped from casks on the bar and is served by its own natural pressure, free from applied gas. The beer is maltier than Diebels with a toasty flavour and a sweet, fruity finish that becomes dry. In common with all Altbiers it is served in a short, stubby glass that is immediately replaced by another as the drinker downs it. Alts are a good companion for local dishes. Im Füchschen's speciality is a huge pickled knuckle of pork.

Zum Uerige offers salted pig's trotter with its Alt. The tavern is at 1 Berger Strasse and the name means the Place of the Cranky Fellow, though the present-day staff are helpful, attentive and friendly, and happy to discuss their beer in English as well as German. The beer is brewed in copper kettles and fermenters viewed from the main bar, part of a warren of rooms. The Alt, dry hopped and made with a dash of roasted malt, is fruity, aromatic and hoppy. Zum Schlüssel, the Key, at 43–47 Bolker Strasse, birthplace of the poet Heinrich Heine, also has its brewhouse on display at the back of the bar. The Alt has a delightful aromatic hop perfume, it is bittersweet in the mouth and has a dry finish.

Rhineland Pilsners

The Rhineland's love affair with Pilsner beers shows the impact which the Bohemian style had in the nineteenth century. For this vast and remote region of Germany is a considerable distance from Pilsen and, before the arrival of the railway, beer and its raw materials moved slowly by water transport. Yet the brewers of the Rhineland switched to cold-fermenting Pils with a fervour matched only in the far north around Hamburg. Several of the leading companies brew just one beer. Their dedication to the style and rigorous attention to the quality of materials and uniformity of production baulks at the notion of such Bavarian largesse as Dunkels, Bocks and Weizens.

Bitburger is a good case in point. It is brewed in the small town of Bitburg in the Eifel Lake district, close to the historic city of Trier, birthplace of Karl Marx. The company was established in 1817 as a humble farmhouse brewery and made warm-fermenting beers. But by 1884 it was producing Pilsner, using ice from the lakes to lager the beer. Its fortunes were boosted when a rail line was built to supply the Prussian army with cannon from the steelworks of Saarbrücken. The Simon family, which still owns the company, began to export its "Pils" to Northern Germany. Today it is one of the most widely exported German beers.

Bitburger's offices, original brewery and "brewery tap" tavern are in the centre of the small town. The superb copper brewhouse is still used but the main production has been switched to a state-of-the-art 1980s plant on a greenfield site on the edge of town. Wort is pumped by underground pipes between the two brewhouses. Enormous care is given to the selection of the finest raw materials: spring barleys – Alexis, Arena and Steiner – and Hersbrucker, Hüller, Perle and Tettnang hops. The beer has three hop additions in the kettle, is 4.6 per cent ABV with 37 to 38 IBUs. It is lagered for three months and is not pasteurized, which helps the delicate balance of malt and hops flavours. Beer for export is sterile filtered.

The Rhineland Pilsners are hoppier than those from the south but less dry and bitter than the interpretation of the style in the far north. Bitburger has a rich malt aroma underscored by floral hops, soft malt in the mouth and a long, complex finish with both bitterness and light citric fruit from the hops, balanced by sweet malt.

The biggest-selling Pilsner in Germany comes from the Warsteiner Brewery. The town of Warstein is in an area of woods and lakes to the east of the Rhine and the Ruhr. The ultra-modern brewery is coy about its ingredients, saying nothing more than "barley malt and Hallertau hops". **Warsteiner Premium** is 4.8 per cent ABV and is lagered for two months. It has a light malt and hops bouquet, rounded and bittersweet in the mouth, and a delicate dry finish with some citric notes from the hops, finally becoming dry.

Krombacher Pils from Kreuztal–Krombach uses Hallertau and Tettnang hops. The beer is 4.8 per cent with 24 to 26 IBUs. It has a comparatively brief lagering of just one month. The aroma is soft and malty, with delicate malt and hops in the mouth, and a dry finish with good hop notes. Brauerei Felsenkeller Herford produces yet another fine example of the style, well-attenuated (1046 degrees original gravity but brewed out to 4.8 or 4.9 per cent ABV). It is brewed from premium Pilsner pale malt and 60 per cent Hallertau Northern Brewer hops for bitterness and 40 per cent Perle and Tettnang for aroma. The hops produce 32 units of bitterness. The beer has a rich honeyed malt aroma, rounded malt and hops in the mouth, and a long, dry, delicate malty finish balanced by some citric fruit from the hops. Herford also brews a malty Export, a pale Maibock and a dark and fruity Doppelbock.

Hamburg and the North

Hamburg and Bremen have had a major influence on German beer and its impact abroad. They are major ports and for centuries have exported German beer to other countries. In common with all ports, they are cosmopolitan, polyglot places, open to many influences. They were at the heart of the great fifteenth-century trading group of cities known as the Hanseatic League. Other countries' beers came into their ports and had an impact on local styles. In particular, hops from Bavaria and Bohemia came up the Elbe, encouraging the Prussians to use the plant in their own brews.

The love affair with the hop married well with a later infatuation with the beers from Pilsen. Pilsner Urquell from Pilsen was given an award in a brewers' competition in Hamburg in 1863. The Prussian interpretation of the style is dry and intensely bitter, almost austere, a reflection of the time when beers were heavily hopped to help them withstand long sea journeys.

The best-known of the region's brewers is Holsten of Hamburg, a major exporter, some of whose beers in other countries are brewed under licence. The company is now owned by Carlsberg.

In its home market, Holsten and its subsidiaries produce more than one million hectolitres of beer a year. Its biggest brand is **Edel**, a 5.0 per cent beer with a good malty/hoppy palate and bitter finish: the name means "noble". The 4.8 per cent **Pilsener** is dry in the finish after a hop-accented start and firm palate. A 5.6 per cent **Export**, with a nod in the direction of Dortmund, has a rounded malty character underscored by rich hops. There is also a seasonal Bock called **Ur-Bock** (7.0 per cent ABV). Its brewery in Lüneburg produced a hoppy and dry **Moravia Pils** (38 IBUs) but the plant has closed and it's not known where the Pils is now produced.

The name of Hamburg's other leading brewer, Bavaria St Pauli, also emphasizes the deep admiration the Prussians feel for the brewers of the south. It was common in the nineteenth century for northern brewers to append either Bavarian or Bohemian imagery to their company name as lager-brewing developed in those regions. The present company is the result of a merger in 1922 of two separate companies, Bavaria and St Pauli: St Pauli is a district of Hamburg. To confuse the issue further, its products are produced under the label of Astra. They include **Astra Urtyp**, lightly hopped, and **Astra Pilsener** with a splendidly aromatic hop bouquet and palate. It also brews a seasonal **Urbock**. Holsten has bought the company and now concentrates all production at its main plant.

The most remarkable beer in the region comes from Jever in the resort town of the same name in German Friesland or Frisia. It was once an independent state, a buffer between Germany, the Netherlands and Denmark. The Frisians like bitter drinks and the Jever Brewery, founded in the 1840s, meets the demand with **Jever Pils** which registers 44 IBUs. It is 4.9 per cent ABV, brewed from two-row barley with Hallertau and Tettnang hops. It is lagered for an impressive 90 days. The brewery uses an infusion rather than a decoction mash. The beer has a massive hop bouquet from Tettnang hops, a malty, hoppy and yeasty palate, and a stunningly dry, bitter and hoppy finish with some honey notes from the malt. Jever Pils is exported widely. The brewery also makes for the local market a rounded, malty **Export** and a **Maibock**. Jever is now part of the Oetker group.

Bremen was once part of the mighty Hanseatic League. The harbour town formed the first brewers' guild in Germany in 1489 and once had a substantial number of brewing companies. Today the three main breweries share a modern brewing factory and are linked through a complex financial structure. The best-known, as a result of its vigorous export policy, is **Beck's**. The 5.0 per cent beer belongs to no clearly defined style, has a light, malty aroma, a bland palate with some hints of hop from Hallertau varieties, and a short finish. As television commercials testify, Beck's has an impressive, traditional copper brewhouse where anchors in stained-glass windows stress the importance of exporting to the company. Haake-Beck, in the same complex, makes far more distinguished and hop-accented **Edel-Pils** and **Pils**. An unfiltered version of the Pils is sold as **Kräusen-Pils** in Bremen taverns. The brewery also produces a Berlin-type wheat beer called **Bremer Weisse** (2.75 per cent ABV), quenching and refreshing, fermented with the aid of a lactic culture to give a deliberate sourness. It has a tart and fruity aroma and palate. Locals underscore the fruitiness by adding a dash of raspberry syrup.

Lower Saxony and Bock

Whatever the Bavarians may think, the origins of strong Bock beers almost certainly lie in the town of Einbeck. Beer has been brewed in the small town near Brunswick and Hanover since at least 1351. It calls itself "Beer City" and marks the fact with three beer casks on its boundary, even though only one brewery survives there today.

Einbeck's beers were sold as far afield as Amsterdam and Stockholm and were brewed strong to help them withstand long journeys by road and water. The early brews would have been dark and top-fermenting, probably made from a blend of barley and wheat malts. Such was their fame that they were referred to by the truncated "Beck", which became "Bock" in the Bavarian accent. At a time when most brewing was undertaken in monasteries or castles, the burghers of Einbeck permitted the production of beer for commercial sale. It was done on a contract basis: citizens would buy malt and hops, which they dried in their lofts. A licensed brewmaster, with a publicly owned brew kettle, would visit their homes and help them make beer which they then sold. Einbeck, despite its small population, became a powerhouse of modern brewing during the life of the Hanseatic League between the thirteenth and fourteenth centuries.

A commercial brewery was built in Einbeck in 1794 and has been rebuilt on several occasions. The present modern brewery, Einbecker Brauhaus, carries the legend: "Ohne Einbeck gäb's kein Bockbier" – Without Einbeck there would be no Bock beer. Three versions of Bock are produced, all with alcoholic strengths of 6.9 per cent ABV and all quite reasonably labelled **Ur-Bock** – Original Bock. Soft water comes from deep springs, malt from the Brunswick area and hops – Northern Brewer, Perle and Hersbruck – from Bavaria. The beers are hoppier and drier than a Bavarian Bock on the sound historic grounds that the original Einbeck beers would have been heavily hopped to help them withstand long journeys. But the main characteristic of the beers is a rich, rounded maltiness that avoids an overbearing, cloying sweetness. The pale **Hell**, with 38 IBUs, has an appealing malt aroma and palate and a late burst of hops in the finish. The **Dunkel** or dark beer has the same bitterness rating. The aroma and palate are dominated by rich malt with hints of dark fruit and coffee, and again the hops make a late entrance in the dry and complex (malt, fruit, hops) finish. A **Maibock**, on sale between March and mid-May, has 36 IBUs, is crisp, quenching and refreshing, an ideal way to celebrate the arrival of spring. It is lagered for six weeks. The Hell and Dunkel have eight to 10 weeks' maturation.

In Brunswick the Feldschlössen Brewery brews a 4.9 per cent **Pilsner** (and spells the word in the correct Czech manner). It also produces two warm-fermenting beers, a **Brunswiek Alt** and the Disney-sounding **Duckstein**, a tawny, fruity ale matured over beechwood chips, with a bitter and tart finish. In the days when there were two Germanys divided by a wall, the East also had a Feldschlössen Brewery. Today both plants are owned by Carlsberg.

Hanover has three major breweries. The Brauhaus Ernst August is a city-centre brewpub that serves one organic beer in large quantities: **Pilsener Naturtrüb**. Gilde, an InBev subsidiary, brews a large portfolio that includes Pilsener, Premium Pils and Spezial. It also runs a tavern, the Gilde Brauhaus in the Heinrich Heine Platz. Herrenhäuser is large company that has managed to remain in family hands. It produces an Ice Beer, a Pilsener and a Weizenbier.

Berlin wheat beers

When Napoleon's troops reached Berlin they described the local wheat beers as the "Champagne of the North". It was a fitting and perceptive description, for the Pinot and Chardonnay grapes of the Champagne region produce such a tart wine that it only becomes drinkable after a long, slow process in which a secondary fermentation in the bottle involves some lactic activity and finally becomes spritzy and sparkling. Berliner Weisse beers are so tart and lactic that drinkers add a dash of woodruff or other syrups to the beer to cut the acidity. The style is traditionally low in alcohol, around 3.0 per cent ABV, is extremely pale in colour, has a light fruitiness and little hop aroma. The origins of the style are unknown but one theory is that the fleeing Huguenots picked up the skill of brewing sour beer as they migrated north from France through Flanders. At its height Berliner Weisse beer was brewed by no fewer than 700 producers in the Berlin area. By 2006 there were just two.

The lactic cultures that work with a conventional top-fermenting yeast to produce Berliner Weisse were isolated early in the twentieth century by scientists who founded Berlin's renowned university research and brewing school, the Versuchs und Lehranstadt für Brauerei or VLB for short. The culture is named *lactobacillus delbrücki* after Professor Max Delbrück, the leading research scientist. The Berliner Kindl Brauerei was the bigger of the two remaining producers but it closed in 2006, with production moved to Schultheiss: both brands and the remaining plant are owned by the Oetker group. The proportion of wheat malt in Kindl is around 30 per cent and the finished alcohol is 2.5 per cent. Bitterness units register a modest 10 from the use of Northern Brewer. After mashing and boiling, the *lactobacillus* is added first to start acidification, followed by a top-fermenting brewer's yeast. Fermentation lasts for a week followed by several days of cold conditioning. The beer is then filtered, bottled with a top yeast and kräusened with partially fermented wort.

The Schultheiss Brewery blends equal amounts of wheat and barley malts in the mash to produce a 3.0 per cent beer. Hallertau hops produce four to eight IBUs. Top-fermenting yeast and *lactobacilli* are blended together with wort that is between three and six months old to encourage a lively fermentation, which lasts for three to four days. The beer is warm conditioned for three to six months. It is then kräusened and *lactobacillus* added for bottling. The finished beer is complex, fruity, sour and quenching, more assertive than the Kindl version. Unlike Bavarian wheat beers, the Berliner Weisse style is not enjoying a revival and is in serious decline.

Black beer of Thuringia

When the wall between East and West Germany came down, West German companies rushed to buy up breweries in the East, many of them run down and in urgent need of an injection of capital. Many old East German beers were lacking distinction, mainly because the old regime did not adhere to the *Reinheitsgebot*. They exported malt and hops for "hard currency" and were prepared to allow all manner of cheap adjuncts to be used in brewing.

Many breweries have closed. Others have been swallowed by such giants as Holsten. Bitburger alone was motivated by affection as much as commercial enthusiasm. The present chairman of Bitburger, Dr Axel Simon, a descendant of the founder, remembered **Köstritzer Schwarzbier** from his youth and thinks he may have drunk it even before the family's Pilsner. Bad Köstritz was a spa town (Bad means bath) near the great cities of Weimar and Erfurt in Thuringia but had disappeared into obscurity along with its beer behind the wall.

But Black Beer from the region is a style in its own right and may even have inspired the black beers of Japan. It is a style different from the dark but not quite black Dunkel beers of Munich and Franconia, and it is likely that the beers were warm-fermented much later than in Bavaria. Certainly under the old Communist regime, Köstritzer Schwarzbier varied between being warm- and cold-fermented and was even exported to the West at one stage as "stout".

When Dr Simon arrived he found a superb red-brick Victorian brewery built in 1907 covered in scaffolding. It had fallen into disuse. Brewing was carried out in an ugly modern brewhouse with East European vessels that looked fittingly like army tanks. A weird tangle of pipework led to wort and yeast being trapped in joins, creating yeast infections. Bitburger could have closed the place and moved production to the Rhineland but Dr Simon was

determined to make the black beer of Köstritz a Thuringian speciality again.

Black beer, rather like stout in Britain and Ireland, was recommended for nursing mothers: Dr Simon's mother drank it when
she was breast-feeding him. It eased rheumatism though, unlike
Mackeson, did not claim to stop drinkers farting. Older drinkers
still like to beat sugar and egg into the beer: the brewery used to
make a sweetened version of the beer but this is now prohibited
by the *Reinheitsgebot*, which has been restored to the Eastern
lands.

Bitburger pumped millions of euros into the brewery to restore
it. When the sweet version of **Köstritzer Schwarzbier** was
dropped, the brewery concentrated on a 3.5 per cent ABV beer
brewed with 50 per cent pale malt from the Erfurt area, 43 per
cent Munich and the rest roasted malt, the last two from Franconia.
Hüller hops for bitterness and Hallertau Mittelfrüh for aroma created 35 units of bitterness. Local spring water is softened for brewing liquor.

Since then Bitburger has dramatically upped the alcohol level
to 4.6 per cent. The beer is bigger and dryer but still has an aroma
of dark fruit/malt loaf and bitter chocolate, a creamy palate and a
long, complex finish with more dark, bitter roasted malt, coffee
and chocolate, underpinned by hops. It is a minor classic but perhaps, in the rush to make an acceptable beer for the whole of a
united Germany, some of the traditional if quaint Thuringian
originality has been lost.

SELECTED GERMAN BREWERS

Altstadthof,
18 Berg Strasse, 8500 Nürnberg (Nuremberg).

Augustiner Brauerei,
Neuhauserstrasse 16, 8000 Munich 1.

Bayerische Staatsbrauerei Weihenstephan,
Postfach 1155, Freising, Munich.

Bitburger Brauerei Theo Simon,
Postfach 189, 5520 Bitburg/Eifel.

Brauerei Inselkammer Aying,
1 Zornedinger Strasse, 8011 Aying.

Brauerei Beck GmbH & Haake-Beck/St Pauli Girl,
Am Deich 18/19, Bremen 1.

Brauerei Binding AG,
Darmstädster Landstrasse 185, Frankfurt 70.

Brauerei Felsenkeller Herford,
Postfach 1351, Herford.

Diebels, Privatbrauerei Diebels GmbH,
Braueurei-Diebels Strasse 1, Issum 1, Düsseldorf.

Dinkelacker Brauerei AG,
Tübinger Strasse 46, Postfach 101152, Stuttgart 1.

Dortmunder Actien Brauerei,
Steigerstrasse 20, Postfach 105012, Dortmund 1.

Eichbaum-Brauereien AG,
Käfertaler Strasse 170, Mannheim 1.

Einbecker Brauhaus,
4–7 Papen Strasse, 3352 Einbeck.

EKU Erste Kulmbacher Unionbrauerei AG,
EKU-strasse 1, Kulmbach.

Erdinger Weissbräu,
1–20 Franz Brombach Strasse, 8058 Erding.

Fürstlich Fürstenbergische Brauerei KG,
Postfach 1249, Donaueschingen.

Gaffel, Privat Brauerei Gaffel-Becker,
41 Eigelstein, 5000 Köln (Cologne).

Gilde Brauerei AG,
Hildesheimer Strasse 132, Hanover 1.

Hacker-Pschorr Bräu GmbH,
Schwanthalerstrasse 113, 8000 Munich 2.

Heller-Trum Schlenkerla,
6 Dominikaner Strasse, 8600 Bamberg.

Heller, Brauhaus Heller,
33 Roon Strasse, 5000 Köln (Cologne).

Henninger-Bräu,
Hainer Weg 37–53, Frankfurt/Main 70.

Holsten Brauerei AG,
Holstenstrasse 224, 22765 Hamburg.

Jever, Friesisches Bräuhaus zu Jever,

17 Elisabethufer, 2942 Jever.

Kaisderdom Privatbrauerei,

Breitäckertasse 9, Bamberg 14.

Köstritzer Schwarzbierbrauerei,

Heinrich Schütz Strasse, Bad Köstritz, 6514 Thüringen.

Krombacher Brauerei,

Hagener Strasse 261, Kreuztal-Krombach.

Kulmbacher Mönchshof-Bräu GmbH,

Hofer Strasse 20, Kulmbach.

Küppers Kölsch Brauerei (Kölne Verbund),

145–155 Alteburger Strasse, 5000 Köln (Cologne).

Löwenbräu AG,

Nymphenburger Strasse 4, Munich 2.

Maisel,

Hindenburger Strasse 9, Bayreuth.

Malzmühle, Brauerei Schwarz,

6 Heumarkt, 5000 Köln (Cologne).

P. J. Früh Cölner Hofbräu,

12–14 Am Hof, 5000 Köln (Cologne).

Päffgen, Gebrüder Päffgen,

Obergarige Hausbrauerei, 64–66

Friesen Strasse, 5000 Köln (Cologne).

Paulaner-Salvator-Thomasbräu,

Hochstrasse 75, Munich 95.

Pinkus Müller,

4–10 Kreuz Strasse, 4400 Münster.

Reichelbräu AG,

Lichtenfelser Strasse 9, Postfach 1860, Kulmbach.

Schlossbrauerei Kaltenberg,

Augsburger Strasse 41, Fürstenfeldbruck, Bayern.

G. Schneider & Sohn,

1–5 Emil Ott Strasse, 8420 Kelheim.

Schultheiss-Brauerei,

28–48 Methfessel Strasse, Kreuzberg, 1000 Berlin 61.

Schwaben Bräu,

Hauptstrasse 26, Stuttgart 80.

Gabriel Sedlmayr Spaten-Franziskaner-Bräu KGA,

Marsstrasse 46–48, Munich 2.

Staatliches Hofbräuhaus in München,

Hofbräuallee 1, Munich 82.

Warsteiner Brauerei,

Wilhelmstrasse 5, Warstein 1.

Zum Uerige Obergarige Hausbrauerei,

1 Berger Strasse, Düsseldorf.

The beer styles of England, Scotland and Wales

- Tomintoul 1
- Orkney Islands 1
- Dollar 1
- Alloa 1
- Dunbar 1
- Edinburgh 1
- Biggar 1
- Innerleithen 1
- Newcastle upon Tyne 5
- Sunderland 5
- Hartlepool 4
- Ripon 3
- Keighley 3
- Tadcaster 3, 4, 5
- Leeds 3, 2
- Manchester 3, 2
- Stockport 3
- Denbigh 1
- Wrexham 1
- Burton-on-Trent 3, 4
- Derby 3
- Wolverhampton 6
- Walsall 3
- Oakham 3
- Southwold 3
- Dudley 6
- Birmingham 2, 3
- Bury St Edmunds 3
- Ipswich 3
- Banbury 3
- South Woodham Ferrers 3
- Llanelli 1
- Henley on Thames 3
- Hertford 3
- St Albans
- Cardiff 1
- Trowbridge 3
- London 3
- Faversham 3, 4
- Devizes 3
- Horsham 3
- Edenbridge 3, 4
- Lewes 3, 4
- Dorchester 3
- St Austell 3

Key

1	Brewery	4	Porter brewers
2	Mild ale brewers	5	Brown ale brewers
3	Pale ale and bitter brewers	6	Milk atout brewers

England

Britain in general and England in particular is enjoying a beer revolution. Britain now has around 550 small craft breweries and, as a result of the arrangement of population, most of them are based in England. Add together all the craft breweries in the United Kingdom and the nation can boast more per head than any other country in the world. Sales of these craft breweries' products are growing by around 11 per cent a year, while the products of the global brewers – mainly premium lagers and "cream flow" keg ales – are in sharp decline. The small brewers concentrate on cask-conditioned beer – also known as "real ale" – and they have touched a chord with drinkers.

ENGLAND	Faversham	**Melmerby**	**Alva**
Alton	Shepherd Neame	Hambleton	Harviestoun
Triple fff	**Helston**	**Netherton**	**Bridge of Allan**
Aylesbury	Blue Anchor	Olde Swan	Bridge of Allan
Chiltern	**Hertford**	**St Austell**	**Edinburgh**
Banbury	McMullen	St Austell	Caledonian
Hook Norton	**Houghton-le-**	**South Woodham**	Innis & Gunn
Bedford	**Spring**	**Ferrers**	**Fraserburgh**
Wells & Young's	Double Maxim	Crouch Vale	BrewDog
Brierley Hill	**Keighley**	**Southwold**	**Orkney**
Batham	Timothy Taylor	Adnams	Orkney
Burton-on-Trent	**Lewes**	**Stockport**	**Shetland**
Burton Bridge	Harvey's	Frederic Robinson	Valhalla
Coors	**Liverpool**	**Tadcaster**	
Marston's	Cains	Samuel Smith	**WALES**
Old Cottage	**London**	**Whimple**	**Cardiff**
Tower	Fuller's	O'Hanlon's	Brain's
Bury St Edmunds	Meantime	**Witney**	Bullmastiff
Greene King	**Manchester**	Brakspear/Wychwood	**Flintshire**
Cockermouth	Hydes	**Wolverhampton**	Facer's
Jennings	Holt's	Banks's	**Llanelli**
Thornbridge	J W Lees	**Woodsetton**	Felinfoel
Thornbridge	**Masham**	Holden's	**Porthmadog**
Devizes	Black Sheep		Purple Moose
Wadworth	Theakston	**SCOTLAND**	**Swansea**
Edenbridge	**Maldon**	**Alloa**	Tomos Watkin
Larkins	Mighty Oak	William Bros/Fraoch	

The growth of the craft sector is all the more remarkable when you consider the plight of the British brewing industry and pub trade. They have suffered severe blows from the government in recent years. A smoking ban in pubs has emptied many of them, and up to 40 a week are closing. The government has compounded the problem by increasing excise duty – the tax on beer – way beyond the rate of inflation. In 2008 two duty increases totalled 18 per cent. The result is that draught beer is expensive while super-markets sell heavily discounted brands cheaper than bottled water. Nevertheless, there are still more than 50,000 pubs and many of them attract discriminating drinkers with a wide range of cask beers, increasingly from smaller, independent producers. Statistics show that a poor copy of European cold-fermenting beer, always called "lager" in Britain, accounts for around half of total beer sales. It's true that packaged lagers dominate the take-home trade. But more than 60 per cent of beer is drunk in draught form in pubs, where ale of all types – mild, bitter, porter, stout, strong and sea-sonal beers – is the preferred choice of pubgoers.

The English are returning to their ale-drinking roots. With Ireland included, the British Isles is the only major centre of population in the world where people have stayed loyal to beer brewed by warm fermentation. In England in particular a growing number of drinkers show a preference for cask beer, a style much admired in other countries but rarely copied. Cask conditioning is to beer what the Champagne method is to wine. Just as real Champagne is allowed to ripen naturally in its bottle, so too does beer that leaves the brewery in an unfinished form and matures in its cask in the pub cellar.

The revival in the fortunes of cask beer in the twenty-first century has been followed by a thirst for knowledge among craft brewers. Old history and recipe books have been ransacked as brewers search for the Holy Grail. What were the first milds, porters, stouts and IPAs really like, they ask? The result has been a new-found fascination with British styles that revolutionized the way beer was made in the eighteenth and nineteenth centuries. Porter and stout were the first mass-produced commercial beers, while the success of India Pale Ale encouraged the development of the first golden lagers in central Europe.

Craft brewers are turning the clock forward as well as back. Golden ale, using just pale malt, attracts young drinkers from lager to real beer. Spring beers, summer beers, autumn beers made with the first malts and hops of the harvest, winter and Christmas beers all add to the pleasure of drinking. Beer mats and pump clips on the bar give information about the ingredients used, deepening both pleasure and knowledge of the national drink.

Mild

Mild ale is the beer that came back from the dead. For decades, the style was confined to a few regions of England. But the craft beer revolution has led to many brewers adding mild to their portfolios, to the satisfaction of drinkers who enjoy the complex flavours created by the darker malts used in its production. Until the Industrial Revolution of the eighteenth and nineteenth centuries and the use of coke in the kilning process, all beer was brown in colour as malt was cured or gently roasted over wood fires. Brown beer was drunk in every country until the development of pale malt. Mild or brown beer was an important constituent of the first porters and stouts in the eighteenth century in England. They were made by blending two or three different beers, one of which was brown. These beers were stored for long periods in wooden vats. But in the nineteenth century, new commercial brewers were anxious to produce beer more quickly to aid their cash flow. They started to make a type of brown beer they called mild. To avoid the harsh taste of immature beer, mild was brewed using a blend of pale, brown and black or chocolate malts, along with brewing sugar. The hop rate was reduced both to cut costs and to allow the rich flavours of the malts to dominate. Historically, the term mild has nothing to do with alcoholic strength but is due to the fact that fewer hops are used than is the case with pale ale or bitter.

Mild appealed to industrial and agricultural workers engaged in hard manual labour as it replaced the energy lost during work. As mild was also cheaper than other beers it was attractive to those on low incomes. Mild – called brown ale when it's bottled – became the dominant beer style of the nineteenth century and early twentieth century. But the decline of heavy industry after the Second World War and changing tastes that saw a movement towards pale-coloured alcoholic drinks sent mild into almost terminal decline. It survives today in the former heartlands of heavy industry. The major mild-drinking region is the Black Country around Wolverhampton. Banks's Brewery in the city is part of the Marston's group, England's biggest regional brewer. **Banks's Original** accounts for 60 per cent of the brewery's annual production, outselling the company's bitter. The beer is 3.5 per cent ABV and is made from Maris Otter malt, with caramel for colour, and whole Worcestershire Fuggles and East Kent Goldings hops. The beer has 40 units of colour and 25 bitterness units. The tawny-red beer is wonderfully drinkable with a pronounced port wine note from the caramel, a gentle but persistent hop presence and light fruit in the finish.

There are fine milds to be found in and around the Black Country town of Dudley. Batham's Brewery stands alongside the Vine pub in Brierley Hill where the pub's facade is emblazoned with a quotation from Shakespeare's *Two Gentlemen of Verona*: "Blessings of Your Heart, You Brew Good Ale". Daniel Batham started to brew in 1881, when he lost his job as a miner, and today, Tim and Matthew Batham represent the fifth generation of the family to run the brewery. Batham's produces 6,000 barrels of beer, with a substantial proportion of that made up of mild. The 3.6 per cent **Mild Ale** is made from Maris Otter malt, caramel for colour, and Goldings and Northdown hops. More Goldings are added in the cask, giving the beer considerable bitterness for the style. A few miles away, Holden's Brewery in

Woodsetton also began life as a brewpub. The great-grandson of the founder, Jonathon Holden, brews 9,000 barrels a year for the small estate of 22 pubs and free trade outlets. **Black Country Mild** (3.7 per cent ABV) is made from Maris Otter malt and a complex blend of amber, crystal and black malts for colour. The hops are Fuggles, specially grown in Worcestershire. Nearby, the Olde Swan brewpub in Netherton, dating from 1835, brews two milds, a 3.5 per cent ABV **Original**, a rare example of a pale mild, and **Dark Swan** (4.2 per cent) a full-bodied, sweet-tasting beer with a robust strength for the style. Another brewpub in Worcestershire, the Cannon Royall at Ombersley, produces a prize-winning **Fruiterer's Mild** (3.7 per cent), a black beer with a rich dark malt and fruit character. In the same county, Hobson's of Cleobury Mortimer won the Champion Beer of Britain award in 2007 for its wonderfully roasty and fruity 3.2 per cent ABV **Mild**.

In Liverpool, Cain's Brewery, a sizeable regional company, produces a 3.2 per cent ABV **Dark Mild** that is roasty and fruity and notably bitter for the style. In Manchester, Holt's **Mild** is also 3.2 per cent yet belies the modest strength with great complexity of aroma and flavour. It's roasty, fruity and hoppy. Two more Manchester brewers produce milds with great character and slightly more alcohol: Hyde's **Traditional Mild** and Lees's **Dark** are both 3.5 per cent ABV. The bitter character of milds from the North-west reflects the fact that the brewers there once competed with Guinness stout imported from Dublin for the large Irish communities in the region.

In Essex, one craft brewer proves that making beer and a good sense of humour go hand in hand. Mighty Oak in Maldon brews **Oscar Wilde** (3.7 per cent ABV), strong for the style and with a roasty, dark chocolate character. What possible connection is there between the notorious playwright – better known for champagne than beer – and mild ale? Oscar Wilde is Cockney rhyming slang for mild!

MILD ALE BREWERS

Banks's (Wolverhampton & Dudley Breweries),
Bath Road, Wolverhampton WV1 4NY.

Daniel Batham & Son,
Delph Brewery, Delph Road, Brierley Hill DY5 2TN.

Cain's Brewery,
Stanhope St, Liverpool L8 5XJ.

Cannon Royall,
Fruiterers Arms, Uphampton Lane, Ombersley, Droitwich, Worcestershire WR9 0JW.

Highgate Brewery,
Sandymount Road, Walsall WS1 3AP.

Hobsons,
Newhouse Farm, Tenbury Rd, Cleobury Mortimer, Kidderminster, Worcestershire DY14 8RD.

Holden's Brewery,
George Street, Woodsetton, Dudley DY1 4LN.

Joseph Holt,
Derby Brewery, Empire Street, Cheetham, Manchester. M3 1JD.

Hyde's,
Anvil Brewery, 46 Moss Lane West, Manchester M15 5PH.

J.W. Lees,
Greengate Brewery, Middleton Junctions, Manchester. M24 2AX.

Mighty Oak,
4b West Station Yard, Spital Road, Maldon, Essex CM9 6TW.

Olde Swan Brewery,
89 Halesowen Road, Netherton Dudley, Worcestershire, DY2 9PY.

Pale Ale, bitter and IPA

Bitter is by far the most popular form of draught beer in England. It's a twentieth-century development of the pale ale brewed primarily for the colonial trade in the previous century. The strongest version, India Pale Ale (IPA), was brewed to high alcohol and hop levels to withstand long sea journeys of three months or more. At the dawn of the twentieth century, as brewers started to develop "tied estates" of directly owned pubs, they wanted beer that would be ready to serve within days of arriving in the pub rather than having to mature for several months.

"Running beers" were the result. They were made possible by using carefully cultured yeast strains that enabled beer to clarify or "drop bright" quickly in cask. New varieties of hops were high in acids and tannins that meant that fewer had to be used to create the required level of bitterness. While the original pale ales were light in colour, the new running beers tended to be copper-hued due to the use of a new type of malt known as crystal, which augmented pale malt. Crystal is stewed malt: during the kilning process, the starches are caramelized by a method similar to the manufacture of toffee. Crystal malt gives fruity and nutty flavours and "mouthfeel" to beer that makes up for the lack of long conditioning enjoyed by traditional pale ale.

Running beer was brewers' terminology. The style was dubbed "bitter" by drinkers as a result of the beer's tangy hoppiness. The term is given only to draught beer – bottled versions are still known as pale ale. The most remarkable aspect of draught bitter is that it conditions in the cask. English brewers remained faithful to a form of technology rejected by the rest of the world when lager-brewing took hold. The running beers of the early twentieth century were the forerunners of today's "real ales".

With the exception of a handful of specialist brewers, every beer maker in England produces at least one bitter. There are usually two, a lower-strength "supping bitter" of around 3.6 per cent ABV, and a stronger best bitter of 4.0 or more. Some produce three versions of bitter. Crouch Vale, a large craft brewery in Essex, which won the Champion Beer of Britain award in successive years in 2005 and 2006, produces **Essex Boys Bitter** (3.5 per cent ABV) and **Brewers Gold** and **Crouch Best**, both 4 per cent. The giant of the region, Greene King, makes the best-selling standard bitter in the UK, **IPA** (3.6 per cent ABV) and the full-bodied and vinous **Abbot Ale** (5.0 per cent). The version of IPA, with such a modest strength, is an ordinary bitter, not a genuine IPA. In London, the revered independent Fuller's brews **Chiswick Bitter** (3.5 per cent ABV), **London Pride** (4.1 per cent), the country's leading premium bitter, and the 5.5 per cent **ESB,** short for Extra Special Bitter, as fruity as a confectioner's shop and a brand that spawned a whole new class of beer in the United States called ESB.

To find a true descendant of the nineteenth-century pale ale that spawned modern bitter, it's fitting that the journey takes us to Burton-on-Trent in the East Midlands where the style was developed. Historians will point out that the first "India Ale" was brewed in East London, by Hodgson of Bow, but Burton rapidly became the capital of pale ale brewing. This was due to the remarkable spring waters of the Trent Valley, rich in natural salts that bring out the full, rounded character of pale ale. Marston, Thompson and Evershed started brewing in Burton in 1834 and moved to its present site, the Albion Brewery, in 1898. Its leading beer today, **Pedigree** (4.5 per cent ABV), is branded as bitter but is truly a pale ale. It's made – in the style of the nineteenth century – with only pale malt (83 per cent) and glucose sugar, and hopped with Fuggles and Goldings that create 26 bitterness units.

The character of Pedigree – at once subtle yet robust, aromatic as well as malty and lightly fruity – is due to the singular method used to ferment it. Marston's is the last remaining brewery to use the "Burton Union" system. It was developed in the town in the nineteenth century as sales of pale ale coincided with commercial glass blowing. Once drinkers could see what was in the glass they demanded clear, sparkling beer and the Burton Unions met the demand with a system that removed yeast from beer. It was based on a medieval method of brewing in which ale fermented in large wooden casks. Yeast and liquid rose out of the open bung holes of the casks and were collected in buckets below. It was a messy system and the Burton Unions simply and effectively turned the medieval system on its head. Troughs, known as "barm trays" – barm is an old Midlands and North Country term for yeast – are placed above large oak casks, each one holding 144 gallons, with pipes slotted into the bung holes. The fermenting liquid rises up the casks and drips into the troughs, which are slightly inclined.

The liquid runs back into the casks, while the yeast settles in the troughs. The result is a well-attenuated and crystal-clear beer.

Marston's yeast strain voraciously turns malt and glucose sugars into alcohol. As a result of the high levels of gypsum in the local water, Pedigree has a renowned sulphur aroma, known locally as the "Burton snatch". Only Pedigree is fermented in the Unions but so much yeast is created that the same culture is used for all Marston's beers. In spite of the great demand for India Pale Ale in the nineteenth century, Marston's never brewed an IPA. But Marston's put that deficiency right early in the twenty-first century with the launch of **Old Empire** (5.7 per cent ABV), a pale bronze beer with sulphur on the nose, bitter hop resins, toasted malt and tangy fruit in the mouth, and a long bittersweet, quenching finish with a late punch of bitter hops. Marston's also brews **Draught Bass** (4.4 per cent ABV), once a world-famous Burton beer but sadly diminished these days. Bass stopped brewing in 2000; the brand belongs to InBev and is brewed under licence for the global giant.

Bass also used to brew the bottle-fermented Worthington's White Shield, a beer that can claim to a direct descendant of the first India Pale Ales. William Worthington was a member of the great Burton brewing clan whose company merged with Bass in the 1920s. **White Shield** (5.6 per cent ABV and with a powerful 40 units of bitterness) is brewed by Coors, the American brewing company that bought the former Bass site in Burton. It's brewed with a blend of Halcyon and Pipkin pale malts and crystal malt, and hopped with Challenger, Fuggles and Northdown hops. At the end of the brewing process, the beer is filtered and then, like champagne, primed with sugar to encourage a second fermentation in bottle. The beer is then re-seeded with a special yeast strain. Although it's an ale culture, the yeast sinks to the bottom of the bottle as though it were a lager strain and slowly turns the remaining sugars to alcohol. The beer is warm-conditioned for three weeks before it leaves the brewery. It can then be drunk but true devotees of White Shield prefer to keep the beer for a longer time. After a year to 18 months it takes on a more rounded and fruity character. This amazingly complex beer has an enticing aroma of spices, peppery hops, light fruit and sulphur. There are malt, hops and spices in the mouth with a nutty finish, bitter hop resins and a hint of apple fruit.

The Burton Bridge craft brewery, based behind the Bridge Inn, produces a fruity/hoppy **Bridge Bitter** (4.2 per cent ABV), using Pipkin pale malt and 5.0 per cent crystal, with Challenger and Target whole hops in the copper and Styrian Goldings for dry hopping in cask. It also brews a magnificent bottle-fermented **Empire Pale Ale** (7.5 per cent ABV), using Pipkin pale malt, invert sugar and Challenger and Styrian hops. This intensely bitter, fruity beer with rich juicy malt is matured in cask for three months prior to bottling to match the length of a sea journey from England to India in the nineteenth century when sailing ships carried precious cargoes of IPA. Two more craft breweries in the town also fly the flag for pale ale. Old Cottage brews **Pail Ale** (3.8 per cent ABV) and **IPA** (4.4 per cent), while Tower recalls a long-lost Burton brewer with **Thomas Salt's Bitter** (3.8 per cent ABV), a 4.2 per cent **Bitter** and **Pale Ale** (4.8 per cent).

Meantime Brewery in Greenwich is determined to reclaim the capital's role as the first home of beer destined for the colonies. Its **India Pale Ale** reflects the true strength of the style in its heyday at 7.5 per cent ABV. The bottle-fermented beer comes suitably sealed with a Champagne-style cork and cradle. The ingredients could not be more traditionally English: Maris Otter pale malt and Fuggles and Goldings hops. Meantime's beer is conditioned in the brewery prior to bottling and additional hops are added at this stage. The finished beer has peppery hops, orange fruit and sappy malt on the nose, with fruit, malt and hops vying for attention in the mouth, followed by a finish that is bittersweet to start and then becomes increasingly dry, fruity and hoppy.

The Yorkshire Square method of fermentation vies with Burton Unions as an early example of how pale ale was cleansed of yeast. Modern Yorkshire Squares are made of stainless steel but were first built from slate. The only surviving slate squares are found at Samuel Smith's Brewery in Tadcaster, a company founded in 1758 and the oldest in the region. The square was invented to cope with the particular problems posed by the yeast strains used in Yorkshire. The yeasts are "flocculent". This means the cells clump together, separate from the wort and refuse to turn malt sugar into alcohol unless they are regularly roused by agitating and aerating the wort. The square is a two-storey vessel invented to tackle the problem. The top chamber is known as the "barm deck". The bottom chamber is filled with wort and yeast. Fermentation forces liquid and yeast through a central manhole where the yeast is trapped by a raised flange while the wort runs back into the bottom chamber via pipes. Every few hours, fresh wort is pumped to the top chamber to aerate it and mix yeast back into the liquid. When fermentation is complete, the manhole is closed, the "green" or immature beer is left to condition in the bottom storey while excess yeast is collected from the top.

Yorkshire beers are not only full-bodied as a result of unfermented sugars but also have the famous "thick, creamy head", the result of high levels of carbonation created during fermentation. Samuel Smith's **Old Brewery Bitter** (3.8 per cent ABV) is a classic of the style: rich, malty and nutty, but with the flavours underpinned by powerful Fuggles and Goldings hop notes.

In the market town of Masham, in the Yorkshire Dales, Paul Theakston opened his Black Sheep Brewery in 1992 and insisted he would use traditional fermenting squares. He bought some, ironically, from a brewery in Nottinghamshire. His **Black Sheep Bitter** (3.8 per cent ABV) has a powerful Fuggles hop aroma, with more peppery hops in the mouth and a long, bitter finish. **Black Sheep Ale** (4.4 per cent) is a complex beer with malt, hops, cobnuts and orange fruit on the aroma, a bittersweet palate and a big hoppy and fruity finish..

Paul Theakston left his family brewery when it was taken over by Scottish & Newcastle in the 1990s, but Theakston's is now back in family hands and brews cheek-by-jowl with Black Sheep. It has a large portfolio of beers but its best-selling brand is **Best Bitter** (3.8 per cent ABV; 24 IBUs), with a delicate fruit and hops aroma and palate. Theakston's also brews the legendary strong ale **Old Peculier** (*see* Special Ales).

In Keighley, Timothy Taylor's brewery has won a shelf-load of prizes in CAMRA's Champion Beer of Britain competition for its outstanding **Landlord Bitter**. The 4.3 per cent ABV beer is brewed only from Golden Promise malt, with Worcestershire Fuggles for bitterness and East Kent Goldings and Styrians for aroma. To keep pace with demand for Landlord and its other beers, Taylor's has invested £10 million in additional brewing vessels that has allowed capacity to double to 60,000 barrels a year. Close by, in Skipton, Copper Dragon Brewery opened in 2003, but had to move to new premises five years later to expand capacity. The range includes a traditional bronze-coloured **Best Bitter** (3.8 per cent ABV), with a fruity and malty aroma and an uncompromisingly bitter palate and finish.

The small Thornbridge Brewery in Derbyshire, set in the grounds of the imposing Thornbridge Hall, has won many prizes since it opened in 2005 for its fine interpretation of an India Pale Ale. **Jaipur IPA** is 5.9 per cent ABV and is brewed from Maris Otter pale malt and American Cascade and Chinook hops. The hops impart citrus fruit as well as bitterness to the beer. It has a bittersweet palate and a fruity and hoppy finish. It's available on draught and in bottle-fermented form.

A rudimentary but effective method of cleansing beer of yeast is the "dropping system". This is in operation at Brakspear's Brewery at Witney in Oxfordshire. The brewery was originally based in

Henley-on-Thames, but when that site closed new owners thought it essential to keep the fermentation system when it moved to Witney, where the water composition is identical to Henley's. Fermentation is based on a two-storey system. The transformation of malt sugars to alcohol begins in the top bank of open vessels. After a few days, the wort is literally dropped from the top storey to vessels below, leaving behind dead yeast cells and unwanted protein. The wort is roused and aerated and a fresh yeast head quickly forms. **Brakspear Bitter** (3.6 per cent ABV) is brewed with Maris Otter pale and crystal malts, with a touch of black malt for colour. The hops are Fuggles and Goldings. The beer, with 38 units of bitterness, is famous for a pronounced "diacetyl nose". Diacetyl is a bi-product of yeast created during fermentation and it gives a pronounced butterscotch or toffee character to beer. Most brewers fight hard to remove diacetyl from their beers and traditional lager brewers incorporate a "diacetyl rest" to allow the beer to purge the butterscotch note. But it's the signature of Brakspear Bitter, loved by its devotees, and it has been maintained in spite of the move to new premises. Brakspear shares the Witney site with the Wychwood Brewery: both are now owned by Marston's.

Hook Norton, another Thames Valley brewery in the village of the same name, is a fine example of a Victorian "tower brewery" in which all stages of the brewing process flow from floor to floor without the need for pumps. Mashing takes place at the top, boiling with hops in the middle, and fermentation and racking into casks at ground-floor level. **Hook Norton Best Bitter** (3.6 per cent ABV) has a fine hop character from Challenger, Fuggles and Goldings varieties, balanced by rich malt and some fruit in the finish. **Old Hooky** (4.3 per cent) is a rich and fruity beer with hints of raisins in the finish.

Traditional brewers prefer to use open fermenting vessels, made from wood, iron, stainless steel, often lined with polypropylene, so they can rouse the wort by hand. But good beer can be made in ultra-modern brewhouses. Charles Wells of Bedford, for example, uses all the trappings of high tech, including mash mixers, lauter tuns and closed cylindro-conical fermenters, a system that allows the company to produce lager as well as ale. Its **Bombardier** (4.2 per cent ABV) is one of the country's biggest-selling cask beers, made from pale and crystal malts with Challenger and Goldings hops. The beer has a complex malt, hop resins and fruit character. The company is now officially Wells & Young's, following the closure of Young's Brewery in London. Young's **Ordinary Bitter** (3.7 per cent ABV) and **Special Bitter** (4.8 per cent) have had to make the transition from traditional vessels to modern ones at Bedford but have settled in well. The Bitter is extremely pale (14 units of colour), brewed with Maris Otter pale malt and Fuggles and Goldings hops that create 32 to 34 bitterness units. It's tart, fruity and uncompromisingly hoppy. Special (32 bitterness units) has a peppery hop aroma balanced by citrus fruit, ripe malt in the mouth and a big finish packed with fruit and hop character. Wells & Young's has also bought the Courage brands from Scottish & Newcastle and **Courage Best Bitter** (4 per cent ABV), copper-coloured, with rich malt and solid hop bitterness, is now the brewery's biggest cask brand.

Down the road in the county town of Hertford, the family firm of McMullen has switched from traditional vessels to modern ones and continues to produce outstanding beers that are well attenuated, with most of the brewing sugars turned to alcohol. **AK** (3.8 per cent ABV, 22 IBUs) – the curious name stems from nineteenth-century cask markings – is hoppy and fruity with hints of orange peel on the aroma, while **Country** (4.6 per cent, 30 IBUs) has massive hops and fruit appeal. Further east, in the grain basket of East Anglia, Adnams in the coastal town of Southwold in Suffolk, has met the growing clamour for its beers with a brewhouse that has been expanded three times in ten years. Both the brewhouse and a new warehouse are environmentally friendly, using recycled water and steam. **Adnams Bitter** (3.8 per cent ABV) is pungent with spicy hop resins from First Gold, Fuggles and Goldings varieties, with a deep bronze colour provided by Maris Otter pale and crystal malts. The premium **Broadside** (4.7 per cent ABV) has massive fruit, malt and peppery hops attack.

South of London in the heart of the Kent hop fields, Shepherd Neame of Faversham is England's oldest brewery, dating from 1698 and still family-owned. This is yet another brewery that has had to invest heavily in a new brewhouse in order to keep pace with the demand for its beers. It brews two bitters and a strong ale, all bursting with a complex blend of Omega, Goldings, Target and Zenith hops. **Master Brew Bitter** (3.7 per cent ABV) and **Kent's Best** (4.1 per cent) have tangy, hoppy and citrus fruit aromas, bittersweet palates and complex bitter and fruity finishes. **Spitfire Premium Ale** (4.5 per cent ABV) is ripe and fruity, balanced by great depth of hop bitterness. A bottle-fermented **1698** (6.5 per cent) celebrates the brewery's birth date.

Harvey & Son of Lewes in East Sussex dates from 1790 and has a superb Victorian tower brewery on the banks of the River Ouse. Demand has seen brewhouse and fermenting capacity double in recent years to 38,000 barrels a year, with beer supplied to 48 of its own pubs and 450 free trade outlets. **Sussex Best Bitter** (ABV 4 per cent ABV) is a magnificent example of a traditional copper-coloured bitter. It's brewed with Maris Otter and Pipkin malts with crystal malt and brewing sugar. No fewer than four hop varieties – Bramling Cross, Fuggles, Goldings and Progress – are used and added at different stages of the copper boil to extract the acids, oils and tannins for maximum effect. The beer has 33 colour units and a pungent 38 IBUs. The amber beer has a grassy and spicy aroma with biscuity malt and tart fruit. The beer fills the mouth with sappy malt, hop resins and citrus fruit while the long finish becomes dry, bitter and hoppy but well-balanced by juicy malt and tart fruit.

Among smaller craft breweries in southern England, the Chiltern Brewery near Aylesbury in Buckinghamshire, was founded by Richard Jenkinson in 1980 and is now run by his two sons, George and Tom. They brew **Ale** (3.7 per cent ABV) and **Beechwood Bitter** (4.3 per cent), both with rich malt, raisin fruit and bitter hop resins. Several beers, including **Three Hundreds Old Ale** (4.9 per cent), are available in bottle-fermented form. In Alton, Hampshire, Triple fff Brewery – founder Graham Trott likes his music fortissimo – has gone from a five-barrel to a 50-barrel plant in 12 years. In 2008 he won the Champion Beer of Britain award with **Alton's Pride** (3.8 per cent ABV), a golden brown standard bitter. He brews two additional bitters, **Moondance** (4.2 per cent) and **Stairway** (4.6 per cent), both fruity and hoppy bronze beers.

Back among the older family-owned breweries, Wadworth's in Devizes, Wiltshire, has an imposing red-brick brewery that produces a clutch of bitters of which the best-known is the 4.3 per cent ABV **6X**. The ale takes its name from the medieval habit of branding casks with Xs to denote strength. 6X is brewed from Pipkin pale malt, crystal malt and brewing sugar, and is hopped with Fuggles and Goldings. With 22 bitterness units, the beer has a rich and enticing aroma and palate of vanilla and sultana fruit, balanced by tangy hop bitterness.

Cornwall, in the far west of England, has breweries old and new. St Austell, in the town of the same name, is family-owned and dates from 1851. Its 3.7 per cent ABV **Tinners** has a delicate aroma of hops and buttercups, with light fruit on the palate and finish. The best-selling **Tribute** (4.2 per cent) is a refreshing, bitter-sweet, copper-coloured beer with good malt, hops and fruit notes. The 5 per cent **HSD** – malty and fruity with a good underpinning of hops – is nicknamed "High Speed Diesel" by locals though the name officially stands for Hicks Special Draught, named after the brewery's founder. Sharp's at Rock opened in 1994 and within just

10 years grew from 1,500 annual barrels to 35,000. It brews a wide range of bitters, from a 3.6 per cent ABV **Cornish Coaster**, through **Cornish Jack** (3.8 per cent), the top-selling **Doom Bar** (4 per cent), **Own** (4.4 per cent) and **Special** (5.2 per cent). All the beers are clean and quenching with a fine balance of biscuity malt, tangy fruit and aromatic hops.

In the far North-west of England, Cumbria has 21 breweries. They range from the substantial Jennings in Cockermouth, founded in 1828, with three bitters – **Bitter** (3.5 per cent ABV), **Cumberland Ale** (4 per cent) and **Cocker Hoop** (4.6 per cent) – to the tiny Hesket Newmarket in the village of the same name that supplies the Old Crown pub with **Blencathra Bitter** (3.3 per cent ABV), **Skiddaw Special Bitter** (3.6 per cent) **Haystacks Refreshing Ale** (3.7 per cent), **High Pike Dark Amber Bitter** (4.2 per cent) and **Catbells Pale Ale** (5 per cent), all splendidly hoppy and fruity beers that take their names from the surrounding mountain peaks and fells.

In Manchester, with its great brewing tradition, Hydes has a malty/fruity **Traditional Bitter** (3.8 per cent ABV, 28 IBUs) while J W Lees offers a copper-coloured 4.0 per cent **Bitter** that is noticeably quenching and hoppy. The finest pale ale in the city is the uncompromisingly bitter and hoppy **Holt's Bitter** (4.0 per cent ABV, 40 IBUs). Joseph Holt is an old-fashioned, traditionalist family firm that refuses to advertise its beers or distribute them beyond a small radius around the brewery. It still supplies its bitter in 54-gallon casks known as hogsheads to some of its bigger pubs. The complex bitter is brewed from Halcyon, Pipkin and Triumph pale malts, with a touch of black malt, flaked maize and invert sugar. The hops are Goldings and Northdown.

Down the road from Manchester, Frederic Robinson in Stockport brews **Unicorn** (4.2 per cent ABV) and **Double Hop** (5 per cent), bitters with pronounced malt, citrus fruit and a peppery Goldings hop character..

PALE ALE, IPA AND BITTER BREWERS

Adnams & Co,
Sole Bay Brewery, East Green,
Southwold, Suffolk IP18 6JW.

Black Sheep Brewery,
Wellgarth, Masham, nr Ripon, North
Yorkshire HG4 4EN.

Brakspear/Wychwood,
Eagle Maltings, The Crofts, Witney,
Oxfordshire OX28 4DP.

Burton Bridge Brewery,
24 Bridge Street, Burton-on-Trent,
Staffordshire DE14 1SY.

Chiltern,
Nash Lee Road, Terrick, Aylesbury,
Buckinghamshire HP17 0TQ.

Copper Dragon,
Snaygill Industrial Estate, Keighley
Road, Skipton, North Yorkshire
BD23 2QR.

Coors,
137 High Street, Burton-on-Trent,
Staffordshire DE14 1JZ.

Crouch Vale Brewery,
12 Redhills Road, South Woodham
Ferrers, Essex CM3 5UP.

Fuller, Smith & Turner,
Griffin Brewery, Chiswick Lane
South, London W4 2QB.

Greene King,
Westgate Brewery, Bury St Edmunds,
Suffolk IP33 1QT.

Harvey's,
Bridge Wharf Brewery, 6 Cliffe High
Street, Lewes, East Sussex BN7 2AH.

Hesket Newmarket,
Old Crown Barn, Hesket Newmarket,
Cumbria CA7 8JG.

Joseph Holt,
Derby Brewery, Empire Street,
Cheetham, Manchester M3 1JD.

Hook Norton Brewery Co,
Brewery Lane, Hook Norton,
Banbury, Oxfordshire OX15 5NY.

Hydes Anvil Brewery,
46 Moss Lane West, Manchester
M15 5PH.

Jennings,
Castle Brewery, Cockermouth,
Cumbria, CA13 9NE.

J. W. Lees & Co,
Greengate Brewery, Middleton
Junction, Manchester M24 2AX.

Marston, Thompson & Evershed,
PO Box 26, Shobnall Road, Burton-
on-Trent, Staffordshire DE14 2BW.

McMullen & Sons,
The Hertford Brewery, 26 Old Cross,
Hertford, Hertfordshire SG14 1RD.

Meantime,
Unit H2, Penhall Rd, Greenwich,
London SE7 8RX.

Burton Old Cottage,
Unit 10, Eccelshall Business Park,
Hawkins Lane, Burton-upon-Trent,

Staffordshire DE14 1PT.

Frederic Robinson,

Unicorn Brewery, Stockport, Cheshire SK1 1JJ.

St Austell Brewery Co,

63 Trevarthian Road, St Austell, Cornwall PL25 4BY.

Sharp's,

Rock, Cornwall, PL27 6NU.

Shepherd Neame,

17 Court Street, Faversham, Kent ME13 7AX.

Samuel Smith,

The Old Brewery, High Street, Tadcaster, Yorkshire LS24 9SB.

Timothy Taylor & Co,

Knowle Spring Brewery, Keighley, Yorkshire BD21 1AW.

Joshua Tetley & Son,

PO Box 142, The Brewery, Hunslet Road, Leeds, Yorkshire LS1 1QG.

T. & R. Theakston,

The Brewery, Masham, nr Ripon, North Yorkshire HG4 4DX.

Thornbridge,

Thornbridge Hall, Ashford-in-the-Water, Bakewell, Derbyshire DE45 1NZ.

Tower,

The Old Water Tower, Walsitch Maltings, Glensyl Way, Burton-upon-Trent, Staffordshire DE14 1LX.

Triple fff,

Unit 3, Old Magpie Works, Station Approach, Four Marks, Alton, Hampshire GU34 5HN.

Wadworth & Co,

Northgate Brewery, Devizes, Wiltshire SN10 1JW.

Wells & Young's

Havelock Street, Bedford, Bedfordshire MK40 4LU.

Special ales

Craft brewers argue that their ales should be treated as seriously as wine. They have underscored the point in recent years by introducing strong bottle-fermented beers that mature and improve with age. Fuller's in London has been in the vanguard of this movement with two beers, 1845 – which commemorates the opening year of the brewery – and Vintage Ale. **1845** (6.3 per cent ABV) is brewed with pale, amber and crystal malts, and hopped with Goldings. The beer stays in conditioning tanks for two weeks following primary fermentation and is then filtered and re-seeded with fresh yeast. It has a peppery hop note balanced by ripe vinous fruit on the nose, with biscuity malt, rich fruit and bitter hops in the mouth and finish. **Vintage Ale** (8.5 per cent) is an annual vintage, based on the company's Golden Pride. Only pale malt is used and both the malt and hop variety change from year to year. Fuggles, Goldings and Styrian Goldings have been used. Tastings of all vintages in the brewery show how the use of different grain and hops along with bottle-conditioning give sharply different aromas and palates from year to year, but consumers can expect rich orange fruit balanced by ripe malt, tangy hops and warming alcohol.

Fuller's also brews **Gale's Prize Old Ale** following the closure of the Hampshire brewery. This 9.0 per cent ABV beer is the closest England will come to brewing a Belgian-style lambic: it has a sour nose with apple and raisin fruitiness and good depth of spicy hops.

Brakspear in Oxfordshire has added **Triple** to its range, a 7.2 per cent ABV that takes its name from the fact that it's hopped three times in the copper and fermenter with Northdown and Cascade varieties. The name also makes a bow in the direction of Belgian Tripel strong ales. The beer is also fermented three times – in the "double drop" fermenters, in conditioning tanks and in bottle. The grains are pale, crystal and black and the end result is an amazingly complex beer with ripe vinous fruit, butterscotch and spicy hops from aroma to finish.

The most famous bottle-fermented English beer is **Thomas Hardy's Ale**. It was launched at a literary festival in 1968 to mark the fortieth anniversary of the death of Hardy, the Wessex writer and poet. The beer was brewed by Eldridge Pope in Dorchester and when the brewery closed it was feared the brand might die. But it has been bought by John O'Hanlon, who brews on a farm in Devon. He has recreated the beer with enormous skill and now sells substantial amounts to the United States. The beer reaches 12.0 per cent ABV in bottle – brewer's yeast cannot work much above that level of alcohol – and is brewed from pale and crystal malts and hopped with Challenger, Goldings, Northdown and Styrian Goldings varieties. The russet beer gets its colour from some caramelization of the malt sugars during a long copper boil with hops. The beer is rich and vinous yet intensely bitter, with 75 units of bitterness.

The Blue Anchor in Helston, Cornwall, is a celebrated home-brew pub with strong Spingo beers. They are available on draught in the pub but are also on sale in bottle-fermented form. They include **Spingo Middle** (5.0 per cent ABV), **Spingo Bragget** (6 per cent) and **Spingo Special** (6.6 per cent). The beers have simple recipes of Pipkin pale malt and Goldings hops, while Bragget has the addition of honey and apple juice. The beers are noticeably fruity – with black-currant to the fore – with great depth of peppery hop bitterness.

Theakston's **Old Peculier**, while not bottle fermented, is an intriguing example of an Old Ale, a style that was once matured for long periods in oak vats. Old Peculier is 5.6 per cent ABV and has a big winey bouquet, roast malt on the palate and a bittersweet, lightly hopped finish. In the far north, the Orkney Brewery's **Skullsplitter** (8.5 per cent) has won many awards in CAMRA competitions. It has a deceptively creamy and silky smoothness, with rich plummy fruit and a good hop balance.

SPECIAL ALE BREWERS

Blue Anchor,
50 Coinagehall Street, Helston, Cornwall TR13 8EL.

Brakspear/Wychwood,
Eagle Maltings, The Crofts, Witney, Oxfordshire OX28 4DP.

Fuller's/Gale's,
Chiswick Lane S, London W4 2QB.

O'Hanlon,
Great Barton Farm, Whimple, Devon EX5 2NY.

Orkney,
North Schoolhouse, Quoyloo, Stromness, Orkney KW16 3LT.

T & R Theakston Ltd.
The Brewery, Masham, Ripon, North Yorkshire HG4 4YD.

Porter and stout

The revival of interest in beer styles has led to a renaissance for porter, the beer that created the modern commercial brewing industry in the eighteenth century. The strongest or "stoutest" version of the beer was called Stout Porter, eventually shortened to just stout. Versions of stout high in alcohol were exported to Russia where they were given a royal warrant, which enabled them to be called grandly Imperial Russian Stout. A true interpretation of the style is **Harvey's Imperial Extra Double Stout** (9.0 per cent ABV), based on a recipe first used in the early eighteenth century by the London brewer Barclays. The grains are Maris Otter pale malt, with amber, brown and black malts and Fuggles and Goldings hops. The beer is matured for a year before being released. It has a massive bouquet of vinous fruits, leather, fresh tobacco, smoky malt and peppery hops. Dark fruit, hop resins, liquorice, roasted grain and bitter hops dominate the palate, followed by a long and complex finish with warming alcohol, burnt fruit, tobacco and spicy hops. In Derbyshire, the Thornbridge Brewery produces a **St Petersburg Imperial Russian Stout** (see oak-aged beer section below).

Two beers that have won major prizes are **Wickwar Station Porter** (6.1 per cent ABV) from Gloucestershire, CAMRA's Champion Winter Beer in 2008, with roasted grain, coffee and chocolate notes, and **Dorothy Goodbody's Wholesome Stout** (4.6 per cent) from the Wye Valley Brewery in Herefordshire, with roasted grain, tangy hops, chocolate and burnt currants on aroma and palate. In Yorkshire, **Hambleton Nightmare** (5.0 per cent) won the Champion Winter Beer award in 1996 for a porter with a rich burnt grain and spicy hop character. In London, **Meantime London Porter** (6.5 per cent ABV) is bottle fermented and has a superb aroma and palate of bitter chocolate, coffee, liquorice and spicy hops.

One of the most highly rated versions of the style is the **Porter** (5.5 per cent ABV) from the small Larkins Brewery, based on a

Kentish hop farm. It has a mighty 59 units of bitterness and is packed with piny, resiny Fuggles and Goldings character, with a bittersweet palate and finish dominated by dark fruit and hops.

PORTER AND STOUT BREWERS

Hambleton Ales,
Melmerby Green Lane, Melmerby, Ripon, North Yorkshire HG4 5NB.

Harvey & Son,
Bridge Wharf Brewery, 6 Cliffe High Street, Lewes BN7 2AH.

Larkins Brewery,
Larkins Farm, Chiddingstone, Edenbridge TN8 7BB.

Meantime,
Unit H2, Penhall Rd, Greenwich, London SE7 8RX.

Thornbridge,
Thornbridge Hall, Ashford-in-the-Water, Bakewell, Derbyshire DE45 1NZ

Wickwar,
The Old Brewery, Station Road, Wickwar, Wotton-Under-Edge, Gloucestershire GL12 8NB.

Wye Valley,
The Barrels, 69 St. Owen's Street, Hereford, Herefordshire HR1 2JQ.

Brown ales

Most brown ales are bottled versions of mild but there is a handful of distinctively different beers that are available exclusively or mainly in bottled form. The 3.0 per cent ABV **Manns Brown Ale** is the last reminder of a malty and sweet London brown ale, once brewed by Mann, Crossman & Paulin in East London. As a result of brewery closures, the beer has moved around the country and now resides at Burtonwood in Cheshire. It's a lightly hopped, sweet and fruity beer.

Brown ale has deep roots in North-east England, a region once famous for its shipbuilding and mining industries. As a result of hard, manual labour, the brown ales there are more robust than southern versions. The best-known version is **Newcastle Brown Ale,** now owned – such is the nature of modern big brewing – by Heineken. To add to the curiosity, the beer is no longer brewed in Newcastle but in Gateshead. The recipe is composed of pale and crystal malts, brewing sugar, syrup and a touch of caramel. A complex blend of Hallertau, Northdown, Northern Brewer and Target hops are used. The beer is nutty and malty with rich vanilla and toffee notes.

In Houghton-le-Spring, the Double Maxim Brewery continues the rich vein of North-east brown ales with **Double Maxim** (4.7 per cent ABV), originally brewed by Vaux of Sunderland. It was launched to mark the derring-do of a member of the Vaux family who had fought with valour in the First World War. Maxim referred to the gun used by his regiment. The beer is made with Maris Otter pale and crystal malts with a touch of caramel and is primed with brewing sugar. Only Goldings hops are used. It has a superb peppery hop aroma with nuts, apricots and plums in the mouth and finish. It has 22 units of bitterness. There's also a cask-conditioned version of the beer.

Further south, Samuel Smith in Tadcaster brews **Old Brewery Brown Ale** (4.8 per cent ABV), a deliciously nutty beer with a rich note of butterscotch. With 34 units of bitterness, it is notably hoppy for the style.

BROWN ALE BREWERS

Double Maxim Beer Co Ltd,
1, Gadwall Rd, Houghton Le Spring,
Tyne and Wear DH4 5NL.
Manns (Thomas Hardy),
Bold Lane, Burtonwood, Warrington,
Cheshire WA5 4TH.

Newcastle Breweries (Heineken),
Dunston Brewery, Lancaster Road,
Gateshead, Tyne and Wear NE11 9JR.
Samuel Smith,
The Old Brewery, High Street,
Tadcaster, Yorkshire LS24 9SB.

Oak-aged beer

A new style of beer has burst on the British scene in recent years. Oak-aged beer is a Scottish development that is discussed in that section of the guide. But the style has spread to England. Thornbridge Brewery in Derbyshire has taken as a base beer its St Petersburg

Imperial Russian Stout and matured it in whisky casks supplied by three Scottish distilleries. The beer is brewed with Maris Otter pale malt, chocolate malt and roasted barley and is hopped with Bramling Cross and Galena. The beer is matured for 55 days prior to bottling and is primed with special brewing sugars. The whisky casks used come from distillers in the Highland, Speyside and Islay areas.

Highland Whisky Reserve is 9.4 per cent ABV and has oak, whisky, berry fruits and rich malt on the aroma. Malt, oak and fruit dominate the palate, with a finish that is woody, with hop notes and burnt fruit. **Speyside Whisky Reserve** is 8.8 per cent ABV and has creamy malt, milk drop confectionery, burnt fruit, vanilla and roasted grain on the nose with rich malt and fruit in the mouth balancing oak, hops and vanilla. The finish has pronounced hop bitterness with roasted grain, oak and vanilla. **Islay Whisky Reserve** (10.2 per cent ABV) has all the characteristics of the island's famous malt whiskies: iodine and seaweed on the nose with smoked malt and light vanilla notes. Burnt grain, tangy herbal notes, bitter hops and orange fruit fill the mouth with seaweed, tart fruit, vanilla and hops in the finish.

Fuller's in London launched bottle-fermented **Brewer's Reserve** in 2008, a blend of its ESB and Golden Pride strong bitters stored in casks from Scotland for 500 days. The casks come originally from bourbon whiskey makers in the United States. The beer (7.7 per cent ABV) has a deep bronze colour with orange fruit and powerful whisky and oak notes on the nose. There are bitter hops, tart fruit, vanilla and whisky in the mouth, followed by a bittersweet finish that becomes dry and warming, with continuing whisky, oak and vanilla characteristics.

OAK-AGED BREWERS
Fuller, Smith & Turner,
Chiswick Lane S, London W4 2QB.

Thornbridge,
Thornbridge Hall, Ashford-in-the-Water, Bakewell, Derbyshire DE45 1NZ.

Scotland

The history, the culture and even the climate have determined the course of Scottish brewing. The end result is a style radically different from that of the bigger country to the south.

Commercial brewing was slower to develop north of the border. Ale production was confined to the home and the farm, and it faced competition from home-grown whisky and imported French wine. The Napoleonic Wars cut off the supplies of wine from Bordeaux and from around 1730 commercial brewers sprang up to meet both local supply and a demand from Scots who had emigrated to the West Indies and North America. The term "export" for a strong and malty brew developed into a generic style and even today one of the major brands in Scotland is **McEwan's Export**.

The new entrepreneurial Scots brewers grew at astonishing speed. Companies such as Younger and McEwan not only became powerful forces in Scotland but exported considerable quantities of ale to North America, India and Australasia while Scotch Ale sent to North-east England via the new railway system out-sold local brews. The brewing industry was mainly confined to the Lowlands, where the finest malting barley grows, and Alloa, Edinburgh and Glasgow became major brewing centres. Although pale malt provides the bulk of the grist in Scottish brewing, amber, brown, black and chocolate versions are widely used even in what are nominally called "pale" ales, while roasted barley and oats add further distinctive tart and creamy flavours.

The cold climate determined the particular nature of Scottish beer. Hops cannot grow in Scotland and as they are expensive to import they are used more sparingly, with a short time in the copper to avoid boiling off the aroma and bitterness. And before temperature control was introduced, fermentation was naturally cooler than in England, around 10°C/50°F. The yeast works more slowly and fermentation lasts for around three weeks, followed by a long conditioning period. Slow, cool fermentation, allied to the large number of Scots who worked abroad and acquired a taste for lager, help explain the enthusiasm to embrace the new style of brewing in Scotland. Tennent's Wellpark Brewery in Glasgow started to brew lager as early as 1885. The rush to merge in the 1960s and 1970s, creating the Scottish duopoly of Scottish and Newcastle, and Tennent-Caledonian (a subsidiary of Bass), was driven by the demands of the lager market and the heavy costs of investing in new brewing plant.

Far more than in England, Scottish ale seemed destined for the scrapheap. But due to a long rearguard action by CAMRA and the enthusiasm of a small but growing number of specialist ale brewers, cask beer is starting to revive to such an extent that the busiest bars in Aberdeen, Edinburgh and Glasgow are those that offer real ale. The revival has also seen a welcome reappearance of the names given to Scottish styles, such as "light", meaning a lightly hopped ale, "heavy" for a standard bitter ale, "export" for a stronger ale, and "wee heavy" for a powerful beer akin to an old ale. Many revivalist ales are also branded with the term shilling, as in 60, 70, 80 and 90 shilling ales, based on a nineteenth-century method of invoicing based on strength. This means that a light may be called Sixty Shilling and so on up the strength table to Ninety Shilling for a wee heavy.

The pacesetter in the Scottish ale revival has been the Caledonian Brewery in Edinburgh. Bought by a handful of enthusiasts in 1987 when its previous owners closed the plant, Caledonian struggled to survive but won through on the sheer quality of its ales and its commitment to traditional methods and ingredients. The brewery uses open-fired coppers that encourage a good rolling boil, according to the brewer, who says his ales are properly boiled with hops and not stewed. While the bitterness units of most Scottish ales rarely exceed 30, Caledonian's are noticeably hoppy due to the generous use of Fuggles and Goldings that give the ales a delectable

aroma and palate of citric fruit. Caledonian ales include a malty/
hoppy **Caledonian 80 Shilling** (4.1 per cent ABV) and a superb
interpretation of an India Pale Ale, **Deuchar's IPA** (3.8 per cent
ABV; 34 to 36 units of bitterness). The beer is brewed from Golden
Promise pale and crystal malts with Fuggles and Goldings whole
hops. It won CAMRA's Champion Beer of Britain award in 2002.
It's now a national brand available as far south as Cornwall in
England. Caledonian is now a subsidiary of the Heineken-owned
Scottish & Newcastle but the new owners have not to date inter-
fered with the brands and have kept the original management team
in place.

The Caledonian management also owns the Harviestoun
Brewery in Alva, which is free from Heineken control or influence.
It produces two award-winning beers, **Bitter & Twisted** (3.8 per
cent ABV) and **Schiehallion** (4.8 per cent). Bitter & Twisted is a
notably hoppy beer by Scottish standards, with a rich malt balance,
a golden colour and a long bitter finish. Schiehallion, named after
a local mountain, is called a "cask-conditioned lager" though the
brewery has no lager equipment. The beer is effectively ale brewed
with lager malt, lager yeast and German Hersbrucker hops and
served chilled. It has a fine hop aroma, a good balance of toasted
malt and hops in the mouth and a dry and bitter finish.

Another Scottish brewer that ploughed a lonely ale furrow for
years before breaking through to plaudits and success is Belhaven in
Dunbar. The brewery, based in old maltings buildings, is in a superb
setting on the coast, close to the English border. It brews the whole
gamut of traditional Scottish ales, from 60 to 90 shilling. Its
Belhaven Eighty Shilling (4.1 per cent ABV; 33 units of colour;
29 of bitterness) is the Scots classic, with a pronounced gooseberry
character on the aroma and palate underscored by peppery, resiny
Fuggles and Goldings.

Two other breweries in Border country offer fascinating examples of the art. Broughton Brewery is in the town of the same name

where novelist John Buchan was born – it names its major product, **Greenmantle Ale**, after one of his Richard Hannay adventures. It also brews a strong **Old Jock** (6.7 per cent ABV; 32 IBUs) and a traditional **Broughton Oatmeal Stout** (3.8 per cent ABV; 28 IBUs) in which the oats give a pleasing creamy sweetness to balance the slight astringency of roasted barley.

Traquair House near Peebles is a restored medieval brewery, based in the oldest inhabited stately home in Scotland. **Traquair House Ale** (7.0 per cent ABV; 35 IBUs) is brewed from pale malt and a touch of black, with East Kent Goldings specially grown for the house.

For many years the most northerly brewery in the British Isles was Orkney. It produces **Raven Ale** (3.8 per cent ABV), **Dragonhead Stout** (4.1 per cent), **Dark Island** (4.7 per cent) and **Skullsplitter** (8.5 per cent). The beers are rich and complex, fruity with good hop balance. Skullsplitter has won CAMRA's Champion Winter Beer of Britain award. But the title of most northerly brewery now goes to Valhalla on Shetland, set up in 1997 by husband and wife Sonny and Sylvia Priest. The beer range includes **Old Scatness** (4 per cent ABV), a pale ale named after an archaeological dig on the island where early evidence of malting and brewing was found, **Simmer Dim** (also 4 per cent), a golden ale named after the long Shetland twilight, and **Sjolmet Stout** (5 per cent), which has a pronounced roast barley aroma and palate and a creamy and malty finish.

Back on the mainland, BrewDog of Fraserburgh brews exceptionally bitter and hoppy beers, including **Hop Rocker** (5.5 per cent ABV), **Punk IPA** (6.2 per cent) and **Rip Tide** (8 per cent). In 2009 it added a properly brewed lager, **Zeitgeist**.

The origins of Scottish – or rather Pictish – brewing have been captured in the remarkable **Fraoch**, an ale that uses heather as well as barley malt in its make-up. Heather was widely used centuries ago to augment the poor quality of the barley grown in the

Highlands. Bruce Williams discovered a woman living on the Western Isles who was able to translate a recipe for heather ale from Gaelic. Fraoch is brewed by Williams Brothers in Alloa and uses ale malt, carapils, wheat malt, ginger root and 12 litres of heather. Hops are used primarily for their preservative quality and did not feature in the original recipe. Part of the heather is added to the copper, the remainder in the hop back, where it acts as a filter for the hopped wort. Fraoch comes in two versions, a 4.0 per cent ABV draught and a 5.0 per cent ABV bottled. It has a crisp heather aroma with a hint of liquorice, a dry herbal palate, and a fruity and minty finish.

The dramatic change in Scottish brewing has been the emergence of oak-aged beers. The trend was started by Innis & Gunn in Edinburgh, run by Dougal Sharp, a former head brewer at Caledonian. His brand, **Oak Aged Beer**, is brewed at Belhaven and then matured in lightly toasted whiskey casks bought from the American Bourbon industry. The beer is 6.6 per cent ABV and is brewed with Golden Promise pale and crystal malts and hopped with the Phoenix variety. The beer has a 77-day maturation period during which time it picks up the toasted and oaky character of the whiskey casks. The beer, only available in bottled form, is smoky and oaky, with rich malt, vanilla and tangy hops on nose and palate.

Harviestoun at Alva produces three oak-aged beers called **Ola Dubh**, Celtic for Black Oil. The beer is a stronger version of the brewery's **Old Engine Oil** ale. It is matured in 12, 16 and 30-year-old whisky casks supplied by the Highland Park distillery on Orkney. The beers range in strength from 6 to 8 per cent ABV and are intensely rich, oaky and smoky, with good underlying malt and hop character.

1488 Tullibardine Majestic Whisky Beer (7 per cent ABV) is brewed by Douglas Ross at the Bridge of Allan Brewery. Douglas takes the "first runnings" of the mash at Tullibardine Distillery and then ferments the wort in his brewhouse using the original whisky yeast. Saaz hops are added. The beer is matured for up to 60 days in American oak Bourbon casks. The finished beer has a rich whisky and fruit aroma and palate with vanilla and woody notes.

Dark Island Reserve on Orkney is 10 per cent ABV and is matured in Highland Park casks while BrewDog's **Paradox Islay Cask** (also 10 per cent) uses casks from Islay that impart the renowned peaty quality of the island's malt whiskies to the beer.

SCOTTISH BREWERS

Belhaven Brewery Co,
Dunbar, East Lothian EH42 1RS.

Broughton Brewery,
Broughton, Biggar, Lanarkshire ML12 6HQ.

Caledonian Brewing Co,
Slateford Road, Edinburgh EH11 1PH.

Maclay & Co,
Thistle Brewery, Clackmannanshire FK10 1ED.

McEwan and Younger,
Scottish & Newcastle Breweries, Fountain Brewery, Edinburgh EH3 9YY.

Orkney Brewery,
Quoyloo, Sandwick, Orkney KW16 3LT.

Traquair House Brewery,
Traquair House, Innerleithen, Peebles-shire EH44 6PW.

Wales

The Welsh beer scene, so long dominated by subsidiaries of Bass and Whitbread along with the Wrexham Lager Company, has been transformed following the demise of those companies. There are now many vigorous independent breweries. They bring greater choice and also full-flavoured brews to a country once in the sway of the church and the temperance movement that led to beers being low in both strength and character.

The major independent brewery in Wales is Brains of Cardiff. Still family-owned, it was founded in 1822. Brains moved from its original site in the city in 1999 when it bought the former Hancock's Brewery, alongside the railway line, from Bass. The expanded capacity has enabled Brains to produce more of its own beer and to take on contract brewing for such giant companies as Coors that don't have the necessary equipment to make cask beer. Brains owns 260 pubs and has 3,000 free trade accounts. It pleases sports fans of most persuasions by sponsoring the Wales Rugby Union team, Glamorgan County Cricket Club and the Football Association of Wales. Its beers include the legendary **Dark** (3.5 per cent ABV), a mild with a fine chocolate malt character, dark grain in the mouth and a quenching finish dominated by chocolate and light hops. The amber-coloured **Bitter** (3.7 per cent) has a good malty/hoppy nose and palate followed by a dry and bitter finish. **SA** (4.2 per cent) takes its name from the initials of Samuel Arthur Brain, one of the founders of the company, but it's known locally by the nickname of "Skull Attack". It has a mellow, malty character balanced by gentle fruit and light but persistent hop bitterness. **SA Gold** (4.7 per cent) is a new, golden interpretation of SA with piny and peppery hop resins balancing rich toasted malt and a touch of vanilla.

Felinfoel of Llanelli is another family-owned independent. It was founded in the 1830s and, as it has remained on the original site, lays claim to being the oldest brewery in Wales. Its **Best Bitter** (3.8 per cent ABV) is bittersweet in the mouth but has pleasing hop bitterness in the finish. The flagship beer is **Double Dragon** (4.2 per cent), a complex bronze beer that is fruity, malty, slightly vinous and lightly hopped (25 IBUs).

Tomos Watkin was founded in Llandeilo in 1995 and moved to Swansea in 2000 with an increased, 50-barrel plant. Its main brand is **OSB** (Old Style Bitter), 4.5 per cent ABV, amber-coloured with a strong aroma and palate of malt and hops. Lapsing into Welsh, the company also brews a 3.7 per cent **Cwrw Braf**, lightly-hopped, quenching beer, **Chwarae Teg** (4.1 per cent) a golden ale with a toasted malt and floral hops character, and **Aber Cwrw**, a strong golden ale of 4.7 per cent.

Bullmastiff in Cardiff was founded in 1987 by a pair of brothers, Bob and Paul Jenkins. Their strong ale, **Son of a Bitch** (6 per cent ABV), raises a few eyebrows but the beer and company name stem from the brothers' love of the Bull Mastiff breed of dog. The beer is rich and warming, with powerful malt, hops and fruit flavours. Other beers in the range include **Welsh Gold** (3.8 per cent), a hoppy and fruity pale beer, **Thoroughbred** (4.5 per cent), with a powerful hop aroma and balancing malt notes, and **Brindle** (5.1 per cent), full-bodied, hoppy, malty and fruity.

Breconshire Brewery in Brecon, Powys, dates from 2002 and supplies beer to mid and south Wales. **Brecon County Ale** (3.7 per cent ABV) is an amber beer with a good smack of hops while **Golden Valley** (4.2 per cent) is hoppy, bitter but balanced by rich malt and tart fruit. **Red Dragon** (4.7 per cent) is a russet beer with wheat as well as barley malt used in the brewing process, with tangy hedgerow hops. **Ramblers Ruin** (5 per cent) is a deep bronze/red beer with a rich biscuit, fruity character and good bitterness in the finish.

Bragdy Sir y Flint Facer's or Facer's Flintshire Brewery is the only brewery in the county and moved to its present site from

Salford, Greater Manchester, in 2006. Its range includes **Clwyd Gold** (3.5 per cent ABV), a pale bronze beer with a malty aroma followed by good hop bitterness in the mouth and finish, **Northern County** (3.8 per cent), straw-coloured with a fine floral hop character, **DHB** or Dave's Hoppy Beer (4.3 per cent), which lives up to the promise of its name with powerful floral hop notes balanced by biscuity malt, and **Landslide** (4.9 per cent), a rich, fruity beer with good hop bitterness breaking through on the palate and finish.

Purple Moose in Porthmadog, Gwynedd, has a number of bi-lingual beers, including **Cwrw Eryi/Snowdonia Ale** (3.6 per cent ABV), a light, golden ale with citrus notes and a dry finish, **Cwrw Madog/Madog's Ale** (3.7 per cent), a malty and nutty beer with a good balance of hop bitterness, and a 4.6 per cent beer that is a mouthful in every way: **Ochr Tywyll y Mws** or **Dark Side of the Moose**, a dark beer with ripe, roasted grain character balanced by fruity hops.

WELSH BREWERS

S. A. Brain & Co,
Crawshay Street, Cardiff CF1 1TR.

Bullmastiff Brewery Co,
Bessemer Close, Leckwith, Cardiff
CF11 8DL.

Facer's Flintshire Brewery,
Tan Y Coed, Bryn Y Garreg, Flint,
Flintshire CH6 5YL.

Felinfoel Brewery Co,
Farmer's Row, Felinfoel, Llanelli
SA14 8LB.

Plassey Brewery,
The Plassey, Eyton, Wrexham
LL1 0SP.

Purple Moose Brewery Ltd,
Madoc St, Porthmadog, Gwynedd
LL49 9DB.

Tomos Watkin (Hurns Brewery),
Unit 3, Century Park, Swansea
SA6 8RP.

The beer styles of Ireland

Key

3 Stout brewery

IRELAND	Murphy's	*Davy Jones*	**Kilkenny**
Belfast	**Dublin**	*Neary's*	E. Smithwick & Sons
Crown Liquor Saloon	Arthur Guinness	*McDaid's*	**Lisburn**
Cork	& Son	**Kilkeel**	Hilden
Beamish & Crawford	*The Brazen Head*	Whitewater	

Ireland

Ireland, in common with the Czech Republic, Denmark and the Netherlands, is a country with a small population that must export beer to have viable breweries. Guinness, far and away the best-known brewery in the Irish Republic, is an international brand, available in 120 countries and brewed in many of them. But it does not neglect the home market. Its domination is so awesome on its own soil that there is no need to ask for the beer by name – "a glass of stout" will suffice. The only exception to the rule is in the city of Cork and the surrounding area where Beamish and Murphy offer alternatives to the ubiquitous Dublin brew.

Stout is rooted in the Irish way of life, to such a degree that Guinness uses the harp, the national symbol, as the company logo. Just like the people, you cannot hurry a glass of stout. Pouring a pint is an art form. Drinkers must wait patiently as the barperson allows it to settle into black body and white head and then tops it up to make sure you receive a full measure. Some bar staff will even inscribe a shamrock in the foam.

Ale is brewed in Ireland but it commands a relatively small share of the market, though that may grow as more new craft brewers appear. Lager has made considerable inroads but stout made a comeback in the 1990s, with clever advertising and pro-motions winning young people to the joys of the black stuff.

Dry Irish Stout – the dryness the result of adding roasted bar-ley to the malted grain along with generous levels of hops – is a style in its own right. But the origins of porter and stout lie in London, not Dublin. Before porter became a major style in the early eighteenth century and found its way across the Irish Sea, Ireland produced sweet and unhopped ales in the Celtic tradition, a tradition that goes back 5,000 years.

St Patrick, the monk who introduced Christianity to the island, is also doubly blessed as the country's first provider of beer. A brewer was an important member of his staff and for centuries the production of ale was controlled by the church. As a result of the damp climate, it's difficult to grow hops in Ireland and the English found to their astonishment that as late as the eighteenth century Irish ales were unhopped. There's even a suggestion that the first ale brewed by Arthur Guinness did not contain hops.

But once large amounts of London-brewed porter and stout began to pour into Ireland, local brewers responded by developing their own versions of the style. A small amount of hops were cultivated in Ireland but most hops had to be imported from England and, later, from the United States.

Guinness

The history of Irish brewing is inextricably linked to Arthur Guinness. He used £100 left to him by a benefactor to open a small brewery in County Kildare in 1756. Three years later he moved to Dublin and took a lease on a disused brewery in St James's Gate at an annual rent of £45. He brewed ale but in 1759 he decided to challenge the English brewers' domination of the Irish market by switching production to porter with the aid of a brewer hired from London. In 2009 Guinness celebrated 250 years of brewing stout. Arthur Guinness's business expanded rapidly and he used canals and the new railway system to sell beer nationally. The brewery produced two beers, **X** and **XX**. The XX was later renamed **Extra Porter Stout** while a third beer, **Foreign Extra Porter Stout**, was developed for export to the British colonies. Eventually the term porter was dropped and the beers became known simply as stout. Single X, which was porter, became better known by its Dublin nickname of **Plain** and was brewed well into the twentieth century.

Arthur Guinness's son, also called Arthur, not only expanded the business at home and abroad but was responsible for developing the generic style known as Dry Irish Stout. Until the 1880s,

British and Irish brewers paid tax not on the strength of beer but on the malt used. In order to avoid paying unnecessary imposts to the London goverrment – the whole of Ireland was then part of the United Kingdom – Arthur Guinness II experimented with blending some unmalted and therefore untaxed roasted barley with the malted grains. The barley added colour and a roasted, slightly charred character to the stout, making it more bitter and drier than a London porter. Arthur II also designed the recipe for Foreign Export Stout, which, in common with English pale ales, was high in alcohol and heavily hopped to withstand long sea journeys. When Arthur II handed over control of the company to Benjamin Guinness, the latter built substantial sales in Belgium – where a taste for strong stout remains undiminished today – and North America. One third of Ireland's population had migrated to the United States following the terrible famine of the 1840s and the Irish there were keen to drink stout from the homeland.

By the end of the nineteenth century Guinness was the biggest brewer in Europe and, by the end of the First World War, was the largest in the world – a remarkable achievement for a company based on an island with a population of five million. Its fortunes were boosted by a decision of the British government in the First World War to ban the use of highly kilned dark malt in order to save energy for the war effort, munitions production in particular. As a result, porter and stout brewing went into steep decline in Britain, leaving the market clear for the Irish.

There are now 19 different versions of Guinness brewed in both draught and packaged versions. The classic Dublin brews use malt, unmalted roasted barley, flaked barley and a blend of English and American hops. Water comes from the Wicklow mountains and is treated with gypsum to harden it. Arthur Guinness's original yeast culture is still used, though it has been reduced from some five strains to one. It's a remarkable type of yeast, highly flocculent, and it works at a warm temperature of 25°C/77°F. Fermentation is rapid, lasting just two days, with the yeast remaining in suspension. The yeast is removed by centrifuge. Bottle-conditioned **Guinness Original** (4.1 per cent ABV; 43 to 47 IBUs), available only in the Dublin area, is produced by blending wort with the fermented beer to create a second fermentation in the bottle. **Irish Draught Guinness** has the same strength and IBUs as the bottled beer. **Export Draught** for Europe is 5.0 per cent ABV, 45 to 53 IBUs, with a pronounced hop aroma, dark and bitter grain in the mouth and a dry finish. Guinness exported to North America has the same IBUs as the European version but is higher in alcohol and has some fruit on the aroma and a characteristically hoppy finish.

Bottled **Guinness** brewed in Dublin for Belgium is 8.0 per cent ABV, IBUs around 50 and has dark fruit on the aroma, great depth of hop bitterness, burnt raisins in the mouth and a long bittersweet finish. But bottled **Foreign Extra Stout** puts even this remarkable beer in the shade. **FES**, as it's known, is a palpable link to the time of the first Arthur Guinness. Fresh stout is blended with beer that has been stored for between one and three months and which picks up a hint of sourness – a beer known as "stale" in the eighteenth century. As a result, the finished beer (7.5 per cent ABV; 60-plus IBUs), brewed from pale malt, 25 per cent flaked barley and 10 per cent roasted barley, has a magnificent and unmistakable hint of sour fruit on the aroma that comes from the wild yeast fermentation, balanced by roasted grain, burnt fruit and intensely bitter hops.

Cork

The stout tradition was also carried out with great fervour by two Cork breweries, Beamish & Crawford and Murphy's. Beamish and Crawford were Protestants of Scottish descent who came south to sell cattle and butter, bought an ale brewery on the banks of the River Lee and were brewing porter by 1792. The company's single X porter disappeared in the 1960s and it concentrated on just one version of stout. **Beamish Stout** (4.3 per cent ABV; 38 to 44 IBUs) is brewed from pale and dark malts, malted wheat, roasted barley and wheat syrup, and is hopped with Irish, German and Styrian varieties.

Murphy's Lady's Well Brewery, across the city from Beamish, is on the site of a religious shrine that once supplied water for the brewery. James, William, Jerome and Frances Murphy, devout Catholics, built their brewery in 1856 and, in common with their rivals, produced porter as well as stout. It is only stout that remains today. **Murphy's Stout** is 4.3 per cent ABV with 35 to 36 IBUs, and is brewed from pale and chocolate malts and roasted barley. It's hopped with Target.

The future of brewing in Cork is now in question. Murphy's has been owned by Heineken for many years while Beamish, after a series of owners, finished up in the hands of Scottish & Newcastle. In 2008, Heineken bought S&N and became owner of both Cork breweries. It plans to close Beamish and concentrate production at Murphy's. It remains to be seen whether both stouts will survive.

New breweries

Guinness will not be quaking in its giant boots, but there is now greater choice for drinkers in Ireland as new small breweries come on stream. Carlow Brewing Co in Carlow brews **O'Hara's Celtic Stout**, **Leann Follain Stout**, **Curin Gold Celtic** wheat beer and **O'Hara's Traditional Red Ale**. The Celtic Brewing Co in Enfield, County Meath, produces **Red Ale**, stout and lager. Hooker Brewery in Roscommon brews **Galway Hooker Irish Pale Ale** and **Dark Wheat Beer**, while Franciscan Well is restoring choice in Cork with **Blarney Blond**, **Rebel Red**, **Shandon Stout** and **Friar Weisse**.

In Dublin, Messrs Maguire at Burgh Quay has a **Plain Porter**, **Rusty Red Ale** and **Weiss** while Porterhouse – the first micro to challenge the hegemony of Guinness in Dublin – produces a cask-conditioned **TSB**, **Porterhouse Red**, **Brainblásta**, **Plain**, **Oyster Stout** and **Wrasslers XXXX**. As new breweries blossom, Guinness plans to close its subsidiaries of Smithwick, Cherry and Macardle and bring all brewing under one roof in Dublin. Plans to close parts of St James's Gate and build a new brewery outside the city have been put on hold as a response to the sharp down-turn in the Irish economy in 2008 and 2009. **Smithwick's Draught**, sold as **Kilkenny Ale** in some foreign markets, is a red ale in the Celtic tradition, with the colour derived from roasted barley blended with pale malt and brewing syrup. A complex blend of Challenger, Goldings, Northdown and Target hops is used and is added three times during the copper boil. The beer is 3.5 per cent ABV with 22 IBUs and has a creamy, malty, lightly fruity aroma with dark fruit in the mouth and bittersweet finish. Cherry's and Macardle's draught ales are indistinguishable from Smithwick's.

Northern Ireland

Stout from the republic is the main beer style in the north. Bass owned Caffrey's Brewery in Belfast but it closed in 2005 following change of ownership to first InBev and then Coors. Cask-conditioned ale in the province comes from Hilden and Whitewater. Hilden in Lisburn opened in 1981, distributes to around 20 outlets and owns two pubs. It produces **Ale** (4 per cent ABV), an amber beer with a malty and hoppy character, **Silver** (4.2 per cent), a pale beer with a floral hop aroma from the Saaz variety, **Molly Malone** (4.6 per cent), a ruby-red porter with a pronounced chocolate character, and two red ales, **Scullion's Irish** (4.6 per cent), a sweetish beer with a nutty flavour, and **Halt** (6.1 per cent) with a malty and biscuit character.

Whitewater in Kilkeel, Co Down, opened in 1996 and has achieved rapid success. Its extensive beer range includes **Mill Ale** (3.7 per cent ABV), **Glen Ale** (4.2 per cent) and **Belfast Ale** (4.5 per cent).

IRISH BREWERS

Carlow Brewing Co,
The Good Store, Station Road,
Carlow, Co. Carlow.

Celtic Bewing Co,
Enfield, Co Meath.

Franciscan Well,
14b North Mall, Cork, Co. Cork.

Arthur Guinness & Son,
St James's Gate, Dublin 8.

Hilden Brewery,
Hilden House, Grand Street, Hilden,
Lisburn, Co Antrim.

Hooker Brewery,
Racecourse Road, Roscommon.

Messrs Maguire,
1–2 Burgh Quay, Dublin 2.

Murphy's/Beamish,
Lady's Well Brewery, Leitrim Street,
Cork.

Porterhouse Brewing Co,
45 Nassau Street, Dublin 2.

Whitewater Brewing Company,
40 Tullyframe Road, Kilkeel,
Co. Down.

Luxembourg

The Grand Duchy of Luxembourg, with its small population of 350,000, is wedged between Belgium, France and Germany. Its influence is Germanic, and it brews mainly Pilsner-type beers, but the country does not adhere to the *Reinheitsgebot*. There is often a high proportion of cereal adjuncts in its beers.

In Luxembourg city, Brasserie Réunies de Luxembourg brews under the names of Mousel, Clausen and Henri Funck. **Mousel Premium Pils** is 4.8 per cent ABV, brewed from 90 per cent pale malt and 10 per cent rice, and hopped with Hallertau and Saaz varieties (28.5 IBUs). It is lagered for five weeks, has a rich malt aroma with some delicate hops, is light and quenching in the mouth, and has some hop character in the finish. **Henri Funck Lager Beer** is brewed with an identical specification to the Mousel Pils. A 5.5 per cent ABV **Altmunster** is in the Dortmunder Export style, with a firm body and a good malty characteristic.

The Brasserie Nationale in Bascharage brews **Bofferding** (4.8 per cent ABV) from pale malt and corn (maize), with Hallertau Northern Brewer and selected aroma hops (25 IBUs). It is lagered for a month. It is a refreshing but rather thin beer with some light hops and malt on the aroma, a medium body, and a short, bitter-sweet finish. Diekirch, from the town of the same name, has an all-malt **Pils** with slightly more character than its rivals. Two tiny breweries, Simon at Wiltz, and Battin in Esch-sur-Alzette, produce occasional **Bocks** along with their **Pils**.

LUXEMBOURG BREWERS

Brasserie Nationale SA (Bofferding), 2 Boulevard John F. Kennedy, L-4930 Bascharage.

Brasserie Réunies de Luxembourg Mousel et Clausen SA, BP 371, L-2013 Luxembourg-Clausen.

The Netherlands

The Netherlands, or Holland as it is often called, is so closely identified with Heineken that casual observers could be forgiven for thinking the Dutch drink nothing else. But prompted by the cross-border interest in Belgian speciality beers, the Dutch market is beginning to change. A number of microbrewers have appeared, producing Pilsners with rather more character than the brand leaders. Some micros are also brewing fascinating versions of ales, some based on old and long-forgotten Dutch styles. They have prompted the beer giants to widen their portfolios to brew brown, dark and Bock beers.

But the speciality beers are pebbles on the Dutch beach, and most of the beach is owned and controlled by Heineken. It not only accounts for well over half of the beer brewed and sold in the Netherlands but is a giant on the world market. As the Netherlands has a small population of around 14 million, all the leading brewers have turned to other markets to boost production and sales. Heineken produces more than 40 million hectolitres of beer a year from both its Dutch breweries and some 100 plants worldwide.

This powerful position is a long way removed from the origins of the Dutch company, though the origins were far from humble. In 1863 Gerard Adriaan Heineken bought De Hooiberg (the Haystack), the largest brewery in Amsterdam, with records going back to 1592. Such was his success that within a few years he built a second brewery and opened a third plant in Rotterdam in 1873.

In the Netherlands, Heineken had a curious on-off love affair for years with its great rival Amstel. In 1941 the two companies took over another leading Dutch brewery, Van Vollenhoven, and jointly managed it. But it was not until 1968 that Heineken and Amstel formally merged. Amstel was founded in 1870 by C.A. de Peters and J.H. van Marwijk Kooy. The awe in which brewers held Munich beer can be seen in the original title of their company: "Beiersch

Bierbrouwerij de Amstel" – the Bavarian Beer Brewery of the Amstel. Amstel is the name of the river that flows through Amsterdam.

The merger in 1968 was prompted by the incursion into the Netherlands the previous year by the large British group Allied Breweries, which had bought the second biggest Dutch brewery, Oranjeboom in Rotterdam. Heineken and Amstel were worried that Allied and other overseas brewers would snap up other Dutch companies and sought strength through merger. The view was heightened when Allied later acquired the Drie Hoefijzers (Three Horseshoes) brewery in Breda. Allied merged Three Horseshoes and Oranjeboom but had little success and sold its interests to Interbrew, now InBev. The group closed Oranjeboom and the brands are now brewed at Dommelsch.

Dutch Pilsner

Heineken today has its headquarters in Amsterdam but no longer brews there. The old Haystack site is now a restaurant and hotel. The second brewery built by the founding Heineken near Museum Square is a visitors' centre with views of superb copper vessels and video shows depicting the history of the company.

Heineken Pilsner is 5.0 per cent ABV and, in keeping with all its pale lagers, has between 20 and 25 bitterness units. This enormously successful beer is something of a hybrid, a half-way house between a true Pilsner and the light-bodied international style. It has a delicate hop and malt aroma, a clean palate and a refreshing finish with some hop notes. **Amstel Bier** is also 5.0 per cent ABV, has a deeper golden colour and a fraction more hop character. These two beers are the ones by which the group is best known internationally. For its home market, Heineken also produces beers of considerably greater character. **Amstel 1870** is also 5.0 per cent ABV but has a decidedly more hoppy edge while **Amstel Gold** (7.0 per cent ABV) is rich and fruity, balanced by great hop character.

The best Pilsners within the Heineken group come from the Brand Brewery, bought in 1989. It is the oldest brewery in the Netherlands, dating from the early fourteenth century, in the village of Wijlre, close to Maastricht – the present brewing site dates from 1743. In the 1970s Brand became the official supplier of beer to the Queen of the Netherlands and now calls itself the Royal Brand Brewery. Its **Brand Pils** is sold in North America in a white ceramic bottle and is called "Royal Brand Beer". It is the standard 5.0 per cent ABV and is brewed from 90 per cent pale malt made from two-row summer barley and 10 per cent maize grits. Hops are German Northern Brewer, Perle and Hersbrucker, achieving 26 to 28 IBUs. The beer is lagered for 42 days. It has a perfumy hop aroma, is malty and hoppy in the mouth followed by a firm, hoppy finish. **Brand-UP** is a premium 5.5 per cent Pilsner, not a soft drink despite the title (UP stands for "Urtyp Pilsner" – Original Pilsner). It is all-malt, uses Hersbrucker, Spalt and Tettnang hops and has an impressive 36 to 38 IBUs. It is lagered for up to 56 days.

The Brand beers are distinguished by their long lagering periods and the company's refusal to pasteurize them. The head brewer declares: "Pasteurization serves to lengthen the shelf-life of a beer but only marginally and at enormous costs to the taste and aroma of the beer".

The most characterful Pilsner in the Netherlands comes from the small St Christoffel Brewery in Roermond in Dutch Limburg. It is owned by Leo Brand, a member of the Brand family. He built his brewery in 1986 after studying brewing at Weihenstephan in Munich and then working in the German brewing industry. His brewery is named after the patron saint of Roermond, once a major coal-mining area, and is distinguished by a fine domed and brick-clad copper kettle which he found in a barn. Leo Brand's main product is **Christoffel Bier**, 5.1 per cent ABV, made only from barley malt, with Hallertau and Hersbrucker hops. It has 45 IBUs, a massive hop-resin aroma, a tingle of hops on the tongue and a big dry and bitter finish. The beer is not pasteurized and Mr Brand answers critics who claim his beer is too bitter with the riposte: "I am not brewing to please everyone!" The beer is also known as Blond and sub-titled Dubbel Hop to underscore the hoppy intent. He has introduced a "double malt" **Robertus** (6.0 per cent ABV) with a tinge of red in the colour from darker, Munich-type malt: the name comes from Robyn, the Dutch for Robin Redbreast. It is rich and malty with a dry finish.

But for the presence of Heineken, Grolsch would be considered a brewing giant. It's based in the Gelderland region of the country and had two plants in Enschede and Groenlo. These were closed and replaced by a vast new site at Enschede in 2004. This is close to the German border and Grolsch has now entered the German market and has turned **Grolsch Pilsener** (5.0 per cent ABV) into an all-malt beer to meet the demands of the *Reinheitsgebot*. Pilsener, known as **Premium Lager** in some export markets, is brewed from a complex blend of spring barley malts from Belgium, England, France, Germany and the Netherlands. Hops are Hallertau and Saaz, with aroma hops added at the end of the copper boil. The beer is lagered for 10 weeks and has 27 IBUs. It's not pasteurized, even for export. The size of the new plant enables Grolsch to brew a wide range of occasional and seasonal beers. The family-owned brewery startled the beer world by selling to SABMiller in 2008.

Alfa is a small independent brewery in Limburg dating from 1870. Its **Edel** (Noble) **Pils** is 5.0 per cent ABV, an all-malt brew made from French and Dutch malts, with Hallertau, Saaz and Tettnang hops. It is lagered for two months but with just 19 IBUs it has only a light hop character.

Oranjeboom, originally of Breda, has a light interpretation of the **Pilsner** style (5.0 per cent ABV) and a drier version called **Klassiek.** As the beers are now brewed at Dommelsch in Dommelen, where a **Dommelsch Pilsener** (5 per cent ABV) is also produced, it's likely there will be some contraction of brands under InBev's ownership.

The village of Gulpen near Maastricht is home to a highly regard-ed independent, Gulpener, established in 1825. Its regular 5.0 per cent ABV **Gulpener Pilsener** is pleasant but unexciting. But the **Gulpener X-pert** premium Pils of the same strength is superb, an all-malt brew bursting with Tettnang hop aroma and flavour with 35 IBUs.

Brown and dark beers

A few breweries produce dark lagers that bear some resemblance to the Dunkel beers of Munich and Bavaria. They are usually called Oud Bruin – Old Brown – and are around 3.5 per cent ABV, lightly hopped, smooth and easy drinking. Heineken has an everyday brown lager and a stronger, 4.9 per cent ABV **Heineken Special Dark** in some export markets. A new micro, Zeeuwse-Vlaamse in Flemish Zeeland, has a strong 6.0 per cent ABV **Zeeuwse-Vlaamse Bruine** while Gulpen and Grolsche have Oud Bruins in their ranges.

The Düsseldorf influence can be seen in a handful of Alt or Old ales. Arcense has a 5.0 per cent ABV **Altforster Alt**, amber-coloured, with a malty, slightly roasty aroma, thin palate and dry finish. (The same brewery has a warm-fermenting Kölsch-type beer called **Stoom** – Steam – **Beer**, also 5.0 per cent ABV, using a blend of barley and wheat malts, Northern Brewer and Hersbruck hops – 22 IBUs – with fruity and peppery hop aromas and flavours.) Grolsch introduced an Alt in the late 1980s called **Amber** (5.0 per cent ABV) with a malty aroma but growing hop character in the big palate and long dry finish. De Leeuw – the Lion – Brewery in Valkenberg, near Maastricht, has **Venloosch Alt** (4.5 per cent ABV) with plenty of dark and roasted malt character. The Us Heit – "Our Father" – micro in Dutch Friesland, founded in a cow shed in 1985, has a 6.0 per cent ABV **Buorren Bier**, copper-coloured, fruity and dry: not strictly an Alt but it fits most easily into the category. The energetic Budels Brewery has a 5.5 per cent ABV **Budels Alt** with massive peppery hops on the aroma, dark chocolate and malt in the mouth, and a deep, dry and intensely bitter finish with some fruit and toffee.

Dutch "Dorts"

The proximity of Dortmund to the Netherlands created great interest in the rounded, malty beers of the great German city. The style has been shortened to the simple expostulatory "Dort" in the Netherlands. Gulpener has a 6.5 per cent ABV **Gulpener Dort**, brewed from pale malt, maize and caramel – hardly *Reinheitsgebot!* – with Hallertau hops. It has 20 IBUs and is lagered for 10 weeks.

Alfa's **Super-Dortmunder** has a redoubtable 7.0 per cent ABV. The beer is ripe and fruity with a clean but sweet finish. De Ridder, originally in Maastricht, was close to Dortmund. Heineken owns the company and it closed the brewery, transferring production to its main plant near Amsterdam. It continues to produce De Ridder's Dort called **Maltezer** (6.5 per cent ABV) – a name that for British drinkers conjures up the name of small chocolate-covered confectionery. It is a fruity lager, smooth from the malt, but with a good hop character in the long finish. De Leeuw produces **Super Leeuw** (5.9 per cent ABV), rich and malty, becoming dry in the finish.

Bocks

The major revivalist beer style in the Netherlands is Bock or Bok. As in Germany, the word means billy-goat and the potent animal features on several labels. For years Bok meant a dark and sweet beer which had little connection with the well-crafted German versions. From the late 1980s Bok has undergone a transformation. Bok beers come in many colours; some are warm-fermented, others are lagered. Strengths vary to accommodate Dubbel Boks and Meiboks.

Brand has an impressive **Imperator**, which should be a double with such a name but is brewed all year round and is a single Bock of great quality. It is all-malt, using pale, chocolate and Munich malts with Hallertau, Hersbrucker and Perle hops (6.5 per cent ABV; 22 IBUs). A 7.5 per cent ABV **Brand Dubbelbock** is a winter beer with a tempting port-wine colour, fruity and malty. The spring

Brand Meibock (7.0 per cent ABV) has a spicy aroma, a citric fruit palate and more spice in the finish.

The Drie Ringen Brewery in Amersfoort makes a 6.6 per cent ABV warm-fermenting **Drie Ringen Bokbier**, amber-coloured, packed with ripe fruit and gentle hops, and a 6.5 per cent ABV **Drie Ringen Meibok**. Interbrew's Dommelsch subsidiary produces a 6.5 per cent ABV **Dommelsch Bokbier**, dry with light fruit. Its **Dominator** suggests it should be a double but it is lower in alcohol (6.0 per cent ABV) than the Bok and is fruity in the mouth. Drie Horne in Kaatsheuvel brews a 7.0 per cent ABV **Drie Horne Bokbier** that is warm fermenting and conditioned in the bottle with a dry, fruity and peppery hop character.

A taste of an old-fashioned Dutch Bok comes from arch-traditionalist Grolsch. It is 6.5 per cent ABV, dark, sweet and potable. Its **Grolsch Mei Bok** (6.0 per cent ABV) is amber-coloured and much dryer, with a good balance of fruit and hops. Heineken has an **Amstel Bock** (7.0 per cent ABV), dark, malty and chewy. Its **Heineken Tarewebok**, also 7.0 per cent ABV, has 17 per cent wheat in its grist and is smooth and fruity with chocolate notes from dark malt. The Lindeboom (Linden Tree) independent in Neer, Limburg, has two Boks: a 6.5 per cent ABV **Lindeboom Bockbier**, dark, dry and bitter, and **Lindeboom Meibock** (7.0 per cent ABV), amber-coloured, bittersweet and fruity. Maasland, a micro in Oss, brews warm-fermenting, bottle-conditioned beers of great character and integrity. Its 7.5 per cent ABV **Maasland MeiBockbier** bursts with dark fruit, malt and resiny hops. A 6.5 per cent **Maasland SummerBock** is amber-coloured, hopped with Hallertau and German Brewers' Gold, rich, spicy and chocolatey.

Ales

Dutch ale was once as rare as a lofty hill in the Netherlands. But brewers are losing their fear of warm fermentation and are re-creating ales of quality and character.

For decades the ale flag was flown by the country's single surviving Trappist brewery near Tilburg. The abbey is called Koningshoeven, a name meaning "King's Garden" – the land was a gift to the monks from royalty.

The brewery has had a chequered history since the end of the Second World War. It was bought by Stella Artois but the monks then raised the money to buy the brewery back from Stella. They had, with great prescience, held on to their brewing equipment and their top-fermenting yeast strain. Today their beers, all labelled La Trappe, are made from pale, Munich and other coloured malts, with Hallertau and English Goldings hops. **La Trappe Dubbel** (6.5 per cent ABV) has a tawny appearance with a superb Muscat aroma and palate underscored by peppery hops. The 8.0 per cent ABV bronze-coloured **La Trappe Tripel** has a big Goldings aroma and a spicy palate and finish. **La Trappe Quadrupel** (10.0 per cent ABV) is an annual autumn vintage, reddish in colour with a smooth palate that belies the rich alcohol. In 1995 the abbey launched a new pale **La Trappe Enkel** (Single), at 5.5 per cent ABV, dry, quenching and hoppy. La Trappe is now owned by the giant Bavaria group, which makes large amounts of own-label beers for supermarkets. For a while the monastic brewery was expelled from the International Trappist Association but its membership was restored when the association was satisfied that the abbot at Koningshoeven controlled the brewery.

In Amsterdam ale brewing has been put firmly on the map by the 't IJ brewpub. It was opened in 1984 by songwriter Kaspar Peterson in an old bath house beneath a windmill. The name of the brew-pub is an elaborate pun. The IJ is the name of the waterway that fronts Amsterdam harbour. The pronunciation of IJ – "ay" – is virtually identical to the Dutch for egg, which explains the ostrich and an egg on the pub sign. In the sign's background, a windmill standing in a desert suggests that Amsterdam was a beer desert until Kaspar Peterson started to brew.

't IJ brews 10 beers but they are not all available at the same time. **Natte**, meaning "wet", is a 6.5 per cent ABV brown ale in the style of a Belgian Dubbel. **Zatte** (8.0 per cent ABV) means "drunk" and is in the Tripel style, pale, with a spicy, hoppy character. **Columbus's Egg** (9.0 per cent ABV), is cloudy bronze in colour with a deep winey aroma, citric fruit in the mouth and more fruit in the finish. **Struis**, also 9.0 per cent ABV, is the Dutch for ostrich and is spicy, fruity and dry. The brewery also produces an autumn Bok, beers for New Year and the spring, an English-style bitter and Vlo, "flea beer".

De Bekeerde Suster – the Reformed Sister – in Kloveniersburgwal is a brewpub on the edge of Amsterdam's red light district. The name commemorates Magdalena van Bethanien, a prostitute in the Middle Ages who saw the error of her ways and joined a convent where the pub now stands. The beers are brewed by Harrie Vermeer, a vastly experienced Dutch brewer who has worked at, amongst others, La Trappe in Tilburg. His regular beers include **Blonde Ros** (White Horse), a 6 per cent ABV ale brewed with Pils malt and hopped with East Kent Goldings, Northern Brewer and Saaz varieties. It has a peppery hops and tangerine fruit aroma and palate with a solid underpinning of toasted malt. **Bock Ros** (6.5 per cent ABV) uses Pils malt, caramalt, roasted grain, wheat and ginger and is hopped with two English varieties, Goldings and Target. It has a dark malt, spicy hops, raisin fruit and ginger character from aromas to finish.

Drie Ringen's Hopfenbier (5.0 per cent ABV) has, as the name suggests, a powerful hop character to offset rich and fruity maltiness. 't Kuipertje (the Little Kettle) in Herwijnen brews a similarly fruity/hoppy pale ale called **Lingewal Vriendenbier** and a strong and ripely fruity **Nicks** (7.0 per cent ABV). Maasland's **D'n Schele Os** means the Dizzy Bull (7.5 per cent ABV) with a label showing a cross-eyed bull suffering over-consumption of this strong pale ale made from barley malt, rye, wheat, spices and hops with a marvellously rich, complex spicy, hoppy and fruity palate and finish. An Easter Bunny beer, **Paasbier** (6.5 per cent ABV) is also spicy, spritzy from hops and with delicious chocolate notes from the use of dark malt. Budels produces **Parel** (6.0 per cent ABV), a golden ale with great hop character, malt and vanilla in the mouth and a bittersweet finish. Its **Capucijn** (6.5 per cent ABV) is an Abbey-style beer, deep brown, with a nutty aroma and some resiny hops, sultana fruit in the mouth and bittersweet finish.

Even Heineken is experimenting with an ale. It refuses to allow top-fermenting yeasts to come anywhere near its Dutch breweries and is test-marketing **Kylian** (6.5 per cent ABV), brewed by its French subsidiary Pelforth, in Lille. It is the same beer as George Killian's Irish Red Ale, sold on the French market, and is smooth but tart with a gentle hop character. (Killian's brewery was in Enniscorthy but closed in 1956.)

Wheat beers

De Ridder (the Knight) brewed a wheat beer in Maastricht as its main product and it is now produced by Heineken at its main plant. **Wieckse Witte** (5.0 per cent ABV) is packed with tart, lemon and spices characteristics and is deliciously refreshing. Wiecske comes from the same Saxon root as the English wick and means a settlement. The original brewery was in an area of Maastricht known as the Wieckse.

The Raaf Bierbrouwerij (Raven Brewery) started life as a farmhouse, brewery and maltings at Heumen near Nijmegen in the 1700s, closed in the 1920s and re-opened in 1984. It was bought by Allied Breweries' Oranjeboom subsidiary, which busily promoted its spicy and tart **Raaf Witbier** (5.0 per cent ABV). Raaf also brewed a Dubbel, a Tripel and a Bok but Allied closed the brewery and the future of the beers is now in the hands of InBev. Whether Witbier survives will depend on whether InBev sees it as a threat to its heavily marketed Hoegaarden wheat beer. Arcen has **Arcener Tarwe** (5.0 per cent ABV), brewed from a 50:50 blend of barley and wheat malts, and Hallertau Northern Brewer and Hersbruck hops. It has 17 IBUs and uses a Bavarian wheat beer yeast culture. There is a delicious aroma of cidery apples, with more tart fruit in the mouth and a bittersweet finish. De Drie Horne has a powerful 7.0 per cent ABV **De Drie Horne Wit**, darker than is usual, sweet and fruity. **De Leeuw's Witbier** (4.8 per cent ABV) is packed with spices and tart fruit.

Old ale

Gulpener has recreated a long-lost speciality of the Limburg area with its **Mestreechs Aajt** (old dialect for Maastricht Old). It is fermented by wild yeasts, based on a style last seen in the 1930s. The wort (made from pale malt and brewing sugar, hopped with Hallertau: 10 IBUs) is exposed to the atmosphere until it is attacked by *Brettanomyces* yeast and *lactobacilli*. The wort is then stored in unlined wooden casks for a year or more while a secondary fermentation takes place. It is then blended with the brewery's dark lager. This complex and fascinating beer (3.5 per cent ABV) has a sweet and sour aroma with hints of cherry fruit, sour in the mouth with a dry and bitter finish.

Stout

Arcener Stout (6.5 per cent ABV) is genuinely warm-fermenting, brewed from pale, chocolate, Munich and coloured malts, with Hallertau Northern Brewer and Hersbruck hops (27 IBUs). It has rich malt and chocolate aromas, coffee and chocolate in the mouth and a dry and bitter finish. Heineken's **Van Vollenhoven Stout** (6.0 per cent ABV) is cold-fermented. The name comes from the Amsterdam brewery founded in 1733 and closed after it was bought by Heineken and Amstel. Its complexity and fruitiness would increase if Heineken took the plunge and converted it to a true ale, fermented with a top-working yeast.

DUTCH BREWERS

Adbij Koningshoeven,
Trappistenbierbrouwerij de
Schaapskooi, Eindhovensweg 3, 5056
RP Berkel-Eschot.

Alfa Bierbrouwerij,
Thull 15–19, 6365 AC Schinnen.

**Amersfoort De Drie Ringen
Bierbrouwerij,**
Kleine Spui 18, 3811 BE Amersfoort.

Arcense Bierbrouwerij BV,
Kruisweg 44, 5944 EN Arcen.

**Koninklijke Brand Bierbrouwerij
BV,**
Brouwerijstraat 2, Postbus 1, 6300
AA Wijlre.

De Bekeerde Suster,
Kloveniersburgwal 6–8, Amsterdam.

Budelse Brouwerij,
Nieuwstraat 9, 6021 HP Budel.

Dommelsche Bierbrouwerij,
Brouwerijplein 84, 5551 AE
Dommelen.

De Drie Horne Bierbrouwerij,
Berndijksestraat 63, 5171 BB
Kaatsheuvel.

Grolsche Bierbrouwerij,
Fazanstraat 2, 7523 EA Enschede.

Gulpener Bierbrouwerij,
Rijksweg 16, 6271 AE Gulpen.

Heineken Nederland NV,
Postbus 28, 1000 Amsterdam.

't IJ Brouwerij,
Funenkade 7, 1018 AL Amsterdam.

't Kuipertje,
Waaldijk 127, 4171 CC Herwijnen.

De Leeuw Bierbrouwerij,
Pater Beatrixsingel 2, 6301 VL
Valkenberg an den Geul.

De Lindeboom Bierbrouwerij BV,
Engelmanstraat 52–54,
6086 BD Neer.

Maaslandbrouwerij,
Kantsingel 14, 5349 AJ Oss.

St Christoffel Bierbrouwerij,
Bredeweg 14, 6042 GG Roermond.

US Heit Bierbrouwerij,
Buorren 25, 8624 TL Uitwellingerga.

Scandinavia

History is hard to hide. While the Scandinavians attempt to control drinking by heavy taxation, and restrictions on strength and availability, the image of roistering Vikings downing foaming tankards of beer contains a germ of truth. Beer has a long, deep-rooted history in these lands of the far north. Home-brewing and distilling are major craft industries in rural communities while the Finns still make sahti, a rye, oats and barley beer flavoured with juniper. Sahti and similar home-brewed beers go back for around a thousand years. The Vikings brewed a barley-based beer they called aul and handed down, via the Finnish olut, the Swedish öl and the Danish ol, the universal term ale for a warm-fermenting beer. Today there are a few dark beers, both warm and cold-fermenting, but Scandinavia is firmly in the lager camp where its mainstream beers are concerned.

Denmark

Denmark is a country with a population of five million. In common with Heineken of the Netherlands and Stella Artois of Belgium, the largest Danish brewing group has had to turn itself into an international giant to achieve success. For many beer drinkers, Carlsberg is as quintessentially Danish as Hans Christian Andersen and his Little Mermaid.

The great brewing dynasty was founded by Christian Jacobsen, a farmer with brewing skills who arrived in Copenhagen from Jutland in 1801. Within 10 years he had saved sufficient money to rent his own brewery where he made wheat beers. He quickly decided that science and technology had to become the allies of modern brewing. When his son, Jacob Christian Jacobsen, heard of the experiments in lager brewing going on in Bavaria he made the long and arduous coach journey to Munich and went to work with Gabriel Sedlmayr at the Spaten Brewery.

217

Jacobsen was fired with enthusiasm for the new beer and determined to brew it in Denmark. When he reached home he made a beer in his mother's wash-tub using Munich yeast and then turned to making lager beer commercially.

His first lager beers were, like those in Munich, dark brown in colour and were well received. He inherited money on his mother's death and built a new brewery outside Copenhagen. It was on a hill – berg in Danish – and Jacobsen named it after his son, Carl. From that simple conjunction of words a legend was born.

The first beers from the new brewery appeared in 1847. They were a great success. Within a decade or two, Jacobsen built a second brewery alongside the old one. It was dubbed "New Carlsberg" and was run by his son, Carl. It was not so much a brewery as an architect's dream, gleaming copper vessels set amid cool tiling and bronze sculptures, all fronted by the world-famous elephant gates modelled on the Minerva Square obelisk in Rome.

In 1875 Jacobsen created the Carlsberg Laboratories that carried out research in brewing technique. He hired a young scientist, Emil Hansen, who isolated the first pure single-cell yeast culture, one of the major breakthroughs in brewing practice. Both the Old Carlsberg brewery and the rival Tuborg plant had been experiencing problems with their beers. Hansen proved that the cause in both cases was multi-strain yeasts which contained bad strains as well as good. By isolating the good strains he was able to allow them to produce beers of consistent quality.

Carlsberg and Tuborg merged in 1970s to form United Breweries. Tuborg closed in the mid-1990s and Carlsberg plans to move all its operations to a greenfield site outside Copenhagen. The New Carlsberg plant is a listed building and will be maintained as a visitor attraction.

Overseas Carlsberg and Tuborg are both identified by pale, clean, quenching but undemanding versions of the Pilsner style. At home they have a wider portfolio. The main Carlsberg brand is a

4.7 per cent **Carlsberg Pilsner** that is often referred to as Hof from the Danish for "Court". It is a well-balanced and refreshing beer with a malty edge, but lacking great hop character. **Let** – "Light" – **Pilsner** is a mere 2.8 per cent ABV and is typical of the thin lagers produced throughout Scandinavia to deter over-consumption of strong alcohol. At the other end of the scale, the 5.8 per cent **Carlsberg Black Gold** is a big, buttery-malty beer of considerable character.

Tuborg was founded in 1873. The brewery launched a pale lager in 1875, the result of research in Germany by head brewer Hans Bekkevold. Its main pale beers today are in the same strength range as Carlsberg's. The best-selling beer is **Tuborg Green**, which takes its name from the colour of the label, similar to Carlsberg Hof but with a shade more hop character. **Tuborg Gold Label**, at the top of the range, has a good balance of malt and hops. **Tuborg Classic**, 4.8 per cent ABV, was brewed to commemorate 100 years of brewing, and has a deep golden colour.

Both companies produce characterful dark beers. Carlsberg has a cold-fermenting beer called **Gammel ("old"), Porter** and **Imperial Stout** – all on one label. It is not a mistake, for the early stouts were called porter stouts and one constituent element of them was a well-aged old or "stale" beer. It is an impressive 7.7 per cent ABV with rich dark fruit, bitter coffee and scorched vanilla notes. Tuborg's **Porter** is similar with a creamy palate and dry finish, dominated by burnt malt and dark fruit. Carlsberg recalls its origins with **Gamle**, a Munich-style dark lager (4.2 per cent ABV), smooth and chocolatey, and Tuborg has a similar beer called **Tuborg Red Label**. Seasonal beers include two for Easter, Carlsberg and Tuborg **Paskebryg** (7.8 per cent ABV), red-gold in colour, and similarly coloured Christmas beers, **Julebryg** (5.5 per cent ABV).

Several Danish brewers produce beers they call Bock in the German style. Carlsberg makes no such claim for its **Elephant** but this rich, malty-sweet, dangerously drinkable beer falls into the category. Named after the brewery's elephant gates, it is 7.5 per cent ABV and is made from pale malt and brewing sugar, with Hallertau hops (38 IBUs). Carlsberg does not declare the lagering period for the beer but its smoothness implies considerably more time than that given to its **Carlsberg Special Brew** (8.9 per cent ABV), brewed by its English subsidiary in Northampton. Like an ageing boxer, the beer punches its weight, but is short on style and easily falls flat on its face. It is heavy and syrupy. A series of small-run beers is made under the Jacobsen name. They are of high quality and include a Summer Wit (white), Dark Lager, Christmas Beer, Brown Ale, Saaz Blonde and Pilsner.

United Breweries controls around 80 per cent of the Danish beer market and owns two subsidiaries, Wiibroe and Neptun. Wiibroe was founded in 1840 at Elsinor, scene of Shakespeare's *Hamlet*, and even brewed a beer under the Hamlet name. It now makes a light lager (3.6 per cent ABV) but concentrates on low-alcohol products. Its one beer of note is an **Imperial Stout** (6.5 per cent ABV), similar to Carlsberg's. Neptun does not brew in the conventional sense: Carlsberg supplies it with wort which it turns into beer.

The second biggest Danish group is Royal Unibrew. Its major plant, Ceres, dated from 1856 and was based in the university town of Aarhus in Jutland. The plant was closed in January 2009 and production has been transferred to its subsidiary plants, Albani and Faxe. Royal Unibrew also produces beers for another Jutland company, Thor. The group brews Heineken under licence and closer ties with the Dutch giant can be expected. Following the closure of Ceres, the beers have undergone rebranding and are known as Royal. There is a fine, cold-fermented dark beer called **Stout**, with the tag line **Gammel Jysk**, which means "old Jutland". It's 7.7 per cent ABV, brewed with Munich as well as pale malt, is delightfully spicy, slightly oily and darkly fruity with hints of liquorice. **Royal**

Red, previously Red Eric (4.8 per cent ABV), is named in honour of the Viking who discovered Greenland and brewed beer there to celebrate. The group has a strong lager of 5.6 per cent ABV, labelled **Export**, with a strong nod over the border to the home of German Export in Dortmund. It has a malty, pear drops aroma, a creamy/malty palate and a long, bittersweet finish. The Aarhus name lives on in **Ceres Julehvidtol** Christmas beer.

Albani is based on the island of Odense, which was much loved by Hans Christian Andersen. The brewery returns the compliment with a strong beer called **H.C. Andersen Eventyr** (9 per cent ABV). Its main brand is **Odense Pilsner** (4.6 per cent ABV) and it competes for attention in the Bock sector with **Giraf** (7.2 per cent ABV), its answer to Carlsberg's Elephant. Faxe on the island of Zealand became famous in the 1970s with **Faxe Fad**, a "draught" beer in a bottle: draught implied the beer was not pasteurized. It has its own interpretation of Dortmunder Export with a strong lager called **The Great Dane**, which caused mirth when it was briefly available in Britain. **Faxe Pils** (5.0 per cent ABV) has delicate malt, hops and vanilla on the aroma, a firm-bodied, malty palate and a gently hoppy finish.

There are several micro plants in Denmark, notably Brockhouse, Norrebo, Orbaek and Thisted.

Norway

Taxation on beer is steep in Norway. In a blinkered approach to drinking problems, the government increased taxes on beer in the 1980s more steeply than on wine and spirits. It is impossible to find beers of more than around 4.5 per cent ABV, which tends to reinforce the production of Pilsner-style lagers. Stronger beers are made mainly for export.

The country's brewers persevere, despite the prohibitionist attitudes of politicians and bureaucrats. As well as pale lagers, there are some Bocks, summer beers, Christmas beers and Munich

Dunkels, rendered respectively in Norwegian as Bokkol, Summerol, Jule Ol, and Bayerol. Beers in the Dortmunder Export style are known as "Gold Beer". The country has its own version of the German Purity Law, which means the beers are all-malt, clean, rounded and quenching. Brewers tend to fully attenuate their beers, leaving them dry and crisp.

The major brewing group is Ringnes. It merged with Pripps of Sweden and both are now owned by Carlsberg. It has a mighty 60 per cent stranglehold on the Norwegian market, with breweries in Olso, Arendal and Trondheim that produce 1.4 million hectolitres a year. Its portfolio includes a 4.7 per cent ABV **Pilsener**, a 6.5 per cent **Gold** and a beer simply called **Strong** that weighs in at 10.2 per cent.

The second major brewing group is Hansa Borg, owned by Royal Unibrew of Denmark. It has breweries in Bergen, Kristiansand and Sarpsborg. The range includes a 4.5 per cent ABV pale lager called **Fatol**, a dark **Bayer** of the same strength, and **Marney's Red Ale**, also 4.5 per cent, a curious attempt in Norway to brew Irish-style ale.

The Aass Brewery in Drammen is independent, family-owned and dates from 1834: *aass*, perhaps surprisingly to English-speaking ears, means summit and is pronounced "orss". The brewery produces a conventional but high-quality **Pilsner** (4.5 per cent ABV), a rich, firm-bodied **Classic** amber (5.5 per cent), a **Bayer Dark** (4.5 per cent), recalling the first Bavarian lagers, and a 6.5 per cent **Bock** that incorporates Munich malt with pale malt and is lagered for an impressive three to six months.

Mack of Tromso is another major independent, based 300 kilometres inside the Arctic Circle – it's the most northerly brewery in the world. Its 4.5 per cent ABV **Pilsener** is pale gold with a pronounced vanilla/toffee aroma, hoppy in the mouth and with a tart, refreshing finish. **Ludwig** (4.7 per cent) is a wheat beer clearly inspired by the German style while **Bock-ol** has an impressive strength of 6.5 per cent. Norwegian micros include Atna, Baatbryggeriet, Hand Bryggeriet, Lervig and Trondheim.

Sweden

The Swedes are troubled more than their neighbours by anxieties over the pleasures and problems of consuming alcohol. As a result beer is taxed to the hilt, to such an extent that scores of smaller breweries have been driven out of business. Beer sold in pubs and bars cannot exceed 3.6 per cent ABV. Stronger beers can only be bought in state shops and restaurants at daunting prices. Confusingly for the consumer, and especially for visitors, beers of the same name are produced in both Class II and Class III strengths, 3.6 and 5–5.6. As in all countries that have attempted to suppress alcohol, production has been concentrated into fewer and fewer hands until there are only three breweries of size left.

The biggest by far is Pripps, founded in Gothenburg in 1828 by Albrecht Pripps. It merged with Stockholm Breweries in 1964 but retained the family name. Pripps was state-controlled for many years after the Second World War. When it was privatized it was sold, incongruously, to car maker Volvo. Predictably, it's now owned by Carlsberg, which has closed the Stockholm brewery and concentrated production at Gothenburg. Its mainstream lager is called **Pripps' Bla**, which is not a critical noise but means blue. It is a sweetish, malt-accented beer with a buttery palate and some light citric fruit in the finish. It is called **Pripps' Fatöl** when sold in draught form. Pripps brews several light lagers under different labels. The most characterful is **Royal**, an all-malt Pilsner bursting with Hallertau hops on the aroma and finish. Pripps' most interesting beers are the darker ones: a malty Munich dark called **Black & Brown**, a warm, rounded, nutty Christmas beer **Julöl**, and a coppery, hoppy **Dart**. But the stand-out beer is **Carnegie Porter**. This intriguing beer dates back to 1836 when a young Scottish brewer named David Carnegie opened a brewery in Gothenburg, one of many Scots who sought work in Scandinavia and the Baltic states. Although interest in the beer waned over the years, Pripps, to its credit, never turned its collective back on the brand.

Interest has risen in recent years and Pripps is giving it some promotion. It has launched a vintage-dated version every year that has six months' maturation in the brewery and is then bottle-matured for the same period. Although the beer is then filtered and pasteurized, it does improve slightly over time, developing what the brewers call a "port-like" note. The 3.5 per cent version is pleasant but the 5.6 one, restored in 1985 after years of abandonment, is superb with a dark malt aroma reminiscent of Dundee cake – appropriate given the origins of the founder – a cappuccino coffee palate and a finish that becomes dry with more dark malt and hops developing. It won a gold medal at Brewex, the international brewing exhibition held in 1992 in England's Burton-on-Trent, for the best foreign stout in the show: the award was given by British judges – quite an accolade.

Spendrup in the Stockholm suburbs, with splendid views over a tree-fringed lake, is the result of a merger between several old-established companies in an attempt to survive both the prohibitionist tendencies of the government and the might of Pripps. It is now part of the Royal Unibrew group of Denmark. From a handsome and traditional brewhouse it produces a malty, flavoursome **Spendrup Premium** and a **Spendrup Old Gold** of quite outstanding quality. Old Gold, in its 5.0 per cent form, has a rich malt and vanilla aroma, a quenching citric fruit palate and an intensely dry and bitter finish. It is a world-class lager beer.

Falken Breweries of Falkenberg was owned by giant agribusiness Unilver but is now part of Carlsberg. The brewery was founded in 1896 alongside a spring of natural pure water and has never moved from the spot. It uses the Anglicized spelling of Falcon for its beers, which include a **Bayer Munich Dark**, a 5 per cent ABV **Pilz** and a 3.5 per cent warm-fermented ale. Krönleins of Halmstad is an independent with close links to Prince Luitpold's brewery in Bavaria. Under licence, it produces **Kaltenberg Pils** (4.8 per cent ABV), **König Ludwig Dunkel** (5.1 per cent) and **Oktoberfest** (5.4 per cent). Nils Oscar in Stockholm is a substantial and admired micro: the beers include **Kalasol** (5.2 per cent ABV), **Amber** (5.3 per cent) and **God** (also 5.3 per cent).

Finland

The Finns are a fiercely independent people who have, to their chagrin, been ruled at various times by the Swedes and the Russians. In spite of a long period of prohibition that lasted from the turn of the century until 1932, the country has a proud brewing record that labours under the same restrictions as its Scandinavian neighbours. Beers are available in four classes and only the weakest Class I versions can be advertised.

The oldest brewery in Finland was built by a Russian, Nikolai Synebrychoff, in 1819 to produce porter and other warm-fermenting beers. By 1853 it had switched to cold-fermentation.

After the Second World War Koff Porter, one of the brewery's original beers, was reintroduced. The brewers were keen to make it in the true warm-fermenting fashion but they didn't possess an ale yeast. They claim they saved the yeast from a bottle of Dublin-brewed Guinness and made a culture which is still going strong today. **Koff Porter** is made only in the strongest Finnish bracket at 7.2 per cent and is the most powerful beer produced in the country. It is made from four malts and is hopped with German Northern Brewer and Hersbruck varieties (50 IBUs). It is conditioned in the brewery for six weeks and is then pasteurized. In common with Pripps of Sweden's Carnegie Porter, the brewery is now producing a vintage version in a fine club-shaped bottle. The company is now owned by Carlsberg.

Synebrychoff – the Finns shorten it to Koff for convenience and to mark a long-nurtured distrust of the Russians – brews a strong lager named in honour of the founder **Nikolai**, a reddish **Jouloulot Christmas beer** of around 5.0 per cent ABV and a copper-coloured ale-type beer called **Cheers**, which is cold-fermented. A 6.8 per cent **Extra Strong Export Lager** – perfumy, sweetly malty – is sold only for export and on ferries to Sweden. It is aimed at the Carlsberg Elephant market.

Hartwall has three breweries, including one in the major city of Turku and another in remote Lapland. **Lapin Kulta** is 5.3 per cent ABV, brewed from pale malt and some unmalted cereals and hopped with Hallertau and Saaz varieties. Brewing liquor comes from a fjord. The beer is lagered for an impressive six months and has a smooth malty aroma, bittersweet malt and hops in the mouth and some light citric fruit in the finish. Hartwall produces other lagers under the Aura and Karjala labels. Its most interesting brew is a **Weizen Fest** wheat beer, the only one in Finland, made to a recipe devised by Sigl of Austria and using an Austrian yeast.

The small Olvi Brewery produces a Bavarian Märzen-style beer called **Vaakuna** (5.5 per cent ABV) with a big malty aroma and palate. Hartwall is now owned by Heineken.

Great interest has been aroused in recent years by the revival of sahti, the traditional rustic beer style of Finland. The basic cereal used in sahti is rye, which gives the finished drink a tart and spicy character. Oats are also used, as is barley malt for its enzymes and husk. Hops are used sparingly, mainly for their antiseptic qualities: the main seasoning comes from juniper berries. **Sahti** was made for centuries as part of the natural way of rural life, using saunas to kiln the grains. The mash is filtered through juniper twigs and then fermented, often using the household's bread yeast.

Perhaps as part of the worldwide revival of traditional brews, several small commercial breweries in Finland are now making sahti, though they tend to use more barley malt and less rye as a result of problems of mashing with the dark, huskless grain. The Lammin Sahti Brewery is the best-known and sells the beer in a container like a wine box. It is around 8.0 per cent alcohol, has a hazy copper colour and a winey, spicy, aromatic "nose" and palate.

Iceland

Brewing was banned in Iceland until 1989 so it's not surprising that beer is in limited supply. Two companies – Egils Bjor in Reykjavik and Vifilfell in Akureyri – are predominantly soft drinks manufacturers but make some light lager beers.

SCANDINAVIAN BREWERS

P. Lauritz Aass,
PO Box 1107, Drammen, Norway 3001.

Carlsberg Brewery,
100 Vesterfaelledvej DK 1799, Copenhagen.

Falken,
Box 164, 311 22 Falkenberg.

Hansa Borg,
Kokstaddalen 3, 5061 Bergen.
Setesdalsveien 17, 4616 Kristiansand.
Per Gyntsvei 2-4, Pb.7, 1701 Sarpsborg.

Oy Hartwall AB,
PO Box 31, SF-00391 Helsinki.

Krönleins,
Bryggaregatan 7-9, 302 43 Halmstad.

Mack,
Storgata 4, 9005 Tromsö.

Pripps,
JA Pripps gata 2, Gothenburg, 400 97.

Ringnes,
Industriv. I 1, 4800 Arendal.
Postboks 7152 M, Thv. Meyers gate 2, 0307 Oslo.
Postboks 714, Strandveien 71, N-7001 Trondheim.

Royal Unibrew,
Albani Bryggerierne A/S, Tværgade 2 DK-5000 Odense C.

Faxe Bryggerie A/S,
Faxe Allé 1, DK-4640 Faxe, Zealand.

Spendrups,
Box 341 02, 100 26 Stockholm.

Synebrychoff,
Sinebrychoffinaukio 1, P.O.Box 87 04201 Kerava.

Southern Europe

Italy

The Italians have discovered beer. Or rather young Italians, concerned with "la bella figura" – life style – have decided that beer is the drink of the moment. They leave wine to their fuddy-duddy parents. In Milan and Rome there are bars and even replicas of English pubs specializing in beer. British brewers have responded by exporting enthusiastically to Italy. Other overseas brewers have moved into the Italian market by acquisition as well as exports. SABMiller has bought the once proudly independent and family-owned Peroni. Heineken owns Peroni's main rival, Moretti. Wünster, founded in the nineteenth century by a Bavarian aristocrat, Heinrich von Wünster, is also part of the giant InBev group, while Poretti belongs to Carlsberg.

Anton Dreher, the great Viennese brewer, opened a brewery in Northern Italy in the 1860s. Today a brewery bearing his name is owned by the omnipresent Heineken. While the ghost of Dreher would be less than impressed by the thinnish lagers brewed in his name he might be amused by McFarland, an attempt at a Celtic "Red Ale", which attempts to cash in on Italian interest in Scotland and its malt whiskies but which unintentionally pays homage to Dreher's "Vienna red" style. **McFarland** (5.5 per cent ABV) is cold-fermented and lacks the rounded and fruity character it seeks to emulate but the company deserves some praise for effort.

Poretti of Varese, to the north of Milan, brought some much-needed variety and innovation to the Italian beer scene with a smoked beer and a red beer. But now under Carlsberg control the emphasis is on a 5 per cent pale lager. There is greater choice from an energetic new player, Castello of Udine. The group bought the former Moretti plant when it was closed by Heineken. Castello has links with Heineken but is not a subsidiary and has freedom to develop a wide portfolio. It includes **Blond** (3.5 per cent ABV), **Blond Castle** (5 per cent), **Reserve Red** (6.2 per cent), and **Kiefer Pils** (4.5 per cent).

Some of the most characterful beers are brewed by Heineken's Moretti, now based in Bergamo. The character is due as much to the labels of the beers as to the contents of the glass. The brewery is famous for its image of a man in a fedora hat and large drooping moustache sipping a glass of beer. Moretti was founded in Udine to the north of Venice in 1859 when the region of Friuli was still annexed to the Austro-Hungarian empire. The Austrian connection lingers on in **La Rossa** – the Red – an all-malt beer of 7.5 per cent and 24 IBUs, made from pale malt and 10 per cent darker Munich malt. **La Bruna** (6.25 per cent ABV) is in the style of a Munich Dunkel, malty, smooth, with hints of roasted grain and chocolate. Moretti also has in **Sans Souci** (4.5 per cent ABV) an interpretation of the German Export style, with a firm malty body and a perfumy hop aroma. The company's main brand, **Birra Friulana**, is marketed as an "Italian Pilsner" – at least the spelling is correct – made from pale malt and 30 per cent maize (corn). A restaurant next to the brewery's offices sells in the winter an unfiltered and more aggressively hopped version of the beer called **Integrale** – whole.

Market leader Peroni, part of global giant SABMiller, has **Nastro Azzuro** – Blue Riband – as its main brand. Brewed from Alexis and Prisma pale malts, with 20 per cent maize, and hopped with Saaz, it is 5.3 per cent ABV and is lagered for 10 weeks. Peroni also brews a similar beer called **Raffo**, named after one of many breweries it has acquired. The company was founded in 1846 in Vigevano and soon moved to Rome. It has plants strategically placed throughout the country and in the 1960s it opened three state-of-the-art breweries in Bari, Rome and Padua. Its **Gran Riserva** (6.6 per cent ABV) is a pale Bock-style beer with a rich malt and hops character.

In the Italian region of South Tyrol and close to the Austrian border, the Forst (Forest) Brewery has not only labels but even its address – Lagundo/Algund – in both Italian and German. **Forst Pils** (4.8 per cent ABV) is brewed from pale malt and maize and hopped with Hallertau (30 IBUs). Forst also produces a 5.0 per cent **Forst Kronen** in the Export style and a 6.5 per cent **Forst Sixtus** made from pale, chocolate and crystal malts that – as the name implies – is in the Belgian Trappist/Abbey tradition, while **Heller Bock** (7.8 per cent ABV) is a golden beer in the German style.

Choice for beer lovers has increased with the emergence in the 1990s and twenty-first century of a number of small craft breweries, many of them no more than brewpubs. The brewers are fascinated with beer styles and create Belgian, German and even British interpretations. One of the best-known is Baladin of Piozzo, which is devoted to beers in the Belgian tradition. Many of the craft brewers are represented by an umbrella organisation, UnionBirra, and their outlets can be found on the website www.unionbirrai.com.

ITALIAN BREWERS
Baladin,
Piazza V Luglio 15, 12060 Piozzo.
Castello,
Via Enrico Fermi 42, I-33058 San Giorgio di Nogaro, Udine.
Birra Forst SpA/Brauerei Forst AG,
Via val Venosata 8, 1-39022 Lagundo.
Birra Moretti SpA,
Bergamo.
Birra Peroni Industriale SpA,
GA Guattini 6/A, 00161 Rome.

Spain and Portugal

Spain has a long association with beer. When the Romans marched through the Iberian peninsula they were impressed by local intoxicants made from soaked grain. Flemish and German members of the court of Charles V set up the first commercial Spanish breweries. The Spanish beer market was closed to outside influence during the long Franco dictatorship but now brewing groups from other countries have arrived in force to exploit the growing interest in beer among both Spaniards and the vast number of tourists.

The only major independent is Damm of Barcelona. It was founded in 1876 by Augusto R. Damm, who had learned his brewing skills in Alsace. It panders to the hordes of Germans who pour into Spain every summer with **Voll-Damm**, a 5.5 per cent lager more in the Dortmunder Export style despite the Franconian term "Voll", which is similar to a Munich Helles. There is a stronger version of **Voll-Damm** at 7.2 per cent ABV. Most of the Spanish brewers make an Extra or an Especial of around 5.0 per cent with a malty rounded character similar to a Dortmunder. Coruña's **Especial Rivera** and **Estrella Extra** are good examples, as are **Ambar Export** from Zaragoza and **Keler 18** from San Sebastian.

El Aguila – the Eagle – has had its seven breweries whittled down to four by Heineken. Its **Aguila Reserva Extra** is a powerful 6.5 per cent ABV with 28 IBUs. **Adlerbrau** is an interpretation of a Munich Dunkel, brewed from pale and caramalts with some corn grits. Northern Brewer and Brewers' Gold produce 28 IBUs. It has an estery, fruity aroma, quenching malt in the mouth and a smooth finish with hints of dark chocolate.

Aguila's everyday beer is **Aguila Pilsener** (4.5 per cent ABV), brewed from pale malt and corn grits with Northern Brewer and Brewers' Gold hops, which are Spanish varieties of German hops. The beer has 23 IBUs and is conditioned for three weeks.

San Miguel's Premium Lager (5.4 per cent ABV, 24 IBUs) is made from pale malt, with Hallertau Northern Brewer and Perle varieties plus Styrian Goldings. **Selecta XV**, also 5.4 per cent, has a fruity and hoppy aroma, with rich malt and hops in the mouth, and a long finish with good hop character. Mahou, now part of San Miguel, has a 4.7 per cent ABV **Lager** which has a pronounced malt and toffee aroma, sweet malt in the mouth and a full finish that becomes dry with some late hops developing.

In general Spanish beers suffer from short conditioning periods, which means they lack the finesse of a Northern European lager and often have yeasty, estery and grainy textures. There are a few new microbreweries, mainly based in bars. See the excellent website www.europeanbeerguide.net for further information.

Two major brewing groups dominate Portugal and, while the influence is yet again Northern European, the quality is high. Brewing records go back to the seventeenth century and there have been French, German and Danish influences since the eighteenth. But, in common with its Iberian neighbour, Portugal was shut off from the outside world during the long years of the Salazar dictatorship.

Central de Cerjevas of Lisbon brews under the Sagres label. **Sagres pale lager** is rich and malty with good hop character on the palate and finish while a brown version in the Munich Dunkel style is smooth and chocolatey. The company has also launched a warm-fermenting beer known incongruously as **Bohemia**, which with its fruity and hoppy character is more akin to Belgium than the home of golden Pilsners. When Portugal joined the European Union, Sagres launched **Sagres Europa**, a firm-bodied, malt-accented, 5.4 per cent Dortmunder-style lager.

Unicer in Oporto was nationalized until 1991, since when it has gone into partnership with Carlsberg of Denmark. Its everyday lager, broadly in the international Pils style, is malty and quenching. A 5.8 per cent **Unicer Superbock** is yet another curious interpretation of practices further north.

Greece

The Greek brewing industry has been virtually wiped out as a result of opening its door to foreign groups. The only Greek brewery of any size or influence, Fix, went out of business in 1984. It was owned by the Greek Minister of Defence and when his political fortunes waned his brewery followed him into extinction.

The market is now dominated by Heineken, which brews both Heineken and Amstel locally. Henninger Hellas was created by the German Henninger group but has been bought by Carlsberg, which plans to concentrate on Kronenbourg. Löwenbräu has built a brewery under the name of Löwenbräu Hellas to promote a Greek version of the Munich beers.

In the north of the country, **Aegean** produces a 5.0 per cent lager with a sweet malty aroma, pronounced toffee on the palate and a bittersweet finish. To English speakers, the term "Hellas" has a certain poignancy when surveying Greek beer. The country had its own Purity Law, which meant the beers were all malt, but this has been abandoned under pressure from foreign brewers. It is a pity there is so little ethnic interest.

Malta

Malta has long been independent but a benign British influence hovers over the beers of the George Cross island. The Farson's Brewery produces lagers under the Cisk name but is best known for its ales. These include a well-hopped **Hop Leaf** pale ale (1040 degrees – the brewery still endearingly declares strength by original gravity), a stronger **Brewer's Choice** (1050), fruity and hoppy, a mild **Blue Label** (1039) and a genuine **Milk Stout** (1045; 3.4 ABV), brewed with lactose (milk sugar) to give a rounded, creamy, slightly sweet palate and a surprisingly dry finish with hints of dark fruit and chocolate. The malts are pale, mild and crystal with some caramel and have a respectable 30 IBUs. The stout is called **Lacto** and carries the claim "Milk Stout with Vitamin B for Extra Energy" – the island has yet to meet Environmental Health Officers. Malta is a beery time warp and Southern Europe could do with a few more of them.

SOUTHERN EUROPEAN BREWERIES

Central de Cerjevas,
Estrada da Alfarrobeira - Apartado 15, 2626–851 Vialonga, Lisbon, Portugal.

Heineken Espana,
Carretera Córdoba, 23005 Jaén, Spain.
Avenida de Andalucía 1 s/n, 41007 Sevilla, Spain.
Carretera Nacional num. III Km. 338, Cuart de Poblet, Valencia, Spain.

Damm,
Rosello 515, 08025 Barcelona, Spain.

Mahou-San Miguel,
Compte DUrgel, 240-8°, 08036 Barcelona.
Paseo Imperial 32, 28005 Madrid.

Simonds, Farsons Cisk
The Brewery, Mriehel, Malta GC.

Unicer,
Via Norte – Leça do Balio
Matosinhos, Apartado 1044, 4466–955
S. Mamede de Infesta, Oporto, Portugal.

Switzerland

Not surprisingly, it is the German region or canton of Switzerland that has the best beer traditions. It was in this canton that an Irish Benedictine monk called St Gall built an abbey in the seventh century, which over time developed several brewhouses. St Gall, who brought learning and Christianity from Ireland to Europe, is considered to be the founder of Swiss brewing and the town where his abbey stood is named St Gallen in his honour.

In modern times the Swiss government has attempted to stop monopolies in brewing appearing by restricting breweries to their cantons of origin. But the system fell apart in the early 1990s when the leading Swiss brewer Feldschlössen signed a trading agreement with Kronenbourg-BSN of France, then merged with the Cardinal group before falling into the cold embrace of Carlsberg. Carlsberg now enjoys close to 50 per cent of the Swiss market, while Heineken has become a major player through its acquisition of Calanda and Chur. The Swiss market is now wide open and the result is likely to be a rapid fall in the number of 30 breweries.

Feldschlössen

The most remarkable aspect of the Feldschlössen beers is the brewery, whose name means "Castle in the Field". It is a former chemicals factory near Basel, set in rolling and verdant grounds, designed, as the name indicates, like a castle. The magnificent interior has a stained glass window that incorporates a picture of the founder Théophil Roninger who had worked in German breweries before launching his own in 1874. The brewhouse is a symphony of burnished copper set on marble floors, the plaster ceiling supported by marble pillars. After all this inspirational architecture, the beers are rather less than dramatic. The 5.2 per cent **Hopfenperle** has some light fruitiness on the aroma along with a delicate hop presence, is lightly malty in the mouth, and with a finish that becomes dry with tart hoppiness. A version of the beer using darker malts is called **Dunkleperle** while the castellated brewery is commemorated by a stronger, maltier **Castello**.

Hürlimann

Hürlimann of Zürich was the country's most energetic exporter and was best-known for the world's strongest beer, **Samichlaus** – Santa Claus. The 14.0 per cent beer was made possible by the brewery's long association with the cultivation of pure yeast strains. Hürlimann was founded in 1865 by Albert Hürlimann – his father had started a brewery in the family's name in 1836 but had gone out of business. The move to cold fermentation for lager beers demanded a more scientific knowledge of the workings of yeast and Hürlimann became a world leader in developing specific strains that would work at the fermenting and conditioning temperatures required for different types of beer. The major problem with producing strong beers is that the yeast is eventually overwhelmed by the alcohol it produces: the yeast "goes to sleep", brewers say. Hürlimann tackled this problem and produced a strain of yeast that could ferment beer to a high level of alcohol. In 1979 it used the yeast to brew a strong Christmas beer as an experiment. The interest created by the beer encouraged the brewery to make it every year and in 1982 it was given the accolade of the strongest beer in the world by *The Guinness Book of Records*, much to the chagrin, no doubt, of EKU in Germany.

Sadly, this rich tradition disappeared in the late 1990s when Hürlimann was bought by Feldschlössen, which announced it planned to discontinue Samichlaus. The last batch appeared for Christmas 1998. After a break of a few years, beer lovers were delighted to hear that Samichlaus had been restored by Schloss Eggenberg in Austria – *see Schloss Eggenberg entry*.

Smaller breweries that have managed to stay free from global

Switzerland

takeover include Adler of Schwanden, which produces a 4.5 per
cent ABV **Hell** and **Spezial Hell** at 4.8 per cent. Baar, in the town
of the same name, was founded in 1862 and remains family-
owned. The German-style range includes **Hell** (4.8 per cent ABV),
Dunkel (4.8 per cent) and **Spezial** (5.2 per cent).

Falken of Schaffhausen is an impressively old brewery, founded in
1799. The beers include **Hell** and **Dunkel** (both 4.8 per cent ABV),
Spezial (5.2 per cent), a dark lager called – suitably – **Schwarz** (5.2
per cent) and a **Weizen**, also 5.2 per cent. Falken brews seasonal Bocks
and, to prove it's not living in the past, **First Cool**, an undemanding
light lager of 4.5 per cent ABV, aimed at younger drinkers.

In the French-speaking Lausanne region, Bière du Boxer dates
from 1960 and offers a Franco-German range that includes **Gold**
(4 per cent ABV), **Old Spezial** (5.2 per cent), a dark lager called
Brunette (5.2 per cent) and **La Forte**, which means strong and
has both a strength of 8 per cent and a 90-day lagering time to
back up the name.

Cardinal, now owned by Carlsberg, in Fribourg has a 4.9 per
cent Helles or pale lager that carries the brewery name and **Anker**,
a dark and top-fermenting beer in the German Alt tradition (5.8
per cent ABV). Cardinal was founded in 1788 and was substantially rebuilt in 1877 when it was bought by the renowned watch-
maker Paul-Alcide Blancpain, who may have some connection
with the French Blancpain who settled in England and became
Whitebread or Whitbread. The brewery's strong **Rheingold** (6.3
per cent ABV) is malty and perfumy, firm-bodied and with a big
and complex malt-and-hops finish.

Heineken's Calanda of Chur, Frauenfeld in the town of the
same name, and the Ueli Brewery in Basel all produce wheat beers
in the Bavarian style. Ueli is a micro based in the Fischerstübe beer
restaurant at Rheingasse 4, founded in 1974 by Hans Nidecker
with the help of a member of the German Binding brewing
family. Ueli means jester but the beers are serious without being

pompous: a delicate, clean, refreshing lager, a 3.5 per cent **Dunkel** with heavy malt and toffee notes, a tart, aromatic, spicy 4.0 per cent **Weizenbier** and a pale **Reverenz**, also 4.0 per cent. The restaurant specializes in dishes cooked with beer.

SWISS BREWERS

Adler,
Hauptstrasse 34, 8762 Schwanden.

Baar
Langgasse 41, 6340 Baal.

Calanda,
Kasernenstrasse 36, 7007 Chur.

Bière du Boxer SA,
route. d'Echallens 32, 1032 Romanel sur Lausanne.

Brasserie du Cardinal,
Passage du Cardinal, 1700 Fribourg.

Braueriei Falken AG,
Brauereistrasse 1, 8201, Schaffausen.

Feldschlössen Getränke AG,
Theophil-Roningerstrasse Postfach 4310 Rheinfelden.

Hürlimann (Löwenbräu),
Brandschenkestrasse 150, 8002 Zurich.

Ueli Brewery,
Fischerstübe Restaurant, Rheingasse 4, Basel.

Beers from the Americas

The first beers in both North and Latin America were native brews using cereals from the fields and plants from the ground or jungle. In North America, English settlers brought an ale culture with them, while the second wave of immigrants from central Europe rapidly spread the lager message. As a result of Prohibition and the Great Depression of the 1930s, a handful of brewers came to dominate the American market with thin versions of the lager style. But now a renaissance led by small craft brewers has resulted in both ales and lagers of great quality becoming available. In Latin America, Spanish, German and even Austrian influences have developed some good examples of the Pilsner and Vienna styles, as well as some bland international brands. The Caribbean's beers range from thin lagers to high-quality Pils-style beers and – as a legacy from colonial times – some fine dry and sweet stouts.

United States of America

The most profound and exhilarating changes have transformed the beer scene in the USA. Some 1,200 craft breweries have brought much-needed choice and diversity to a country for too long dominated by bland lagers. The growth of the craft brewing sector has been phenomenal: yearly growth of 10 and 11 per cent has given it a 10 per cent share of the world's biggest beer market and forced the brewing giants to rethink their policies.

The major brewing cities and regions of the USA

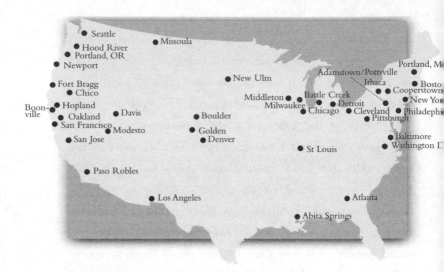

UNITED STATES	**Davis, CA**	Pabst Brewing	**Pittsburgh, PA**
Abita Spings, LA	Hübst Sudwerk	**Missoula, MT**	Penn Brewery
Abita Brewing	Privatbrauerei	Bayern Brewing	**Portland, ME**
Adamstown, PA	**Denver, CO**	**Modesto, CA**	Allagash Brewing
Stoudt's Brewing	Blue Moon Brewing	St Stan's Brewing	D. L. Geary Brewing
Atlanta, GA	Wynkoop Brewing	**New Ulm, MN**	Shipyard Brewing
Atlanta Brewing	**Detroit, MI**	August Schell Brewing	**Portland, OR**
Baltimore, MD	Stroh Brewery	**New York, NY**	BridgePort Brewpub
Clipper City Brewing	**Dublin, CA**	Brooklyn Brewery	Hopworks Brewery
Battle Creek, MI	*Lyons Brewery*	*American Festival Café*	Portland Brewing
Arcadia Brewing	**Fort Bragg, CA**	*Bohemian Hall Beer and*	**Pottsville, PA**
Boonville, PA	North Coast Brewing	*Garden*	D.G. Yuengling & Son
Anderson Valley	**Golden, CO**	*Brewsky's*	**St Louis, MO**
Boston, MA	Coors Brewing	*Fraunce's Tavern*	Anheuser-Busch
Atlantic Coast Brewing	**Hood River, OR**	*Jimmy Armstrong's Bar*	**San Francisco, CA**
Boston Beer	Full Sail Brewing	*Peculier Pub*	Anchor Brewing
Bull & Finch	**Hopland, OR**	*Peter's Waterfront Ale*	*San Francisco Brewpub*
Doyle's	Mendocino Brewing	*House*	*20 Tank*
Boulder, CO	**Ithaca, NY**	*Peter Doelger's*	*Marin Brewing*
Avery Brewing	Ithaca Beer	*Zip City*	**San Jose, CA**
Boulder Beer	**Juneau, AK**	**Newport, OR**	Gordon Biersch
Chicago, IL	Alaskan Brewing	Rogue Ales	**Seattle, WA**
Goose Island	**Middleton, WI**	**Oakland, CA**	Pike Place Brewery
Chico, CA	Capital Brewery	Pacific Coast Brewery	**Washington DC**
Sierra Nevada Brewing	**Los Angeles, CA**	**Paso Robles, CA**	*Brickseller*
Cleveland, OH	*Gorky's*	Firestone Walker	**Woodinville, WA**
Great Lakes Brewing	**Milwaukee, WI**	**Philadelphia, PA**	Redhook Brewery
Cooperstown, NY	Lakefront Brewery Inc	Dock Street Brewery	
Brewery Ommegang	Miller Brewing		

Before the rise of the revivalists, it was a remarkable fact that, in a country that lauds the free market, brewing was concentrated to an astonishing degree. More than 90 per cent of all beer sales were controlled by just a handful of producers, the biggest of which accounted for almost half the beer brewed. But dramatic change has transformed the beer scene. As well as the rise of craft brewers, global producers from outside the US have had the temerity to challenge and take over the once all-powerful giants. The unthinkable has happened. Anheuser-Busch, producer of Budweiser, the world's biggest beer brand, is now owned by a Belgian and Brazilian conglomerate with the ungainly name of InBev while Miller now resides under an equally clumsy title, SABMiller. SAB stands for South African Breweries but the group is registered in London and trades on the British Stock Exchange. The brewing eagles' wings have been well and truly clipped.

Nevertheless, it would be a mistake to assume that visitors to the United States will find craft beers in every bar. Bland and watery lagers still abound thanks to the awesome power of the big brewers. It's illegal to both brew and retail beer in the US. As a result, the national brewers have long-standing arrangements with distribution companies to sell their beers – and no one else's. Senator John McCain, the unsuccessful Republican candidate for the presidency in 2008, lives in some style in several mansions with a fleet of expensive cars due to the fact that his wife is the heiress to a fortune made by distributing beer. You can see how the dollars mount up when you consider that Budweiser's owner, A-B InBev, formerly Anheuser-Busch, makes more than 90 million barrels of beer a year.

American beer for several centuries was locked into a culture and economy that had to grow, compress, rush and cut corners in order to catch up with the rest of the industrialized world. Other great brewing nations – Britain at first, then Ireland, Germany, Bohemia and the Netherlands – brought their styles and the ability to make them to the New World. But Americans applauded when Henry Ford declared that history was "bunk" and those pioneering styles were ignored, denied and subsumed by mass-produced and massively promoted pale lagers that were once from the European mould but have long lost any authenticity or credibility. The familiar American cry "Let's have a cold one" suggests that aroma and flavour are not high on the agenda of the average beer drinker. There's a cynical saying in the brewing industry that "people drink the advertising". It's as true of the perpetrators as it is of the recipients. If you call your main product "the King of Beers", you'd better believe it or the whole corporate structure falls apart like castles built of sand.

But, slowly from the 1960s, and now with gathering speed, a counter-culture has developed. Alongside the everyday beers there is now a remarkable surge of small breweries dedicated to the consumer rather than the production chart. Beers rich in choice and heritage are available, some based on long-forgotten but indigenous styles, others that look to Europe for their inspiration. There's a pleasing irony in the fact that, while many European brewers now ape the American giants by neutering their beers of flavour, the new wave of American craft brewers is rediscovering the joys of the barley corn and hop flower. If you fancy a juicy Märzen, a warming Bock, a roasty stout, a chocolaty porter, or an India Pale Ale so hoppy your eyeballs pop, then the United States is the place to drink. It's a counter-culture that points to a country at ease with itself. Conformity in beer drinking was a bi-product of an immigrant nation in which people were not anxious to over-stress their Dutch, German or Italian roots. They ate and drank "all-American" products. Now that pasta and Pilsner are no longer seen as a threat to the American way of life, a thousand beers can flourish.

The market share of the craft brewers grew from 2 per cent at the turn of the century to around 10 per cent by 2009. That proportion will continue to increase but the craft brewers don't aim to supersede the national giants. That's not the aim of the operation. They are not planning to muscle in on the big producers' sectors. In a country where packaged beer for home consumption accounts for around 80 per cent of sales, the smaller producers are offering a specialist product unashamedly aimed at those prepared to pay a dollar more for a beer than those who pack the supermarket trolleys high with Bud or Miller Lite.

Prohibition is another facet of the American beer story. At a time when many European governments and their advisers call for greater restrictions on the availability of alcohol to counter "binge drinking" by a tiny but vociferous minority, it's worth considering the implications of such policies. While the right to manufacture and sell alcohol was restored in 1933 after 13 years of illegality, the shadow of this frightening period – when bootleg liquor was in the hands of the Mob, hung over the brewing industry for many decades. Only the biggest brewers survived Prohibition, able to make a living from soft, drinks, yeast production and ice cream. Thousands gave up the ghost and more followed during the Depression of the 1930s. Brooklyn, once the greatest brewing borough in the whole country thanks to its Dutch settlers, lost all its producers. With a mass market to themselves, the giants went for the hard sell and the soft option of national brands. The country lost much of its regional diversity and traditional beer styles. In particular, it lost its ales.

Brewing existed in North America before the first settlers. The Indians and Mexicans made porridge-type beers, quickly produced and spiced with herbs and plants. When the British arrived on the East Coast they began to brew to keep their communities healthy as well as happy. Brewers from the old country were cajoled into joining the settlers in the New World. They brought with them ale yeasts while farmers grew barley and other cereals and began to nurture a hop industry. As in Europe, beer-making moved out of the home and hearth and into specialist factories. The first commercial brewery was set up in New Amsterdam (now New York City) in 1623. Ale, porter and stock ale – a strong, long-matured beer similar to old or stale in England – were the staple products of the first brewers. George Washington brewed his own ale at Mount Vernon. Thomas Jefferson was a brewer and his recipe at Monticello has been preserved. Another of the great American revolutionaries, Samuel Adams in Boston, was a significant brewer as well as one of the organisers of the Boston Tea Party that signalled mass opposition to British rule and taxation. He is now immortalized by a modern brewery in Boston that bears his name.

From 1840 the beer scene changed dramatically and fundamentally. The second wave of immigrants, a vast army of central Europeans, turned their backs on despotism, unemployment and the drudgery of semi-feudal rural life and moved to the New World. Many brought with them the skills and the thirst to make the new cold-fermented beers developed in Munich, Pilsen and Vienna. Lager brewing established itself rapidly and the Germanic influence can be seen in such famous names as Anheuser and Busch, Heilemann, Miller (originally Müller), Pabst, Schlitz and Stroh. Samuel Adams in Boston may commemorate a great American patriot but the owner is Jim Koch, descendant of German immigrant brewers, though to avoid bringing a blush to American cheeks he delicately pronounces it "Cook".

The British settlers were no match for the central Europeans. Determined to stamp their mark on the New World, they grasped all the technologies made possible by the Industrial Revolution to produce beer in enormous quantities. They used the railroad to speed their products outside their home bases and they signed Faustian pacts with the new service industries of marketing and advertising to tell the American people their beers were the best, the greatest, the kings. By the dawn of the twentieth century, there were 4,000 American breweries. Before the marketing men took over with a mission to turn beer into a commodity, those breweries served cities, towns and neighbourhoods with a vast range of styles.

The triple attacks of Prohibition, the Great Depression and the mass-market mentality caused such havoc that by the 1980s just six national giants and 20 independent regional brewers remained. It has been the enthusiasm of the craft brewers that has restored choice and style – in every sense of the word – to the American beer scene. Charles Finkel, founder of Pike Place Brewery in Seattle, says: "It's not a beer revolution, it's a renaissance. We're going back beyond Prohibition and the second wave of immigrants with their lager culture to the Founding Fathers. Americans are going back to their roots."

Note: American brewers are not required by law to state the strength of their beers. A growing number do but in some cases we are not able to give beer strength.

The giants

No study of world beer is complete without looking at the remarkable Anheuser-Busch empire that brews the biggest beer brand ever known. Its origins lie in St Louis, Missouri, significantly at the heart of Middle America. With the advent of the railroad, a far-sighted brewer in St Louis could send beer across the Rockies to the West Coast, down the Mississippi river to the South, up to the Great Lakes and Chicago in the North, and to the burgeoning cities of the East. It was the genius of Adolphus Busch to seize these opportunities. On a vaster scale, he followed in the footsteps of Arthur Guinness and William Bass by building national brands while others were content to stay loyal to their localities.

In 1861 Eberhard Anheuser bought a failed brewery in St Louis from a fellow German, George Schneider. Anheuser was born in 1805 in Kreuznach in the German Rhineland. He moved to the United States in 1843 and settled first in Cincinnati but then moved to St Louis. He had trained as a soap manufacturer and became first general manager and a partner in a soap business called Schaffer, Anheuser & Co. He moved into brewing courtesy of Herr Schneider and when Anheuser died in 1880 at the age of 75 his brewing business had become one of the biggest in the country. Among the many tributes to him was a lengthy obituary in a German language paper published for German-Americans, *Anzeiger des Westens*.

In 1861, Adolphus Busch married Eberhard's daughter Lilly Anheuser. Three years later he joined his father-in-law at the Anheuser Bavarian Brewery. Busch was born in 1839 in Kastel, near Mainz, in the Hesse region of Germany, the son of an inn-keeper. He arrived in America in 1857 and reached St Louis, via New Orleans and the Mississippi. He worked on the riverfront as a clerk and gradually made his way into business until he owned a successful wholeselling company. Five years after joining Anheuser, Busch bought the half-share in the Bavarian Brewery owned by William D'Oench, who retired back to Stuttgart, and became a full partner in the company. In 1879 the Bavarian name was dropped and the company became Anheuser-Busch Brewing. When Anheuser died, Busch became president and the company remained in his family, until it was bought by InBev in 2008. A-B has plants carefully placed in all the key parts of the union: Newark, New Jersey; Los Angeles; Tampa, Florida; Houston, Texas; Columbus, Ohio; Jacksonville, Florida; Merrimack, New Hampshire; Williamsburg, Virginia; Fairfield, California; Baldwinville, New York State; Fort Collins, Colorado; and Cartersville, Georgia.

Adolphus Busch had a flair for marketing. He grasped the opportunities for selling beer outside its city of origin, using the new means of transport at his disposal. Ice-making and refrigeration made not only cold fermentation possible on a commercial scale but enabled beer to be transported in refrigerated trucks by rail and road. Busch also recognized that commercial success would come from producing a type of beer acceptable to the great bulk of Americans, not just those of German origin used to the dark and heavy Bavarian style.

Encouraged by Anheuser, Busch travelled widely in Europe in the late 1860s and early 1870s, concentrating on Bavaria and Bohemia. He closely studied the brewing process in Pilsen, but knew that Pilsen-style beers were already being made extensively elsewhere in Europe and in parts of the United States, especially in Michigan and Wisconsin. He wanted something different and he found it in Budweis. This small town in southern Bohemia was a brewing legend. For centuries, the quality of its beers – called generically, in the German fashion, Budweisers – had made them popular at the Bohemian court to such an extent that they were known as "the beer of kings". The marketing appeal of such a noble title was not lost on Busch. He enjoyed, too, the style of beer, maltier and less aggressively hopped than Pilsner, and with a delicate hint of tart fruit.

While he was in Europe, Busch became acquainted with the work of Louis Pasteur on yeast propagation and the heat treatment called "pasteurization" that prevented beer being attacked by bacteria, giving it a longer shelf life. Busch's experience coalesced into a determination to make a pale, golden lager with a soft and appealing palate, pasteurized to withstand long journeys throughout the United States. It's not known whether he took any Budweis yeast back with him but he did introduce European two-row barley to his adopted country. It's a variety that produces a sweeter beer than the native six-row. He also picked up the Franconian habit in northern Bavaria of maturing and clarifying beer over a bed of beechwood chips. Adopted by Busch, the method was to become an important though largely irrelevant element of the Budweiser myth.

Back in St Louis, Busch put his plans into action. He called in Carl Conrad, a St Louis wine merchant and restaurateur, to help him develop a beer that, in his own words, "would be acceptable to all tastes – a beer lighter in colour and with a more delicate taste than Pilsner beer". It is claimed that after much thought, Busch chose Budweiser as the name for this new "national beer", because it had a slightly Germanic sound, but was easily pronounced by Americans of different origins. Busch also claimed that, as no other American brewery was using the title, he could not be accused of passing-off or copying an existing brand. Budweiser was launched in 1876. It was not an overnight success. Until the turn of the century, A-B's leading beer was called St Louis Lager Beer. It also had a second beer with the extravagant name of Anheuser-Busch St Louis White Label Pilsener Exquisite. If the company's own description is anything to go by ("it combines all the virtues of the European Pilsener – the excellent aroma of hops; the strengthening, pure taste of malt; the clear Rhine Wine color, the small-beaded, creamy, white-as-snow foam which covers the last drop left in the glass"), it must have been quite a beer.

But sales of Budweiser climbed in step with the growth of the company. In 1870, A-B was producing a modest 18,000 barrels a year. By 1901 it had passed the million-barrel mark. Budweiser was now the flagship brand and it had been joined in 1896 by a "super premium" called Michelob, which also took its name from a Bohemian town (it's pronounced with a hard "ch": Mickelob). A-B had gone national and such local and regional specialities as a Munchener, an Erlanger (Märzen), a Bock and an Old Burgundy barley wine fell by the wayside.

By the 1890s, Budweiser was promoted as the "King of Beers" and the "Original Budweiser". The first claim is devoid of meaning: who crowned it? And by no stretch of the imagination could it claim to be original, for the beers beloved of the Bohemian court were called Budweiser and the Burghers' Brewery founded there in 1795 used the term long before A-B. When the Czech Joint Stock Brewery – the first name for Budweiser Budvar – was formed in 1895, it exported to the US using the name Budweiser Aktienbier. But its sales in North America were thwarted by a series of legal actions brought by A-B.

The A-B catalogue for 1899, with a charming naivety, described its Budweiser as a "pale and innocuous beverage". The company claims today that the recipe for the beer has never changed in its long history. That is remarkable, for few beers have never been "tweaked", to use a brewer's term. New varieties of malt and hops appear in every generation and brewers are always experimenting to improve the aroma, flavour and colour of their brews. If the A-B claim is true, it means that from the outset the company used substantial amounts of rice as an adjunct to barley. Rice is listed before barley malt on the label of the modern beer and is thought to account for between 30 and 40 per cent of the grist. Yet the first labels for the beer in the nineteenth century said, in German, that it was brewed from the finest Bohemian malt and Saaz hops, with no mention of rice. All the big American brewers use substantial amounts of unmalted adjuncts, usually corn (maize) rather than rice. This is because the high levels of enzymes in native six-row barley can convert the starches in unmalted grains as well as in the malt. In the case of rice, it's cooked to break down the cell walls and then added to the mash, where the malt enzymes add rice's sugars to the wort. Rice is a useful adjunct if the aim is an exceptionally pale beer with a light flavour.

Budweiser is brewed from a blend of two-row and six-row pale malts and rice. The hops are both American and European varieties and are used as whole flowers. A single decoction mash is used and the beer lagered for a maximum of a month – 21 days is usual. The beer has a starting gravity of 1044 degrees and a finished alcohol by volume of 4.8 per cent: it's well attenuated or fully brewed-out, with few malt sugars left behind. In spite of the careful choice of hops and their skilful blending, the units of bitterness range between 10 and 12 (Budweiser Budvar has 20 units). With such a low level of malt, too high a hop rate would overpower the flavour. During maturation, strips of beechwood, about a foot long and a couple of inches wide, are placed in the conditioning tanks where they attract yeast particles. During lagering, the beer is kräusened by adding a portion of partially fermented wort to the beer to encourage a second fermentation. The finished beer has no discernible aroma, a light, clean, quenching palate and a short finish. The brewery calls the finish "fast", which says it all. Even these characteristics are masked by a house rule that the beer must served at 42° Fahrenheit/6°C. When the beer warms up there is the faintest hint of apple fruit.

The premium **Michelob** (4.8 per cent ABV; 10 IBUs) has a similar specification to Budweiser but a lower rice ratio. As a result it has a pleasant malt aroma and palate, and a smooth finish with a hint of hop. There are several Budweiser and Michelob spin-offs from the main brand, including **Bud Lite** and **Dry** and **Michelob Lite** and **Dry**. But from the late 1990s and accelerating in the new century, A-B launched a new range of beers that recognised that sales of its main brands were in slight decline and that a new generation of consumers wanted to drink more than the advertising and packaging. The range includes **American Ale** (5.3 per cent ABV), an amber beer with a good dash of crystal malt and Cascade hops and, all under the Michelob name, **Amber Bock**, an all-malt brew with 19 bitterness units, mahogany colour and Hallertau and Strisselspalt hops; **Dunkel Weisse** dark wheat beer brewed with pale, wheat and chocolate malts and Hallertau and Tettnang hops; **Irish Red Ale** with 25 bitterness units from Cascade and Willamette hops; a **Märzen** in the Oktoberfest style, copper-red, with 20 bitterness units from Hallertau hops; **Pale Ale** (3.9 per cent) "brewed in the English style" with a resounding 37 units of bitterness from Cascade, Hallertau and Saaz varieties, with a floral and citrus character; and a 3.6 per cent **Porter**, brewed with pale, crystal and chocolate malts and hopped with Cascade, Willamette and Saaz. It's not known whether the ales are properly warm fermented but the levels of malt and hops must have shocked not only drinkers but also suppliers of rice and hops to Anheuser-Busch.

Whether this range will survive the takeover in 2008 by InBev remains to be seen. It was the biggest takeover in brewing history and created the world's biggest brewer. Perhaps the most surprising aspect of the takeover was the weak fight put up by the Busch family. They may have become even more fabulously wealthy as a result but their passion and commitment to brewing went missing. A top manager at Budweiser Budvar told me in 2009: "Anheuser-Busch was my enemy but I respected the company as it was run by brewers. With InBev I am faced by accountants." And accountants have little interest in quality and tradition: their commitment is to the "bottom line".

Life for the other national brewers has been no less turbulent. Several once-famous names have disappeared and there has been a series of major mergers. The second biggest brewing group in the US, Miller of Milwaukee, had a slower rise to fortune than Anheuser-Busch. It was founded in 1855 as Charles Best's Plank Road Brewery and was bought by Frederic Miller, who turned it into one of the region's major brewers. In 1965 it was in eleventh place in the national pecking order but in 1969 Miller became part of the Philip Morris tobacco group, which began aggressively to build the brewery's market share. For years, the company's flagship brand had been **Miller High Life** (4.67 per cent ABV), a pale lager that pre-dated Prohibition. Under Morris's tutelage, the company launched **Miller Lite** (4.18 per cent), one of the first low-calorie beers. Fully brewed-out to turn the maximum amount of sugar into alcohol, light beers appealed to Americans concerned by health and expanding waistbands. Miller Lite was an enormous success though this "fine Pilsner beer brewed from the finest ingredients" had to undergo some rapid changes in the 1980s when the company was charged by the Center for Science in the Public Interest of using foam enhancer, propylene glycol alginate, chill-proofing the beer with papain, using amyloglucosidase to speed up starch conversion and preserving the finished beer with potassium metabisulphite. Miller said it stopped using all chemical aids in the beer. The shock waves caused other large brewers to take greater care with the ingredients they used.

Miller improved its image in the late 1980s with **Miller Genuine Draft** (4.67 per cent ABV), a dark golden beer that, despite its name, comes only in bottled form. It uses the Japanese system of cold filtering, rather than pasteurization, to enhance aroma and flavour. It added some new products, including **Red Lager** and **Genuine Bock**, when it bought the Jacob Leinenkugel Brewery of Chippewa Falls, Wisconsin, founded in 1867. Then in 2002, Miller was bought by South African Breweries, and became SABMiller, a global giant, with head offices in London. Further concentration took place in 2007 when the American operations of Coors and Miller were merged. SAB owns 58 per cent of the new company, the remaining 42 per cent going to Coors. Part of the deal excludes Miller operating in Canada, where Coors merged with Molson in 2004. Coors and SABMiller operate as independent companies in the rest of the world.

Adolph Coors of Golden, Colorado, until the merger mania of the early twenty-first century, was fiercely independent, the third biggest brewer in the United States. As a result of its isolated base high in the Rockies, it's often dismissed as the Mr Nobody of American brewing. But it runs the single biggest brewing plant in the country, producing some 20 million barrels a year. The site was chosen by Adolph Coors in 1873 because of its easy access to the fine spring waters from the Rockies: the company makes great play of the quality of its water. Locked in its mountain fastness, Coors is as famous for its corporate and political conservatism – it staunchly supports the Republican Party, finances right-wing think-tanks and fought long and hard against trade union recognition – as it is for its beer.

The Golden Brewery is magnificent to look at, packed with burnished copper vessels. Enormous care is taken in choosing the finest ingredients. Coors owns its own barley fields and hop gardens. Its beers are a blend of pale malted barley and cereal adjuncts, along with whole hops. The finished products have the minimum of taste and character. Drinkers could be forgiven for thinking the acclaimed Rocky Mountain water was the most memorable characteristic. Since 1874 its flagship brand has been Coors **Banquet**, also known as **Original** (5.0 per cent ABV). **Coors Light** (4.2 per cent) is a pale shadow of even the thin-tasting Original. In recent years, Coors has recognized the changing nature of the American beer market and has introduced **Killian's Irish Red** (4.9 per cent) and **Blue Moon** (5.4 per cent), a Belgian-style wheat beer. Killian's started life as a genuine Irish ale but moved to France where Pelforth turned it into an amber-red lager. Coors now owns the brand. Blue Moon is a surprisingly full-tasting beer in the Belgian white beer tradition: the company ran into trouble when it first launched the beer in the 1990s, labelled a "Belgian wheat beer" and now calls it "Belgian-style". It's brewed in the Belgian tradition with barley malt, wheat malt and oats and, along with hops, is spiced with coriander and orange peel. In order not to shock its core base of drinkers, there is no mention of Coors on the label. The beer is brewed by the Blue Moon Brewing Company, using a small Coors' plant in Denver. It's thought some production may be based at Molson in Canada.

In 1987 Coors opened a second brewery in the Shenandoah Valley near Elton, Virginia. The group makes much of the fact that, in the wake of the Miller Lite furore, it brews without preservatives and additives. It does not pasteurize its beers, preferring to sterile-filter them.

Stroh of Detroit became the fourth biggest American brewing group by taking over one of the most famous names in beer, Schlitz. The fall of Schlitz, with the renowned slogan "the beer that made Milwaukee famous", is testimony to the fact that you can fool some of the drinkers some of the time but not all the drinkers all of the time. Schlitz was founded in 1849 and grew until at one stage it challenged Anheuser-Busch in size. Disaster struck Schlitz in the 1970s. It attempted to undercut its national rivals by reducing the barley and hop content of its brews, saving 50 cents on each barrel brewed. In order to give the beers shelf-life and a foaming head, Schlitz replaced a silica-gel containing enzymes with a stabilizer called Chillgarde. Unfortunately for Schlitz, Chillgarde reacted with another ingredient called Kelcoloid, a foam stabilizer. As a result the beers, lacking natural malt proteins to give a good natural head went, according to one wholesaler, "as flat as apple cider". Schlitz's sales nose-dived and in 1982 the company was saved from extinction when it was bought by Stroh. Stroh had been founded in Detroit in 1850 by Bernard Stroh, whose family came from Kirn in the German Rhineland. Bernard brewed "Bohemian" in the Pilsner style and adopted the European fashion of heating the brew kettles by direct flame. The method encourages what brewers call "a good rolling boil" to extract the maximum aroma and flavour from the hops. It also causes a slight caramelization of the malt sugars, which leaves a distinctive port-wine note in the beer. This was most evident in Stroh's **Signature** (4.84 per cent ABV). It moved into more flavoursome beers using the Augsburger title with such brands as **Golden** (4.93 per cent) and **Weiss**, a wheat beer with some fruitiness.

In 1996, Stroh bought another American giant, Heileman, for 290 million dollars. Heileman was founded in La Crosse, Wisconsin, in 1858 and along the way bought a number of well-known brewing companies, including Blitz of Oregon, Henry Weinhard, Rainier of Seattle and Lone Star, the famous Texan beer. Heileman's beers were thin in the extreme and it became famous – or perhaps infamous – for **Colt 45**, a "malt liquor" consumed mainly by people who prefer to keep their beer cans hidden inside paper bags and drink them on park benches. In the 1980s Heileman had the misfortune to lose control to the Australian business tycoon Alan Bond. When Bond's empire, which stretched from Australasia to Asia and central Europe, crashed – with Bond serving a stretch in prison – the Heileman brands were bought by Pabst, which in 1999 divested some of the former Heileman beers to Miller. Pabst now owns Colt 45, Schlitz and Old Milwaukee while Miller has the Henry Weinhard brands and a malt liquor with the risible name of **Mickey's**. Is this aimed at talking mice with a drink problem?

Pabst, another Germanic giant of Milwaukee, was the biggest brewer in the United States at the turn of the twentieth century but its fortunes declined, though it remains a national force. It was founded in 1844 by Jacob Best from Rheinhessen, who joined forces with Captain Frederick Pabst from Leipzig. Pabst's fortune was made by its **Blue Ribbon** beer (4.56 per cent ABV), which became the drink of industrial workers, known fortuitously in America as "blue collar workers". The decline of Pabst mirrored the decline of American industry. In 1996 new owners of Pabst, who had also bought the Falstaff and Pearl breweries, closed the Pabst plant and moved production of all brands to the former Stroh/Heileman complex in La Crosse.

The revivalists

Two men played a pivotal role in the revival of craft brewing in the United States. They came from different stock. One is the scion of a rich family of German origin, an amiable man who used his wealth to save a brewery and revive the country's only indigenous beer style. The other was a gruff, bluff man of Scottish-Canadian stock who brewed ales with great devotion to style in the hop fields of Washington State. Their impacts have been nationwide, encouraging a generation of beer lovers to invest in mash tuns, brew kettles and fermenters, and produce ales and lagers of often startling quality.

The first man is Fritz Maytag, a member of the powerful washing machine dynasty. He was a student at Stanford University and enjoyed a local speciality called Steam Beer. One day in 1965 he went into his favourite bar, asked for a glass of Steam and was told it would be his last as the Anchor Steam Brewery was about to close. So Maytag cashed in his shares in the family firm and bought the brewery. There are cynics who scoff at the suggestion that Maytag was playing out a part in the American Dream, but he did stand to lose every cent of his fortune by taking over a failed business that produced a beer that only a handful of people wanted to drink.

Steam Beer is a San Francisco speciality that dates from the California Gold Rush of the 1890s. When gold diggers poured into the small town with a mainly Mexican, wine-drinking population, they demanded beer – and they wanted the cold, refreshing lagers beers they had enjoyed on the East Coast. The few ale brewers in San Francisco had neither ice nor mountain caves in which to store beer. The one ingredient they could get was lager yeast and they used it to brew beer at ale temperature. They developed special shallow vessels, a cross between a fermenter and a cool ship, which exposed more of the beer to the atmosphere, causing it to cool quickly. The high level of natural carbonation created by the system caused casks to "hiss like escaping steam" when they were opened in bars.

Fritz Maytag inherited a rundown brewery with just one employee. It was so broke it was using baker's yeast to ferment the beer. It took 10 years for Maytag to turn Anchor Steam into a profitable concern. Eventually he was able to move from the site under a freeway to an Art Deco building in Mariposa Street that once housed a coffee roasting company. As well as turning Anchor into a successful brewery, Maytag toured the world in order to immerse himself in the history and practice of brewing. In particular, a visit to some of Britain's finest producers of cask ales encouraged him to branch out from his flagship beer into ale brewing, where he adopted with some fervour the English habit of "dry hopping" – adding hops to the finished casks to give beer improved aroma and keeping quality. His new brewery is magnificent, packed with gleaming copper vessels built to his specification in Germany.

Following mashing and boiling, **Anchor Steam Beer** is fermented separately from the ales to avoid any cross-fertilization of yeast cultures. Fermentation takes place in open vessels just two feet deep, using lager yeast but at a warm temperature of 16–21° Celsius/60–70°F. The beer has a finished strength of 5.0 per cent ABV. The grist is a blend of pale and crystal malts: no brewing sugar is used. Hops are Northern Brewer, added three times in the brew kettle. Following fermentation, the green beer is warm-conditioned for three weeks and is then kräusened by adding some partially fermented wort to encourage a second fermentation. The beer is bronze-coloured and highly complex, with a rich malty-nutty aroma, malt and light fruit in the mouth, and a finish in which the hops slowly dominate. It has 30 to 35 units of bitter-ness. While it's clean and quenching in the lager fashion, it also has an ale-like fruitiness.

The other beers are fermented in conventional vessels that are six feet deep. **Liberty Ale**, launched in 1975, was inspired by Maytag's tour of British breweries even though it has an anti-British theme, inspired by the ride by Paul Revere from Boston to Lexington to warn the American revolutionaries that the Redcoats were marching to arrest them. His ride signalled the start of the American War of Independence. Liberty Ale is a world classic, 6.0 per cent ABV, brewed from pale malt and hopped with Cascades.

American hop varieties, like the grapes of California, are big, bold and assertive, adding a citrus fruitiness to beer that often borders on a grapefruit note. In the case of Liberty Ale, Cascades are added to the kettle and the maturation tank, giving the beer an intense lemon citrus aroma and palate, and a dry and hoppy finish.

The remaining Anchor beers include **Porter** (6.0 per cent ABV), with a smooth coffee character, a refreshing **Wheat Beer** with delicate apple notes, made with 70 per cent wheat malt, **Old Foghorn** barley wine style ale (8.75 per cent ABV), winey and intensely bitter with a massive 85 IBUs, and **Our Special Ale**, brewed every year for the Thanksgiving and Christmas periods. It's brewed with a different specification each year and always includes a secret spice, which in the past has included cloves, coriander, cinnamon and nutmeg.

From his redoubt in the Yakima Valley, surrounded by the snow-topped Cascade Mountains, Bert Grant was a tough and committed practitioner of the brewers' art. He worked in a region that still has a powerful feel of the old frontier about it, where visitors are asked to check in their guns before entering a bar or a hotel. Grant was born in Scotland but left for Canada at the age of two. He became an analytical chemist for Canadian Breweries, which became Carling O'Keefe. When the company went into terminal decline, Grant crossed the border and worked for Stroh in Detroit for four years before moving to Yakima to rebuild a hop processing plant in the heart of the American hop fields. He started to brew at home and friends appreciated his efforts. When production reached 500 barrels a year, he decided to go commercial. His first brewpub was in the former Yakima Opera House. He moved to a greenfield site on the edge of town where he had the capacity to make 25,000 barrels a year. He also ran a brewpub in Yakima's old railroad station where his ales were cask conditioned.

Bert Grant was a stickler for style. His **Scottish Ale**, which he described without a blush as "the best beer in the world", had an amber colour and nutty roastiness from dark crystal malt. His **Celtic Ale** was perhaps too generously hopped to be a true Irish ale but his **India Pale Ale**, with a label showing British troops in front of the Taj Mahal, was closer to style. Other beers included a **Porter** with a pronounced hint of peat smoke from imported Scottish malt and a 7.0 per cent ABV **Imperial Stout** with stunning aromas of liquorice, fresh leather, coffee and apple fruit.

Grant sold his beers in 27 states, as far south as Florida. He died in 2002 and the wine company that bought the brewery failed to make the transition from grape to grain and closed the plant in 2005. But, for a legion of American craft brewers, Bert Grant's name and achievements remain an inspiration.

West Coast breweries

The Sierra Nevada Brewing Company was founded in 1981 by Ken Grossman and Paul Camusi in the northern California university town of Chico. It was one of the first of the new wave of specialist craft breweries. Grossman made the leap from home-brewing to commercial production and concentrated at first on ale for the simple reason that he lacked conditioning tanks for lager. A new brewhouse was installed in 1987 and by 1993 production had grown to 70,000 barrels a year. Today, you can add another nought, and at 700,000 barrels a year, the company is second in size only to the Boston Beer Company in the craft-brewing sector.

The flagship beer is bottled **Pale Ale** (5.3 per cent ABV); in draught form it's called simply **Sierra Nevada** and is a fraction lower in strength. It has a spicy, citrus Cascade hop aroma, malty on the palate and with a dry hoppy finish. Sierra Nevada also brews a coffeeish **Porter**, a 6.0 per cent **Stout** with a roasted malt character, and **Big Foot Barley Wine**, at 12.5 per cent ABV one of the strongest beers brewed in the United States. It has a big aroma of hops and dark malt, massive alcohol and hops in the mouth and a rich and warming finish. The hops are Nugget for bitterness with a late addition of Cascade for aroma, with more Cascades along with Centennial added during conditioning. A recent addition to the line is a 7.2 per cent ABV **Torpedo Extra IPA** with a massive 70 IBUs from Crystal and Magnum hops. The grains are pale, carapils and crystal malts.

Mendocino Brewing is based in the perfect town: Hopland, about 90 miles north of San Francisco. Hops were once grown in California but the industry moved north to Oregon and Washington State where the rain is more plentiful and the sun less searing. The founders of Mendocino did plant hops alongside their tavern and brewery but most supplies now are sourced from the major hop-growing areas of the country. The company is now owned by the Indian entrepreneur Vijay Mallya who owns United Breweries in India and plans to make Mendocino the biggest craft brewery in the US. The main brands are named after birds of the region and include **Peregrine Pale Ale**, hoppy and fruity, **Blue Heron Pale Ale**, full-bodied and with great hop character, a copper-coloured **Red Tail Ale** (5.5 per cent ABV), with nutty crystal malt and a superb hop aroma and finish from Cascade and Cluster varieties. **Black Hawk Stout** is as smooth and dangerously drink-able as a chocolate liqueur. Mendocino has joined the India Pale Ale bandwagon with **Imperial IPA** (7.5 per cent ABV).

Anderson Valley is also based in Mendocino County in California and makes great play of the natural ingredients and unpasteurized nature of its award-winning beers. They include a **Boont ESB** (6.8 per cent ABV), packed with citrus fruit, rich malt and bitter hop resins, **Amber Ale** (5.8 per cent) with a big crystal malt character, **Hop Ottin' IPA** (7.0 per cent), with a massive bitter hop character, and **Dark Porter** (5.5 per cent).

Across the bay from San Francisco, in Oakland, Pacific Coast offers a range of English-style ales: a dark **Mariner's Mild**, a hoppy **Gray Whale Ale**, a rich, firm-bodied and malty **Blue Whale Ale** and a dry and tart **Killer Whale Stout**.

In sharp contrast, the Gordon Biersch Brewing Company, founded in Palo Alto in 1988, concentrates on European lager styles. The title of the company is an amalgam of the names of the two founders, Dean Biersch and Dan Gordon. Restaurateur Biersch's antecedents are obvious while Gordon studied brewing skills in Germany. The company, has brewpubs in Honolulu, Pasadena, San José and San Francisco with a new outlet in the unlikely setting of Taiwan. It produces **Dunkel, Maibock, Blonde Bock, Märzen** and **Hefeweizen**.

In Modesto, St Stan's Brewing has established a reputation for its Alt beers, modelled on the warm-fermenting style of Düsseldorf. The main brand is **Amber** (5.8 per cent ABV) which, as the name implies, uses some darker, roasted malt alongside the pale for colour and flavour. Owner Garith Helm and his German-born wife Romy Graf also brew a **Dark Alt**, rich with chocolate malt character, a **Winterfest Alt**, and two English-style pale ales, **Red Sky Ale** and **Whistle Stop Pale Ale**. The label of the Alt shows a monk with a foaming tankard and the slogan "Conceived in heaven, brewed in California". American brewers don't lack chutzpah.

The Sudwerk Privatbrauerei Hübsch has an authentic German ring. Founder Ron Broward took his mother's German maiden name for his brewpub in Davis, bought Steinecker equipment from Germany and employed a trained German brewmaster. The success of his venture enabled him to open a second brewpub in Sacramento. His **Pilsner** (5.0 per cent ABV) uses Hallertau and Tettnang hops that give a fragrant floral lilt to the beer. Other beers include a 5.3 per cent **Märzen** and a **Hefewiezen** wheat beer.

Firestone Walker of Paso Robles, California, brews notably hoppy beers, including **Double Barrel Ale** (5.0 per cent ABV), a pale ale with a portion of the beer aged in oak casks. The resulting beer has woody, smoky and vanilla notes with a balance of spicy hops. **Union Jack IPA** (7.5 per cent) makes a deep bow in the direction of Britain with a beer with massive grapefruit and herbal notes, rich meal-like maltiness and a long bitter and oaky finish.

In Fort Bragg, California, North Coast Brewery makes a phenomenal **Imperial Stout** of 11.6 per cent ABV, with rich chocolate and coffee aromas, burnt grain and spicy hops in the mouth and finish. There's a jazz joke in **Brother Thelonius** – the 9.3 per cent strong pale ale is brewed in the Belgian style, so think Monk. The complex ale has a rich candy sugar, banana fruit, spicy hops and warming alcohol character.

The North-west

Portland, Oregon, is one of the major revivalist brewing centres in the United States. The Portland Brewing Company started life in an Irish-style bar with a small brewery attached in the city centre and moved to a custom-built, German brewery on a greenfield site in 1995. The new plant has a capacity of 70,000 barrels a year. The company was founded by Fred Bowman, a keen home-brewer, whose inspiration was a somewhat obscure English strong ale called Bishop's Tipple. The success of Portland Brewing led to its takeover by Pyramid Brewing of Seattle, which in turn was bought by Magic Hat. The brewery has been re-named MacTarnahan's after a major shareholder, Robert MacTarnahan. Unsurprisingly, the main brand today is **MacTarnahan's Ale** (6.0 per cent ABV), brewed with pale and crystal malts and hopped with Cascades. It has a rich, nutty aroma, dark sultana fruit on the palate and a bittersweet finish. **Portland Ale** (5.0 per cent) is brewed with pale malt only and has a big citrus fruit character from Cascades. The brewery also produces a Bavarian-style **Weizen** and **Porter**.

The Bridgeport Brewing Company is based in Portland's oldest warehouse, brick-built and smothered in climbing ivy. The brewery was opened in the early 1980s by the Italian-American wine-making Ponzi family. They sold the company to Gambrinus of Texas in 1995. The stainless-steel brewhouse produces a cask-conditioned ale in the English style called **Coho** (4.4 per cent ABV). The hops are English Goldings and Nugget and the beer is dry hopped in cask. It has a citrus fruit aroma from the hops, more bitter hops in the mouth and a dry and bitter finish. Other beers in the range include a peppery-hoppy **Bridgeport Ale** and **Blue Heron Ale** named after Portland's emblem, made from pale, crystal, black and chocolate malts, with a hoppy aroma, soft malt in the mouth and a tart and quenching finish. Its **IPA** is 5.5 per cent and has a citrus hop character balanced by sappy malt, and **Blackstrap Stout** (6.0 per cent), with molasses, chocolate, roasted grain and burnt fruit dominating aroma and palate. The annual barley wine, **Old Knucklehead**, is named each year after someone who has brought dishonour on the city, such as a local politician caught with his fingers in the till: knucklehead is the politer American equivalent of the British dickhead.

Also in Portland, Hopworks specializes in organic beers. They include **Velvet ESB** (5.2 per cent ABV), with butterscotch, rich malt and tart hops on the aroma, and ripe fruit and hops on palate and finish, while **Organic IPA** (6.6 per cent), has a big grapefruit and lemon nose, and juicy malt and tangy hops in the mouth and finish.

In Seattle, Redhook is the major craft brewery in the Northwest. It was launched in 1982 by Gordon Bowker and Paul Shipman. Six years later they moved the brewing kit to a converted trolley barn (tramshed) in the old Swedish Fremont district of the city. The barn remains the company's flagship bar and restaurant but, in 1994, a brand-new brewery, capable of producing 90,000 barrels a year, was built on the edge of the city. In 1994, Redhook rocked the industry when it agreed to sell 15 per cent of its shares to Anheuser-Busch. A-B promised to use its marketing skills and muscle to sell Redhook beers nationally. Today the A-B share has grown to 25 per cent and Redhook has built a new, $30 million brewery in Portsmouth, New Hampshire, opening the East Coast to its products.

The arrival of A-B was seen by some independent brewers as a sinister threat, by others as recognition that the brewing giants needed quality craft-brewed beers. It's not known whether the takeover of A-B by InBev will change the relationship with Redhook but the quality of the beers remains high.

The brewery's main beer is **Extra Special Bitter** (5.8 per cent ABV), brewed with pale and cara malts and hopped with Tettnang and Willamette (28 IBUs). It has an amber colour, a juicy malt character balanced by a touch of butterscotch and a floral and spicy hop note. **Long Hammer IPA** has a strength of 6.5 per cent in keeping with the Victorian origins of the style and a pungent 38 bitterness units. The grains are pale, crystal and Munich and the hops Cascade, Northern Brewer and Willamette. **Blackhook Porter** is 5.23 per cent and has a chocolate and roasted grain character from cara and black malts and roasted barley. The hops are Cascade, Northern Brewer and Willamette (40 IBUs). There's a rolling programme of seasonal ales.

The Seattle-based Pike Brewery was founded by Charles Finkel, a man with enormous passion for creating beers true to style. As well as the brewery, in the elegant Pike Place harbourside area, with noted fish restaurants, Finkel also runs a brewery museum and a store selling books and home-brewing supplies. His beers include **Pale Ale** (5.0 per cent ABV), brewed with pale, crystal Munich and wheat malt and hopped with Magnum, East Kent Goldings and Willamette (32 IBUs). Finkel is a great believer in using authentic materials and imports Maris Otter malt and Goldings hops from England. Pale Ale has a floral and peppery hops character balanced by nutty malt. His **XXXXX Stout** (7.0 per cent) uses pale, crystal and roasted malt, along with Chinook, Goldings and Willamette hops and has a roasted grain and coffee character. **Kilt Lifter** (6.5 per cent) is a Scotch Ale, introduced following the death of Bert Grant in Yakima, which signalled the demise of his renowned Scotch Ale. The beer uses peated malt along with pale, crystal and Munich grains and is hopped with Magnum and East Kent Goldings (27 IBUs). The smoked malt gives a rich whisky note to the beer, with malt and light hops. **Pike's Old Bawdy** barley wine commemorates the fact that the brewery is on the site of a former brothel. The 10.0 per cent ale is brewed with pale and wheat malts and hopped with Chinook, Columbus and Magnum varieties. It's rich and warming, bursting with candied fruit, alcohol and tangy hops.

Full Sail Brewing in Hood River, Oregon, enjoys one of the finest settings of any brewery in the world, overlooking the Columbia River Gorge at its confluence with the Hood River. Its main beer is **Amber** (5.5 per cent ABV) with a citrus and spice aroma, juicy malt in the mouth and a clean, quenching finish. **Session Lager** (5.1 per cent) has a toasted malt and light citrus fruit nose and palate with a long hoppy finish, while **Imperial Porter Bourbon** (9.8 per cent) is stored for 12 months in bourbon casks and emerges with a smoky, oaky, coffee and chocolate character, with contributions from roasted grain and peppery hops. Pale Ale is brewed with pale and crystal malts and hopped with local varieties, while its interpretation of **IPA** has 60 units of bitterness and a big hop character balanced by biscuity malt.

John Maier, head brewer at Rogue Ales in Newport, Oregon, is what Americans call a "hop head". He loves hops and the subtle and not-so-subtle aromas and flavours they add to beer. Maier is able to buy some of the choicest hops from both Oregon and Washington State and he adopts the British practice of dry hopping his finished ales in kegs. **Shakespeare Stout** (6.1 per cent ABV) is brewed from pale, crystal, English chocolate malt, rolled oats and roasted barley. The hops are Cascade. It has a smooth chocolate aroma with a creamy note from the oats. Burnt currants, roasted grain, chocolate and bitter hops fill the mouth, while the deep and complex finish has tangy hops, dark fruits, roasted grain and silky oats. The 11.0 per cent **Imperial Stout** has a massive hop attack, with Cascade, Chinook and Willamette creating an astonishing 87 units of bitterness. It's brewed with pale malt, English crystal and chocolate, black and Munich malts. The aroma conjures up spices, espresso coffee, black chocolate and bitter oranges. It's chewy, oily and perfumy in the mouth followed by a long finish that has surprisingly sweet glacé fruit notes balanced by dark grain and bitter hops, burnt fruit and smoky and roasted grain. The beer in bottle is not filtered and will improve with age. John Maier recommends letting it develop in bottle for a year. He also brews a phenomenal barley wine, **Old Crustacean**, bursting with fruit and hops (11.3 per cent) and, tongue-in-cheek, his own face appears on the label of his 6.0 per cent **Maierbock**, a warming beer fermented with ale yeast.

Alaskan Brewing in Juneau is famous for its **Smoked Porter** (5.5 per cent ABV). Founded by Geoff and Marcy Larson, the beer is made from pale, black, chocolate and crystal malts, with Chinook and Willamette hops. A local smokehouse takes the dark malts, spreads them on racks and smokes them over alder wood for three days. The finished beer is brewed once a year and is then vintage dated. It has an intensely smoky aroma and palate, overlain by spicy hops and dark malt and chocolate. The smoked dark malts, allied to an intense bitterness, mean that beer brewed close to the Arctic Circle is the closest we may ever come to the aroma and flavour of an eighteenth-century London porter. Other beers in the portfolio include a 5.3 per cent **Amber**, based on the German Alt style, brewed with pale and cara malts and hopped with European and Pacific North-west hops. It has a smooth, malt-loaf character balanced by gentle, fruity hops (18 bitterness units). **Pale** is 5.2 per cent, brewed with two-row barley malt and European and American hops. It has 24 IBUs and a good hoppy, citrus fruit and sappy malt character.

East Coast

The Brooklyn brewing tradition has been revived by former journalist and keen home-brewer Steve Hindy and banker Tom Potter. When they planned their business, they sought the advice of veteran brewer Bill Moeller who was keen to recreate a pre-Prohibition Brooklyn recipe. **Brooklyn Lager** (5.5 per cent ABV) is a revelation, an indication of how rich and full-bodied American lagers were before Prohibition and the national giants suppressed flavour in beer. It's a brilliant example of the now hard-to-find Vienna Red style, brewed with crystal as well as pale malt and is dry hopped. The beer has 30 bitterness units and a floral and piny hop aroma balanced by toasted malt. The mouth is filled with juicy malt and caramel flavours with a big punch of spicy hops. The finish is a fine balance of rich malt, a hint of citrus fruit and crisp, bitter hops.

The brewing side is run by Garrett Oliver, former brewmaster at the Manhattan Brewery and a leading writer and lecturer on beer styles. His **Brooklyn Brown Ale** (5.6 per cent) created the style in the US. It's a warm-fermented beer with a blend of English pale ale malt, Belgian aromatic malts and American caramalt and roasted barley. The hops create 28 IBUs and are all home-grown varieties: Cascade, American Fuggles and Willamette. The beer has a burnished mahogany colour and a rich aroma of chocolate, burnt fruit, roasted grain and tangy hops. Caramel, roast and chocolate dominate the palate, followed by a finish that is dry from malts and roast, with a continuing chocolate note and a solid underpinning of tart hops.

Additions to the portfolio include **Pennant Pale Ale** (5.0 per cent ABV), using Scottish Maris Otter pale malt and crystal malt, with Cascade, Perle and Willamette hops, a 5.1 per cent **Pilsner** that uses imported German pale malt and American Fuggles blended with Mittelfruh, Perle and Saaz hops, and a 5.1 per cent **Weisse** with German barley and wheat malts and Perle hops.

The brown ale revival has been taken up by another brewery in the region. Ithaca is in upstate New York's rural Finger Lakes area and the brewery of the same name is in the town. It was set up in 1998 using equipment from a closed brewery in Texas. **Nut Brown** is 4.9 per cent ABV, brewed with pale, crystal and chocolate malts and hopped with American varieties. It has a nutty/malty nose and palate with chocolate and floral hop notes. **Pale Ale** (5.8 per cent) is brewed with pale, crystal and Munich malts and hopped with Cascade, Centennial and Willamette varieties. It has a piny, resinous, floral hop nose with ripe malt and hop resins in the mouth and some citrus fruit in the dry and hoppy finish. **Old Habit** rye beer (9.0 per cent) uses four rye malts and a portion of the beer is aged in whisky casks. The finished beer is bready, grainy and oaky with a big hop bitterness balancing the wood and whisky character.

Boston Brewing Company is now the biggest craft brewery in the US due to the tireless work of its founder, Jim Koch. His beers are better known by the Samuel Adams name, with the stern face of the American revolutionary and brewer glaring out from the labels. Koch is a descendant of Bavarian brewers who brought their skills to the United States but were forced out of business during a bout of merger-mania in the 1950s. The Harvard-educated Koch gave up a business career to restore his family's traditions by selling beer from 1985. **Samuel Adams Boston Lager** (4.8 per cent ABV), sold door-to-door by Koch, was an almost instant success. The beer was contract-brewed at first but eventually Koch built a small brewery on the site of the former Haffenreffer Brewery in Boston's Jamaica Plain. Koch has added brewing plants in key parts of the US to offer fresh beer to customers. He has bars at several airports, including one at St Louis, Missouri, under the gaze of Anheuser-Busch. His lager has fine toasted malt and piny hops character, with Mittelfruh and Tettnanger varieties imported from the German Hallertau.

Boston Ale (5.0 per cent) has an amber colour, a big peppery-resiny aroma from English Fuggles and Czech Saaz hops – the beer is hopped three times during the boil and again during conditioning. It's tart and fruity in the mouth with a big malt-and-hops finish. Koch endlessly tries new styles, including a **Cranberry Lambic** in the Belgian fashion (though no wild yeast is used) and a Triple Bock that reached a staggering 17.5 per cent ABV. Fermentation was finished with a champagne yeast culture. This has now been scaled down to a **Double Bock**.

Harpoon is also based in Boston and brews a 5.9 per cent **IPA** with a floral hops and citrus fruit nose, with chewy malt and tangy hops in the mouth and a long hoppy and fruity finish. In sharp contrast, **Munich Dark** (5.5 per cent) has a toasted malt character with strong chocolate and coffee notes and gentle hop bitterness. Also in Massachusetts, the Berkshire Brewery in Deerfield produces a **Drayman's Porter** (6.2 per cent ABV) with coffee and chocolate on the nose from dark malt, with caramel and hop notes in the mouth and finish.

A superb pale ale is brewed by the Geary Brewing Company in Portland, Maine. David Geary produced his first ale in 1986 after learning brewing skills in England: his brewery was designed by Peter Austin, founder of the Ringwood Brewery in Hampshire, and Geary uses Ringwood's yeast culture. **Pale Ale** (4.5 per cent ABV) is brewed with pale and crystal malts with a touch of chocolate malt: the grains are imported from England, while the hops are American varieties. The beer has a piny, resinous hop nose and palate with a restrained but consistent fruitiness in the finish and a delicate malt-loaf grainy note. Geary's **Hampshire Special Ale** (7.0 per cent) pays respect to the brewer's time at Ringwood. It has a rich, warming and spicy hop character with powerful hints of caramel and butterscotch.

Geary worked for a while with Alan Pugsley, an English brewer who also picked up the brewing skills with Austin at Ringwood.

Pugsley moved from Geary to co-found with Fred Forsley Shipyard Brewing, also in Portland. The portfolio includes **Old Thumper** (5.6 per cent ABV), a one-time winner of the Champion Beer of Britain trophy and brewed under licence by Shipyard. All the Shipyard brews have the characteristic Ringwood yeasty fruitiness, as Pugsley brought a supply with him. His range includes an **IPA** and **Longfellow Winter Ale** (5.5 per cent). Following Anheuser-Busch's example at Redhook, Miller has taken a half-share in the company, with the aim of giving the beers greater distribution. Pugsley and Forsley have the freedom to stick to their recipes and develop new beers.

A third brewery in Portland, Allagash, brings a different and Belgian influence to its beers. **White** (6.2 per cent ABV) uses coriander and orange peel in the Hoegaarden style, and the beer is tart, spicy and quenching. **Curieux** (10 per cent) is a Belgian-style Triple matured in bourbon casks. The result is a beer rich in vanilla and tangy fruit, with oaky and smoky notes.

Brewery Ommegang is in Cooperstown, New York State, a town best known as the home of the National Baseball Hall of Fame. The brewery was founded by Don Feinberg and Wendy Littlefield, who share a passion for Belgian ales. Their brewery is designed like a Belgian farmhouse and their beers have been phenomenally successful, to such an extent that they sold the company to the Belgian brewery Moortgat, producer of the famous blond ale, Duvel.

The main beer from Ommegang is **Abbey Ale** (8.5 per cent ABV), in the style of a Belgian Dubbel. It's brewed with pale, Munich and cara malts and hopped with American and Belgian varieties. It's burgundy coloured, with a deep collar of foam, a complex aroma of fruit, hops and spices, and a palate rich in caramel, liquorice, toffee, chocolate and earthy hops, and a dry finish in which vine fruits, peppery hops and ripe grain dominate. Other beers include **White**, the brewery's first draught beer – the other

products are bottle-conditioned – **Hennepin**, a Belgian-style sai-
son, **Rare Vos** (Dark Horse), a strong amber ale, and **Three
Philosophers**, a Quadrupel that is a blend of strong dark ale and
Lindemann's Kriek.

Jeff Biegert at Atlantic Coast Brewing in Boston is heavily
influenced by English brewing practice. He, too, uses Ringwood
yeast. His flagship **Tremont Ale** (4.8 per cent ABV) is tart and
hoppy, with a hint of sulphur. It's sold in cask-conditioned form
on draught. He brews a hoppy and fruity **IPA** (6.4 per cent) and
a rich and hoppy **Old Scratch Barley Wine** (9 per cent). He has
recently added a **Porter**.

One day, the joke ran, Carol Stoudt would brew a stout.
Eventually, she gave in and added a stout to her range but the
Stoudt Brewery in Adamstown, Pennsylvania, has built its
reputation on dedicated interpretations of German cold-fermented
beers. Carol trained in Germany and the brewery she runs with
her husband Ed has won more than 20 medals at the annual Great
American Beer Festival. She brews a **Pils** (4.5 per cent ABV) that,
in her own words, is "assertively hopped with Saaz", a rich, malty
Gold (5 per cent) in the Dortmunder Export style, and a smooth,
full-bodied **Honey Double Mai Bock** (7.5 per cent).

There's more German influence behind the Penn Brewery in
Pittsburgh, where owner Tom Pastorius is a descendant of the
Germans who first settled in "Germanstown". Pastorius learnt the
brewing skills in Germany and installed German equipment to
produce a range that includes a **Dark** (Dunkel) at 5 per cent ABV,
packed with roast and chocolaty malt character, a wonderfully rich,
nutty and spicy **Oktoberfest** (5.8 per cent), and a big-bodied **St
Nikolaus Bock** (8.4 per cent).

The Yuengling Brewery in Pottsville, Pennsylvania, is the oldest
surviving commercial brewery in the US. It was founded by a
German immigrant, David Yuengling, to supply thirsty workers in
the local coal mines. The current brewery, built in the 1830s, was

designed in the European style on a hill so that deep cellars could be dug to store or lager the beer. Today it produces a wide range of beers, all cold-fermented. Its stand-out product is a 4.7 per cent ABV **Porter** – actually a dark lager that is more in the style of a Bavarian Dunkel.

In Philadelphia, the Dock Street brewpub produces beers in both the Central European and English styles. The range includes two IPAs, **Rye IPA** at 6.8 per cent ABV and **Magnum IPA** (6.3 per cent) that, as the name suggests, uses Magnum hops, and a rich and malty **Amber** (5 per cent). **Royal Bohemian Pilsner** (5 per cent) has soft and nutty malt and a fine, floral hop note.

The Midwest

The powerful influence of German immigrants underscores the beers from August Schell Brewing in New Ulm, Minnesota. This is an "old German" brewery, complete with a large beer garden, not a new-wave micro. It survived Prohibition, introduced some bland lagers to compete with the giants, but kept tradition going with an acclaimed hoppy and malty **Pils** (5.5 per cent) that uses imported Hallertau hops. The range of speciality beers includes a rich and full-bodied **Maifest Bock** (6.9 per cent) and a **Weizen** wheat beer.

Goose Island in Chicago, founded by John and Gregg Hall, is one of the most innovative craft breweries in the US. It's named after an island in the Chicago River and started life as a brewpub but moved to a new, custom-built site to keep pace with demand. The main beer is **Honker's Ale**, with a squawking goose on the label, a 3.8 per cent pale ale with an orange-gold colour and a tart hop character from Styrian Goldings and some tangy fruit on the palate. **Goose Island IPA** is arguably the finest interpretation of the style in both the US and Britain. It's bottle-fermented and is truly pale, with just 10 units of colour, and is heavily hopped with 58 IBUs. The pale and crystal malts are a blend of American and

European varieties while the hops are Cascade and Mount Hood from the US and Czech Saaz and Styrian Goldings. It has a superb aroma of bitter oranges, spicy hops and cracker biscuit maltiness, with juicy malt, bitter hop resins and tart fruit in the mouth. The persistently bitter finish has an iron-like intensity from the hops with more bitter and tangy fruit and a lingering malt character. The remarkable **Bourbon County Stout** (11.5 per cent) is aged for a minimum of one hundred days in oak casks supplied by Jim Beam. The beer has a powerful sweet whisky, oak and vanilla character with contributions from roasted malt and hops. Goose Island has branched out with a range of bottle-conditioned Belgian-style beers, including **Sofie**, a 6.8 per cent saison, **Matilda**, a pale ale, **Juliet**, a sour beer in the lambic tradition, and **Père Jacques**, an 8.5 per cent Abbey Ale.

Arcadia in Battle Creek, Michigan, brews English-inspired beers, including a **London Porter** (7.2 per cent ABV) with an image of Sir Winston Churchill on the label and a coffee and dark chocolate character, **Angler's Ale** (5.4 per cent), spicy and peppery from English Goldings hops, a sweet and fruity **Scotch Ale** (7.5 per cent) and an 8.4 per cent **Imperial Stout**.

Great Lakes has restored Cleveland's once vibrant brewing tradition with some of the most highly regarded beers in the Midwest. The **Eliot Ness** (5.6 per cent ABV) is a Vienna Red lager that commemorates the pioneering work of Anton Dreher. It's full-bodied, with toffee malt and spicy Tettnang hops. It's named after Eliot Ness, the Director of Public Safety, who took on the mobsters when Cleveland was a tougher and rougher city between the two world wars. **Burning River Pale Ale** (6 per cent) is deliciously hoppy and packed with citrus fruit: the name comes from the time when the heavily polluted Cuyahoga River which runs through the city caught fire. **Conway's Irish Ale** (6.8 per cent) is malty and delicately hopped while **Edmund Fitzgerald Porter** (5.4 per cent) takes its name from a freighter that sank with all hands in the Great Lakes in 1975. Hopped with Cascade, Northern Brewer and Willamette varieties that produce a mighty 60 units of bitterness, the porter has floral hops on the aroma, dark roasted grain and chocolate in the mouth and a gentle fruity finish. **Dortmunder Gold** (5.8 per cent) celebrates the fast-disappearing German style and is a fine balance of juicy malt and tangy hops, while **Commodore Perry** (7.5 per cent) has 80 units of bitterness and a big hoppy and fruity character.

Capital in Middleton, a northern suburb of the Wisconsin state capital, Madison, brews a **Munich Dark** (5.4 per cent ABV) with a big caramel and butterscotch character, backed by raisin fruit and gentle hops. Its **Special Pilsner** (4.8 per cent) has floral hops, toasted malt and citrus fruit on the aroma and palate, followed by hoppy finish.

Lakefront Brewery in Milwaukee is based in a former bakery and has restored flavour to beer in a city once synonymous with the bland offerings of national brewers. Its main brand is **Riverwest Stein Beer** (5.9 per cent ABV), yet another interpretation of Vienna Red, with toffee malt and spicy Cascade and Mount Hood hops. Lakefront also produces an **Organic ESB**, an **IPA** and a **Pilsner**.

Rockies, South and South West

Denver, high in the Colorado Rockies, used to be a city dominated by Coors of nearby Golden. There is now such improved choice in the city that Coors had to respond with a brewpub serving ales and stout in the local baseball stadium it sponsors. The pacesetter in the Denver revival is the Wynkoop brewpub close to the railroad station. Launched by John Hickenlooper, who also runs a major book store in Denver and has been mayor of the city, it was the first brewpub in the Rockies and claims to be the biggest brewpub in the US, and, by definition, the world. Some of the beers are sold in cask-conditioned form in the pub, including **Sir Charles ESB** (4.5 per cent ABV), an English-style, copper-coloured bitter with toasted malt and bitter hop character. The pub's main brand is **Railyard Ale** (5.2 per cent), a cross, says Hickenlooper, between English pale ale and a Bavarian Oktoberfest. **Wixa Weiss** (5.4 per cent) is a German-style wheat beer with a banana, cloves, bubblegum and creamy malt character, while **Patty's Chile Beer** (4.5 per cent) has chilis added to each cask. It's pale, tart, tangy, spicy and refreshing.

Boulder, Colorado, has two craft breweries. Avery brews a 6.3 per cent ABV **India Pale Ale**, with citrus fruit and piny hops, and **Salvation**, a 9 per cent Belgian-style golden ale, with rich fruit and spices on the nose and palate, and a long bittersweet finish. The Boulder Brewery offers **Planet Porter** (5.1 per cent ABV), with dark, burnt fruit, roasted grain and bitter chocolate, while **Hazed & Infused** (4.8 per cent) has a big hop character with citrus fruit and spices.

Bayern in Missoula, Montana, was, as the name suggests, founded by Germans from Bavaria. Its 5 per cent ABV **Pilsner** has a floral hop aroma with toasted malt, light fruit balancing malt and hops in the mouth and a long, hoppy finish. The brewery's 5.3 per cent **Amber** is a fine example of a Munich Märzen with a toasted malt nose, a hint of butterscotch along with rich fruit in the mouth and gentle hops in the long bittersweet finish.

Clipper City, of Baltimore, Maryland, is a substantial brewery founded by Hugh Sissons that honours the long history of clipper ships in the area. **Loose Cannon Hop** (7.2 per cent ABV) is an IPA with a citrus fruit aroma of grapefruit and oranges, balanced by piny hops. **Small Craft Warning** (7.2 per cent) is a pale Bock with soft, creamy malt, "fruit gums" confectionery notes and spicy hops. An English-style **Pale Ale** is 4.9 per cent while a **Gold Ale** has a similar strength.

The Atlanta Brewery was founded in Atlanta, Georgia, in 1993. It produces a wide range of beers under the Red Brick label. **Red Brick Ale** (7 per cent ABV) has a big chocolate, caramel, coffee and butterscotch character balanced by fruity hops. **Red Brick Oatmeal Porter** (7.7 per cent) has a creamy malt note with chocolate and roasted grain and a good under-pinning of hop resins.

Abita in Abita Springs, Louisiana, is 30 miles north of New Orleans. It opened in 1989 and its beers include **Purple Haze** (4.7 per cent ABV), a wheat beer with raspberries, fruity and quenching, and **Turbodog** (6.1 per cent), a dark beer with choc-olate and butterscotch on the nose and palate, and an espresso coffee finish.

UNITED STATES BREWERS

Abita Brewing Company,
PO Box 1510, Abita Springs,
Louisiana 70420.

Alaskan Brewing Company,
5429 Shaune Drive, Juneau, Alaska
99801.

Allagash Brewing Company,
50 Industrial Way, Portland, Maine
04103.

Anchor Brewing Company,
1705 Mariposa Street, San Francisco,
California 94107.

Anderson Valley Brewing Co,
PO Box 505, 17700 Highway 253,
Boonville, California 95415.

Anheuser-Busch Inc (A-B InBev),
One Busch Place, St Louis, Missouri
63118.

Arcadia Brewing Company,
103 Michigan Avenue W, Battle
Creek, Michigan 49017.

Atlanta Brewing Co,
1219 Williams Street, Atlanta, Georgia
30309.

Atlantic Coast Brewing Co,
25 Drydock Avenue, Boston,
Massachusetts 02210.

Avery Brewing,
5763 Arapahoe Ave. Unit E, Boulder,
Colorado 80303.

Bayern Brewing,
1507 Montana Street, Missoula,
Montana 59801.

Blue Moon Brewing Co,
2145 Blake Street, Denver, Colorado
80205.

Boston Beer Co,
1 Design Center Place, Boston,
Massachusetts 02210.

Boulder Beer Company,
2880 Wilderness Place, Boulder,
Colorado 80301.

BridgePort Brewing Co,
1318 N.W. Northrup, Portland,
Oregon 97209.

Brooklyn Brewery,
79 N 11th Street, Brooklyn, New
York 11211.

Capital Brewing,
7734 Terrace Avenue, Middleton, nr
Madison, Wisconsin 53562.

Clipper City Brewing Company,
4615 Hollins Ferry Road, Suite B,
Baltimore, Maryland 21227.

Coors (Molson Coors),
Coors Brewing Co, PO Box 4030,
NH475, Golden, Colorado, 80401.

Dock Street Beer,
701 S 50th Street, Philadelphia,
Pennsylvania 19143.

Firestone Walker Brewery,
1400 Ramada Drive, Paso Robles,
California 93446.

Full Sail Brewing Co,
405 Portway, Hood River, Oregon
97031.

D.L. Geary Brewing Co,
38 Evergreen Drive, Portland, Maine
04103.

Goose Island Beer Co,
1800 West Fulton Street, Chicago,
Illinois 60612.

Gordon Biersch Brewing Co,
357 E Taylor Street, San Jose,
California 95112.

Great Lakes Brewing Co,
2516 Market Avenue, Cleveland,
Ohio 44113.

Hopworks Urban Brewery,
2944 SE Powell Boulevard, Portland,
Oregon 97202.

Hübsch Sudwerk Privatbrauerei,
2001 Second Street, Davis, California
95616.

Ithaca Beer Company,
606 Elmira Road, Ithaca, New York
14850.

Lakefront Brewery Inc,
1872 N Commerce Street,
Milwaukee, Wisconsin 53212.

Mendocino,
Hopland Brewery, 13351 S. Highway
101, Hopland, California 95449.

Miller (SABMiller),
4251 W State Street, Milwaukee,
Wisconsin 53208.

North Coast Brewing Co Inc,
455 N. Main Street, Fort Bragg,
California 95437.

Brewery Ommegang,
656 County Highway 23,
Cooperstown, New York 13326.

Portland (MacTarnahan's) Brewing,
2730 NW 31st Street, Portland,
Oregon 97210.

Pabst/Stroh,
  Pabst, PO Box 736 Milwaukee,
  Wisconsin 53201.

Stroh, 100 River Place, Detroit, Michigan 48207.

Pacific Coast Brewing Co,
906 Washington Street, Oakland, California 94607.

Penn Brewery,
800 Vinial Street, Pittsburgh, Pennsylvania 15212.

Pike Brewing Co,
1415 First Avenue, Seattle, Washington 98101.

Redhook Ale Brewery,
15300 NE 145th Street, Woodinville, nr Seattle, Washington 98072.

Rogue Ales,
2320 OSU Drive, Newport, Oregon 97365.

St Stan's Brewing Co,
821 L Street, Modesto, California 95354.

August Schell Brewing,
1860 Schell Road, New Ulm, Minnesota 56073.

Shipyard Brewing Co,
86 Newbury Street, Portland, Maine 04101.

Sierra Nevada Brewing Co,
1075 E 20th Street, Chico, California 95928.

Stoudt's Brewing Co,
Route 272, 200 N. Reading Road, Adamstown, Pennsylvania 19501.

Wynkoop Brewing Co,
1634 18th Street, Denver, Colorado 80202.

D.G. Yuengling & Son, Inc
5th & Mahantongo Streets, Pottsville, Pennsylvania 17901.

Canada

Canadians understandably bridle when Europeans think of their country as an appendage to the United States. But there are striking similarities in the development of the Canadian beer market, with substantial cross-border trading and link-ups. This is most marked by the 2004 merger between Coors of the US and Molson, Canada's biggest brewer. The introduction of "ice beer" in the 1990s was spearheaded by Canadian brewers and taken up by the giants south of the border.

The shape of Canadian brewing, in common with its neighbour, was determined in large measure by Prohibition, which ran for longer, throughout the First World War and until 1932. The result was an industry dominated by a few giants. The big three all started as ale brewers but, encouraged by what they saw in the US, have concentrated on lagers in the 5.0 per cent ABV bracket. Six-row barley enables them to use substantial levels of adjuncts, usually corn. With low bitterness rates of around 10 IBUs, mainstream lagers tend to be sweet, creamy, undemanding and underhopped. The domination of the giants was intensified in 1989 when Molson and Carling merged, giving the new group around 50 per cent of the market. Labatt, for a period, owned the American beer Rolling Rock, but ownership has now passed to Anheuser-Busch in the US: both A-B and Labatt are now owned by InBev, the world's biggest beer maker.

The beer scene is changing slowly but for the better. Micros are emerging and there are now some characterful ales. But brewpubs are illegal in many provinces and the new generation of entrepreneurial brewers has had to fight a guerrilla war to establish their outlets.

Molson is the oldest brewery in Canada and the whole of North America. Its origins date from the nineteenth century when John

Molson emigrated from Lincolnshire in England, clutching a copy of John Richardson's *Theoretical Hints on the Improved Practice of Brewing*. In 1786 he opened a brewery in Montreal and the company he founded is still controlled by his descendants. Carling O'Keefe dates from a merger in the nineteenth century between the breweries founded by Sir Thomas Carling in 1840 and Eugene O'Keefe in 1862. Today Molson brews in Ontario, Vancouver, Edmonton, Winnipeg, Prince Albert, Regina, and St John's, Newfoundland. Its main brands are **Export** (4.9 per cent ABV), **Lager**, **Canadian** and **Carling** (all 5.0 per cent). They are all light tasting, though Carling is rather more firm-bodied than the other beers. **Rickards Red** (5.2 per cent) is an Irish-style beer with malt and butterscotch notes while **Rickards White** (5.4 per cent) is spiced in the Belgian white beer tradition. **Molson's Pilsner** is 5 per cent and is a light-tasting interpretation of the Czech style. Following the merger with Coors, Molson also brews Coors Light for the Canadian market. In the 1990s, the brewery announced it was cutting out the use of all preservatives in its products. Specialist all-malt brews include a smooth, fruity **Cream Ale** with a hint of hop and a malty and nutty **Amber Lager**. **Molson's Ice** has a slightly skunky, perfumy aroma but no discernible palate or finish.

Labatt dates back to a small brewery built in 1828 in London, Ontario, by an innkeeper named George Balkwill. He sold the business to William and George Snell in 1828 who in turn sold it to Samuel Eccles and John Labatt in 1847. Labatt became the sole owner in 1853.

In 1995 Labatt was bought by Interbrew, now A-B InBev. Labatt's beers are bland in the extreme and most have the same strength of 5.0 per cent ABV. The main brand by far is **Labatt Blue**, which also comes in a **Lite** version. **Cristal** has a faint hop note from Saaz, while **Labatt 50** is brewed with ale yeast and has some faint malt and fruit character. Its Alexander Keith subsidiary in Nova Scotia produces **IPA** (surprisingly, 5.0 per cent) that has nothing in common with the style and a **Red Amber Ale** (5.0 per cent) that is smooth and undemanding.

Ice Beer, launched with a crescendo of hype in 1993, started the craze for the style. During the brewing process the temperature of the beer is lowered until ice crystals form. These are removed, according to the company, to take out proteins and other undesirables. Although the finished beer is high in alcohol, 5.8 per cent ABV, most of the flavour is also removed. Beers brewed in this fashion can only have rounded flavours if they are lagered for lengthy periods. In the case of American and Canadian ice beers, the rapid brewing method leaves behind some rough esters that give a perfumy, nail-polish aroma and finish.

Moosehead is the largest and longest-surviving independent in Canada. Its remote plants in New Brunswick and Nova Scotia have had a turbulent history. Its story began with John and Susannah Oland brewing in their backyard in Dartmouth, Nova Scotia, in 1867, using old family recipes brought from Britain. Their ales were sufficiently popular for the Olands to win a contract to supply the armed forces. Renamed the Army & Navy Brewery, the company moved to new premises on the waterfront at Dartmouth. Three years later John Oland was killed in a horse-riding accident and his widow was forced to sell a controlling interest in the brewery. With the help of an inheritance, she bought back her stake in 1877 and renamed the company S. Oland, Sons & Co. When Susannah died, her youngest son George took over control of the brewery, but again they faced tragedy. When two ships collided in Halifax Harbour in 1917 brewmaster Conrad Oland was killed and his brother John injured. The family soldiered on. With the help of the insurance money, George Oland and his son moved to a new site in St John, New Brunswick. Even though Prohibition was still in operation and beer was restricted to 2.0 per cent ABV, the Olands prospered and returned to Halifax. Their fortunes soared in 1931 when George Oland rechristened his main ale brand with the charismatic name of Moosehead. Such was the success of the brand that the company name was changed in 1947 from New Brunswick to Moosehead. Today Moosehead has breweries in St John, New Brunswick and Dartmouth, Nova Scotia.

Moosehead has had enormous success in the United States but the brewery's beers have paid the price. **Moosehead Pale Ale** has some light hop aroma from the use of Czech Saaz and is dry in the finish but has little ale character, while **Canadian Lager** (5.0 per cent ABV) is in the inoffensive but unexciting mainstream.

It is scarcely surprising that ale brewing has taken root in Victoria on Vancouver Island, British Columbia, for this is the most English of Canadian regions, its population packed with ex-patriates. Spinnakers, on the outskirts of the town, was the dream of Paul Hadfield and John Mitchell, both from Vancouver town on the mainland. Mitchell returned home in 1982 from a trip to Britain with samples of 14 English ales. When the two men and their friends tasted them they were fired with enthusiasm to build a small brewery to produce beers along similar lines. They faced major legal obstacles. The city of Victoria refused to grant a licence for a brewpub but later said it would give planning permission as long as local people supported the idea in a referendum – 95 per cent voted yes. Permission to brew and retail beer needed an amendment to federal law; it came just two months before the brewpub was due to open. Spinnakers, with superb views out over the sea, was packed from opening day in May 1984.

The small attached brewhouse, built by an English firm in Manchester, has been expanded twice to meet demand. Paul Hadfield's main brew is **Spinnaker Ale** (4.2 per cent ABV). It is made from pale malt with a dash of crystal and is hopped with Cascades from Yakima and Centennial from Oregon. It has an apple fruit aroma, more tart fruit in the mouth and a light dry finish. **Mount Tolmie**, also 4.2 per cent, uses caramalt, chocolate and crystal blended with pale malt. Mount Hood hops are added in the copper and the beer is dry hopped with Cascade. It has a citric fruit aroma, dark, tart fruit in the mouth and a dry and bitter finish. **Doc Hadfield's Pale Ale** (4.2 per cent ABV) uses Mount Hood for aroma and bitterness. The ale has a piny aroma with citric fruit in the mouth and a light, dry finish with fruit notes. **Mitchell's ESB**, named in honour of the other founding partner, is 4.6 per cent, copper-coloured, with a grapefruit aroma and palate from Chinook hops and a citric finish, with hints of sultana fruit from crystal and chocolate malts. There is a late addition of Cascade hops.

A 4.9 per cent **India Pale Ale** is hopped with Centennials and is mashed with pale malt only. It has a resiny hop aroma, tart fruit and hops in the mouth and a citric fruit finish. A complex **Porter** (4.9 per cent ABV) uses pale, crystal, chocolate and roasted malt and malted wheat, with Centennial and Hallertau hops. It has a herbal, slightly lactic aroma, and is tart in the mouth. **Empress Stout** is the same strength, with bitter chocolate and hops in the mouth. As a sight for sore British eyes, the beers are served by beer engine and handpump. Paul Hadfield has now branched out with a Hefe-Weizen and a lambic.

There are handpumps on view in Swan's Hotel in the centre of Victoria. The hotel, restaurant and attached Buckerfield's Brewery were founded by Michael Williams, from Shropshire in England. He emigrated to Canada and became a sheep farmer before moving into property. He bought an old warehouse in Victoria and turned it into Swan's. He died in 2000 but his legacy lives on in the brewery. Malt, including pale, crystal, chocolate and roast plus oatmeal, are supplied by the major English malting company, Bairds. The main brand is **Buckerfield's Bitter** (5.0 per cent ABV), with a nutty, malty aroma, piny hops, dark raisin fruit in the mouth and a dry, bitter finish. An impressive 8.0 per cent **Scotch Ale** has vinous fruit and hops on the aroma, raisin and sultana fruit in the mouth, and a complex finish with malt, nuts and late hops. **Appleton Brown Ale** (5.0 per cent) is named after the brewery's designer, Frank Appleton. It has pronounced apple fruit and cinnamon aromas, dark fruit in the mouth, and a creamy, bittersweet finish. **Oatmeal Stout** (5.4 per cent) has a rich, dark coffee and hops aroma, creamy malt, chocolate and hops in the mouth, and a tart and bitter finish. Other beers include **Legacy Ale**, in Michael Williams' honour, **Smooth Sailing Honey Ale**, **Pumpkin Ale** and a Belgian-style wheat beer.

German brewer Hermann Hoerterer helped develop the beers at Vancouver Island Brewery, one of Canada's earliest micros. **Hermann's Dark Lager** (5.5 per cent ABV), rich in chocolate malt character, pays homage to him. The brewery also produces a splendid **Weizen**, rich in banana aroma and flavour. Other beers in the range include a **Pilsner** with a good toasted malt character balanced by floral Saaz hops, and **Piper's Pale Ale**, hopped with Hallertau and Willamette varieties, dark for the style with the addition of caramalt and chocolate malt.

Okanagan Spring Brewery in Vernon, British Columbia, also has strong Germanic influences. It was founded by German immigrants and is now the biggest microbrewery in the province. Starting with a fine **Premium Lager**, it has spread to a more eclectic range that includes a pale ale, brown ale, porter, stout and wheat beer. The **Old English Porter** (8.5 per cent ABV) is especially highly regarded. It is bottle-fermented and has a delicious chocolate malt character balanced by bitter hops and dark fruit. The brewery has added a **Bavarian Helles** and **Munich Dark** to the range to cement the German connection.

Upper Canada Brewing Company in Toronto uses the early settlers' name for the province of Ontario. The sizeable micro was founded in 1985 by Frank Heaps. The 5.0 per cent **Dark Ale** is a cross between a strong English mild with a dash of Belgian red ale sourness. It has an intensely fruity aroma and palate with more tart dark fruit and bitter hops in the finish. while **Upper Canada Lager** is malty and firm bodied while a new **Pale Ale** celebrates the brewery's 20 years of production. **Red** is available only on draught and is a malty, ruby-red beer, lightly hopped with Galena and Hersbrucker varieties.. A 4.3 per cent **Wheat Beer** has more than 35 per cent wheat malt blended with pale barley malt. Hops are Northern Brewer (18 to 20 IBUs). The beer is filtered and has a tart and fruity aroma and palate with some light spiciness in the finish.

In the old brewing town of Guelph, the Wellington County Brewery produces an **Arkell Best Bitter** to mark a family connection with the Swindon brewing family of Arkell in Wiltshire, England. The 4.0 per cent cask-conditioned ale has a peppery Goldings hops aroma, malt and fruit in the the mouth and a long, hoppy-fruity finish. The brewery also produces a fruity **Wellington SPA** (4.5 per cent ABV), a hoppy **County Ale** (5.0 per cent ABV), a rich and fruity strong ale called **Iron Duke** (6.5 per cent ABV), and a roasty and chocolatey **Imperial Stout** (8.0 per cent ABV).

The Francophone areas of Canada are also joining the beer revival. Many of the first French settlers came from Normandy and Flanders and have an ale-brewing tradition. Les Brasseurs du Nord in St Jerôme, north of Montreal, which labels its beers Boréale, brews a dry **Blonde**, a fruity **Rousse** and a smooth, dark **Noire**. La Cervoise in the heart of Montreal brews **Blond**, **Dark Ale** and a **Stout**.

Le Cheval Blanc, also in Montreal, has a chocolatey **Ambrée**, an espresso-like **Brune** and a tart **Weissbier**.

Unibroue in Chambly, Quebec, is now the leading small brewery in the French-speaking area. One of the founders was Canadian rock singer Robert Charlebois, and the company was initially helped by the Belgian Riva group, producers of Dentergems Witbier. The main brand, **Blanche de Chambly** (5 per cent ABV) is delicious, with tart orange and lemon fruit flavours. **Maudite**, meaning "damned", is 8 per cent, styled in the fashion of a Belgian strong ale, and packed with fruit and spice character. A fetching label shows a flying canoe with the devil waiting below: it is taken from a legend concerning a party of trappers who sold their souls to the devil to get home in time for a party. The alarmingly named **Le Fin du Monde** (End of the World) is 9 per cent and is in the style of a Belgian Tripel. **Trois Pistoles** (9.0 per cent) has ripe fruit and chocolate on aroma and palate and a port wine note in the finish, **Chambly Noire** (6.2 per cent) has a roasted grain and coffee character.

Creemore Springs, in a small town of the same name in Ontario, is based in a converted hardware store in a ski resort. It concentrates on one main beer, **Pilsner** (5.0 per cent ABV), brewed with spring water, malt, hops and "loving care". It has a rich malt, vanilla and floral hops character. A strong **Urbock** is also brewed.

CANADIAN BREWERS

Amsterdam Brewing Co Ltd,
21 Bathurst Street, Toronto, ON
M5V 2N6.

La Cervoise,
4457 Blvd St Laurent, Montreal, PQ
H2W 1Z8.

Le Cheval Blanc,
809 Ontario Street, Montreal, PQ
H2L 1P1.

Creemore Springs Brewery,
139 Mill Street, Creemore, Ontario,
LOM 190.

Labatt Brewing Co Ltd,
150 Simcoe Street, PO Box 5050,
London, ON N6A 4M3.

Molson Breweries of Canada Ltd,
3300 Bloor Street W, Suite 3500,
Toronto, ON M8X 2X7.

Moosehead Breweries Ltd,
89 Main Street, PO Box 3100,
Station B, St John, NB E2M 3H2.

Okanagan Spring Brewery,
2801-27A Avenue, Vernon,
BC V1T 1T5.

Spinnakers,
309 Catherine Street, Victoria BC
V9A 3S8.

Swan's Hotel/Buckerfields,
506 Pandora Street, Victoria BC,
V8W 1N6.

Unibroue,
80 Des Carrières, Chambly,
Quebec J3L 2H6.

Upper Canada Brewing Company,
2 Atlantic Avenue, Toronto, Ontario
M6K 1X8.

Wellington County Brewery Ltd,
9500 Woodlawn Road W, Guelph,
ON N1K 1B8.

Latin America and the Caribbean

Latin America has a fascinating and long brewing tradition and it is tragic that the tradition has largely been submerged and suborned in recent years by modish thin lagers from Mexico that are neither typical of that country nor the continent as a whole. Yuppies in Manhattan, London and Berlin who drink Corona and Sol straight from the bottle with a wedge of lime stuck in the neck may be making a statement about their lifestyle – raspberry would be a better fruit – but are denying the quality and the heritage of good Latin American beer.

Long before Europeans arrived in Latin America the natives were making a variety of beers from the ingredients to hand. The Mayans of Central America brewed from fermented corn stalks while the Aztecs of northern Mexico produced a more advanced beer made from maize that had been allowed to sprout. According to legend, it was the task of specially chosen maidens of the Inca tribe living around Lake Titicaca to chew the cooked maize pulp used in brewing. Only their beauty and the purity of their saliva would start fermentation, it was believed. Even when the Spanish had conquered vast areas of the continent, peasants continued to make *pulque* from the juice of the algave plant. The name comes from a Spanish word meaning "decomposed", as the drink will keep for only a day before going off.

Pulque and other native drinks survive in Latin America. In the remote areas of the Upper Amazon a black beer has been made since at least the fifteenth century. The colour comes from the use of roasted barley and grain that are dark brown in colour. It is flavoured with lupin plants. The American beer writer and anthropologist Alan Eames – nicknamed the "Indiana Jones of Beer" – searched and found the beer in remote areas and encouraged a Brazilian brewery, Cervejaria Cacador in Brazil, to make it commercially. It is called **Xingu** (5.0 per cent ABV), pronounced shin-gu, the name of a tributary of the Amazon River. It is a modern, conventionally brewed interpretation of the style, using hops for both flavouring and as a preservative.

Small Spanish breweries – *cervecería* – were established from the sixteenth century but distilled spirits such as mescal and tequila were more popular than beer until the arrival of ice-making machines in the nineteenth century. The first lager beers were known as *sencilla* or *corriente* and were matured for short periods.

Some earlier breweries achieved remarkable success, however. In December 1543 Don Alonso de Herrera from Seville, known as a citizen of "New Spain" (Mexico), built a brewery in Mexico City and launched a beer called **Zerbeza**. It means Desire, the sort of name that modern marketing departments of breweries would pay a lot of money for. Such was the local desire for Zerbeza that Don Alonso had to add 100 additional vats to keep up with demand.

The modern influences in Mexican brewing are Germanic. Some of the first lager breweries were established by Bavarians, Swiss and Alsatians. The country was briefly and incongruously a colony of the Austrian empire, with Archduke Maximilian doubling as Emperor of Mexico. One of the few benefits of the association was the influence of the great Viennese brewer Anton Dreher, who invented the style of amber beers. The style has virtually vanished from Austria but is alive and well in the former colony.

Today two giants dominate Mexican brewing. In Mexico City, Modelo runs the biggest brewing plant in the country, which rivals all but the top five American groups in size. It is best-known today for **Corona**, the beer that spawned the Mexican lager-and-lime craze. Like its competitor, Sol, **Corona Extra** (4.6 per cent ABV) has been around for decades and was a bottom-of-the-range product made cheaply for poor peasants and industrial workers. It comes in a utilitarian plain glass bottle with an embossed label. It has around 40 per cent rice in its recipe and a low hop rate that creates around 10 to 12 IBUs. Served extremely cold, it is a refreshing drink for those engaged in hard manual labour, which is more than can be said for the well-heeled young Americans on surfing holidays. They took up the beer with enthusiasm and extolled its peasant-cum-worker attributes when they returned to California and Manhattan – a middle-class attitude known as being "prolier than thou". It was the Americans who added lime to the beer, which caused amusement and consternation in Mexico, though sad to say the habit has now been taken up there as well.

A beer with not only pedigree but taste is Modelo's **Negra Modelo** – Black Modelo. It is dark brown rather than black, a cross between a Vienna Red and a Munich Dunkel, 5.3 per cent ABV, 19 IBUs, with a chocolatey aroma with some hop character, sweet dark malt in the mouth and a long finish with a hint of spice, more chocolate and hops, ending with a dry roastiness. Modelo also owns the Yucatán Brewery which produces a similar dark beer called **Negra Leon**. The dark colour of these beers owes only part of its inspiration to Vienna. Before modern malting developed, Latin American brewers dried their grain in the sun, giving beers a russet hue as a result.

Modelo, in which A-B InBev has a 50 per cent stake, has the largest brewing plant, but the group has been overtaken in size by the merger of Moctezuma and Cuauhtémoc. They both belong to a holding company called Valores, which runs seven breweries in Mexico. Moctezuma dates from 1894 when it was built by Henry Manthey, William Hasse, C. von Alten and Adolph Burhard in Orizaba, Veracruz. Cuauhtémoc, named after an Aztec emperor, took on the name in 1890 when the Casa Calderón Brewery in Monterrey was extended. Moctezuma is best known today for **Sol** (4.6 per cent ABV), a Corona lookalike also produced in a clear glass bottle. It is believed to have an even higher level of adjuncts than Corona. Of far greater interest is **Dos Equis** – Two Crosses –

dark lager (4.8 per cent ABV), widely available in foreign markets. It is in the Vienna style, a fraction paler than Negra Modelo, and with a rich dark fruit and chocolate aroma and palate, with more chocolate and light hops in the finish. **Superior** (4.5 per cent ABV) is a far more interesting pale lager than Sol, with some hop bite.

Cuauhtémoc also has a thin quencher in the Corona/Sol style with the risible name – to outsiders – of **Chihuahua**, which is a Mexican state as well as a small dog. Tecate – once advertised as "the Gulp of Mexico" – is another pale ("clara") beer useful for quenching the thirst, as is **Carta Blanca** ("white label") launched in 1890 in the Pilsner style but now another thin mainstream beer. **Bohemia** is in a different league, an indication of what Mexican brewers can achieve when they turn their gaze away from their neighbour to the north. At 5.4 per cent ABV it has some clout and good hop character – Saaz are used – that complements the rich malt and vanilla aroma and firm malty body.

Mazatlán in Sinaloa state is now owned by Modelo. It opened in 1900 and was established by Jacob Schuehle who also built the original Moctezuma Brewery. **Pacifico Clara** is a light lager while **Pacifico Oscura** is a thin amber beer.

Brazil was invaded by the Portuguese rather than the Spanish but the modern brewing tradition is Germanic. **Brahma**, owned by AmBev, the local arm of InBev, is a fine Pilsner-style beer (5.0 per cent ABV) with a rich malt and vanilla aroma, a malty palate and a bittersweet finish with late developing hops. The group produces more than 31 million hectolitres a year and, surprisingly, its brands include a warm-fermenting, 8.0 per cent ABV **Porter**. Some zealous porter sniffers suggest another possible origin of the beer style's enigmatic name: they say it comes not from London street porters but from Portugal!

In Peru, the similarly named Compañia Cervecera brews **Peru Gold** with a striking native face mask on the label. The beer is 5.0 per cent ABV, has a rich corn and vanilla aroma, is tart and quenching in the mouth, and has a dry finish with some citric fruit notes from the hops. It also produces **Cuzco Peruvian Beer**. In Venezuela, the Polar brewing company's **Polar Lager** (5.0 per cent ABV) is so remarkably thin that it makes Corona and Sol seem malty and hoppy by comparison. It is nevertheless a major brand, responsible for more than 12 million hectolitres a year. The Cardenal group in the same country has a more distinctive range, including **Nacional "Cerveza Tipo Pilsen"** – Beer Type Pilsen, which indicates the astonishing impact of Pilsen beer and deserves marks for honesty of promotion. A German influence can be seen in the brewery's **Tipo Munich** beer, a malty, burnished gold lager, while **Andes** is more typical of the light beers of the continent.

Cervecería Bieckert in Buenos Aires, Argentina, despite being a former Spanish colony, is also heavily influenced by German and Czech styles. **Cerveza Pilsen** (4.8 per cent ABV) is brewed from pale malt, rice and maize and is hopped with American Cascades. It has 13 IBUs. Pilsen is more of an illusion than an allusion, for the lightly hopped and heavily adjuncted beer is low on aroma, body and flavour. **Especial** (5.0 per cent ABV) has 14 IBUs and the same grist recipe and has a shade more character. The most interesting product is **Africana** (5.5 per cent ABV), a cold-fermenting beer that is a hybrid Munich Dunkel and Vienna Red. It is brewed from pale, crystal and chocolate malts with rice and maize and is hopped with Cascades (14 IBUs). It has a tempting roasted malt aroma, a smooth chocolate palate and a dry finish with hints of dark fruit, more chocolate and a tart Cascade note.

LATIN AMERICAN BREWERS

Cervecería Bieckert SA,
Ponsato 121 Llavallol (1836) Pcia,
Buenos Aires, Argentina.
Cervecería Moctezuma,

Avenida Alfonso Reyes 2202, Nte,
Monterrey NL 64442, Mexico.
Cervecería Modelo,
156 Lago Alberto, Mexico City
11320, Mexico.

The Caribbean

The islands of the Caribbean have brewed beer for centuries. The quickly made native porridge beers, known by a welter of names in the different islands – *tesguino, chicha, izquiate, sendecho, zeydetha* and *zeyrecha*, the last two sounding like derivatives of the Spanish *cerveza* – succumbed to both the imported beers of the British, Spanish and French and to the comfort of locally made rum. Guinness's **West Indies Porter** had a profound impact in the early nineteenth century. Known today as **Foreign Extra Stout** (7.3 per cent ABV), it is brewed in Spanish Town, the former capital of Jamaica, and by the Carib company in Trinidad.

The main beers today are light lagers but several Caribbean brewers keep a stout in their lockers. There is even a **Prestige Stout** from the unlikely location of Haiti where there is a morbid joke that under the old Duvalier regime all beers were lagered or stored for very long periods. Cuba's main brewery was founded in the last century by two brewers of German extraction, Obermeyer and Liebmann, who went to Havana from Brooklyn. The Nacional Dominicana Brewery in Santo Domingo, Dominican Republic, produces more than two million barrels/2.4 million hectolitres a year and is the biggest brewery in the region. **Bohemia** is the main product, a 5.0 per cent lager that is a rather thin interpretation of the Pilsner style.

The major brewery in the former British West Indies is Desnoes & Geddes of Kingston, Jamaica. It was founded in 1918 as a soft drinks business by Eugene Desnoes and Thomas Geddes. The families are still in control, with Peter Desnoes and Paul Geddes running the company, though Heineken now has a small shareholding. The flagship brand is **Red Stripe** (4.7 per cent ABV; 14 IBUs), a malty, sweetish rather perfumy beer, the product of a short lagering regime. Its grist is made up of 70 per cent barley malt and 30 per cent corn. In common with many Australian beers, Red Stripe began life as an ale but switched to cold fermentation in the 1930s. Red Stripe is brewed under licence in Britain by Charles Wells and is popular in the West Indian community. The company's **Dragon Stout** (7.0 per cent ABV) is also a lager, with a sweet malt character overlain by chocolate and dark fruit with some hop character. The Jamaicans do not shy away from stressing the alleged aphrodisiac qualities of the beer. Its most famous promotion declared that "Dragon Puts It Back".

On Barbados, the Banks Brewery produces **Banks Beer**, a 4.5 per cent lager made from two-row pale malt and brewing sugar. It is hopped with Yakima Clusters and Styrian Goldings and has 16 IBUs. The beer has a delicate, citric hop aroma, smooth malt in the mouth and a finish that becomes dry with good hop notes. It is lagered for a month. **Carib Lager** from Trinidad is a fully brewed-out beer, dry and quenching in the finish with some hops on the aroma and a firm, malty body.

IMPORTANT ADDRESSES

Banks (Barbados) Breweries Ltd, PO Box 507C, Wildey, St Michael, Barbados.

Desnoes & Geddes Ltd, 214 Spanish Town Road, PO Box 190, Kingston 11, Jamaica.

Beers from the Rest of the World

Modern brewing methods – for both ale and lager – were part of the baggage of imperialism in the eighteenth and nineteenth centuries. British, French, Dutch and German settlers brewed for themselves and their troops but the taste for beer remained and spread when the troops and sometimes the settlers returned home. Lager is now the dominant beer style in Africa, India and Asia and often of the highest quality. But there are residual pockets of ale brewing, including the post-imperial stouts of Sri Lanka and a warm-fermenting beer or two in Japan.

Africa and the Middle East

Africa was the birthplace of brewing. Although no records exist, it is likely that beers similar to those in Ancient Egypt were widespread throughout the vast continent. They exist today in the traditional "porridge beers" in which a mash made of millet, sorghum, cassava flour, palm sap, maize and even banana is allowed to ferment spontaneously with wild yeasts in the atmosphere and in the brewing pots and is then spiced with bitter herbs. In countries still struggling to throw off the last vestiges of colonialism and create modern societies, porridge beers are an important part of the diet of poor people, containing vitamin C and several important B vitamins. The beers have many different names such as *chibuku* in Central Africa and *dolo* in West Africa.

The survival of these traditional beers is important, for conventional modern brewing is expensive, as barley and hops do not grow in most parts of Africa and have to be imported. The Kenyan government is attempting to create barley and hop industries in the cooler altitudes: so far the barley grown can only be used as an unmalted adjunct in brewing as its quality is not sufficiently high for malting. Hops are also grown in South Africa. European brewing groups with interests in Africa have been reluctant to experiment with beers made from local cereals, though the Nigerian government decided in the mid-1980s that 25 per cent of local grain should be used in brewing. Nigeria has the biggest number of breweries in Africa, around 30. The main brewing group, Nigerian Breweries, is jointly owned by Heineken and the United Africa Company and they made it plain to the government that if it pressed ahead with plans to make all breweries use only local cereals then some beers would be withdrawn from the market. They consider that cereals such as sorghum do not contain sufficient starch to convert into fermentable sugar.

Southern Africa

Modern brewing in Africa came as part of the baggage of colonialism. British, French, Dutch and Germans needed to refresh themselves and they set up rudimentary breweries, often on farms, that blossomed into substantial commercial plants once the newcomers had set down firm roots. Southern Africa, in particular, became a melting pot of brewers. In 1820 the Mariendahl Brewery was set up at Newlands; the Germans arrived in Natal in the 1840s and began brewing; the British opened a brewery in Durban; and in 1862 a Norwegian named Anders Ohlsson bought the Mariendahl Brewery. Ohlsson opened a second brewery and rapidly became a brewing giant on the Cape, eliminating most of the competition and establishing his Lion Beer as the principal brand.

The gold rush in the Transvaal created an enormous demand for beer. Ohlsson now faced serious competition from the British. The leading British-owned brewery was Castle and Castle Beer soon vied with Lion as the main brand in the region. Castle, owned by Frederick Mead, merged with smaller companies to form South African Breweries. SAB expanded from the traditional heartland of beer-drinking in Johannesburg, Durban and Cape Town to Port Elizabeth and Salisbury, Rhodesia (now Harare, the capital of Zimbabwe). After many years of talks and stand-offs, SAB and Ohlsson finally merged in 1956, making the enlarged SAB the biggest brewing group in the whole of Africa.

SAB experimented with lager-brewing as early as 1896. Today **Lion Lager** and **Castle Lager** (5.0 per cent ABV) dominate the market from the Zambezi to the Cape. Anders Ohlsson's memory is recalled in **Ohlsson's Lager**, also 5.0 per cent. In the 1980s a microbrewery started to produce an all-malt lager at Kynsa in Cape Province and tested occasional cask-conditioned ales and stouts. A second micro called Our Brewery opened in Johannesburg, brewing an unpasteurized ale.

During the years of apartheid, blacks were not encouraged to drink conventional beer. They were confined to insultingly named "kaffir bars" where the only beer was a porridge-type called "kaffir beer". The end of race discrimination and rising expectations among the black population are likely to cause a demand for modern beer. The demise of porridge beer in South Africa and Zimbabwe will be a mixed blessing, marking the end of years of oppression but also the loss of a link with brewing's past.

Kenya

The most characterful Pilsner-style beer in the whole of Africa comes ironically from a brewery in Kenya founded by British settlers, including a gold prospector. East African Breweries – now Kenya Breweries – imported both equipment and a brewer from the old country: the brewer came from the famous brewing town of Burtonwood, near Warrington. Hops were imported from Kent and the main products were ale and stout. Lager brewing was developed in the 1930s. White Cap and Tusker rapidly became admired lager beers, not only winning prizes at international competitions – including two gold medals and one silver at the World Beer Competition in 1968 – but gaining even more chutzpah from the fact that Ernest Hemingway pronounced them his favourite beers when he was hunting in Kenya.

Tusker Premium Lager is a well-attenuated beer, with a starting gravity of 1044 degrees but reaching 4.8 per cent ABV. It is brewed from 90 per cent barley malt and 10 per cent cane sugar and is hopped with imported Hallertau and Styrian hops. A regular, everyday version of **Tusker** and the more fruity **White Cap** are around 4.0 per cent ABV. Pilsner Lager is almost identical to Tusker Premium. Kenya Breweries has subsidiaries in Uganda and Tanzania and supplies the Zimbabwe market.

Nigeria

Nigerian Breweries built its reputation on the quality of **Star Lager**, brewed to mark the opening of the first of the group's plants in Lagos in 1949. Additional breweries were built in Aba, Kaduna and Ibadan to quench the thirst of the Nigerians, the greatest beer drinkers in Africa. The influence of Heineken is clear to see in **Gulder**, also 5.0 per cent but with a shade more hop character than Star. Gulder has become the flagship brand, with a gentle malt and citric hops aroma, tart and refreshing in the mouth and a finish that starts malty and becomes dry with good hop character. The company also produces a 7.0 per cent **Legend Stout**, roasty and chocolatey, brewed to meet the enormous demand for stout in Nigeria and to counter the challenge of Guinness.

Guinness has three breweries in Nigeria producing an 8.0 per cent version of the stout. These breweries make a beer using conventional pale malt. Guinness sends out from Dublin a concentrate made by making dark stout and removing the water. The concentrate (the recipe of which is a closely guarded secret) is blended with the pale beer to make **Nigerian Guinness**.

Golden Guinea Breweries in Umuahia is another leading Nigerian company. It started life as the Independence Brewery in 1962 and came under state control. It receives support today from Holsten of Hamburg, which advises on raw materials and technical processes. **Golden Guinea Lager** is 5.0 per cent with a good balance of malt and hops on the aroma and palate. The brewery also produces **Eagle Stout**.

Francophone Africa

The biggest non-African brewery group operating on the continent is the French BGI – Brasseries et Glacières Internationales. Founded in Tonkin, Indochina, in the nineteenth century, BGI has been active in all the countries that were French colonies in Africa and Asia. It is best known for its **33 Export** lager but also brews for the African market such brands as Beaufort, Castel, Flag, Gazelle and Regab. It has a powerful presence in Benin (main brand **La Béninoise**), Cameroon, Central African Republic (**Mocaf** and **Mocaf Blonde**), Gabon, Niger (**Bière Niger**), Ivory Coast, Mali, Tunisia and Zaire. The main producer in Zaire, formerly the Belgian Congo, is the Belgian giant InBev, best known for Stella Artois. It brews under the name of Brasimba and produces two lager beers, **Simba** and **Tembo**. In the finest Belgian tradition, the first brewery in the Belgian Congo was founded by Jesuits in 1902 at Ki-Santu.

In the Republic of the Congo, the SCBK Brewery at Pointe Noire near Brazzaville brews **Ngok**, local dialect for Le Choc – crocodile. One of the most highly regarded lagers in Francophone Africa, **Mamba**, is brewed in Abidjan, capital of the Ivory Coast by Solibra, owned by InBev. The brewery also produces a strong Bock lager and a tawny Brune, the latter with a faint hint of an Abbey-style beer from Belgium.

The island of Madagascar's Star Brewery has three plants devoted to just one lager brand called **Three Horses Beer**. The smaller island of Réunion has a lager with the enticing name of **Bourbon**, which takes its name from the town where the brewery is based and has no whisky connections. Mauritius, for a small island, has had impressive success with the lager beers produced by the Mauritius Brewery. **Phoenix** (4.5 per cent ABV) won a gold medal at the International Brewers Exhibition (Brewex) in 1983 and a gold at Monde Sélection in 1989. Stella Lager – no connection with Stella Artois – has also won two golds. **Blue Marlin** (5.6 per cent ABV) was introduced in 1989 and won a Monde Sélection gold three years later.

North Africa and the Middle East

The surge of Islamic fundamentalism in North Africa and the Middle East makes the future of brewing in the region uncertain. All the Iranian breweries have closed since the ayatollahs came to power. The fate of Iraq's state-controlled breweries, producing **Ferida, Golden Lager** and **Jawhara** beers, is unknown. Egypt has a state-controlled brewery in Cairo producing **Pyramid** lager. Arab Breweries in Amman, Jordan, brews **Petra** lager.

Tempo Beer Industries in Israel dominates the market through five brewing plants. Its flagship brand is **Maccabee** (4.9 per cent ABV) with a pronounced malt aroma, bittersweet malt and hops in the mouth, and a dry finish with some hops and vanilla notes. Tempo also produces **Gold Star** and **Malt Star** lagers.

The major brewing group in Turkey, Anadolu Industri, brews **Efes Pilsen** (5.0 per cent ABV) with a tangy malt and hops aroma, rich malt in the mouth, and a long bittersweet finish that becomes dry and hoppy. The beer is exported widely throughout the Middle East, Africa and Europe. A smaller company, Türk Tuborg, is a subsidiary of the Danish Carlsberg/Tuborg group and brews Tuborg under licence. The island of Cyprus has **Keo Beer**, a 4.5 per cent lager, with a good balance of malt and hops on the aroma, some vanilla notes and hops on the palate, and a bittersweet finish.

AFRICAN AND MIDDLE EASTERN BREWERS

Anadolu Industri (Efes),
Anadolu Efes Biracılık ve Malt San.
A.Ş, Esentepe Mah. Anadolu Cad.
No: 1, Kartal 34870 Istanbul/Turkey.

Arab Breweries,
Prince Muhammad Street, Amman,
Jordan.

Brasimba,
Avenue du Flambeau 912, Kinshasa,
Zaire.

Brasseries et Glacières Internationales,
Brasserie El Harrach, Boite Postale 22,
El-Jazair (Algiers), Algeria.

Golden Guinea Breweries,
5 Route de Coyah, Conakry, Guinea.

Kenya Breweries,
Thika Road, Ruaraka, Nairobi, Kenya.

Mauritius Brewery,
Pont Fer, Vacoas-Phoenix Mauritius.

Nigerian Breweries,
PO Box 496, Aba, Nigeria.

SCBK Brewery,
Kronenberg, Point Noire, Brazzaville,
Republic of Congo.

Solibra,
01 Boite Postale 1304, Abidjan 01,
Côte d'Ivoire (Ivory Coast).

South African Breweries,
Sandton 2146, South Africa.

Star Brewery,
Route de Majunga Andranomahery,
Tanjombato, Antananarivo, Madagascar.

Tempo Beer Industries,
New Industrial Zone, POB 127
42101 Netanya, Tel Aviv, Israel.

The beer styles of Australia

AUSTRALIA	Matilda Bay Brewing	Two Brothers	Sydney
Adelaide/Thebarton	Co	*James Squire Brewhouse*	Redoak Boutique
Cooper's Brewery	*Sail and Anchor*	*Prince's Bridge Hotel*	Beer Cafe
South Australian	**Hobart**	*Cookie*	*Pumphouse Brewery*
Brewing Co	Cascade Brewery Co	**Mornington**	*Brewpub*
Beechworth	Moo Brew	**Peninsula**	*Lord Nelson Hotel*
Bridge Road Brewers	**Launceston**	Red Hill	*The Hero of Waterloo*
Brisbane/Milton	Boag's	**Perth/Swan Valley**	*Hotel*
Castlemaine Perkins	**Margaret River**	Feral Brewing Co.	*Australian Hotel*
(Lion Nathan)	Bootleg Brewery	Swan Brewery Co	**Taylors Arm**
Brisbane German Club	**Melbourne**	(Lion Nathan)	Murray's
Fremantle/Canning	Foster's/Carlton and	**Richmond**	**Woodend**
Vale	United Breweries	Mountain Goat	Holgate Brewhouse
Little Creatures	Three Ravens		

Australia

If Foster's is your favourite tipple, don't go to Australia. What was once considered an iconic Australian beer – the "amber nectar" – hardly features. Even Crocodile Dundee shuns it now and the company that makes it has reverted to its original name of Carlton and Union Breweries. Foster's today is an export brand. CUB's main beers are Victoria Bitter, the biggest-selling beer in Australia (and a lager in spite of the name) and Carlton Draught.

With Lion Nathan, which brews **Castlemaine XXXX**, **Toohey's** and **Swan**, the two giants command 95 per cent of the Australian market. Cooper's of Adelaide, doughty brewers of the famous **Sparkling Ale**, has a further 3 per cent, which doesn't leave much room for anyone else. But an astonishing number of small craft breweries have sprung up, like flowers in the Australian desert after a rainstorm, to grab the remaining 2 per cent of the market.

Thanks to their efforts, Australians can now move beyond ice-cold lagers and savour British-style pale ales, IPAs, porters and stouts, alongside Belgian and German-inspired wheat beers, strong ales and true Pilsners.

One of the main driving forces behind the craft brewing revolution is an American, Dr Charles Hahn. Better known simply as Chuck Hahn, he has built a chain of brewpubs under the Malt Shovel and James Squire names. Hahn was born in New York City and worked for Coors in Colorado for 10 years before being head-hunted by Tooth's in Sydney. He was brewery general manager there but lost his job in 1983 when Foster's bought Tooth's.

Hahn moved to New Zealand where he worked for Lion for 3½ years before launching his own Hahn Brewery in New South Wales. He built **Hahn Premium Lager** into a successful brand but his business collapsed when banks withdrew their support during a recession in the 1990s. He teamed up with Lion Nathan and opened the Malt Shovel Brewery in Camperdown, New South Wales, named after the tavern where James Squire brewed in the late eighteenth century.

Squire is commemorated as Australia's first brewer. He was a convict transported from England to Australia. He continued a life of crime until he settled down to run his tavern and brew beer. Chuck Hahn launched **James Squire Original Pilsner** and then rolled out a number of James Squire brewpubs. There are two in Melbourne and one in Sydney, with a fourth due to come on stream in Perth in 2009. The aim is to have a brewpub in every major Australian city.

The brewing kit on view in the James Squire Brewhouse on Russell Street, Melbourne came from a former Firkin brewpub in London. In common with the other brew-pubs, the Russell Street site produces small volume beers such as IPA and Porter and occasional "off the wall" brews, including a raspberry wheat. Bigger brands such as **Pilsner**, **Golden Ale** and **Amber Ale** come either from the Malt Shovel brewery in New South Wales, which produces 2.5 million hectolitres a year, or Lion Nathan's South Australian Brewery in Adelaide.

Western Australia

For a state with a population of around just one million, Western Australia has a surprising number of micros. Feral in the Swan Valley won three awards and was named overall champion at the International Brewing Awards in Melbourne in 2009. Its beers include a powerfully hopped American-style IPA, **Hophog** (5.8 per cent ABV), a lemony and spicy Belgian-style wheat beer, **Feral White** (4.6 per cent), **Rust**, a 6 per cent Belgian ale, and **Farmhouse Ale** (4.3 per cent), unfiltered, cloudy, with big citrus fruit and spicy notes.

Bootleg is the first craft brewery in the Margaret River region of the state. Its beer range includes a malty dark beer, **Raging Bull** (7.1 per cent) with coffee, chocolate and toffee notes, a seasonal German-style **Hefe** wheat beer, **Tom's Amber Ale** (4 per cent) and **Wil's Pils** at 4.9 per cent.

Little Creatures in Fremantle is a fast-growing craft brewery with national coverage whose range includes a 5.2 per cent ABV **Pale Ale**, with grapefruit and floral hop notes balancing rich malt, and **Bright Ale** (4.5 per cent), packed with citrus hops and juicy malt. **Roger's Beer** (no relation) at 3.8 per cent has chewy caramel notes and spicy hops, while a 4.6 per cent **Pilsner** has toasted malt, light citrus fruit and good hop bitterness.

Matilda Bay in Fremantle is one of the earliest craft breweries in the country and revives memories of David Bruce's Firkin chain in England with a 5.2 per cent ABV **Dogbolter** – a big malty beer with roasted grain and chocolate notes. The brewery also produces a 4.7 per cent **Bohemian Pilsner**, rich and malty with a late burst of hop bitterness, **Alpha Pale Ale** (5.2 per cent), and its best-known brand, the 4.7 per cent Bavarian-style wheat beer, **Redback**, with a pronounced banana and cloves character.

New South Wales

In Sydney, the Lord Nelson brewpub offers **Old Admiral** (6.1 per cent ABV), with vinous fruit and ripe malt notes, and **Three Sheets** (4.9 per cent), a pale ale that has juicy malt, fruity hops and a long bittersweet finish. Also in Sydney, the Redoak boutique beer cafe, run by David and Janet Hollyoak, has an eclectic range including a Belgian-inspired raspberry beer, **Framboise Froment** (5.2 per cent ABV), a 6.5 per cent **IPA**, which is served on handpump in the cafe, and has a big citrus fruit and bitter hop character, and **Rauch** or smoke beer (5.5 per cent) using malt from Bamberg in Germany, with toffee notes, spicy hops and a long, smoky, complex finish. Redoak also produces a 5 per cent **Blackberry Wheat**, tart and quenching.

Murray's at Taylor's Arm, produces **Nirvana Pale Ale** (4.5 per cent ABV) with big spicy and peppery hops, cracker-wheat maltiness and a good bitter finish, and **Sassy Blonde** (4.5 per cent), a Belgian-style ale with spicy hop notes, juicy malt and a long bittersweet finish.

The Wig & Pen in Canberra in the Capital Territory is another bar with handpumped beer. The influence is firmly British, with a **Bulldog Best Bitter** (4 per cent ABV), bursting with cracker-wheat malt, spicy hops and rich fruit, with a long and bitter finish, and **Creamy Stout** (6 per cent), a silky smooth beer with chocolate and mocha flavours and a roasty and fruity finish.

South Australia

The South Australian Brewing Co in Thebarton, Adelaide, was a major independent until it was bought by Lion Nathan. The company grew by a succession of mergers that started as far back as 1888 when the Kent Town Brewery and the West End Brewery joined forces. Later acquisitions included Broken Hill Brewery and Southwark Brewery. Several of the former breweries are recalled in the current range of beers. **West End Premium** (5.0 per cent ABV) is dry in the finish with 25 bitterness units created by Pride of Ringwood and Hersbrucker Hallertau varieties. **Southwark Premium** (5.5 per cent) has a good balance of malt and perfumy hop while **Old Australia Stout** (7.4 per cent) is a dark lager with an abundance of roasted grain and chocolate character. **Broken Hill Lager** (4.8 per cent) also has some roasted barley in its make-up. It's one of the more characterful of mainstream Australian lagers with a good hop aroma from Pride of Ringwood, a rounded palate and a quenching, bittersweet finish.

Cooper's of Adelaide

Cooper's of Adelaide is a world-famous brewery once laughed to scorn in its homeland by remaining true to ale while the rest of the country was switching to lager. But the brewery had the last laugh. It's a flourishing company and it has broken out of South Australia and enjoys national and international sales. It's family-owned and run by the fifth generation of the Coopers, who believe in tradition and quality. When Lion Nathan attempted to buy Cooper's in 2005, 94.6

per cent of the 117 shareholders, mainly family members, turned down an offer worth A\$450 million – that's around £200 million.

The brewery was founded by a Yorkshireman, Thomas Cooper, who emigrated from Skipton with his wife, the daughter of an inn-keeper. While Thomas worked as a dairyman and a cobbler, his wife brewed at home. When she became ill, Thomas tried his hand at making beer. Not only was his wife cured but his friends raved about Thomas's beer and encouraged him to open a brewery.

For most of its life, the brewery was based in the Leabrook district of Adelaide. It used a brewing method similar to the Burton Unions in England: primary fermentation took place in vessels made from the hardwood called jarrah. The beer was then dropped into wooden puncheons or hogsheads where it continued to ferment. In 2001, Cooper's moved to a new site at Regency Park: Leabrook could produce 700,000 hectolitres a year while Regency Park has a poten-tial capacity of 250 million hectos. It's typical of the Cooper family, represented today by Glenn and Tim, that the modern yet tradi-tional new brewhouse, based on mash tuns, mash filters and coppers, was designed by Briggs of Burton-on-Trent in the historic home of pale ale. The old vessels are on view in a museum on the site.

The beers are brewed using malted barley grown in South Australia, with Pride of Ringwood hops also sourced from the home state. The pale beers are made with pale and crystal malts, with roasted barley added to the stout. The renowned hazy character of the beers, despite being called "sparkling", is the result of the house yeast culture, which is powdery and remains in suspension in the beer. The main brand, **Pale Ale** (4.5 per cent ABV) has a fruity and hoppy nose, with juicy malt, some citrus fruit and bitter hops in the mouth and the finish. The flagship **Sparkling Ale** (5.8 per cent) has 26 units of bitterness. It's intensely fruity, with apple and banana dominating, a peppery hop aroma, citrus fruit in the mouth, and a long, quenching finish with more hops and fruit.

Cooper's Stout (6.8 per cent) has an oily aroma and palate with rich coffee and bitter chocolate notes. The company aims for a creamy and malty stout: it's not looking for the bitter and roasty character of Guinness. **Cooper's Dark** (4.5 per cent) is made from pale, crystal and roast malt and has a fruity and chocolate character. It's based unashamedly on Brain's Dark in Cardiff, discovered by a member of the Cooper family on a visit to Wales. The brewery has introduced **Mild** (3.8 per cent), a light coloured interpretation of the style, and an annual bottled **Vintage Ale** (7.5 per cent), with massive vinous fruit and bitter hops. The beer will improve with age.

Victoria

The Three Ravens Brewery is in the up-market residential Thornbury area of Melbourne, the brainchild of brewer Marcus Cox and partners Matt Inchley and Ben Pattison. They supply cask-conditioned beer to one local pub, the Sherlock Holmes, run by a British ex-pat. But the bulk of their production is in bottle-conditioned form. Marcus uses Pilsner and Maris Otter malts and darker grains for colour and flavour with Fuggles, Goldings, Hallertau and Saaz pellet hops in brewing kit built in New Zealand.

The range includes a 5.2 per cent ABV **Blond**, with fine, floral Saaz notes and juicy malt, 4.6 per cent **Bronze** with spicy hops, sultana fruit and a dry, hoppy finish, and 55, a 5.5 per cent beer with a massive peppery hop aroma (40 bitterness units), orange and tangerine fruit on the palate and a rich fruity and spicy finish. **White** (5.2 per cent) is a Belgian-inspired wheat beer with a coriander and peppery hops character, balanced by toasted malt on the nose, spices in the mouth and a bittersweet finish with continuing coriander and citrus notes. **Dark** (5.2 per cent) is ruby coloured and uses smoked malt from Bamberg. It has a smoky, woody aroma with notes of vanilla on the palate and finish. **Uber Special**, weighing in at a powerful 6.5 per cent, uses brown sugar with Challenger hops added to Fuggles and Goldings. The beer has a powerful aroma of acetate, with banana fruit in the mouth and long, sweetish finish. Finally, **Black** (5.5 per cent) is an English-style stout matured in bottle for six months. Pale malt is augmented by roast barley and Munich malt, with oatmeal making up 10 per cent of the grist. The hops are Fuggles and Goldings and the beer has a chocolate and coffee aroma with a smooth, silky palate dominated by dark fruit, chocolate, coffee, bitter hops and a hint of charcoal from the roasted grain in the finish.

In sharp distinction, the Two Brothers Brewery is in a downtown area of Melbourne, on an industrial estate. Founders Dave and Andrew Ong have a spacious warehouse that houses a bar as well as brewery. They welcome blue-collar drinkers from the surrounding units, who drop in after work for a cold lager but Dave and Andrew hope to entice them on to more flavoursome beers. Two Brothers has an impressive modern plant built in Canada that can produce ale as well as lager. It has a mash kettle that doubles as the copper for the boil with hops following clarification of the wort in a lauter vessel. Two-thirds of the annual 100,000 litre production goes in kegs to pubs, the rest is sold on the premises, with beers served from conditioning tanks.

The standard lager is **Taxi** (4.7 per cent ABV), brewed from Pilsner malt and Saaz hops. It has a corn aroma, light citrus fruit and gentle, floral hops. **Chief** at 6.3 per cent is a complex beer in the Vienna Red style, brewed with Pils, Vienna, Munich and carapils malts and Perle hops. It has a rich malt nose with tart orange fruit. There is juicy malt in the mouth balanced by fruit and gentle hops. The finish is bittersweet with malt and fruit dominating. **Growler** (4.7 per cent) is fermented with English ale yeast and is made with pale, crystal, chocolate and wheat malts. The hops are German Perle and two American varieties. It has a rich malt loaf aroma with a powerful hint of chocolate. Chocolate comes through strongly in the mouth with a bready/yeasty note and light hops. The finish is bittersweet with sultana fruit, chocolate and gentle hop bitterness. **Rusty** (4.7 per cent) is in the style of Belgian pale ale, brewed with

Pils, crystal and Vienna malts and hopped with Saaz. It has a power-ful aroma of burnt fruit and spicy hops, with a fruity and hoppy palate and a long finish that is balanced between sappy malt, dark fruit and hops.

Mountain Goat in Richmond brews **Hightail Ale** (5 per cent ABV), an English-style beer, amber-coloured with good hop notes and toffee-like malt. **Surefoot Stout** (also 5 per cent), brewed with roasted grain, has chocolate, coffee and a light bitterness.

The Red Hill Brewery is in an idyllic location in the Mornington Peninsula region of Victoria. This is wine country and the hills and slopes are smothered in vines. Owners Karen and David Golding attract many visitors to the rustic location that includes a log cabin restaurant serving excellent food. With a name such as Golding, David and Karen had to grow hops. They have possibly the smallest hop garden in the world where they cultivate Goldings, Hallertau, Tettnang and Willamette.

David's spick-and-span brewhouse is based around a similar American system to Two Brothers: a mash kettle that doubles as the boiling copper and a lauter tun. Rain water is collected on the roofs of buildings to supplement local water. The water is exceptionally soft and David adds salts to harden it for some of his beers. All the beers are bottle conditioned and sold to bars and hotels in the area.

Golden Ale (5 per cent ABV) is a warm-fermented Kölsch-style German beer that uses pale and Pilsner malt and ten per cent wheat. Only German hop varieties are used and the beer has a spicy hop and vanilla-like malt nose, with light citrus fruit, malt and hops in the mouth, and a spicy hop and fruity finish. A 5 per cent **Wheat Beer** is exceptionally fruity, with banana to the fore. It's brewed with Pils malt, wheat and Tettnang hops. **Pale Ale** (5 per cent) is dry hopped with Hallertau and fermented with a Kölsch yeast strain. It has a big lemon and orange fruit aroma and palate, with nutty malt in the mouth and a long fruity and hoppy finish. **Scotch Ale** (5.8 per cent) is highly complex: Maris Otter pale malt is the backbone, with the addition of brown, crystal and carapils. The hops are Goldings and Willamette. The aroma and palate are dominated by ripe sultana fruit and peppery hops. Finally, a 6.5 per cent **Belgian Blonde** is big in every way. It's brewed with Pils and Vienna malts and white sugar. It has an enormous peppery hop nose from a blend of the local hops, with chewy malt and fruit in the mouth, followed by a long bittersweet finish with plum fruit, malt and spicy hops.

Bridge End Brewery in Beechworth responds to the interest in Belgian styles with a **Chevalier Saison** (6.2 per cent ABV), a fruity and spicy beer, along with **Robust Porter** (5.2 per cent) with a big roast and chocolate character balanced by peppery hops, and – flying the flag – **Australian Ale** (4.4 per cent), a fruity, cloudy ale with good hop bitterness and more than a nod in the direction of Cooper's Sparkling Ale in Adelaide.

There's a different and English influence in the Holgate Brewhouse's 5 per cent ABV **ESB** from Woodend, with nutty malt, floral hops and a long bitter and fruity finish.

Tasmania

The island of Tasmania is one of the major barley-growing regions of Australia and, along with Victoria, supplies most of the continent's hops: Pride of Ringwood is the leading variety. There are two major breweries, well placed at either end of the island. The Cascade Brewery in Hobart is the oldest continuously working Australian brewery. It started to produce ale and porter in 1832 and draws both its inspiration and water from the Cascade Mountains. In 1922 it merged with Boag's of Launceston and in 1927 switched to lager brewing. Both breweries are now owned by Lion Nathan. **Cascade Premium Lager** (5.2 per cent ABV) is noticeably full-bodied and crisp, with some citrus fruit notes. **Cascade Draught**, **Cascade Bitter** and **Cascade Stout** are all cold-fermented. The Stout has plenty of roasted malt and chocolate character.

Boag's traces its origins to 1927 and uses a traditional European double decoction mashing system. **Boag's Draught** (4.7 per cent ABV) is a lager with a perfumy hop aroma and a dry finish. **Boag's Lager** (5.4 per cent) is hoppy by Australian mainstream standards while **Boag's Stout** has less character than Cascade's.

The island now has a few new craft breweries. Mou Brew in Hobart produces a 5 per cent ABV golden **Pilsner** with light citrus fruit, toasted malt and floral hops. Hazard's Ale produces a **Raspberry Chilli Beer**, St Ives Bay makes a no-nonsense **Old Bastard** while Dark Isle brews **Oyster Stout** and **Leatherwood Porter**.

Queensland

If Elder's dominates Victoria, Queensland is the undisputed home of Castlemaine XXXX. What was once a simple cask marking handed down from medieval monks has become, in the hands of modern marketing gurus, a secular synonym for "Stuff you, Jack". Queensland drinkers couldn't give a XXXX for any other beer, according to the advertising, and at night the four letters blaze out from the Castlemaine Brewery like a neon-lit, two-fingered salute.

The Brisbane version of XXXX, still sold as **Bitter Ale**, uses whole hops rather than pellets, an unusual practice in modern Australia. The 4.8 per cent lager does have a hint more hoppiness than its main rivals but like them is malty sweet. **Gold Lager** is 3.5 per cent and even more malt-accented. **Malt 75** (4.8 per cent ABV) is an additive-free lager, drier than XXXX. The most characterful beer from the brewery is **Carbine Stout**, named after a famous racehorse. It is the last surviving stout from a brewery that once made several. At 5.1 per cent ABV, it is now cold-fermenting with a roasty palate and a dry finish.

Powers was set up near Brisbane in 1987 to bring some much-needed choice to the region. Busily promoted, especially at major sports events, Power's success annoyed the giants and it succumbed to the blandishments of Foster's. Powers produced **Big Red**, a more flavourful lager than most.

AUSTRALIAN BREWERS

Boag's,
21 Shields Street, Launceston,
Tasmania 7250.

Bootleg Brewery,
Pusey Road, Willyabrup, Margaret
River, Western Australia 6285.

Bridge Road Brewers,
Tanswells Old Coach House, Ford
Street, Beechworth, Victoria 3747.

Cascade Brewery Co,
156 Collins St, Hobart, Tasmania 7000.

Castlemaine Perkins (Lion Nathan),
11 Finchley Street, Milton,
Queensland 4064.

Cooper's Brewery Ltd,
9 Statenborough Street, Leabrook,
Adelaide, South Australia 5068.

Feral Brewing Company,
152 Hadrill Road, Baskerville, Swan
Valley, Western Australia 6056.

Holgate Brewhouse,
41 South Rd, Woodend, Victoria 3442.

Little Creatures,
40 Mews Road, Fremantle, Western
Australia 6160.

Lord Nelson Brewery Hotel,
19 Kent Street, The Rocks, Sydney
NSW 2000.

Malt Shovel,
99 Pyrmont Bridge Road,
Camperdown, NSW 2050.

Moo Brew,
Moorilla Pty Ltd, 655 Main Road
Berriedale, Hobart, Tasmania 7011.

Mountain Goat,
Warehouse 1, 18 River Street,
Richmond, Victoria 3121.

Murray's,
Taylors Arm Road, Taylors Arm,
NSW 2447.

Redoak Boutique Beer Cafe,
201 Clarence St, Sydney NSW 2000.

Red Hill,
88 Shoreham Road, Red Hill South,
Mornington Peninsula, Victoria 3937.

**South Australian Brewing Co
Ltd (Lion Nathan),**
107 Port Road, Thebarton, South
Australia 5031.

**Swan Brewery Co Ltd (Lion
Nathan),**
25 Baile Road, Canning Vale, Western
Australia 6155.

Three Ravens,
1 Theobald Street, Thornbury,
Melbourne, Victoria 3071.

2 Brothers Brewery,
4 Joyner Street, Moorabbin,
Melbourne, Victoria 3189.

Wig & Pen,
Alinga Street, Canberra ACT 2601.

New Zealand

"In common with Australia" is not a term that endears itself to New Zealanders but where beer is concerned both countries are dominated by two brewing giants. There is a more palpable link: the biggest producer in New Zealand is Lion Nathan, which is also a major player in Australia. Its Kiwi rival is Dominion Breweries (DB) and both are owned by foreign companies. Kirin of Japan runs Lion Nathan while DB is controlled by Asia Pacific Breweries, in which Heineken is the majority shareholder.

Lion Nathan dominates the beer scene with the country's best-known beer, **Steinlager** (4.8 per cent ABV; 22 IBUs). There have been several Steinlager spin-offs such as Blue and Green, but they have been phased out in favour of **Steinlager Pure** (5.2 per cent) while the original beer is now branded as Classic. There are several other bland lager brands in the portfolio.

DB also concentrates on pale lagers, including **DB Draught** and **Export**. It has been criticised for promoting **Tui** (4 per cent) as "East India Pale Ale" when the beer is a lager. DB's main activity is brewing and promoting Heineken.

The once conservative New Zealand drinker now has a greater choice and is prepared to experiment with beers that offer aroma and flavour. Emerson's of Dunedin brews **Old 95** (7 per cent ABV), a bittersweet ale with chewy malt, butterscotch and hop resins, and a fruity **Organic Pilsner** (4.9 per cent) with toasted malt and floral hops.

Galbraith's of Mt Eden, Auckland, brews an English-style **Best Bitter**, copper coloured with toffee and earthy hops on the aroma and palate, and a long, dry finish. Its **Bob Hudson's Bitter** (4 per cent) is another English-style beer with a deep hoppy and malty character and a refreshing fruity and hoppy finish.

Harrington's of Christchurch was founded in 1991 and has grown to become a major independent with an impressive range of beers. The company prides itself on using no preservatives and imports Cascade, Fuggles and Goldings hops. The portfolio includes **Classy Red** (5.2 per cent ABV), a copper-coloured American-style pale ale with a big hop nose, rich malt and orange fruit on the palate and finish, **Rogue Hop Organic Pilsner** (5 per cent), **Razor Back Premium Bitter** (5 per cent), two dark beers of British ancestry **Clydesdale Stout** and **Wobbly Boot Porter** (both 5 per cent) and, to prove the growing interest in Belgian beers, **Belgium Tempest** (8 per cent). There's also a German-style **Doppelbock** at 8 per cent.

Mac's in Nelson produces **Sassy Red** (4.5 per cent ABV), a beer dominated by fruity American hops but balanced by butterscotch, chocolate and chewy grain. **Black Mac** (4.8 per cent) is a dark lager with chocolate, liquorice and roasted malt notes.

Moa in Blenheim is based in Marlborough wine country and claims its beers are made by the Méthode Champenoise, which conjures up a fascinating image of a member of staff rotating each bottle a few centimetres every day and then disgorging the yeast from the neck. **Original Pils** (5.5 per cent ABV) is a dry, crisp lager with toasted malt, lemon fruit and floral hops while **Blanc** (5.5 per cent), despite the name, is a German rather than a Belgian-style wheat beer, with banana and cloves on the palate and finish.

Monteith's of Greymouth also brews a **Pilsner** (5 per cent) with lots of floral and grassy hops on nose and palate, toasted grain and light, tangy fruit. Its **Black Beer** (5.2 per cent) has coffee, chocolate and caramel notes in a smooth, satiny, easy-drinking dark beer.

Shakespeare of Auckland was the country's first brewpub and is run by former All Blacks rugby international Ron Urlich. He plays up the Bardic connection with a range that includes **Falstaff's Real Ale** (4.5 per cent), with a peppery hop character from imported English hops (the beer is dry hopped), **King Lear Old Ale** (8 per cent), a russet-coloured beer with rich sultana and raisin fruit, butterscotch, chocolate and a long hoppy finish, **Regan's Raspberry Weiss** (4.3 per cent), **Willpower Stout** (4.0 per cent) and the curiously named **Puck's Pixi(l)lation**, an 11.1 per cent Belgian strong ale with warming alcohol, rich malt, floral hops and a long bittersweet finish.

NEW ZEALAND BREWERS

Dominion Breweries,
80 Greys Avenue, Auckland.

Galbraith's Alehouse,
2 Mount Eden Road, Mount Eden, Auckland.

Harrington's Breweries,
199 Ferry Road, Christchurch.

Lion Nathan,
54–65 Shortland Street, Auckland.

McCashins Brewery & Malthouse,
660 Main Road, Stoke, Nr Nelson.

Moa Brewing Company,
Jacksons Road, RD3, Blenheim.

Monteith's Brewing Company,
cnr Turamaha & Herbert Streets, Greymouth.

Shakespeare Tavern and Brewery,
61 Albert Street, Auckland.

The beer styles of the Far East

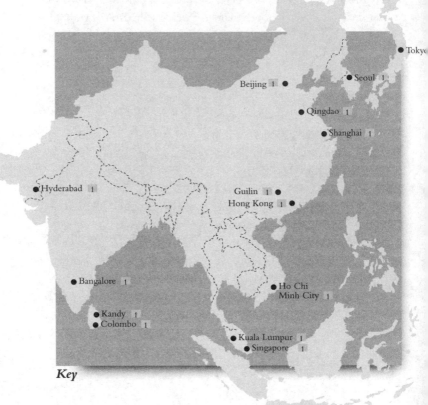

Tokyo

Beijing 1

Seoul 1

Qingdao 1

Shanghai 1

Hyderabad 1

Guilin 1
Hong Kong 1

Bangalore 1

Ho Chi
Minh City 1

Kandy 1
Colombo 1

Kuala Lumpur 1
Singapore 1

Key

1 Brewery

JAPAN AND THE FAR EAST	Ho Chi Minh City	Kuala Lumpur	Shanghai
Bangalore	My Tho/BGI	Asia Pacific Breweries	Shanghai Lager
Mohan Meakin	**Hong Kong**	**Qingdao**	Swan Lager
United Breweries	Hong Kong Brewery	Tsingtao	**Tokyo**
Beijing	**Hyderabad**	**Seoul**	Asahi Breweries
Mon-Lei	Vinedale Breweries	OB Brewery	Kirin Brewery Co
Colombo	**Kandy**	**Singapore**	Sapporo Breweries
McCallum's	Ceylon Brewery	Asia Pacific Breweries	Suntory Brewery
Guilin	UKD Silva		*Beer Bar Brussels*
Wei Mei			*Rising Sun*

316

Japan and the Far East

Japan has come a long way in a short time in brewing terms. Beer was introduced, almost by accident, by the Americans in 1853. The United States was keen to develop trade with Japan but placed a knuckleduster inside the velvet glove by sending the US Navy under Commodore Matthew Perry to negotiate a treaty. A Japanese who went on board one of Perry's ships was offered a beer. Intrigued, he found a handbook on brewing – written in Dutch – and managed to make beer for home consumption.

Following the Meiji reforms of 1868, when Emperor Mutsuhito encouraged Westernization and industrialization, efforts were made to establish commercial breweries. The Americans gave a hand and a brewery was established in Yokohama by Wiegand and Copeland. Eventually the brewery became wholly owned by Japanese and was named Kirin after a mythical creature, half dragon and half horse.

Black beer

The black beer influence may come from the Franconia region of Bavaria but the dark lagers there are brown rather than black. Schwarzbier is now confined to Saxony and the opaque, cold-fermenting beer from Köstritz may be the historic link with Japan's black beers.

Kirin and Sapporo, the oldest of Japan's breweries, produce the most interesting versions of the style. **Sapporo Black Beer** is the classic. At 5.0 per cent ABV, it is brewed from pale, crystal, Munich and chocolate malts with a small amount of rice.

Kirin Black Beer, also 5.0 per cent, has a pronounced roasted coffee and liquorice palate after a gentle, grainy start. The finish is light and quenching with some gentle hop character. **Asahi Black** (5.0 per cent ABV) is less dark, with a hint of red/brown in the colour. It is by far the sweetest of the Japanese black beers and many drinkers blend it with lager to balance the caramel character.

Suntory's Black Beer (5.0 per cent ABV; 23 IBUs) is jet black and opaque. All the black beers are minority brands, sold on draught or packaged for specialist bars or restaurants. The brewers deserve credit for maintaining a style that in most modern brewing climates would have been consigned to the grave decades ago.

Pilsners and lagers

Kirin **Lager** is the most distinctive of the Japanese mainstream Pilsners, lagered, it is claimed, for an impressive two months. At 4.9 per cent ABV and 27.5 IBUs from Hallertau and Saaz hops, it is full-bodied and rich-tasting and is firmly in the Pilsner mould. A stronger lager (6.5 per cent ABV) stresses the German influence with the remarkable name of **Mein Bräu** – My Brew. More recent beers include a hoppy **Spring Valley**, an all-malt **Heartland, Ichiban Shibori**, made from the first runnings of the mash tun that leads to a full-bodied, malty beer, and Golden Bitter, which is cold-fermented in spite of the name and has a fine, resiny hop character.

Sapporo's most impressive brand is **Yebisu**, a fragrant malty/hoppy beer broadly in the Dortmunder Export style and hopped with Hallertau Mittelfruh and Hersbruck. It is 5.0 per cent ABV and has an enticing golden colour. It takes its name from a Shinto god. Other lagers include 4.5 per cent **Sapporo Draft Beer** (which comes in bottles and cans) and has a grainy aroma, malt in the mouth and a dry finish with some hop notes; and a German-influenced **Edel-Pils** with a delightful hop aroma.

Suntory's state of the art breweries can be programmed to produce almost any type of beer. In general Suntory's range is mild and light-tasting, dry in the finish but with only delicate hoppiness. **Suntory's Malt's**, as the name suggests, is on the malty side while **Suntory's Light's** (4.5 per cent ABV), aimed at the calorie-conscious, may be "a healthy delight" but has little else to recommend it. **Dynamic Draft** is fermented with a Canadian yeast.

Asahi's Super Dry is brewed out or fully attenuated to turn all the malt sugars to alcohol. It launched a brief craze for dry beers in several countries, the United States in particular, but the decline was almost as rapid as the rise: it seems that beer drinkers, contrary to the views of marketing departments, do like taste and flavour. Asahi also produces **Asahi Z**, another well-attenuated beer, and a more flavoursome **Asahi Gold**. Orion of Okinawa was founded in 1957, with close links to Asahi. It brews a wide range of beers including Special, Original and Dry.

Japanese specialities

Kirin brews a superb 8.0 per cent ABV **Kirin Stout**, a complex bittersweet, cold-fermenting beer with delicious dark toffee notes. A microbrewery set up in Kyoto produces a German-style, warm-fermenting **Kyoto Alt**, copper coloured and with a delectable nuttiness from crystal malt. Sapporo brew **Yebisu Stout**, soft and mellow, while **Asahi's Stout** is big-bodied, full of dark bittersweet fruits. Suntory has experimented with a Bavarian **Weizen** wheat beer, beautifully made and with a delicious apple-and-clove quenching palate.

A change in the law in the early 1990s made obtaining a brewing licence easier. As a result, several brewpubs and microbreweries have opened. The best-known is Chojugura in Itami, which produces a hoppy **Blond** (5.0 per cent ABV) and a fruity/malty **Dark** (5.5 per cent ABV).

JAPANESE BREWERS

Asahi Breweries,
23-1 Azumabashi 1-chome,
Sumida-ku, Tokyo 130.

Kirin Brewery Co,
26-1 Jingumae 6-chome, Shibuya-ku,
Tokyo 150.

Orion,
2-2-1 Agarie, Nago-shi, Okinawa

905-0021.

Sapporo Breweries,
7-10-1 Ginza, Chuo-ku, Tokyo 104.

Suntory Brewery,
1-2-3 Motoakasaka, Minato-ku,
Tokyo 107.

Chojugura,
Chuo 3-4-5, Itami.

China

China is now the world's biggest beer market, though this is due to the size of the population: consumption per head is low though this will rise as incomes increase, especially in major urban areas. The Chinese potential has not been lost on the global brewing giants, most of which are now represented in the country, either as co-owners or direct owners of breweries. Today there are thought to be 100 breweries in the country but the number could be far higher as China slowly opens up to Western influence and technology. But only one beer is well known outside China and it comes from a brewery set up with the aid of German technology in the late nineteenth century.

When the Germans leased the port of Tsingtao on the Shantung peninsula close to Japan and Korea they naturally built a brewery which survives and thrives. The name of the port is now Qingdao in Shandong province but Tsingtao is still used as the name of the extremely pale Pilsner-style lager brewed there and exported widely. Tsingtao was owned by the world's biggest brewing group, A-B InBev but in June 2009 the global giant sold the brewery to a Chinese entrepreneur.

China now has its own barley and hop industries though supplies and quality are erratic. The 5.2 per cent **Tsingtao**, when it is on form, has a good Pilsner malt and hop attack with some vanilla notes in the finish. Its 4.8 per cent ABV **Harbin** is one of the most widely distributed beers in the country.

Hangzhou Qiandaho Beer Company in Zhejiang province is 25 per cent owned by Kirin of Japan. Asahi, also of Japan, has built a brand-new brewery in the same province.

A malty, lightly hopped beer from Shanghai known either as **Shanghai Lager** or **Swan Lager** from the emblem on the neck label has occasionally been seen in the West. It has no connection to the Swan subsidiary of Lion Nathan in Australia. Shanghai also produces a dark lager called **Guangminpai**. The capital, Beijing, has a lager called **Mon-Lei** with a reddish hue as though influenced by Austrian "red" lagers. A similar beer, **Wei Mei**, comes from Guilin. The Hong Kong Brewery has a 5.0 per cent **Sun Lik Beer** with a traditional Chinese dragon adorning the label. The brewer admits it is identical to San Miguel from the Philippines.

The Hong Kong SAR Brewing Company brews an impressive **Vienna Lager** (4.9 per cent ABV) with a deep amber colour and a biscuity/malty palate balanced by floral hops. Shanghai has two brewpubs and Beijing has one. Japanese influence is growing: Suntory owns three large plants in Greater Shanghai where it brews Suntory and Suntory Gold as well as local beers.

Across the border in South Korea, the OB Brewery in Seoul produces two lagers, **OB** and **Crown**.

The rest of Asia

German technology built the Singha Corporation (formerly Boon Rawd) in Thailand and the German influence continues with the superb **Singha Lager**. The Singha is a mythical lion-like creature and the beer named in its honour is suitably powerful. The rival **Amarit**, in contrast, is a much milder and malty-sweet brew that contains some ale-like fruitiness.

One of the best-known Asian beers, Tiger of Singapore and Kuala Lumpur, refreshed the British during the colonial period and the Second World War. It was immortalized by the British writer Anthony Burgess in his novel *Time for a Tiger*, a marketing slogan used by the brewery since the late 1940s. **Tiger** (5.1 per cent ABV) and **Anchor** of the same strength are both clean-tasting, quenching light lagers. Tiger has the greater hop character and is now much influenced by the Heineken style. APB also brews a roasty/creamy, cold fermenting **ABC Stout** with a powerful 8.1 per cent ABV rating. APB introduced a **Tiger Classic** seasonal beer for the New

Year festivities as well as **Raffles Light**, named after Raffles Hotel in Singapore, a legendary watering-hole in colonial times.

The microbrewery Brewerkz in Singapore offers **Lager**, **Kölsch**, **Oatmeal Stout**, **Dunkel Weizen** and **Steam Beer** – something for all types of ex-pats. The Riverside Brewpub in the city will delight Brits with its 6 per cent ABV **IPA**. In Laos, the Laos Brewery Company is a 50:50 venture with Carlsberg. The 5 per cent ABV **Lao** is crisp, dry, and hoppy, with a tart finish. The Thai Beverage Company in Thailand produces the best-selling, 5 per cent ABV **Chang**, which sponsors Everton FC in England.

The Bintang Brewery in Indonesia produces beer with a Dutch influence, down to the familiar stubby Dutch bottle. **Bintang** is 5.0 per cent ABV with a grainy aroma, a malty/perfumy palate, and a finish that becomes dry with some light hop notes.

One of the most famous beers in Asia and the Pacific is **San Miguel** of the Philippines. The company is a giant concern with several breweries as well as interests in food and agriculture. **San Miguel Pale Pilsen** is 5.0 per cent ABV with around 20 IBUs. It is made with 80 per cent malt and is lagered for a month. **Gold Eagle** is similar to San Miguel, a fraction lower in alcohol and a shade darker in colour. **Cerveza Negra** (Black Beer) is 5.2 per cent ABV with a pleasing roasted malt character. **Red Horse** (6.8 per cent ABV) is a full-bodied, malty lager in the Bock style.

Indian Sub-continent

The British stamped their mark on India with India Pale Ales brewed in Burton-on-Trent for export to the sub-continent. By the 1880s German lagers had replaced ales as they were more suited to both brewing and consumption in the torrid climate. Even today some lagers have a fruity, ale-like character caused by problems of temperature control. Burma's **Mandalay Beer**, for example, is a notably fruity brew even though it is cold-fermenting. Nepal's **Star Beer** is more in the lager mould with a hoppy intensity.

While some Indian states are strictly prohibitionist, breweries range from the far north in the Simla Hills to Bangalore and Hyderabad in the south. The main brewing groups are Mohan Meakin and United Breweries. Lager beers tend to be malty and sweetish with only light hop character. The best-known brands are **Cobra** and **Kingfisher**, both widely exported; Kingfisher is brewed under licence in Britain by Shepherd Neame in Kent. Mohan Meakin, founded in 1855, brews a large portfolio of lagers for the home market, including **Baller, Gymkhana, Lion, Krown** and **Golden Eagle**, ranging from 4.0 per cent to 5.0 per cent ABV. In Hyderabad, Vinedale Breweries produces two premium lagers called **Flying Horse** and **Jubilee**, both around 5.0 per cent ABV, and two stouts called **Kingfisher** and **London**.

Stout is a hangover – a pleasant one – from British colonial times, the finest examples of which are found in Sri Lanka. McCallum's Three Coins Brewery in Colombo has a rich, fruity, chocolatey **Sando Stout** (6.0 per cent ABV), named after a Hungarian circus strongman who toured the country. It is cold-fermenting, along with the all-malt **Three Coins Pilsener**.

A remarkable stout is found at the Ceylon Brewery in Nuwara Eliya in the tea-planting area and close to the Holy City of Kandy. **Lion Stout** (7.5 per cent) is warm-fermenting, using Czech, British and Danish malts, Styrian hops and an English yeast strain, all transported up precarious roads to the brewery 3,500 feet above sea level. It is served in cask-conditioned form by handpump in the Beer Shop in the brewery's home town and in UKD Silva, Kandy.

ASIAN BREWERS

Asia Pacific Breweries,
459 Jalan Ahmad Ibrahim, Singapore.

Bintang Brewery,
Jalan Raya Mojosari-Pacet Km. 50,
Sampang Agung, Jakarta, 61303
Indonesia.

Ceylon Brewery,
Nuwara Eliya, Kandy, Sri Lanka.

Hangzhou,
Pingshan Industrial Park, Qiandaohu
Town, Chun'an County, 311700.

Hong Kong Brewery,
13 Miles Castle Peak Road, Shan
Tseng NT, Hong Kong.

Hong Kong Brewery (Sun Lik),
New Territories, Hong Kong.

Hong Kong SAR Brewing Co,
29 Wong Chuk Hang Road, Vita
Tower Unit A1, 1/F, Aberdeen,
Hong Kong.

McCallum's Brewery,
299 Union Place, Colombo, Sri Lanka.

Mohan Meakin,
Solan Brewery, Himacar, Tredesh,
India.

Oriental Brewery,
Hanwon b/d, 1449-12 Seocho-dong,
Seocho-gu, 137-070 Seoul, S. Korea.

San Miguel,
40 San Miguel Avenue,
Mandaluyong, Manila, Philippines.

Singha Corporation,
Samsen Brewery, 999 Samsen Road,
Kwang Tanon, Nakronchaisri, Dusit,
Bangkok 10300, Thailand.

United Breweries,
24 Grant Road, Bangalore, India.

Vinedale Distilleries,
Hyderabad-Bangalore Highway,
Gaganpahad, Hyderabad-509, India.

South Pacific

Papua New Guinea

The South Pacific Brewery of Port Moresby, Papua New Guinea, was the inspiration of Australians who had gone to the territory to work in the gold fields. Imports of beer were erratic and the quality variable – Allsopp's beer from England was dubbed "Allslopps". In the late 1940s Joe Bourke, a gold prospector, applied for a licence to build a hotel in the town of Wau. Annoyed by the lack of beer from Australia and other countries, he planned a brewery. With other Australians he founded a syndicate which raised £150,000 to launch South Pacific Brewery in Port Moresby, the capital of the islands. They were fortunate to discover Rudolf Meier, a Hungarian who had trained and brewed in Germany.

Production started in 1952 on a small basis. In spite of problems getting supplies of ingredients and often running short of water – the brewery uses rain water collected in tanks – the company prospered. Sales soared in the 1960s when Prohibition was ended for the islanders – until then only settlers had been allowed access to alcohol. Today the company is run largely by Papuans, though Australians are still involved.

The brewery made headlines in 1980 when its **Export Lager** won the gold medal in the Brewex international beer competition. It has also won awards in the Monde Sélection competition. Although it faces competition from a San Miguel brewery built by the Filipino giant, South Pacific is the brand leader with a modern plant. In the 1990s it added a stout to its range, a reflection perhaps of the residual support for the style in Australia. **SP Lager** (4.5 per cent ABV) has a perfumy aroma, a malt and vanilla palate and a cornflour finish that becomes dry. The estery character of the beer suggests a brief lagering,

SP Export Lager (5.5 per cent ABV) has a delicate aroma with a faint malt note, a light malt palate and short finish that becomes dry with faint hop notes. It doesn't drink its strength.

Niugini Gold Extra Stout (8.0 per cent ABV) is a deep brown-black in colour and has a rich chocolate and cappuccino coffee aroma, with dark fruit in the mouth and a big finish packed with hops and tart fruit.

Hawaii

In the spring of 1995, Hawaii got its first microbrewery, the Kona Brewing Company. It was the dream of Spoon and Pops Khalsa, who both grew up in Oregon, US, and became lovers of good beer. When they planned their brewery they called in Ron Gansberg, John Kittredge and John Forbes from the BridgePort micro in Portland, Oregon. Together they planned two ales for the 25-barrel brewery. Brewing liquor is water naturally filtered through the volcanic aquifer. Barley and hops are imported from the US along with BridgePort's top-fermenting yeast strain.

The two beers are **Pacific Golden Ale** (3.5 per cent by weight; 22 IBUs), using a blend of pale and honey malts and hopped with Bullion and Willamette, and **Fire Rock Ale** (4.1 per cent by weight; 40 IBUs), a darker, amber beer using pale and Munich malts and hopped with Cascade, Galena and Mount Hood varieties.

The beers should appeal not only to Hawaiians and Americans but also to the British, for a half acre of the main island is still British territory and the site of an obelisk commemorates the site of the death of Captain Cook. Ships of the Royal Navy regularly visit Hawaii and the crew will now have some good ale to enjoy.

IMPORTANT ADDRESSES

Kona Brewing Company,
PO Box 181, Kealakekua, HI 96750.

South Pacific Brewery,
Spring Garden Road, Boroko, Port Moresby, Papua New Guinea.

Gazetteer of Pubs, Bars and Taverns

Beer can be enjoyed at home but it is a convivial drink, best consumed in the company of others in the cheerful surroundings of a public house, bar or café. It is in pubs and bars that beer on draught, whether ale or lager, is at its best and freshest, drawn from the cellar and lovingly cared for by experienced staff. We offer a selection of some of the best outlets throughout the world for enjoying beer in all its glory.

Belgium

Brussels
Falstaff, 17 rue Henri Maus.

More a restaurant than a pub, the Falstaff is famous for its many extraordinary features. Its location ensures a well-heeled clientele – it's right next to the Bourse or Stock Exchange. The decor is an odd mixture of art deco, art nouveau and rococo, characterized by elaborate mirrors and stained glass. The opening hours are unbelievable and better defined by the closing times: the Falstaff shuts at 5 a.m. – and opens again for breakfast two hours later. The full menu, though, is only served between noon and 2 p.m. – but the huge range of Belgian beers, especially Trappist ales, is available virtually round the clock.

A La Morte Subite, 7 rue Montagnes aux Herbes Potagères.

All visitors to Brussels find themselves gawping open-mouthed at the splendours of the Grand' Place. When you've finished gawping, just nip up the Galeries Royale St Hubert arcade for traditional gueuze at the Morte Subite. You won't die – the café is named after a card-game once played there regularly (and the beer Morte Subite is named after the café). The café itself is very basic – just a single long bar, with prices painted up on the mirrors and a few tables and chairs. The range of food is basic, too, more snack than meal. But then, you're only here for the beer.

Moeder Lambic Ixelles, Boendaalse Steenweg 441, Elsene.

Take a number 95 or 96 bus from outside the Falstaff and get off at the Ixelles Cemetery in the suburb of Elsene, and you find yourself at a café which serves more than 50 Belgian beers on draught alone and a range of bottled beers. For avid beer tourists this is the place to find many of the rarities and oddities for which Belgium is justly famed.

't Spinnekopke, 1 Place du Jardin aux Fleurs.

Just five minutes' walk from the Grand' Place is the Spinnekopke or Little Spider where the speciality is not just drinking beer but cooking with it – owner Jean Rodriguez is an acknowledged authority and author on the subject. The beer-list runs to 70 or so brews, the cooking is excellent and you'd never believe beer was such a versatile ingredient. If all you want is a drink, try the draught faro and lambic from the local Cantillon Brewery.

Bruges

't Brugs Beertje, Kemelstraat 5.

Is this Belgium's most famous bar? It deserves to be, for although there's nothing special about the setting, the building, or the decor, there's something very special about owner Daisy Claes.

The evangelist of native styles, Claes has spearheaded the Belgian beer revival of recent years and refuses to give Pils-style lagers house room. She does, however, have room for some 200 proper native ales, and in the back bar, known as the Beer Academie, she holds tutored tastings for parties of acolytes from all over the world.

Ghent
De Hopduvel, Rokerelstraat 10.
Ghent's huge medieval prosperity was founded on textiles, and its architectural heritage is worthy of a city that was the wealthiest in Northern Europe. De Hopduvel is a stiffish walk from the city centre but the café does not disappoint. A maze of tiny rooms hung with assorted breweriana, the café also has a covered garden at the back and a popular grill upstairs. The list of 120 beers includes a range specially commissioned from the Van Steenberge Brewery.

Antwerp
Kulminator, Vleminckveld 32.
Although not much of a tourist trap, Antwerp, and especially the Old Town round the cathedral, is extremely attractive and boasts many fine cafés. On the edge of the Old Town is the elegant, candle-lit Kulminator with its staggering list of 500 beers. This is an embarrassment of riches even by Belgian standards, but then the Kulminator is the unofficial headquarters of Belgium's beer consumers' association, the Objectieve Bier Proevers.

France

Lille
Les Brasseurs, Place de la Gare.
Opposite the railway station, this is a large and opulent brewpub, the first of a small chain in northern France. A tiny brewhouse produces

a range of top-fermenting ales, including an amber and a wheat beer plus seasonal offerings. The front bar has alcove seats while to the rear a restaurant area offers a range of dishes including the Lille speciality, a thin pizza-style bread with a choice of toppings.

Paris

A La Pinte du Nord, 38 rue Saint-Quentin.

One minute from Gare du Nord, this small bar specializes in French and Belgian beers, including Pelforth Brune and Leffe Blonde. There is also simple food and accommodation as well.

Frog and Rosbif, 116 rue St Denis.

This Parisian brewpub is based on the famous Firkin chain in London. The bar is decked out with old church pews and food includes steak and kidney pudding, Scotch eggs, Cornish pasties and bangers and mash. The microbrewery produces 800 litres a week of Inseine (4.2 per cent ABV) and Parislytic (5.2 per cent ABV) brewed with English malt, hops and yeast.

The Cricketer, rue des Mathurins.

Near the Opéra, this is a traditional English pub – the fixtures and fittings were brought over, lock, stock and barrel, from Ipswich – and offers Adnams of Suffolk's Extra Bitter and Broadside. The walls are awash with fascinating (to a cricket lover) old prints of the game but must cause great head-scratching among the locals.

Czech Republic

Prague

U Fleku, 11 Kremencova, New Town.

Named after the proprietors in the eighteenth century, Jakob and Dorota Flekovskymi, U Fleku is the last survivor of Prague's long tradition of brewpubs. The recipe for its black beer is reputed to go back to the late fifteenth century. It has become one of the most popular meeting places in Prague for foreigners, even though it is some way outside the centre, partly because of its size (pub and beer garden together can seat 500), partly because of its heritage, and partly because most of the staff speak German and even a little English. One peculiarity of U Fleku, perhaps because of its tourist-trap status, is that drinks are paid for one by one rather than by running up a tab.

U Kalicha, Na bojisti 12, Nové Mesto, Prague 2.

The Chalice is a shrine to the Good Soldier Schweik (Svejk in Czech) the anti-hero of all anti-heroes, the conscripted militia man who did his best to avoid fighting and dreamed of the girls, the plum brandy and the beer in U Kalicha. There are drawings and extracts from the book decorating the walls of the large tavern. Writer Jaroslav Hasek modelled Schweik on a regular in the pub.

U Cerného Vola, Loretánské námesti 1, Hradcany, Prague 1.

The Black Ox is in a superb location, across the road from the Loreto church and close to the castle and cathedral. The small tavern has stained glass windows, rustic benches, sausage snacks and the sublime beer from Velké Popovice.

U Zlatého Tygra, 17 Husova.

The Golden Tiger owes much of its present good fortune to the fact that its thirteenth-century cellars are regarded as ideal for storing beer – and Czechs like their beer properly kept. However, it has also gained fame as a gathering place for artists and writers: President Václav Havel was a regular during his spells out of prison, and still has the place opened up after hours occasionally to give official guests a taste of what Czech beer ought to taste like. As a result, the pub is rather too small for its popularity, so a back room is set aside for VIPs. The present building is baroque and was one of the first in Prague to take to the new Pilsner beer which was introduced in the 1840s. It is very typical of Prague pubs, which means it's permanently packed, the air is opaque with tobacco smoke, and the waiters are brusque.

České Budějovice
The Meat Market, off main square.

This spacious beer hall with a long central corridor and side
alcoves has been fashioned from a meat market and the food on
offer is still heavy going for herbivores. But the beer is magnificent,
fresh from the Budweiser Budvar Brewery down the road and
served at great speed by black-suited and white-aproned waiters
who run up a tab on the back of a beer mat.

Germany

Cologne and Düsseldorf
See brewpubs listed in the section on Germany in The World A–Z
of Beer (see pages 145–149) for Kölsch and Alt beer outlets.

Munich
Augustiner Gaststätte, Neuhauserstrasse 16.

The flagship for the smallest of Munich's six breweries, Augustiner,
the Gaststätte is an art nouveau gem in the middle of the city's
pedestrianized shopping area between Karlsplatz and Marienplatz.
As well as a big basic beer hall, the tavern boasts an ornate restaurant and an oval garden. Bavarian dishes such as pork chops in beer
sauce are served all day alongside Augustiner Hell, Dunkel and
wheat beer on tap, and bottled Maximator Doppelbock in spring
and Märzen in the autumn.

Donisl, corner of Marienplatz and Weinstrasse.

This is the bierkeller with everything. It's got history: built in the
fourteenth century as a gaol, it eventually became a weinstube and,
in the seventeenth century, a bierkeller; in the last days of the
Second World War it was flattened by the Allies but has been lovingly recreated. It's got variety: an oompah band serenades (if that's
the right word) from a minstrel's gallery, while one of the bars is a
noted gay hang-out. It's got a good story: in 1983, when it used to

open all night every night, it was the centre of the celebrated Knockout Drop Affair, with staff slipping mickeys into the drinks of the small-hours customers and then rifling their wallets. And it's got beer: Hell, wheat beer and Pilsner from Hacker-Pschorr on tap, with Dunkel in bottle.

Hofbräuhaus, Platzl 9.

The Hofbräuhaus is so much the quintessence of everybody's idea of a Munich beer hall that one suspects that all the stiffish old boys with Tyrolean hats and toothbrush moustaches are actually paid extras. This great cavern of a place has rustic benches, many side alcoves and a large, sunlit garden in spring and summer. There's the obligatory oompah band, and the hefty barmaids moving like icebreakers through the throng, five steins in each hand, plus the association with Adolf Hitler (although no blue plaque, surprisingly) – the Brownshirts met here in the 1930s. The only unpleasantness these days comes from the occasional shouting-matches between Australian and New Zealand visitors. The beers are from the Hofbräu, once owned by the Bavarian royal family. And the secret of carrying so many steins, incidentally, is not to fill them more than half-full.

Mathäser Bierstadt, Bayerstrasse 5.

If you hate oompah bands, the whole of Munich is to be avoided but especially the Mathäser Bierstadt, where for a small fee they actually let punters conduct one. This is the biggest of the Munich beer halls and is the Löwenbräu flagship. Its two halls and profusion of smaller rooms can accommodate 5,000 drinkers, and for those who overindulge there is a genuine vomitorium.

Schneider Weisses Bräuhaus, Tal 10.

Bomber Command was here in the Second World War and when the Lancasters left there was no Schneider Brewery left. Rather than rebuild on the site, however, the company decided to relocate to the greenbelt and convert the old Bräuhaus into a beer hall. Schneider had taken over the brewery in the nineteenth century when the traditional cloudy wheat beer was being superseded by Pilsner. Wheat beer is still the speciality although Dunkel and Pilsner are served from the wood during the evening in this large, often crowded tavern a few yards from the Marienplatz. Service is fast and furious, food is simple and basic – wheat beer and white sausage is the staple – and on the way to the toilets you can look at photos showing the results of Allied bomb damage.

Paulaner Bräuhaus, Kapuzinerplatz 5.

This big brewpub with its marble-clad main entrance and gleaming coppers is the home of Pilsner beers in Munich. The style was brought back from Bohemia by two brewing students, Eugen and Ludwig Thomas, who started up the brewery more than 100 years ago. Eventually it was taken over and converted into a beer hall by Paulaner, which started brewing on the site again in 1989. A draught Pilsner is still on the menu, but the unfiltered wheat beer and Hell are the house specialities. The pub also has a restaurant and, curiously, a library.

Forschungsbräustuberl, Unterhachingstrasse 76, Perlach.

This pub takes five months of every year off. The Jakob family, who have been brewing their Pilsissimus Export and St Jakobus Bock here since 1936, take the whole business very seriously and spend their annual holiday researching and experimenting for other brewers. While the bräustuberl is open – from March to October – the two beers are served in earthenware litre jugs, with only cold sausage and cheese on the food menu. This is a place for people who like – and understand – their beer.

Unionsbräu Keller, Einsteinstrasse 42.

Heretical to say that Germany has followed where Britain and America led, but in the field of brewpubs it is true. This one was established in 1991 by Löwenbräu, which had taken over and closed down the Unionsbräu in 1922. It still serves the Löwenbräu range, but the real stars are the unfiltered Hell from the wood and the traditional seasonal ales brewed and lagered in the cellar. A plus is that all the ingredients are organic. The tiny brewhouse is open to view at the back and, fascinatingly, the wooden fermenters are tilted at an angle in exactly the same manner as the now redundant ones at Pilsner Urquell in Pilsen.

Munich beer gardens
Am Nockherberg, Hochstrasse 77.
This is one of the original beer gardens, which sprang up beside the cool caves used for lagering before artificial refrigeration was invented. Here Paulaner beers are served on draught, but customers are welcome to bring their own picnic lunches. During the Starkbierfest in March drinkers spill out of the beerhalls and into the Nockherberg, completely filling its 3,000 seats. The garden also fulfils the need for a public park for the inhabitants of the surrounding flats.
Chinesischer Turm, Englischer Garten Park.
A Chinese Tower in an English garden in a German city may seem unreal enough but what gives it a surreal air is that the 50-foot pagoda around which the 6,500 seats are arranged is also a platform for ... you've guessed it, an oompah band. The beers are from Löwenbräu and an added attraction is an antique wooden carousel and organ. In the summer the park is home to the MCC – Munich Cricket Club – whose arcane rituals bemuse the Germans. The club has a special rule that a batsman cannot be given out if his concentration was disturbed by a nude jogger.
Hofbräu Keller, Innere Wienerstrasse 19.
This garden, one of the city's oldest, was attached to the original Hofbräu Brewery until it was demolished in 1990 to make way for a hotel. The old bierkeller, though, is still an integral part of the garden. Hofbräu beers are served, including the full range of seasonal specialities.

Great Britain

London
Argyll Arms, 18 Argyll Street, W1.

The Argyll is just off Oxford Street, next door to Oxford Circus tube station and almost opposite the world-famous Palladium music hall. This splendid Victorian pub, with its giant mirrors and maze of little bars, is consequently always packed with tourists and office-workers. The "gents" toilet is a masterwork of mid-Victorian craftsmanship, while a unique survival is the manager's office, sited so that he can see what his patrons are up to in all five bars.

George, 55 Great Portland Street, W1.

The BBC's local, the George, was once patronized by the beer-drinking luminaries of the great days of radio – Dylan Thomas, Louis MacNeice, George Orwell. A magnificent Victorian pub with gas mantles, polished panel work and old wine casks, it is familiarly known as the Gluepot. The name was often given to pubs frequented by furniture workers, joiners and cabinet makers and was attached to the George, rather scornfully, by the conductor Sir Henry Wood who used the Queen's Hall next door to rehearse the BBC Symphony Orchestra.

Lamb, 94 Lamb's Conduit Street, WC1.

With London's pubs so beset by fake Victoriana, it's refreshing to find one where the real thing survives, right down to the "snob-screens" above the bar which supposedly prevented Victorian and Edwardian middle-class patrons being recognized from the public bar when they were entertaining ladies other than their wives. Another big plus for the Lamb – once the Bloomsbury Set's local and long a favourite with London University academics – was its stubborn adherence to real ale when all about was keg. The Lamb is a particularly pleasant resort on a hot summer's night as it stands on a pedestrian precinct. It is one of the finest outlets for Young's superb ales.

Princess Louise, 208 High Holborn, WC1.

Long a London landmark with its peerless location, long bar and palatial gents' loo, the Princess Louise was dying on its feet in the 1970s as a Watney house where only Red Barrel keg beer was served and where few ever ventured. But when Watney sold the dingy and dilapidated wreck, it turned into a flourishing and vibrant free house, well maintained and awash with a grand selection of the finest ales the kingdom has to offer. The pub has magnificent moulded ceilings, ornate columns, glass screens, imposing mirrors and snug side alcoves.

Cittie of Yorke, 22 High Holborn, WC1.

An amazing Victorian recreation of a fifteenth-century gothic Great Hall. The clientele, too, represent a Victorian recreation of a medieval original: they're mainly barristers, clerks and judges from the nearby Law Courts and Inns of Court. Other Victorian survivals include a gantry over the great wine-butts, used until the Second World War by the staff who had to keep the casks topped up, private booths of the sort once common in central London pubs but now a rarity, and the capital's longest bar counter. In keeping with its name, the pub is now owned by Yorkshire brewer Sam Smith's. In winter the bar is always toastingly warm thanks to the heat from open stoves.

Castle, 34 Cowcross Street, EC1.

Blood once mixed with money in this pub on the edge of the City, where Smithfield Market "bummarees" or meat porters in their offal-spattered overalls rubbed shoulders with Savile Row-suited stockbrokers and investment bankers. The bummarees have gone but there are still plenty of City gents. The Castle is the only London pub that is also a pawnbroker. A large mural on the wall, not quite obscured by the out-of-place Wurlitzer juke box, says that George V, strapped for cash after gambling, "popped" or pawned his watch for £5 in the pub. In more modern times, the "pop shop" side of the business allowed bummarees to spend their wages before they got them.

Old Mitre, Ely Court, Ely Place, Hatton Garden, EC1.

This ranks as one of London's most hidden pubs, for although tourists by the thousand surge past within yards, few find its secluded courtyard entrance. Not that it's ever less than packed, for plenty do know it, not least for its place in the chaotic legal history of a country which has never completely shaken off its medieval cobwebs. The pub was, in the late medieval period, part of the "liberty" of the Bishop of Ely, Cambridgeshire: that is, it had earlier been the Bishop's town house and he still had the licensing of it, so London constables had no jurisdiction there. This situation, once repeated in odd corners of many cities, has now been regularized, so if you have just robbed one of the diamond-merchants of Hatton Garden, do not count on the pursuit stopping at the gates of Ely Place. The courtyard of the pub has the stump of a tree round which Queen Elizabeth I is reputed to have danced.

Old Red Lion, 418 St John Street, EC1.

One of the best-known of London's many theatre pubs, the Old Red Lion is a handsome four-storey, red-brick building, dating from the turn of the century but on a site which has been a tavern for centuries. This small patch of London once contained many interesting pubs: the Angel, Islington, itself has long gone and is now buried under a Co-op Bank; next to it was an ancient inn called the Peacock; the Crown & Woolpack, derelict for a long time, was a haunt of red revolutionaries and had a bust of Lenin; and the Empress of Russia, insensitively modernized, was long a favourite of both cast and audiences from the Sadler's Wells theatre nearby. The Old Red Lion itself, with its tiny upstairs auditorium, its well-preserved and plush interior, and its good food, thrives. It claims that Tom Paine wrote the first draft of *The Rights of Man* there.

Dirty Dick's, 204 Bishopsgate, EC2.

The original Dirty Dick was an eighteenth-century London ironmonger called Nathaniel Bentley, whose shop stood on the site.

Bentley was tragically transformed into a dirty and ragged recluse after his fiancée died on the eve of their wedding, and he was so grief-stricken, it is said, that he never washed again. The modern Dirty Dick's dates back to about 1870 and has bars in the vaults and on the first floor as well as at ground level. The main bar, until a few years ago, was decorated with ghastly relics such as two mummified cats which were said to have been in Bentley's shop – although why an ironmonger should be selling mummified cats is anyone's guess. All that is gone now in favour of bare bricks and stripped floors, along with ales from Young's of Wandsworth.

Black Friar, 174 Queen Victoria Street, EC4.

London's only no-holds-barred art nouveau pub was designed in 1903 as a celebration in bronze and coloured marble of the Dominican friars whose monastery once stood on the site. It has recently been restored to its full florid glory at a cost of nearly a million pounds. The wedge-shaped building has a welter of designs showing monks carousing. The great marble-topped bar serves a small area with a vast open fireplace while marble alcoves offer some comfortable seating areas. A marvellous and unique pub.

Olde Bell, 95 Fleet Street, EC4.

Not all the journalists have fled Fleet Street; and those remaining (at Reuters and the Press Association) use the Olde Bell as their watering hole. Supposedly designed by Sir Christoper Wren who rebuilt St Paul's Cathedral after the Great Fire of London, the Olde Bell is one of central London's oldest pubs, having been constructed in 1670 to remove the wages from the armies of workers refashioning London after the fire. The pub's size does not match its present popularity, and on hot days drinkers spill out into St Bride's churchyard next door.

Olde Cheshire Cheese, Wine Office Court,
145 Fleet Street, EC4.

Did Dr Samuel Johnson really drink here? He's not actually recorded as having done so, but since he lived next door it's reasonable to assume that he did – and often. The site was once a friary: its well is still visible in the cellar, which has its own oak-beamed, stone-floored bar, and a medieval tunnel running down towards the Thames. The present building is post-Great Fire with many Georgian alterations producing a warren of small rooms with high-backed wooden settles and open fires. An upstairs restaurant serves such traditional English fayre as roast beef, steak and kidney pie, and the sort of "nursery puddings" that still haunt men who survived the rigours of private schools.

Punch Tavern, 99 Fleet Street, EC4.

The Punch was one of the most famous pubs of Fleet Street in the great days of the newspaper industry and either gave its name to or took its name from (accounts vary) the once-great but now defunct satirical magazine, *Punch*. Cartoons from *Punch* are an important component in the decor, as are huge pub mirrors. The interior has been knocked into one but is still divided into small intimate seating areas, and what used to be a separate public bar is now a busy dining area.

Prospect of Whitby, 57 Wapping Wall, E1.

London often disappoints those in search of real antiquity: there is very little of the original City of London that survived the Great Fire of 1666, and so much of London outside the City dates from the eighteenth, nineteenth or twentieth centuries. The Prospect of Whitby, however, is an exceptional survival from the early 1500s, complete with low ceilings and stone-flagged floors. A rustic beer garden and riverside terrace complete its charm. The infamous Judge Jeffreys, it is said, would feast in lodgings upstairs while watching the bodies of those he had condemned swinging from the Thames-side gallows. Samuel Pepys, diarist, roisterer, and Secretary to the Navy Board, was another contemporary user of the pub. The name relates to a sail-barge engaged in the coastal trade with the north-east of England, bringing coals from Newcastle.

Market Porter, 9 Stoney Street, SE1.
This splendid old London boozer is in the heart of the rejuvenated Borough Market, where stalls sell fruit, vegetables, meat and flowers. The pub has a spacious interior that dog-legs round a large bar where handpumps dispense a wide choice of cask beers: the range constantly changes but Harvey's Sussex Best Bitter is a regular. There's a more intimate seating area at the back and also tables on the pavement. The pub is handy for the Globe Theatre – the recreation of Shakespeare's original – and the Vinopolis and Brew Wharf complex that are a wine showcase and brewpub, respectively.

Anchor, Bankside, SE1.
London's river is perhaps its greatest glory, and the many pubs that line its banks are the best places from which to appreciate it. One of the oldest of them is the Anchor, a maze of little rooms built in 1750 when the old brothel-and-slum district Shakespeare knew was largely redeveloped. The Anchor, built by a brewer named Thrale after whom one of the bars is named, was an instant hit with the literati of the day, and pub-goers from north of the river queued up to rub shoulders with stars such as Dr Johnson and Boswell, Oliver Goldsmith, David Garrick and Edmund Burke. But the Thames is the real star, and can be watched either from the Chart Restaurant upstairs or the terrace across the way.

George, 77 Borough High Street, SE1.
Supposedly a true Shakespearean survival, the George is in fact only a fragment of its original self, two wings having been demolished to make way for railway warehouses (now gone). Actually the courtyard itself is the only bit Shakespeare would have known: he is said to have performed in it as a member of a company of strolling players before fame beckoned. The actual building he knew, though, was pulled down a century later and replaced with a galleried coaching inn. But even if the George is not quite all it pretends to be, it is still a landmark pub, unique in London as the last survivor of the great age of coaching inns, and is a fascinating and lovely place to visit.

Westminster Arms, 7 Storeys Gate, SW1.

If you want to get an honest answer out of your MP, lie in wait for him here. He's bound to turn up eventually – they all drink here and the pub even has a division bell in the bar – and without the array of policemen, ushers, clerks and what-have-you to protect him, he's at your mercy. This is parliament's "local" and, with its cellar bar, its restaurant and its fine range of beers, it's well worth a visit in its own right.

White Horse, 1 Parsons Green, SW6.

This huge Victorian pub would be (and was) an unexceptional Bass house were it not for the dedication of publican Mark Dorber. With Bass's blessing, the pub has been turned into a more or less permanent beer festival where the brewery's standard range, kept in immaculate condition, makes room for guest ales from many regional breweries and even occasional rarities such as draught wheat beer. The annual winter festival of old ales is a must in the diary of every true beer lover. The insistence on quality maintained in the cellar is also at work in the kitchen: the food is on a much higher plane than pub food anywhere else in the capital.

Dove, 19 Upper Mall, Hammersmith, W6.

Another riverside pub, the Dove was a very grand retreat, a morning's journey from London when it was built in the reign of Charles II. At the time, the western reach of the Thames was very fashionable – the poet Pope lived in Twickenham, the Duke of Sussex had a house next to the Dove, and "Rule Britannia" was written upstairs by a man with no other claim to fame whatever, James Thomson. Since those early days, the Dove has maintained its appeal – William Morris, Graham Greene and Ernest Hemingway are all associated with the pub. The Dove is one of the oldest Fuller's houses – the brewery brought it in 1796 – and a pint or three of London Pride on the terrace overlooking the Thames is possibly the best way to idle away a summer's afternoon that London has to offer.

St Albans, Hertfordshire
Ye Olde Fighting Cocks, off George Street, through Abbey gateway.

You can drive down to this old ale-house, though a walk is better, taking in the awesome bulk of St Albans Abbey, dedicated to the first Christian martyr, Alban, whose shrine was built by King Offa and around which the modern cathedral stands. The Fighting Cocks claims to be England's oldest licensed premises though the licence was granted for the "sport" of cock-fighting. The small sunken seating area inside reached via steps was the cock-fighting pit in Stuart times. The pub has a conical roof atop a round building that was known for several centuries as the Round House. The main bar is spacious and comfortable with low beamed ceilings and there is a large and attractive beer garden. The pub is on the edge of Verulam Park with its Roman remains and large lake.

Farriers Arms, Lower Dagnall Street.

A splendid example of an endangered species, a no-frills and unvarnished street-corner "boozer" with two simple bars, magnificent hand-pumped beer from the Hertford brewery McMullen, where darts, dominoes, cribbage and whist are played and pub grub is of the cheap and cheerful sausage-egg-and-chips variety. The locals are friendly and the toilets are in the yard. Outside there is a plaque commemorating the pub – wrongly – as the meeting place of the first branch of the Campaign for Real Ale, but let's not quibble. Go and marvel before the modernizers ruin it.

Leeds
Whitelocks, Turks Head Yard, Briggate.

Leeds's handsome city centre has been enjoying a major wash and brush-up in recent years, emerging from its coating of soot as a wonderland for lovers of decorative Victorian architecture. Undoubtedly, the place for a lunch break is Whitelocks, an unspoilt gem with bars arranged in line alongside a long narrow courtyard secluded from the main drag and full of original carved wood, etched and coloured glass, and brasswork. Popular with office workers and the growing number of tourists who are discovering post-industrial Leeds as the ideal centre for touring Yorkshire.

York
Black Swan, Peasholm Green.
Before the Industrial Revolution, York was England's second city. What is today the Black Swan started life in the fourteenth century as one of its grandest private houses, the home of the Bowes family, ancestors of the Queen Mother. William Bowes was MP for York four times, sheriff in 1407 and Lord Mayor twice. His son was also Lord Mayor, and his grandson was Lord Mayor of London and Court Jeweller to Elizabeth I. The house probably became an inn in 1715, still equipped with all the refinements of a great house: moulded plaster ceiling and fine Jacobean panelling and doorcase in the front parlour; elegant stairs of about 1700; and, in the upstairs dining room, panelling covered with seventeenth-century chiaroscuro paintwork. Luckily the inn declined in the nineteenth century, and was thus never vandalized by the Victorians; a restoration of 1930 revealed intact many fine original features.

Cumbria
Masons Arms, Strawberry Bank, Cartmel Fell.
One of Britain's best-known brewpubs, the Mason's Arms range includes a celebrated damson beer and the pub also makes its own cider. But the in-house brewery is far from being the pub's only attraction: it stocks more than 250 bottled beers from all over the world, many of them imported by the licensee, while the range of home-cooked food is celebrated across a wide area – especially by vegetarians, who are so often badly catered for in pubs. Another bonus is the setting, with its breathtaking views across the Winster

Valley. But perhaps its greatest asset is its interior, which is basically that of a seventeenth-century farmhouse with kitchen, parlour, Jacobean panelled saloon and now an upstairs room as well. The celebrated children's writer Arthur Ransome lived just up the lane in a cottage where he wrote some of his *Swallows and Amazons* novels.

Manchester
Peveril of the Peak, 127 Great Bridgwater Street.
This classic urban pub takes its name from a stagecoach which used to ply the cross-Pennine route to the Derbyshire Peak District. The coach itself took its name from a very ancient North Midlands land-owning family: William de Peverel was a natural son of William the Conqueror, who commanded Nottingham Castle from 1068, and subsequent Peverils owned land around Castleton. Sir Walter Scott's novel, *Peveril of the Peak*, came out in 1823. The pub itself is unusual in being triangular in shape and boasts a Victorian tiled exterior with original mahogany and stained glass in the three bars, which are grouped around a central servery and are homely rather than plush.

West Midlands
Vine (Bull & Bladder), Delph Road, Brierley Hill, near Dudley.
This famous Black Country pub is also the brewery tap for the small family firm of Batham's, whose mild and bitter it sells. The brewery, which owns another eight pubs in the area, is just behind the Vine, whose nickname stems from the fact that part of the building used to be a slaughterhouse and butcher's shop – a combination which may not be obvious but is not uncommon in the Black Country: Sally Perry's brewpub in Upper Gornal is another example. The Vine is a rambling many-roomed pub in a basic style which owes nothing to the rather self-conscious "no frills" style of

modern ale-house decor but is simply the way the pub has evolved down the years. You can stand and quaff in the corridor if you prefer, served through a hatch. The pub grub is simple and plentiful and there are regular live jazz concerts in the large back room at weekends.

East Midlands
Olde Trip to Jerusalem, Brewhouse Yard, Castle Road, Nottingham.
The current building is a seventeenth-century development of a twelfth-century inn and can claim with some historical justification to be the oldest inn in England. There is also a brewhouse that once served the castle – this even pre-dates the original inn. The upstairs bar of the pub, reached by a winding stone staircase, is carved from sandstone below the castle. The walls, panelled at the bottom, disappear into the Stygian gloom of the rock. Side alcoves have been cut from the sandstone. The downstairs bar is also hewn from the rock face and has old oak settles and barrel tables set on flagstoned floors. Soldiers had their last draft of ale here before setting out to fight in the Crusades, hence the name of this wonderfully atmospheric and unspoilt ale-house.

Edinburgh
Bow Bar, 80 West Bow, off High Street and Grassmarket.
Once a rarity in Scotland, and still not common enough, are pubs which sell a variety of real ales from different breweries. One such is the Bow Bar, a single-room traditionally decorated urban classic in the heart of the Old Town where English ales such as Draught Bass and Timothy Taylor's Landlord share the counter with the Caledonian range of Edinburgh-brewed real ales. Often there are as many as 12 real ales at a time – added to which is a fine collection of more than 100 single malt whiskies.

Café Royal, West Register Street.
A design flagship of the late nineteenth century, the Café Royal boasts big Victorian-style chandeliers, marble floors and stairs, a great gantry over the island bar, and incredible Doulton tilework murals portraying such leading lights of science and technology as James Watt, Michael Faraday, George Stephenson, William Caxton and Benjamin Franklin. An air of sophistication is maintained by the selection of morning newspapers and by the fringe productions put on here during the Edinburgh Festival. Scottish and English real ales are complemented by a choice of 40 malt whiskies. There is an acclaimed Oyster Bar that specializes in sea fish.

Glasgow
Babbity Bowster, 16–18 Blackfriars Street.
A highly individual conversion of a Robert Adam townhouse in the heart of the rejuvenated Merchant City district of Glasgow, the Babbity Bowster takes its name from a folk song and dance, Bab at the Bowster, illustrated at the pub by a ceramic plaque of kilted piper and dancer. It is the only pub in the district with an outdoor drinking area – none of your boulevardiers in "Glasgae" – and until recently was the only pub in the whole of Scotland to serve real cider. Its restaurant has a bias towards Scottish produce, though not to the exclusion of all else, and it serves Maclay's range of real ales, including one specially brewed for it.

Ireland

Dublin
The Brazen Head, 20 Lower Bridge Street.
Built on the site of a tavern dating back to the twelfth century, The Brazen Head claims to be the oldest drinking establishment in Ireland, if not the whole of Europe. The place is steeped in history, and is redolent of the secret meetings of rebels and smugglers. In

1798 it was the meeting place of Oliver Bond and Thomas Reynolds, and in the late nineteenth century it was frequented by Robert Emmett, Wolfe Tone and Daniel O'Connell. Tucked away off an alleyway close to the River Liffey, it is splendidly atmospheric and has been mercifully left alone by modernizers.

Davy Byrnes, 21 Duke Street.

Renowned as Dublin's most literary pub, Davy Byrnes is one of the city's finest bars. Although at times patronized by many great literary figures, such as James Stephens, Liam O'Flaherty and Padraig O'Conner, it is best known for its connections with James Joyce. *Dubliners* has mention of Davy Byrnes, but the Joycean character with which the premises is most associated is Leopold Bloom of *Ulysses*. There is a portrait of the writer by Harry Kernoff on one wall, and other splendid decorations include paintings of Dublin and Bacchanalian murals. The pub is well-known in Dublin for its excellent seafood.

Neary's, 1 Chatham Street.

Neary's is a fine old bar that has long been a favourite haunt of the acting fraternity – the back door is conveniently situated across an alleyway from the stage door of the Gaiety Theatre.

McDaid's, Harry Street.

To be found down a lane opposite Neary's, this splendid Dublin pub was once the watering-hole of the poet Paddy Kavanagh and the boisterous writer Brendan Behan.

Belfast

Crown Liquor Saloon, 46 Great Victoria Street.

The Crown is owned by the National Trust and is a Victorian gem, with a long granite-top bar and seating in "donkey boxes" – partitioned private drinking areas separated by carved wood and painted glasswork. The floor is tiled and there is a plethora of mirrors and ornately moulded ceilings. It is said locally that you haven't been to Belfast until you've been to the Crown.

The Netherlands

Amsterdam
In De Wildeman, Nieuwe Zijdskolk.
The Wild Man Inn is well-named since its owner, Henk Eggens, stands at a magnificently moustached 6 feet 8 inches. Eggens was a leading character in Holland's beer revival during his years as manager of the Gollem Café (see below). Now he has a billet of his own down a side street just off the pedestrianized Nieuwedijk and close to Centraal Station – and what a find it is. Its 160 beers include 30 from the Netherlands, it sells spirits from the cask, and – unusually for a country addicted to cheroots – it includes a no-smoking bar. Beer specialities are chalked on a board. The Wild Man is rather like Dr Who's famous Tardis: it is small on the outside but surprisingly spacious inside, with a raised area at the rear that allows drinkers to overlook the long bar. Light snacks are also served.
Café Gollem, 4 Raamsteeg.
Gollem was so popular in the 1980s when its management led the Dutch beer revival that habitués are bound to say it's not what it was. But this small café in its little alley still has the biggest beer list in Amsterdam, with 200 choices from around the world. The food is more limited – just bread, cheese and ham – but who really needs more? House specialities include the rarely sighted sour wheat beers of Berlin.
De Bekeerde Suster, 6-8 Kloveniersburgwal.
Cafe, restaurant and brewery all in one, "The Reformed Sister" is on the edge of the red light district and celebrates a medieval prostitute who became a nun in a convent on the site. The bar opened in 1992 and one remarkable feature is that the brew kettles are not just visible but are a central feature. The two beers are Blonde Ros (White Horse), with East Kent Goldings among the hops – the beer has tangerine fruit, peppery hops and chewy malt – and Bock

Ros, a dark beer with a roasted grain, bitter chocolate, ginger and hop resins on aroma and palate. Good food is available.

't IJ Proeflokaal, 7 Funenkade.

Amsterdam's independent brewery, 't IJ, was founded in 1984 in a converted bathhouse in the city's dockland. Its brewery tap only opens from 3 p.m. until 8 p.m. from Wednesday to Sunday but, with all of the 't IJ beers – Struis, Columbus, Zatte, Bockbier, Natte, Mug Bitter and Plzen – regularly on draught, it's a golden opportunity to sample beers which are all too hard to find elsewhere. To add to the fun, the bar has a collection of 2,000 empty beer bottles from all over the world. Food is limited to drinkers' snacks, but children are welcome and there's a selection of board games to keep them happy. There is a cavernous downstairs room when the ground floor bar gets overcrowded.

Rotterdam

Cambrinus, 4 Blaak.

Between the Blaak railway and metro station and the waterfront is Cambrinus. The name is a variant of Gambrinus, itself a nickname for Jan Primus, Duke of Brabant 1251–95, reputed to be capable of downing 144 mugs of beer at a single sitting. But it would take even such a doughty drinker as Jan Primus more than two sittings to taste his way through the beer-list at this café – it stocks some 300. The modern bar has a dining room at the back which takes *cuisine à la bière* seriously; beyond that, a terrace overlooks the old harbour.

Utrecht

Jan Primus, 27 Jan van Scorel Straat.

Another tribute to the Prince of Beer is this street-corner café in the unassuming suburb of Wilhelmina Park. There's no music, no gaming machines, and not a lot in the way of food; what there is is a list running to 130 beers and a regular clientele who are genuinely pleased to see strangers and – horror of horrors for the reserved English visitor – are likely to try to engage you in conversation!

United States of America

Boston, Mass.
Bull & Finch, 84 Beacon Street.
If you've seen *Cheers* on TV you'll feel at home here for this is the inspiration for the series, more suds than soap. A large central bar is the focus of the roomy, comfortable old saloon where the humour is drier than the beer.
Doyle's, 3484 Washington Street, Jamaica Plain.
Stresses the Irishness of Boston with rooms dedicated to the Kennedys and Michael Collins, the Irish nationalist who negotiated the treaty with Britain in 1921 that created the Free State and sparked a civil war in which he was killed. But all are welcome – even Brits these days – and the style, beer and cuisine are multicultural.

Manhattan, New York City
American Festival Café, Rockefeller Center, 20 West 50th Street, Midtown.
Has superb views out over the famous ice-skating rink. From the comfort of the plush surroundings customers can choose from a beer menu built around American craft breweries, including Catamount, Brooklyn, Grants and Yuengling.
Brewsky's, 41 East 7th Street.
A tiny bar with strong Ukrainian associations, sawdust on the floor, a collection of canned beers, photos of old movie stars on the walls, 400 bottled beers and many independent brewers' draught beers.
Fraunce's Tavern, 54 Pearl Street.
This is one of the oldest taverns in the country, dating from 1790

when New York was still under British rule. George Washington said goodbye to his troops from the steps of the tavern. Inside it has the atmosphere of a period London chop house, with lots of wood panelling, settles and long tables. There is usually a beer from at least one independent brewery, often Brooklyn.

Jimmy Armstrong's Bar, corner of 10th Avenue and West 57th Street.

A splendid bar in an otherwise unremarkable part of Manhattan, just before the island falls into the river. The bar, with its comfortable seating, wood and glass partitions and a Double Diamond mirror from Burton-on-Trent in England, offers a wide range of American craft brewers' beer, from Anchor Steam in San Francisco to Brooklyn.

Bohemian Hall and Beer Garden, 19–29 24th Avenue, Astoria.

There were once no fewer than 800 beer gardens in New York City catering for Czech and Slovak refugees from the Austro-Hungarian Empire. The Bohemian is the only remaining one and is a haven for descendants of central European immigrants. As well as the opulent interior, there's a large outdoor area with tables and benches, food sizzling on the grill and drinkers enjoying pitchers of beer from both the modern Czech Republic and other countries.

Peculier Pub, 145 Bleecker Street, West Broadway, Greenwich Village.

The in place for students from New York University, where beer connoisseurs know the correct spelling of Peculier in the manner of Theakston's of Yorkshire. The narrow tavern, dominated by a long bar, specializes in Belgian and British ales.

Zip City, 3 West 18th Street.

If you want to know where to get unfiltered Helles, Pilsner, Märzen, Vienna Red, Dunkel, Bock, Doppelbock or Maibock, Zip City is the best place outside of Munich. The large bar, where young Manhattans "stand in line" to get in, is the creation of Kirby Shyer near Union Square Park in the old Flatiron garment district.

The brewpub is a converted wrought-iron building from 1895 that once, with delicious irony, housed the National Temperance Society. The brewplant comes from Austria and the food is international. Zip City is a nickname for New York City in Sinclair Lewis's novel *Babbitt*.

Brooklyn, New York City
Peter's Waterfront Ale House, Atlantic Avenue.
Stunning views of Manhattan from outside. Inside this small, smart tavern is reminiscent of a Scots or Irish bar. Peter the owner has an ironic sense of humour – a sign promises "Honest warm beer, lousy food and an ugly owner". All the threats are unfulfilled: the beer in particular is eclectic and in fine form and includes Fuller's Extra Special Bitter from London, Paulaner Oktoberfest from Munich and a clutch of US microbrewers' products.
Peter Doelger's, Berry Street.
More than 100 years old, it was once owned by Doelger's Manhattan Brewery. It is comfortable and well lived-in, with large plate-glass windows, a cracked tiled floor, a small raised platform for musicians, Polish food – always fish on Fridays – and good beer, including Brooklyn Lager, Warsteiner and Bass Ale. Baseball on TV in the season.

Washington, DC
Brickskeller, 1523 22nd Street NW.
On the edge of Georgetown, it has the biggest selection of craft brewers' beers in the United States. Regular tutored beer tastings are held there.

Chicago, Ill.
Goose Island, 1800 North Clybourn.
Few bars can boast a range of beers as wide as Goose Island's. To his three regulars – Lincoln Park Lager, Golden Goose Pilsner, and

Honker's Pale Ale – brewer Gregory Hall adds no fewer than 15 seasonal and special brews inspired by beers as diverse as Irish stout, Weizen and barley wine. The cuisine is just as diverse, with dishes of Mexican, Belgian and German ancestry. The pub itself was once the Turtle Wax factory and now aims for an English pub atmosphere with exposed beams and wooden floors. It is the home of the Chicago Beer Society, which meets here on the first Thursday of every month.

San Francisco, Calif.
San Francisco Brewpub, 155 Columbus Avenue.
Unlike many brewpubs in the US, this is not an imaginative conversion of an old warehouse or a factory or a fire station: it was built as a tavern in 1907 and was originally called the Andromeda Saloon. It later changed its name to the Albatross Tavern and became as colourful as the surrounding Barbary District: Jack Dempsey worked here as a doorman, and Baby-Face Nelson was captured here in 1929. One of its four regular brews, Albatross Lager, recalls its history. Others are Emperor Norton Lager, Gripman's Porter and Serpent Stout, and there are three seasonal beers including Andromeda Wheatbeer. The decor features stained glass windows, tables made from old sewing machines, and a brass-inlaid mahogany bar.
20 Tank, 316 11th Street.
Just south of the Market District, near Folsom, is a brewpub that's all-American: the glass frontage bears a five-foot neon beer mug and the exposed ductwork is a major feature of the warehouse-style interior. The food is all-American, too, with chilli and nachos high on the menu. Kinnikinick Club Ale and Kinnikinick Old Scout Stout are the best-known beers, but other regulars include Mellow Glow Pale Ale and Moody's High Top Strong Ale, and there are up to seven seasonal and special brews.

Marin County, Calif.
Marin Brewing Co, 1809 Larkspur Landing Circle.
A drive across the bridge or a ferry ride from San Francisco brings you to a large, plush and welcoming restaurant and bar with attached microbrewery owned by Grant Johnson. He supplies the bar with a hoppy pale ale, a roasty stout and two fruit beers, raspberry and blueberry. The food is wide-ranging and imaginative and service is wonderfully attentive and friendly. From the deep seats of bar and restaurant there are magnificent views of the bay and the island that once housed a prison. Grant Johnson, with a nice irony, calls his dark beer Breakout Stout.

Dublin, Calif.
Lyons Brewery, 7294 San Ramon Road.
This is a bar, not a micro. Brewing ceased decades ago and there are no known Irish connections in the small town where Judy Ashworth runs a roomy tavern dedicated to quality beers from far and near. The long bar groans with taps for such specialities as Celis White, Pyramid Peach and Lind India Pale Ale. Judy, who is a great enthusiast, will show fellow connoisseurs her tiny but immaculate cool room where beers are stored and will debate the merits of such English ales as Sam Smith's and Greene King.

Los Angeles, Calif.
Gorky's, 536 East 8th Street.
Gorky's bills itself as a café and Russian brewery, and the all-grain, cask-conditioned beers include an Imperial Russian Stout and a "Russian" Red Ale. The menu continues the theme, with Russian pastas a speciality, and the decor is billed as "Bolshevik Modern". Not surprisingly this highly subversive set-up, just in front of the flower market in downtown Los Angeles, attracts students and artists – in fact some of the artists may even have works on show in Gorky's permanent exhibition.

Gazetteer of Pubs, Bars and Taverns

Portland, Oreg.

BridgePort Brewpub, 1313 NW Marshall Street.

This is the place for clear-sighted drinkers – smoking is banned throughout. Founded in 1984 as Columbia River Brewing, this is Oregon's oldest surviving microbrewery. The pub was opened two years later in this century-old building in the city's North-west Section. To three regular brews – BridgePort Ale and Blue Heron and Coho Pacific Light Ale – brewer William Lundeen adds four seasonal ales including a stout and a barley wine. The kitchen specializes in pizzas made with home-made sourdough crusts.

Seattle, Wash.

Redhook Brewery & Trolleyman Pub, 3400 Phinney Ave N.

British drinkers might feel familiar with some of the names on brewer Al Triplett's list, with names like Ballard and ESB. They might feel at ease in the pub, too – modern, comfortable, spacious and friendly, with a big open fire to give a homely atmosphere. Like so many US microbreweries, Redhook is housed in a building with a fascinating past of its own: it was the Fremont Trolley-Car Barn and home to the Seattle Electric Railway, and has national landmark status. Those who like to taste their beer and the home-made pub food that accompanies it will be pleased that the Trolleyman is non-smoking. Redhook is one of America's oldest craft breweries: it was founded in 1982, and the pub was opened in 1988.

Canada

Montreal, Quebec

Le Cheval Blanc, 809 Ontario Street.

Le Cheval Blanc has been a pub since 1937, and in the hands of the family of current owner/brewer Jerôme Denys for all that time. Jerôme relaunched it as a brewpub in 1987 and, although a limited menu includes Hungarian sausage and tacos, the beer is the thing. Jerôme's regular brews are an amber ale, a pale ale, Golden Wheat Ale, and a brown ale, but his specials include a maple syrup beer and bottle-conditioned kriek and frambozen.

Toronto, Ontario
Rotterdam, 600 King Street.
A bar for homesick ex-pats, Rotterdam Brewing serves Younger's Tartan, Guinness, Murphy's, Stone's and Smithwick's on draught. But why drink keg beer from the wrong side of the country when you could be drinking cask-conditioned Scotch Ale, Nut Brown Ale, Milk Stout or any one of 18 other ales and lagers produced on the premises? The menu is long, too: calamari, guacamole, nachos, steaks, sausages, pastas, fish, smoked turkey, sandwiches, and falafel are just some of the dishes on offer. The red-brick building which houses the brewpub is a century old, and the decor goes in for street lamps, stone walls, and marble-topped tables. A slightly disquieting note: look up, and through the glass ceiling you will see several tons of brewery perched right over your head.

Vancouver, British Columbia
Swan's Brewpub, Buckerfield's Brewery, 506 Pandora Street, Victoria.
Located in an 80-year-old seed warehouse in Victoria's Old Town district, Swan's was established in 1989 along the lines of a tradi-tional English local, right down to hanging baskets, plenty of exposed timbers, and a polished oak bar with brass hand pumps. The beers brewed up by Frank Appleton and Chris Johnson include a bitter, a pale, a stout, a brown ale, and a barley wine at Christmas – although the average English pub-goer might be sur-prised to be offered a "Ragin' Cajun Halibut Burger!"
Spinnakers, 308 Catherine Street.
This is a place that really brews. In fact Jake Thomas produces no fewer than 20 beers in all sorts of styles – an India Pale Ale and

four different stouts rub shoulders with four Weizens, one of them mit hefe, a bock and a dark lager. All beers are unfiltered and cask-conditioned. The building itself dates back to the 1920s and has a ground-floor restaurant and an upstairs taproom. It has been a brewpub since 1984, claiming to be Canada's first. As at Swan's, halibut is a speciality.

Australia

Adelaide
Cooper's Alehouse, 316 Pulteney Street.
Cooper's flagship pub and restaurant in its home town. A large, wood-panelled main bar serves the full range of the brewery's beers plus many international brands. Beyond the bar, a bistro has excellent food: why not match freshly caught oysters with Cooper's Stout?

Brisbane
Brisbane German Club, 416 Vulture Street, East Brisbane.
Opposite the world-famous "Gabba" cricket ground, the club offers a vast range of authentic German beers. You can match a hefeweizen with sauerbraten, leberkäse or frikadellen: close your eyes and imagine you're in Munich.

Melbourne
James Squire Brewhouse, Russell Street, near junction with Little Collins Street
A single storey, modern bar with bare wood floors, large windows overlooking the street that open out on warm days, and lots of artefacts about James Squire, convict and brewer. To the right of the entrance is a small brewery that produces some of the James Squire range. The beers on offer include Pale Ale, Gold and Porter. Good value food is served at a fast pace.

Prince's Bridge Hotel, 1 Swanston Street
Better known as Yates & Jackson, this opulent hotel stands opposite
Flinders Street railway station. There are two main bars downstairs
plus a small restaurant, with more bars and a larger restaurant one
floor up. Don't miss Chloe's Bar on the first floor with a once-
notorious nude painting of Chloe. The house beer is Naked Ale,
along with beers from Cooper's, Little Creatures, James Squire and
Redback.
Cookie, 252 Swanston Street.
On the top floor of Curtin House, the long bar dominated by a
large serving counter has an astonishing choice of imported beers,
including Budvar, Chimay, Erdinger, Hoegaarden, Orval, Rochefort
and Young's. There's loud music at night but the bar is quiet and
contemplative during the day.

Sydney
Pumphouse Brewery Brewpub, Little Pier Street, Darling
Harbour.
Built on the site of an old water-pumping station that generated
the energy to power Sydney's elevators at the turn of the last century, the Pumphouse still features an enormous cast-iron water
tank. It has a large beer garden and an attractive balcony.
Lord Nelson Hotel, 19 Kent Street, The Rocks.
The Lord Nelson, at Millers Point, an extension of Sydney's
historical Rocks area, is the city's oldest continuous licensed hotel,
built in 1841 and named after Horatio Nelson. The handsome
sandstone building has been lovingly restored and its small brewery
produces six house beers all brewed without chemicals or adjuncts
and fermented with an English yeast culture. The beers are Old
Admiral, Victory Bitter, Quayle Ale, Trafalgar Pale Ale, Three Sheets
and Nelson's Blood. The ales all have strong associations with
Admiral Nelson save for Quayle Ale, a wheat beer named after a
visit by former US Vice-President Dan Quayle. The hotel also

produces Two Dogs, an alcoholic lemonade that has become a cult drink in Australia and was launched in Britain in 1995 by Bass.

The Hero of Waterloo Hotel, 81 Lower Fort Street, The Rocks.

The Hero of Waterloo is another impressive sandstone building, this one dating from 1843. It was a favourite drinking place for troops in colonial times and it has retained open, log-burning fires. It is popular with British and Irish visitors today as well as locals, and offers Bass, Guinness and Newcastle Brown Ale. Don't miss the stone cellars and the infamous tunnel linking the hotel to the harbour, used for rum smuggling and the involuntary recruitment of sailors. Young men who got drunk at the bar would be dropped through a trap door into the cellar, dragged along the tunnel and Shanghaied aboard a waiting clipper.

Australian Hotel, 100 Cumberland Street, The Rocks.

The Australian Hotel was built in 1913 and retains not only many original features but a ban on poker machines and pool tables. Its beers are supplied by Scharer's Little Brewery based in the George IV inn in Argyle Street, Picton. The microbrews are chemical and additive free and include a 5.0 per cent lager and a 6.4 per cent dark Burragorang Bock. The hotel has an acclaimed menu that includes kangaroo fillet, crocodile marinated in herbs, and marinated emu.

Fremantle

Sail and Anchor, 64 Station Terrace.

Situated opposite Fremantle market, this pub-brewery was set up in 1984 when the Victorian red-brick Freemason's Hotel was bought and refitted. When the brewery was up and running it became the first new brewery in Australia for more than 50 years. The success of the Sail and Anchor prompted its owners to expand and build the Matilda Brewing Company which has achieved great national success with its two leading brands Redback and

Dogbolter. Brewmaster Ken Duncan produces three regular beers for the Sail and Anchor: Seven Seas Real Ale (4.6 per cent ABV), a fruity and hoppy English-style bitter, Brass Monkey Stout (6.0 per cent), a roasty, coffeeish oatmeal stout, and Ironbrew Strong Ale (7.0 per cent), a rich and warming dark ale. The pub is next door to the popular Markets area packed with stalls selling antiques, bric-à-brac and clothes.

New Zealand

Auckland
Shakespeare Tavern, 62 Albert Street.
Brewpub with Sir Toby Belch's Ginger Beer and King Lear Old Ale.
Nags Head, St Georges Bay Road, Parnell.
Six draught beers in a welcoming atmosphere.

Japan

Tokyo
Beer Bar Brussels, 75 Yarai-cho, Kagurazaka.
As you would expect, the Beer Bar Brussels has a good selection of Belgian brews. It is one of a small chain of bars specializing in Belgian beers and offers 80 brands, including Hoegaarden Wit, Chimay, Orval and lambic and gueuze.
Rising Sun near Yotsuya Station.
Irish landlord, international beers and shepherd's pie.
Sapporo
Sapporo Brewery's renowned beer garden is at North 6, East 9, Higashi-ku.

The Great Beer Festivals
of the World

Antwerp Beer Festival

In November, the Belgian beer drinkers' movement Objectieve Bier Proevers (OBP) stages the 24-hour beer festival in Antwerp, a fast-moving celebration of traditional beers in Belgium. Information: 32 3 2324538.

The Munich Oktoberfest

The Munich Oktoberfest is the world's oldest celebration of beer and, in terms of the amount of beer consumed, is also the biggest festival, though more modern events in Britain and the US offer greater choice. Potential visitors should be aware that, despite its name, the festival ends on the first weekend in October and runs for 16 days from the middle of September. During that time more than 10 million pints of beer will be consumed and the millions of visitors will also despatch 600,000 sausages, 750,000 roast chickens and 65,000 pork knuckles. The Oktoberfest is not exactly gemütlich for vegetarians.

The origins of this lederhosen and lager extravaganza date from 1810 when the Crown Prince Ludwig of Bavaria married Princess Theresa. The locals organized a festival on a meadow just outside the city centre and called it the Theresienwiese – Theresa's Meadow – or the 'Wiese for short. That first festival was "dry" – there was just a horse race and fair – but this is Bavaria and the annual event soon attracted the Munich brewers and the thirsty locals. Once the railway reached Munich, the festival started to attract revellers from all over Germany and Central Europe.

Ten giant canvas beer halls are the centre of the modern festival. Only the Munich brewers are allowed to have a tent and some of them cheat. For example, both Hacker and Pschorr have separate tents even though they have been one company for years and are now owned by Paulaner, which also has its own tent. On the other hand, Crown Prince Luitpold of Kaltenberg has been refused permission to have a tent, even though he has opened a brewpub in the city and brews some of the most interesting beer in the area.

The tents are all similar in style: row after row of benches where drinkers down great mugs of beer. In the centre of each tent is a podium for the inevitable oompah band which in between other ditties plays an interminable number called *Ein Prosit* (A Toast) with which all and sundry join in. On the Saturday of the opening day of the festival a parade of brewers' horse-drawn drays, bands and representatives of every craft in Bavaria winds it way through the city centre. The following day, a shorter parade which is confined to brewers' drays puts on a vivid display at the Theresienweise. It all adds up to a carnival of bibulous pleasure. The only disappointment is the disappearance of the true Oktoberfest beers, the Märzen beers brewed in March and lagered until September. Corner-cutting brewers have switched instead to Oktoberfest beers, pleasant, well-rounded and highly quaffable but a shadow of the traditional beers that made this festival a benchmark for all others to follow.

Beer-lovers planning to visit the festival are advised to book accommodation months in advance as every hotel and guest house in Munich and the suburbs fill to bursting point. The tourist office will book rooms but will accept only written requests: The address is Fremdenverkersamt, Postfach, 8000 Munich 1 and the fax number is (49) 89-239-1313.

Not to be outdone by the Müncheners, the people of Stuttgart also have an Oktoberfest called the Cannstatter Volksfest. It takes place in a suburb of the city called Cannstatt on a meadow known in the local dialect as the Wasen.

The Great British Beer Festival

The Great British Beer Festival is, according to its organizers, the Campaign for Real Ale, the "biggest pub in the world". CAMRA also believes that GBBF is the world's biggest beer festival as far as choice is concerned. Whereas the Oktoberfest offers just 10 beers, GBBF is a showcase for cask-conditioned ales, with around 450 on offer each year, celebrating the unique British beer style that would have disappeared but for CAMRA.

The festival has been staged since the mid-1970s and has enjoyed a peripatetic existence. It was held in London for several years but the campaign then took it to Brighton, Leeds and Birmingham in order to stress the regional diversity of cask beer. But the festival has been held in London for more than a decade and is now staged at Earl's Court during the first week in August. See www.camra.org.uk.

The cask beers are ranged on gantries that run the length of the hall and are divided into regions of Great Britain in order to underline the fact that real ale is a British not an English phenomenon, with beers from Scotland and Wales as well. Great emphasis is placed on style, with promotions for mild, porter, stout, old ales, barley wines and bottle-conditioned beers as well as pale ale or bitter. British ciders and perries are also on show as the campaign is keen to preserve these fruit-based drinks.

The festival also features beers from other countries. Belgian and German wheat beers, Trappist ales, lambic and gueuze, dark lagers and genuine Pilsners are just some of the styles that can be found. In 1995 the festival, for the first time ever, had cask-conditioned ales from the East Coast of the United States, a significant example of the deep impression CAMRA has made on the American microbrewing movement.

The festival is enormous fun. There is live entertainment, ranging from rock and jazz to classical music, during every session while children have a room with clowns and other attractions. The serious side of the festival is expressed through the Champion Beer of Britain competition, held on the opening day. Beers voted for by both CAMRA members and the general public are tasted blind by panels in categories ranging from mild ale to barley wines. The winners in each category then go forward to a final panel and the beer with the most marks is declared Champion Beer of Britain.

As well as the Great British, CAMRA organizes beer festivals throughout the country, often as many as 15 in a month, stressing regional choice and such seasonal styles as winter ales. Information concerning all CAMRA festivals: 01727 867201; fax 01727 867670.

Bock Beer Festival

Every October, the Dutch beer drinkers' organization PINT runs the Bock Beer Festival in Amsterdam, a two-day extravaganza featuring the strong beers, both top- and bottom-fermenting, of the Netherlands. Information: 31 2520 22909.

The Great American Beer Festival

The Great American Beer Festival was clearly inspired by the British festival but has developed into a major showcase not only for beer but for brewing as well. It is run by the Association of Brewers, a subsidiary of the American Homebrewers' Association, which inspired a legion of beer-lovers to forsake bland, cold lagers and rediscover the joys of the grain and the hop. Held every October in Denver, Colorado, GABF invites all American brewers, from Anheuser-Busch to the tiniest micro, to participate. The centrepiece of the festival is the judging of beers, broken down punctiliously into dozens of styles. You don't just find porters, for example, but brown porters and dark porters, while stouts come in all colours and ratings, from dry Irish to imperial Russian. The entire style range encompasses light beers at one end of the spectrum to barley wines and Doppelbocks at the other, stressing the enormous variety and diversity of American beer. The winners of each category are awarded gold medals, which are much coveted. Information from: Great American Beer Festival, PO Box 287, Boulder, Colorado 80306; tel 303 447 0816; fax 303 447 2825.

Other beer festivals are beginning to develop in the US. One of the largest on the East Coast is the Under the Brooklyn Bridge Festival, held in mid-September and featuring around 70 American and overseas beers. Information from Brooklyn Brewery, 118 North 11th Street, Brooklyn, New York 11211, tel: 718 486 7422. More information on American beer and beer festivals is in the national magazine *All About Beer*, published in Durham, North Carolina, tel: 919 490 0589.

The Culture of
Beer-drinking

The places where we drink are often steeped in history, none more so than the English pub with its fascinating collection of names and inn signs as well as traditional pub games. Pubs, bars and cafés have also conjured up some great literature, and given rise to some funny and ribald stories.

"We dined at an excellent inn at Chapel-house, where he expatiated on the felicity of England in its taverns and inns, and triumphed over the French for not having, in any perfection, the tavern life. 'There is no private house, (said he), in which people can enjoy themselves so well, as at a capital tavern'... He then repeated, with great emotion, Shenstone's lines:

> *Who'er has travell'd life's dull round,*
> *Where'er his stages may have been,*
> *May sigh to think he still has found*
> *The warmest welcome at an inn.*"
> **James Boswell**,
> The Life of Samuel Johnson.

Every beer-drinking country has public places in which to drink the staple beverage. The reason why the English pub is always singled out as the quintessential environment in which to enjoy beer can be explained in one word: history. In most other countries, bars, bier kellers and cafés are modern buildings. They carry little historical baggage. But even though most English pubs go back no further than the late nineteenth century, and most are more recent, they have a direct lineage with the ale-houses, taverns and inns that date back as far as Roman and Saxon times. Even the design of the modern pub, with several rooms and corridors, replicates the earliest ale-houses, which were extensions of people's homes, chosen because the ale wife or brewster made the finest ale in the village.

What's in a name

And while most bars in other countries carry the names of the owners by way of identification, the English pub comes with a fascinating variety of curious rubrics that delve deep into history. As the chain of ale-houses spread through England, it was no longer sufficient for the ale wife to stick an "ale stake" through a window or hang a garland of evergreens above the door to show that fresh ale was available. Ale-houses became commercial propositions and needed clear identities. Elaborate signs appeared outside them.

As the people were largely illiterate, these signs had to be instantly recognizable. And as the people were frequently at war, many signs were taken from the crests of the "noble" families that organized the fighting. Some famous pub signs still in use, such as the Red Lion (John of Gaunt), Bear and Ragged Staff (Earl of Warwick), and Eagle and Child (Earl of Derby), have heraldic origins. Some names pre-date Christianity, such as the Chequers, of Roman origin – the sign indicated both a wine shop and a place where money could be exchanged – and the Green Man, a pagan man who covered himself in greenery and then attacked villagers. Pubs called the Green Man that use an idealized image of Robin Hood on their signs are wrong by several centuries.

The impact of Christianity can be seen in pubs called the Crossed Keys (the insignia of St Paul), the Mitre, the Lamb (a reference to Christ), the Bell, and the Hope and Anchor (Paul described hope as the "anchor of the soul") while the Bull is a corruption of "bulla", a monastic seal. New Inn is actually a very old name, a shortened form of Our Lady's Inn, the common name given to taverns built alongside churches and monasteries. During the brief Cromwellian republic, all Popish names were banned. The Salutation, a reference to the annunciation of the Virgin Mary, became the Flower Pot. Austere taverns of the time given the firmly Protestant name of God Encompasses Us were refashioned as the Goat and Compasses by opponents of Cromwell.

Publicans were always quick to touch their forelock to the monarch of the day, hence the profusion of Queen's and King's Heads. But as capitalism developed out of feudalism, inns were often the meeting places of trade associations that allowed their crests to be used, hence the survival of the Baker's Arms, the Dolphin (watermen), the Lamb and Flag (merchant tailors), the Three Compasses (carpenters), Noah's Ark (shipwrights), and the Ram or Fleece (wool trade). In fact, in 1393 King Richard II brought in legislation that impelled landlords to erect signs to show they sold drink: "Whosoever shall brew ale in the town with intention of selling it must hang out a sign, otherwise he shall forfeit his ale."

Many pub names have a strong sporting theme, if fox hunting or cock fighting count as "sports". Cricket is far and away the most popular subject, with countless Cricketers. The Bat and Ball at Hambledon in Hampshire staged famous matches and is regarded as the home of the modern game. It was a brewpub where the landlord's ale "flared like turpentine". The most famous of all English cricketers, Dr W.G. Grace, has a pub named in his honour while The Yorker in London's Piccadilly commemorates a particularly wicked type of bowler's delivery. (There is no known American equivalent called The Spit Ball.)

369

Although football (soccer) has a bigger following than cricket, it has less support on pub signs. Nevertheless the Gunners (Arsenal), the Spurs (Tottenham Hotspur), the Hammers (West Ham), the Saints (Southampton) and United (the internationally recognized shorthand for Manchester United) all have pubs named after them.

The drinker's code of honour

The etiquette of pub drinking is also sharply different in English pubs. Whereas in most bars and cafés, drinkers will run up a tab, often marked by waiters on a beer mat or given as a receipt with each drink, in an English pub (or a Welsh or Scottish one for that matter) each beer is paid for as it is ordered. The British drink in "rounds", which means that each member of a group will take it in turns to buy drinks for the ensemble. The name is derived from "going the rounds", or serving everyone in turn with goods or services, which in turn probably comes from King Arthur's egalitarian round table. Woe betide any drinker who does not "stand his round". In order to avoid being considered a skinflint, a member of a round will declare his intention of buying drinks by declaring "It's my shout". The buying of beer in this fashion helps explain the comparative weakness of British draught beer. The rising price of beer in recent years has restricted large rounds. Friends tend to split up into smaller groups of two or three to keep costs down at a time when a pint in some areas can be as much as £3.50.

Waiter service is rare in an English or Welsh pub. The middle- and working-class inhabitants of the British Isles have never been at ease with the notion of being "waited on" and, apart from fish-and-chip takeaways, only started to eat out in large numbers when pubs offered food with buffet-style service. In Scotland the tradition is different: there are pubs in the "Borders", the areas abutting the boundary with England, and also in the great cities of

Aberdeen, Dundee, Edinburgh and Glasgow. But elsewhere drinking is largely confined to hotels.

Last orders, gentlemen, please

Britain was famous – or infamous – throughout the world for its restricted pub opening hours. The restrictions dated from the First World War when the government wanted to keep munitions workers out of pubs and in their factories. Since the 1980s permitted opening hours have gradually been relaxed. First pubs were able to open from 11am to 11pm Monday to Saturday. In 1995, pubs were allowed to open all day on Sunday. Finally in 2006 a sweeping new law allows pub owners to apply for flexible opening hours within a 24-hour cycle. This means that while many pubs still open from 11am to 11pm during the week, they stay open until midnight, 1am or even 2am at weekends. Some sections of the media dubbed the new law "24-hour opening" but this is seriously misleading. The majority of pubs still close at 11pm on weekdays. Flexibility has had the major advantage of not all pubs in city centres closing at the same time on Friday and Saturday nights, cutting back on the risk of disorder. Visitors to Britain will find a far more relaxed attitude to public drinking: it's now possible to buy a beer when you fancy one, not when the government decrees.

Irish pubs have a reputation for being more easy-going and laid-back than their British counterparts, mainly as a result of less restricted opening hours. Irish pubs open all day, though, being a Catholic country, do shut for a contemplative period in the afternoon, known as the "holy hour". The Irish, like the Welsh, tend to burst into song when they are "drink taken". Sometimes worse things happen. The famous writer-cum-boozer Brendan Behan, an acknowledged expert on Dublin pubs, recorded a poem written by the owner of O'Meara's pub to commemorate a punch-up in the bar:

Then Hoolihan hit Hannaghan and Hannaghan hit McGilligan
And everyone hit anyone of whom he had a spite,
And Larry Dwyer, the cripple, who was sitting doing nothing,
Got a kick that broke his jawbone for not indulging in the fight.

Behan also recalled "Being in the Blue Lion in Parnell Street one day and the owner said to me: 'You owe me ten shillings', he said. 'You broke a glass the last time you were here'. 'God bless and save us,' I said, 'it must have been a very dear glass if it cost ten shillings. Tell us, was it a Waterford glass or something?' I discovered in double-quick time that it wasn't a glass that you'd drink out of he meant – it was a pane of glass and I'd stuck somebody's head through it."

European sophistication

In mainland Europe there are occasional pastiches of the English pub – Japanese firms build them, complete with plastic beams – but a different culture prevails. The French café ranges from the large and plush to the small and overcrowded, dense with pungent cigarette smoke. In either, beer competes with wine, spirits and coffee, while food, ranging from the obligatory *croque monsieur* to full meals, is always available. In northern France, where beer has deeper cultural roots, specialist bars, in common with those in Belgium, will offer beer menus with a wide range from several countries. The pace is slower than in a British pub and there is no pressure to drink up and leave – until waiters change shift and all tabs have to be cleared in a rush. Belgian cafés are often large, plush, multi-mirrored and with waiters well versed in the wonder and variety of beer – and ever-ready to offer chips with every dish.

There is no such thing as a German bar. There are Prussian bars and Bavarian bier kellers. The former tend to be formal and quiet, with service spilling out on to pavements in warm weather.

In the Catholic south, bars and kellers are fun, large, roisterous barns of places, with waiters and waitresses often dressed in traditional lederhosen, serving beer at a fast and furious pace, accompanied by dishes in which the choice is pork, pork or, for a change, pork sausages.

Pork is also much in evidence in Czech bars. With the exception of the sumptuous *fin de siècle* hotels that ring Wenceslas Square in Prague, bars tend to be utilitarian by Western European standards but that will change as they meet the expectations of younger Czechs and tourists. Until the end of the old totalitarian regime, conversation tended to be limited for fear of police spies and informers. There was nothing new in that. The Good Soldier Schweik or Svejk was often in trouble for speaking his mind during the First World War in his favourite Prague bar, U Kalika (The Chalice). In one episode Schweik's drinking companion, Bretschneider, turns out to be an unwelcome one when he calls Schweik out into a corridor: "He showed him [Schweik] his eaglet and announced that he was arresting him and would take him at once to police headquarters. Schweik tried to explain that the gentleman must be mistaken, that he was completely innocent and that he had not uttered a single word capable of offending anyone. However, Bretschneider told him that he had in fact committed several criminal offences, including the crime of high treason. Then they returned to the pub and Schweik said to Palivec [the landlord]: 'I've had five beers, a couple of frankfurters and a roll. Now give me one more slivovice and I must go, because I'm under arrest.'"

Other national idiosyncrasies

Australia and Scotland have two things in common: a lot of drinking is done in public houses euphemistically called "hotels" and both countries were once bedevilled by severe restrictions on opening hours. In Australia, when hotel bars were forced to close early in the evening, the "six o'clock swill" was a short period in which beer was poured down parched throats with indecent haste. In Scottish cities, a similar experience accompanied the "ten o'clock swill". Both countries are now more civilized places and their bars more pleasant since the shackles were removed.

In the United States, many bars tend to be dimly lit as though they still live in the shadow of Prohibition. They range from the spartan to the palatial, larger ones having areas set aside for the ubiquitous pool table. Service is usually highly attentive and polite, spoilt only by the shortage of choice and the wickedly low temperature at which beer is served. Sometimes drinkers are handed a frosted mug from the fridge to make the beer temperature even lower. It is difficult to decide whether this tendency is more or less distressing than drinking beer straight from the bottle.

Glossary:
The Language of Beer

Here are the key terms you need to help you widen and deepen your appreciation of ale and lager. By speaking the language of beer, you can better grasp both its many styles and the centuries-old techniques used to make them.

Abbey	Commercial Belgian beers licensed by abbeys. Not to be confused with Trappist ales.
Adjuncts	Materials used in place of traditional grains for cheapness or lightness of flavour. Common adjuncts are rice, maize (corn) and brewing sugar.
Ale	The world's oldest beer style produced by top or warm fermentation.
Alpha acid	The main component of the bittering agent in the hop flower.
Alt	Literally Old in German, a top-fermenting beer mainly confined to the city of Düsseldorf.
Attenuation	The extent to which brewing sugars turn to alcohol and carbon dioxide.
Beer	Generic term for an alcoholic drink made from grain; includes both ale and lager.
Bitter	British term for the pale, amber or copper-coloured beers that developed from the pale ales of the nineteenth century.
Bock/Bok	Strong beer style of Germany and the Netherlands.
Bottle-conditioned	A beer that undergoes a secondary fermentation in the bottle.
Cask-conditioned	Beer that undergoes a secondary fermentation in the cask, a style closely identified with British beers. Popularly known as "real ale".

Copper Vessel used to boil the sugary wort with hops. Also known as a brew kettle.

Decoction mashing A system mainly used in lager brewing in which portions of the wort are removed from the mashing vessel, heated to a higher temperature and then returned. Improves enzymic activity and the conversion of starch to sugar in poorly modified malts.

Dry-hopping The addition of a small amount of hops to a cask of beer to improve aroma and bitterness.

Dunkel A dark lager beer in Germany, a Bavarian speciality that predated the first pale lagers.

EBC European Beer Convention that indicates the colour in malts and beers.

Entire The earliest form of porter, short for "entire butt".

Ester Flavour compounds produced by the action of yeast turning sugars into alcohol and carbon dioxide. Esters may be fruity or spicy.

Fining Substance that clarifies beer, usually made from the swim bladder of sturgeon fish; also known as isinglass.

Framboise/frambozen Raspberry-flavoured lambic beer.

Grist The coarse powder derived from malt that has been milled or "cracked" in the brewery prior to mashing.

Gueuze A blend of Belgian lambic beers.

Helles/Hell A pale Bavarian lager beer.

IBU International Units of Bitterness, scale for measuring the bitterness of beer.

Infusion Method of mashing used mainly in ale-brewing where the grains are left to soak with pure water while starches convert to sugar, usually carried out at a constant temperature.

Kölsch   Top-fermenting golden beer from Cologne.

Kräusen   The addition of partially fermented wort during lagering to encourage a strong secondary fermentation.

Kriek   Cherry-flavoured lambic beer.

Lager   From the German meaning "store". The cold-conditioning of beer at around 0°C/32°F to encourage the yeast to settle out, increase carbonation and produce a smooth, clean-tasting beer.

Lambic   Belgian beer made by spontaneous fermentation.

Lauter tun   Vessel used to clarify the wort after the mashing stage.

Malt   Barley or other cereals that have been partially germinated to allow starches to be converted into fermentable sugars.

Mash   First stage of the brewing process, when the malt is mixed with pure hot water to extract the sugars.

Märzen   Traditional Bavarian lager brewed in March and stored until autumn for the Munich Oktoberfest.

Mild   Dark brown (occasionally pale) English and Welsh beer, lightly hopped. The oldest style of beer that once derived its colour from malt cured over wood fires. One of the components of the first porters.

Milk stout   Stout made with the addition of lactose, which is unfermentable, producing a beer low in alcohol with a creamy, slightly sweet character.

Pilsner/Pilsener/ Pils   International brand name for a light-coloured lager. In the Czech Republic the term is confined to beers brewed in Pilsen or Pilzen where the style was perfected.

Porter   Dark – brown or black – beer originating in London, deriving its name from its popularity with street-market porters.

Priming	The addition of sugar to encourage a secondary fermentation in beer.
Reinheitsgebot	Bavarian beer law of 1516 , the "Purity Pledge", that lays down that only malted grain, hops, yeast and water can be used in brewing. Now covers the whole of Germany.
Shilling	Ancient method of invoicing beer in Scotland based on strength. Beers are called 60, 70 or 80 shilling.
Sparging	Sprinkling or spraying the spent grains in the mash tun or lauter tun to flush out any remaining malt sugars. From the French *esparger*, to sprinkle.
Square	A traditional open fermenting vessel.
Steam beer	American beer style saved by the Anchor Brewery in San Francisco.
Stout	Once an English generic term for the strongest or "stoutest" beer in a brewery; came to be identified with porter. Porter stout eventually became modified to just stout. Now considered a quintessentially Irish style.
Trappist	Ales brewed by monks of the Trappist order in Belgium and The Netherlands.
Union	Method of fermentation developed in Burton-on-Trent using large oak casks.
Ur/Urtyp	German for original. Urquell as in Pilsner Urquell means "original source Pilsner".
Weizen/weisse	German term meaning wheat or white beer Wit in Flemish.
Wort	Liquid resulting from the mashing process, rich in malt sugars.

Index

Note: (B) indicates a brewery; (P) indicates a pub (or equivalent) listed in the Gazetteer.